A History of Modern Ireland

MODERN IRELAND

A HISTORY OF
Modern Ireland
WITH A SKETCH OF
EARLIER TIMES

GIOVANNI COSTIGAN

Bobbs-Merrill Educational Publishing
Indianapolis

ACKNOWLEDGMENTS

Lines from ANCIENT IRISH POETRY, Kuno Meyer, ed., reprinted by permission of Constable & Company Limited.

"Farewell to Sarsfield " from KINGS, LORDS, AND COMMONS by Frank O'Connor. Copyright 1949, © 1959 by Frank O'Connor. Reprinted by permission of Alfred A. Knopf, Inc.

"The Hosting of the Sidhe." Reprinted with permission of The Macmillan Company from COLLECTED POEMS by William Butler Yeats. Copyright 1906 by The Macmillan Company renewed 1931 by William Butler Yeats.

Lines from "In the Seven Woods" reprinted with permission of The Macmillan Company renewed 1931 by William Butler Yeats.

Lines from "The Wanderings of Oisin" reprinted with permission of The Macmillan Company from COLLECTED POEMS by William Butler Yeats. Copyright 1906 by The Macmillan Company renewed 1934 by William Butler Yeats.

Lines from "The Statues" reprinted with permission of The Macmillan Company from COLLECTED POEMS by William Butler Yeats. Copyright 1940 by Georgie Yeats renewed 1968 by Bertha Georgie Yeats, Anne Yeats, Michael Butler Yeats.

Lines from "Michael Robartes and the Dancer" reprinted with permission of The Macmillan Company from COLLECTED POEMS by William Butler Yeats. Copyright 1924 by The Macmillan Company renewed 1952 by Bertha Georgie Yeats.

Lines from "The Tower" reprinted with permission of The Macmillan Company from COLLECTED POEMS by William Butler Yeats. Copyright 1928 by The Macmillan Company renewed 1956 by Georgie Yeats.

The Bobbs-Merrill Company, Inc.
4300 West 62nd Street
Indianapolis, Indiana 46268

First Edition
Second Printing—1979
Library of Congress Catalog Card Number 69–15699

ISBN 0-672-63547-X

TO MY ANCESTORS BOTH
CATHOLIC AND PROTESTANT

PREFACE

Although Britain and Ireland are both islands surrounded by the ocean, the influence of the sea upon their respective destinies has been remarkably different. For nine hundred years, in Shakespeare's phrase, the sea protected England as a "moat defensive to a house." Until the coming of air power in the twentieth century it served to guard her against invasion from abroad—whether from Philip II of Spain, from Napoleon, or from Adolf Hitler. In the popular phrase, the sea was always "Britain's sure shield."

The ocean was also valuable to Britain as a vehicle of colonization and conquest, and as the high road to empire. Its control ensured her dominion over India. Britain's attitude to the sea was as purposeful and commanding as the fervent words of the popular anthem suggest: "Rule, Britannia! Britannia rules the waves!" Churchill no doubt would have agreed with Trevelyan's remark that Nelson, whose statue looks down on London from Trafalgar Square, "is still the best-loved name in English ears."

For Ireland, however, the sea has been the means not of dominion but of subjection, the vehicle not of purposeful colonization but of despairing emigration. Despite the fabled voyages of early saints like Brendan the Navigator, the Irish have never been a seafaring people. Generally speaking, their attitude to the sea has been passive and resigned. For over ten centuries, the sea was the element of their enemies and the high road of their conquerors. Hence from an early time it served as a symbol of sorrow. As early as the Dark Ages, an unknown Irishman lamented:

> I do not know of anything under the sky
> That is friendly or favorable to the Gael,

But only the sea that our need brings us to
As the wind that blows to the harbor
The ship that is bearing us away from Ireland.
And there is reason that these are reconciled with us,
For we increase the sea with our tears
And the wandering wind with our sighs.

A thousand years later the Irish still associated the sea with exile and sorrow—as is evident in a lyric from the *Love Songs of Connacht* that Douglas Hyde took down from the lips of an old crone living in a hovel amid the bogs of Roscommon.

My grief on the sea
How the waves of it roll,
For they heave between me
And the love of my soul. . . .

If during the Famine in the nineteenth century the ocean enabled millions of Irishmen and Irishwomen to escape their stricken land and find a new home in America or Australia, it also interposed between them and any hope of their return an almost insuperable barrier. The last cry that sounded in the ears of the emigrant was often the bitter lament of the "keen," wrung from weeping friends and relations. In *Riders to the Sea,* Synge moved audiences by his poignant representation of the harsh, inexorable dominance of the sea over the lives of the Aran islanders. Yet in more subtle and indirect fashion the sea had taken its toll through generations of Irish history. From the Flight of the Earls in 1607 and the flight of the "Wild Geese" in 1691 down to the "coffin ships" of Famine times, the sea was the transporter of Irish manhood—to the enrichment of Spain and France, of Britain and America. With sure instinct, the young poet Lionel Johnson expressed Ireland's mourning for the death of Parnell by evoking once more the ancient symbol of her grief:

The wail of Irish winds,
The cry of Irish seas,
Eternal sorrow finds
Eternal voice in these.

CONTENTS

MAPS

A History of Modern Ireland

Miles
0   25   50

N

SCOTLAND

RATHLIN IS.
(795)

ATLANTIC
OCEAN

+ Derry

R. FOYLE

ULSTER

Carrickfergus

Bangor

St. Patrick's
+ Purgatory

LOWER
LOUGH
ERNE

LOUGH
NEAGH

R. LAGAN

Armagh
(444)

Downpatrick

UPPER
LOUGH
ERNE

Faughart
(1318)

Knocknarea

LOUGH
CONN

CARLINGFORD
LOUGH (851)

Dundalk

Monasterboice (923)

CONNACHT

Mellifont
(1150)

Drogheda

+ Croagh
Patrick

LOUGH
CARRA

LOUGH MASK

R. SUCK

Kells

R. BOYNE

Newgrange

LAMBAY
IS.

INISHBOFIN
IS.
(651)

Cong

LOUGH
CORRIB

LOUGH
REE

Trim

Tara

Clontarf
(1014)

Maynooth
(1536)

Howth (819)

Galway

LEINSTER

Dublin
(841)

Clonfert
(583)

Clonmacnois

R. LIFFEY

IRISH

ARAN
IS.
(530)

Kildare
(c. 500)

Glendalough
(622)

Wicklow

LOUGH
DERG

R. SHANNON

R. NORE

R. BARROW

Arklow

SEA

Limerick

R. SLANEY

BLASKET
IS.

Ardagh

Lough Gur

Caskel

Kilkenny
(600)

R. SUIR

Wexford

MUNSTER

Waterford

R. BLACKWATER

Cork

R. LEE

IRELAND TO 1500

▲   Pre-historic Sites
+   Christian Foundations
□   Norman Castles
○   Danish Towns

palacios

I

Prehistoric Ireland and Its Significance for Modern Times

The Neolithic and Bronze Ages

There are two ways in which a people may approach the problem of its earliest origins: one way is through the patient accumulation of knowledge and the use of the scientific method; the other is through imagination and poetry, ever impatient to fill the void of ignorance that exists in every civilization before it has developed the intellectual maturity that makes scientific investigation possible.

In Ireland, as elsewhere, archaeology has uncovered traces of prehistoric times—of Neolithic, Bronze, and Iron Ages; but popular belief spurns knowledge laboriously acquired, preferring instead the mythological heroes with whom generations of poets had peopled the unknown past. Yet here, as everywhere, reality is no less exciting than myth, and no less challenging to the imagination.

It seems to have been about fifty thousand years ago that Ireland finally became an island, having been gradually detached from the Eurasian land mass to which Britain still belonged. Indeed, it was not until some forty thousand years later that Britain, too, became an island. One result of Ireland's much longer separation from the Continent has been a relative paucity of flora and fauna, various species of snakes and reptiles, for example, which are common in Europe, being unknown to Ireland. What geology and botany account for prosaically, folk imagination long ago ascribed to the thaumaturgic powers of St. Patrick.

Other basic features of modern Ireland were similarly determined thousands of years ago. Geology and climate long ago decreed that about a quarter of her soil (five million acres out of twenty million) should be mountain and bog, unfit for cultivation. Bogs, of course, occur also on the Continent—with an average depth of between ten and twenty feet, but in Ireland, because of the abundant rainfall, they average a depth of between forty and fifty feet. Not until the age of scientific technology—and the Turf Electricity Board—would Irish bogs yield their full economic potential.

Abundance of rain also makes Ireland a land of brimming rivers—237 in all, not including tributaries—a fact of which the Vikings and other invaders took full advantage. The same climatic factor determined that Ireland should be more a pastoral than an agricultural country; and that horses and cattle, grazing on the rich central plain that overlays the limestone base, should form a large part of the natural wealth of the island. The relative absence of coal, on the other hand, and the almost complete lack of iron, has deprived Ireland of the possibility of ever becoming a modern industrial nation.

No traces of human occupation in Ireland in Paleolithic times have as yet been found. The earliest human artifacts—flints in County Antrim—are dated about 6000 B.C. The Neolithic Revolution, which consisted of the discovery of agriculture and the domestication of animals, having spread slowly westward over Europe from central Asia, reached Ireland probably somewhere toward the end of the third millennium B.C. At sites like Lough Gur, County Limerick, and Lyle's Hill, County Antrim, many traces of the life of Neolithic man have been uncovered. For Ireland, as elsewhere, the Neolithic Revolution must have meant the earliest settled communities, the first appearance of social classes, and the beginning of organized religion. It meant also the development of arts like weaving and pottery of such excellence that not until the Middle Ages do we again find pottery in Ireland of a quality comparable with that of Neolithic times.

Somewhere about 1750 B.C. metallurgy was introduced into Ireland. The land being rich in copper, tin was imported from Cornwall and Spain, and the island soon became one of the leading centers of the Bronze Age. Rich deposits of gold were also discovered, and by 1500 B.C. Ireland had become one of the chief gold-producing countries in Europe. Gold was exported to the Mediterranean—most of the gold found in Mycenae is said to have come from Ireland—as well as to Britain, Germany, and Scandinavia. Dublin owes its origin to this earliest wealth from the mines of Wicklow. The treasures in the National Museum in Dublin today bear witness to the reality of this "Golden Age" in Ireland.

Everywhere across Eurasia, from Western Europe to China, the fusion of Neolithic and Bronze cultures produced the great stone monuments above the graves of important chieftains, raised in the hope, no doubt, of procuring immortality for them. Though Ireland has nothing to compare in size or dignity with Stonehenge—which indeed appears to be unrivaled anywhere—it is unusually rich in megalithic remains. In the Yeats country, at Carrowmore, County Sligo, for example, there lies scattered through the fields a collection of megalithic tombs which—excepting only Carnac in Brittany—is the largest in Europe.

From the Bronze and Iron ages there still remain in Ireland more than thirty thousand raths (circular stone or earthen works enclosing dwelling places), attesting the presence of a numerous population—perhaps several hundred thousand. For nearly two thousand years country people have deemed these raths the haunted homes of fairy hosts and have accordingly avoided any interference with them.

The two most famous Bronze Age sites in Ireland are the great oval cairn at Knocknarea, County Sligo, which long fascinated the imagination of Yeats, and the chambered tomb at Newgrange, County Meath, into which AE once took the skeptical George Moore. It has been estimated that the stones of Knocknarea weigh forty thousand tons—a small relative of the Great Pyramid of Egypt. So dramatic a site—rising abruptly from the Atlantic to confront Ben Bulben grandly across the plain of Sligo—could only have been a royal burial place, and accordingly mythmakers of later ages saw in Knocknarea the burial place of Maeve, Queen of Connacht—"where passionate Maeve lies stony-still." Knocknarea has never been excavated, but Newgrange was plundered by the Danes in A.D. 861. Recent excavations at the burial mounds of Dowth and Knowth, close to Newgrange, promise exciting new revelations about life in Bronze Age Ireland.

Less imposing than either of these, but erected in the same spirit, are the hundreds of smaller monuments—dolmens, menhirs, cromlechs, and circles of standing stones with which the crests of many Irish hills are crowned. These, too, were invested with poetry by popular imagination. A hoary megalith might well become for later ages a trysting place for lovers (as in the story of Diarmid and Grania), a pulpit for priests, or perhaps a sacrificial altar for victims.

The Iron Age: The Gaels

In Ireland the Iron Age began about the middle of the fourth century B.C. with the coming of the Gaels. Cousins of the Britons, they constituted the extreme right wing of that Celtic invasion that swept into Europe from the east—from Greece to the British Isles. The new technique of ironworking which the Gaels like other Celts brought with them not only gave them victory in war—through the superiority of iron swords over bronze—but also meant improved agriculture, through deeper plowing with iron plowshares. This brought increase of food and hence of population.

The Gaels soon overran the whole island, which they called "Erin" (Eriu) from the name of the first people, the Eirann, whom they had conquered in southern Ireland. For more than a thousand years, the Gaels were to dominate Ireland, unchallenged till the coming of the Vikings about A.D. 800. During this long period, they established, on a tribal basis, a social organization that in the west of Ireland was to last until the seventeenth century. The Gaels gave Ireland a common culture, a common language, and a common religion—with a Druid priesthood. Like their near relations in Britain, however, the Gaels failed to achieve political unity, so that Ireland was torn for many centuries by the endless small-scale warfare of conflicting tribes. Despite the shadowy claims to the High Kingship of various provincial rulers, not until the reign of Brian Boru (1002–14) was Ireland effectually united—and then but briefly—under a single sovereign.

Throughout the greater part of its history, Gaelic Ireland was divided into five or even seven leading kingdoms, and these in turn were subdivided into about 150 petty kingdoms or "tuatha." The basic social unit was the "derbfine," a family group that might embrace several successive generations. Gaelic society appears to have consisted of a hierarchy of nobles, freemen, and slaves. The nobility included not only warriors but also Brehons (interpreters of unwritten law handed down by custom) and ollaves (bards, scholars, and genealogists). At a lower social level were the "filidh," popular poets who were the distant ancestors of the wandering harpists and storytellers of the eighteenth century.

Under the Brehon laws, land was held communally rather than individually. This system, known as "rundale," corresponded to the "folk land" of the Anglo-Saxons. A man's social position depended not so much on the amount of land he held but on the number of cattle he possessed. The power of kings was not absolute but was limited by custom. New kings were usually chosen, not by hereditary succession but by choice of the nobility from among the male relatives of the ruler while he was still alive. This custom of tanistry led to numerous disputes about succession. Tanistry survived in parts of the west of Ireland until the seventeenth century.

Punishment took the form of fines paid in kind—usually in cattle, or perhaps in metals or in cloth. Death sentences were rarely inflicted. The absence of capital punishment was another aspect of the Brehon laws which the Elizabethans later regarded as both barbarous and incomprehensible. The object of these laws, however, was to discourage vendettas and to enable those who had been wronged to seek arbitration rather than private revenge. The position of women under the Brehon laws was an honorable one, wives having in general equal rights with husbands.

The customs and literature of the Gaels were never committed to writing. However, perhaps as a result of later contact with the Christian world, a native alphabet was devised—the cumbrous Ogham script, consisting of inscriptions carved upon stone. More than three hundred of these, mostly dating from the fifth to the seventh centuries, have survived into modern times; but nothing that could be called literature exists in Ogham.

The two chief centers of Gaelic Ireland were Tara, County Meath, and Emain Macha, County Armagh, places celebrated in heroic poetry. The royal place of Tara was built on a low hill overlooking the fertile valley of the Boyne. Its banqueting hall was seven hundred feet long, but since like all other Gaelic buildings it was constructed of wood, in course of time it was utterly destroyed, so that today only the site can be traced. The chief figure connected in early times with Tara is Cormac, who is said to have reigned as High King of Ireland from A.D. 227 to 266. Though most modern scholars reject his authenticity, some, like Professor Myles Dillon, are inclined to regard him as the first recognizable personality in Irish history. To Cormac's reign, tradition ascribed the founding of the Fenians, a chivalric warrior band, by the legendary Finn MacCool. In the seventeenth century, Geoffrey Keating, the "Irish Herodotus," maintained that Cormac had been granted a vision of Christ and the true Faith, in consequence of which he had the Druid idols shattered.

Tara today is a desolate grass-grown mound, rising above the elms and chestnuts that surround it. Of its ancient glory not a trace remains. Gone are the decorations of burnished bronze, the gold and silver ornaments, the lofty roof tree. For Tara was often ravaged by the Danes. Yet the hold of Tara upon the folk imagination was never broken, and when the oppressed peasants of Ireland rose in 1798, it was upon the hill of Tara that thousands of them, as if moved by some ancestral memory, assembled. To Tara also, in 1843, Daniel O'Connell summoned his ragged followers to hear his loud defiance of the British government, as numerous priests celebrated Mass from open-air altars upon the hill that once had witnessed Druid rites. In the twentieth century, Tara was to become for Yeats the symbol of a nobility and dignity which he believed to have vanished from the world.

> I have put away
> The unavailing outcries and the old bitterness
> That empty the heart. I have forgot awhile
> Tara uprooted, and the new commonness
> Upon the throne. . . .

The Legacy of Gaelic Ireland

Modern Irishmen, struggling for independence from England and seeking a national symbol free from any English association, have idealized the Gaels and Gaelic Ireland. Over a century ago, the Young Irelander Thomas McGee, in exile in Canada, thus evoked the memory of his forebears:

> Long, long ago, beyond the misty space
> Of twice a thousand years,
> In Erin old there dwelt a mighty race
> Taller than Roman spears.

Contemporary Ireland has in fact inherited three main legacies from the Gaels: the basic physical stock, the language, and the literature of the sagas transmitted orally for centuries before being finally committed to writing by Christian monks. Gaelic is the oldest living vernacular of the West, and its sagas—save for the classics of Greece and Rome—provide us with the most complete account of any pre-Christian society in Europe. Like the Homeric Greeks and the ancient Britons, the Gaels never acquired—perhaps never even desired—the art of writing.

Unlike the Homeric epics with which they have so often been compared, the ancient Irish sagas never received the final impress of a single poetic genius and were never organized into a supreme and lasting unity. For the most part they remained in prose, with poetic fragments interspersed. Thus the failure of the Gaels to achieve political unity was curiously matched by their failure to organize a coherent body of literature. Nor did the Gaels produce drama of any kind. Ireland, indeed, had to wait till the nineteenth century for Douglas Hyde to write drama in Gaelic. Compared, however, with the literary remains of the rest of the far-flung Celtic peoples, the quantity of the Gaelic literature that survives is astonishing—especially considering the extinction of whatever sagas the ancient Britons might have possessed. From this point of view it is no doubt fortunate that Ireland was never conquered by the Romans, for had she been incorporated into the Roman Empire it is highly probable that the adoption of Latin culture would have led, as in Britain, to the total submergence of the native poetic inheritance.

Three main collections of Irish sagas have survived: the Mythological cycle, which deals with pre-Christian times; the Ulster, or Red Branch cycle, which covers roughly the first two centuries of the Christian era; and the Fenian cycle, which deals with the third and subsequent centuries. The earliest existing manuscripts in which the sagas are recorded are of course much later in date. Thus the earliest version of the Red Branch, containing the famous narrative of the Cattle Raid of Cooley, and of the conflict between Cuchulain, young hero of Ulster, and Maeve, Queen of Connacht, dates only from the twelfth century; while the history of the Fenians was not put into writing until the fifteenth. The story of the memorable encounter between Oisin, last of the Fenians, and St. Patrick was not written down until as late as 1750. There is something extraordinary in this survival through many centuries, despite the hazards or indifference of an alien culture, of the slender thread of a purely oral tradition.

Attached to these cycles are two of the most famous love stories in Western literature—the tragic tale of Deirdre and Naisi, which occurs in the Red Branch cycle and is referred to as early as the tenth century, although the earliest surviving MS is from the seventeenth; and the equally ill-starred love of Diarmid and Grania, which belongs to the Fenian cycle and likewise dates back to the tenth century, the oldest MS being from the fifteenth. Unlike many of the sagas, these tragic stories continued for centuries to be cherished by the peasantry of Ireland. The Fenians, too, were preserved as heroes in the folk imagination, whereas Cuchulain virtually disappeared from popular memory until his triumphant revival at the end of the nineteenth century by the poets and dramatists of the Irish Literary Renaissance.

The Mythological History of Ireland

The mythological cycle furnished an account of the origins of the Gaels which innumerable generations of Irishmen accepted as fact and

Cuchulain. This image of the dying Cuchulain is the work of the Irish sculptor Oliver Sheppard. It was unveiled in the Dublin General Post Office in 1936.

which even today with its fabled races and heroic names has not been wholly supplanted in the folk mind by the results of the prosaic labors of scholars. Science may talk of Neolithic, Bronze, and Iron, but children of all ages still remember Fomorians, Firbolgs, Danaans, and Milesians.

The Fomorians, whose last refuge was said to be the bleak, forbidding cliffs of Tory Island off the coast of Donegal, were thought to be the earliest inhabitants of Ireland: sinister, dim, superhuman figures, in some ways like the Titans of ancient Greek mythology. The Giant's Causeway (County Antrim) was their stony stairway. Many regarded the Fomorians as the embodiment of Evil in the world.

The Fomorians were said to have been vanquished by the Firbolgs, who, according to Geoffrey Keating, had fled to Ireland from Thrace to escape the tyranny of the Greeks. If the Fomorians represented aspects of elemental Nature, the Firbolgs were fabled as small, shrewd, and mean, as overcoming the race of giants by superior cunning. (It is not unamusing to find how early in folklore we find that scorn for intelligence which has by no means ceased in the world today.) Since the name "Firbolgs" is thought to mean "Men of the Leather Bags," some have conjectured that this lowly race might have represented some ancient servile caste, perhaps engaged in the universally despised occupation of tanning. Others have fancifully suggested that the tinkers who figure in Synge's plays, and who still roam the roads of Ireland, are the descendants of the Firbolgs. The term itself survives in modern Irish idiom as a term of contemptuous raillery.

As they had overcome the Fomorians, so the Firbolgs were in turn vanquished by the Danaans, who, it was said, anticipating Cromwell, left the bogs and mountains of Connacht to the Firbolgs while they took the rest of Ireland for themselves. Another version relates how the defeated Firbolgs fled to Rathlin Island, thence dispersing to the Isle of Man and the Western Isles of Scotland; while still another account tells how the Firbolgs made their last stand against the Danaans on the cliffs of Aran at the prehistoric fortress of Dun Aengus.

Keating thinks that the Danaans came from Achaia and Boeotia, where they had learned the arts of sorcery. He is uncertain whether Gaedheal, the eponymous founder of the Gaels, had also come from these provinces, or whether, as some Latin authors asserted, he was the son of Cecrops. In his History of Ireland, Keating severely censures the Elizabethan historian, William Camden, for failing to mention the Danaans in his work.

In the Celtic sagas, the Danaans are usually depicted sympathetically and their contest with the Firbolgs is represented as a struggle between the powers of Light and Darkness. The Gaels attributed their own love of poetry and desire for knowledge to the Danaans. Lugh himself, the sun god, and Eriu, earth goddess of Ireland, were said to have been Danaan in origin. Banba and Fodha, other early names for Ireland, were also attributed to this favored people. Even the Lia Fall, the sacred stone of Tara, was said to have derived its magical powers from the Danaans.

When there appeared a fourth race of invaders, the Milesians, the sagas report how the Danaans tried to prevent their landing by sending clouds black as ink to envelop their ships. Possibly this is the earliest reference to the sea fogs rising from the Atlantic, which today can still be seen obliterating cottages, fields, and mountains as they sweep inland from the coast. Eventually the Danaans were forced to accept a diminished, subterranean existence, haunting raths and mounds in the guise of fairies.

With the Milesians we are at last close to the threshold of actual history, since the name itself may possibly have been a generic term for the various dark-haired peoples who had come into Ireland from the south, bringing with them over the centuries the techniques of the Neolithic and Bronze Ages. Although the Gaels seem to have regarded the Milesians, whom they themselves had dispossessed, factually enough—their chronicles enumerate 179 Milesian kings, of whom 71 were said to have been killed in battle, 60 to have been murdered, and 48 to have died naturally—they continued to speculate fondly about the vanished Danaans, whose memory they refused to relinquish.

The World of the Fairies

In course of time, the tall and once proud Danaans were transformed into "the little people," known likewise as leprechauns, or more poetically as the Sidh (pronounced "Shee"). Waving cornfields caressed by the wind or the shifting patterns on the surface of the sea might mark their soundless passing. Whirlwinds and eddies of autumn leaves were sure signs of their presence, as one of the most beautiful of Yeats's early poems, the "Hosting of the Sidhe," reminds us.

> The host is riding from Knocknarea
> And over the grave of Clooth-na-Bare;
> Caoilte tossing his burning hair,
> And Niamh calling Away, come away:

Empty your heart of its mortal dream.
The winds awaken, the leaves whirl 'round,
Our cheeks are pale, our hair is unbound,
Our breasts are heaving, our eyes are agleam,
Our arms are waving, our lips are apart;
And if any gaze on our rushing band,
We come between him and the deed of his hand,
We come between him and the hope of his heart.
The host is rushing 'twixt night and day,
And where is there hope or deed as fair?
Caoilte tossing his burning hair,
And Niamh calling Away, come away.

Innumerable superstitions gradually wove themselves around this fairy world, attaching it to human existence in countless ways. The red berries of the rowan tree (the mountain ash), once sacred to the Druids, were now precious because they belonged to the fairies, and woe to the mortal that plucked them. A thousand years of Christianity could not destroy popular belief in "these bright, beautiful, happy beings," in whose fantasied existence one may perhaps discern the work of the unconscious compensating for the sorrows of daily life. Some people sought to reconcile their belief in fairies with orthodox Christian doctrine by assuming them to be "fallen angels."

Yet the relationship of "the little people" to ordinary human life was by no means a simple one. They had a propensity for stealing children. They were willful and capricious, quick to take offense and apt to seek revenge on anyone who intruded on their fairy haunts or chanced to behold them dancing in the woods or combing out their long yellow hair in the sunshine. Death itself might be visited upon anyone who observed their mysterious ways too closely. The wail of the banshee was a fearful revelation of another aspect of their dread existence. Surely it was better to talk about them than to meet them face to face.*

*A. P. Graves, the father of Robert Graves, told how in the nineteenth century the peasantry of Kerry refused to descend into the subterranean chambers of old forts lest they be carried off by the fairies, and Lady Gregory described how, two centuries after the battle of Aughrim in 1691—where the last hope of Irish freedom was extinguished—the country people of Connacht still believed that the "Danes" (for so the name "Danaan" had been corrupted) danced on the burial mounds of those killed in battle. "The greenest spots are the tumuli," wrote Stopford Brooke in the 1890s, "of which there are many here, that cover the burial places of ancient heroes and chiefs. But the peasantry will not allow their cattle even to walk over these green mounds, for that would offend the Fairy Folk who dwell in them, and some misfortune might befall the cattle or their owners. One lives in Ireland in the constant presence of the fairy world. They touch life at every point—as fully believed in as the Virgin and the Saints. No

Nor was the belief in fairies confined to simple, or to simple-minded, people. An almost militant belief in the reality of their existence was for many years a part of Yeats's poetic creed. "I say to myself," he wrote, "that they are surely there, the divine people, for only we who have neither wisdom nor simplicity have denied them, and the simple of all times and the wise men of ancient times have seen them and even spoken to them. They live out their passionate lives, not far off, as I think, and we shall be among them when we die, if we but keep our natures simple and passionate." As a young man in Sligo, Yeats used to wander through the country lanes seeking out people who might acquaint him with fairy lore. On one occasion, however, when he lectured on the fairies of Sligo in London, he appears to have met his match for, as W. P. Ryan recalls, "the south had a sturdy champion in John Augustus O'Shea, who gave it as his experience that there were more fairies in a square foot of Tipperary than in all the County Sligo."

Close friends of Yeats like AE (George Russell, the poet) and Maud Gonne were equally devoted to the fairy world, and together they planned to establish the headquarters of a new fairy cult on an island in Lough Key, County Roscommon, believing, as Miss Gonne wrote, that "the land of Ireland was powerfully alive and invisibly peopled." The mountains of Ireland, Yeats thought, were truly "sacred mountains, along whose sides the peasant still sees enchanted fires and the divinities which have not faded from the belief, if they have faded from the prayers of simple hearts." For the peasants who

matter from what scientific world one comes, the fairy faith grows into one's imagination in the West of Ireland. I seemed to see the gods of the sea swimming far below the blue depths as I looked down from the cliffs, and I went . . . in the moonlight to see the Shee come riding out of the grassy mounds—nor was it difficult to see them."

When so powerful a prelate as Archbishop McEvilly of Tuam, whose name, according to Frank O'Connor, is still a terror in the West of Ireland, continued to believe in fairies—for fear of them he once forbade Ballintubber Castle to be re-roofed—how should not simple people also be afraid? Some peasants added to the sum of theological knowledge the belief that fairies were angels doing penance for venial sins; others, more prudent, believed that a drop of holy water or the sign of the cross was a specific against them. In his *Recollections*, the old Fenian O'Donovan Rossa mentions his absolute belief in fairies as a child: but when in old age he returned to Ireland after long years in New York, he found to his regret that such beliefs had almost vanished. The implacable old man ascribed the change to English tyranny which, not content with injuring the living, had killed off "the little people" as well.

An event which took place recently in Belmullet, County Mayo, shows that Rossa's pessimism was unfounded. "A fairly big fairy crisis erupted this week," reported Reuters in 1958 when twenty employees of the State Land Commission refused to build a fence which would have cut across a fairy-haunted mound. After a Cabinet meeting summoned by De Valera to deal with the emergency, Erskine Childers, Minister of Lands, announced that the rights of the fairy domain would be respected, and the proposed fence was accordingly re-located.

were the repositories of such lore Yeats had a profound respect. "When we passed the door of some peasant," he once wrote, "we passed out of Europe."

Yet another theme that persistently haunted the imagination of Gaelic Ireland was that of the enchanted islands of the west lying submerged in ocean depths—Tir-na-Og, land of Eternal Youth, connected with the Fenian legend of Oisin, and Hy-Brasil, "island of great desire." The legendary sixth-century voyages of St. Brendan—who is believed by ultra-patriotic Irishmen to have preceded Leif Erickson by more than four centuries as the discoverer of America—helped to keep alive in Christian times this belief in a western paradise. Some medieval chroniclers—Dalerto (1325) or Fra Mauro (1459)—still marked Hy-Brasil as lying off the west coast of Ireland. The story of Brendan the Navigator and his celebration of Mass on the back of a whale was translated from Irish into Welsh, English, French, and Spanish.

The Sagas and Modern Ireland

The mythology created by the Gaels was submerged by the coming of Christianity. It was to remain buried for over a thousand years, during which time the gods and heroes of Celtic fantasy were to become the devils and demons of the new religion. Yeats depicts this vividly in his *Wanderings of Oisin,* a long poem written, as he tells us, under great emotional stress, at the age of twenty-three. In it, St. Patrick mercilessly taunts Oisin, the last survivor of the Fenians, now an old and broken man, threatening him with the everlasting torments of hell.

> You who are bent, and bald, and blind
> With a heavy heart and a wandering mind,
> Have known three centuries, poets sing,
> Of dalliance with a demon thing.

To which Oisin replies indignantly that, were he young again, he "would leave no saint's head on his body from Rachlin to Bera of ships." He adds with dignity that he would prefer to live in hell with his old companions than in heaven without them. "It were sad to gaze on the blessed and no man of old I loved there. . . . I will dwell in the house of the Fenians be they in flame or at feast."

Yet so strong was the hold of the old pagan sagas that when after the lapse of centuries the warlike Gaelic ethic had ceased to be a challenge to the new religion, Christian monks sometimes felt the stirrings of an unexpected tenderness toward the ancient myths and saved them from oblivion by recording them, as in the twelfth-century Book of Leinster, upon vellum. To this devotion of monastic scribes to the fabled past of their own country we owe the texts that tell us about such things as the warfare between Cuchulain and Maeve, the chivalry of the Fenians, or the tragic love of Deirdre.

Sometimes the monk whose fancy had been taken by these ancient legends experienced a curious conflict of sentiment as he transcribed them. "I who have written this history, or rather fable"—so runs one monastic gloss upon the Cattle Raid of Cooley—"am doubtful about many things. . . . For some of them are figments of demons, some are poetic imaginings, some true, some not, and some for the delight of fools."

In the nineteenth century the old heroic legends were even more astonishingly revived as a means of reasserting the sentiment of Irish nationality, still vibrant after seven more centuries of foreign rule. It was a stroke of genius to name the new revolutionary organiza-tion—the Irish Republican Brotherhood, founded in New York in 1858—after the Fenians of old. No name touched such chords of na-tional feeling, or stirred such depths of national consciousness; no name more completely fused past and present in a single glowing sense of union.*

John O'Leary, the old Fenian returned to Ireland in 1885 after twenty years of prison and exile, was the living incarnation of the imagined chivalry of ancient Ireland. "Glory O! Glory O! to the bold Fenian men." For a whole generation of young Irishmen—for poets like Yeats and militants like Pearse—the magnificent physical presence of O'Leary with his great luminous eyes and patriarchal beard symbolized the indomitable spirit of Irish resistance. Nearly fifty years later, Yeats could still evoke the magic of romantic na-tionalism by recalling "beautiful lofty things, O'Leary's noble head."

At St. Enda's school Patrick Pearse quoted as his educational ideal the words attributed to Oisin himself: "Strength in our hands, truth in our lips, and cleanness in our hearts." In that spirit, Pearse was to lead the Easter Rising in 1916. For him the end of the Fenian saga was death before a firing squad in Kilmainham jail.

Though the Fenians had never lost their hold entirely upon the minds of simple people—in the eighteenth century, a devout priest named Shemas Cartan deplored that women were still given to "la-

---

*As a child in Boston in the 1920s, John Fitzgerald Kennedy was taught to cherish the memory of the Fenians.

menting, tearing their hair, and keening pitifully after the Fenians"—
Cuchulain, the young god-hero of the Red Branch cycle, had been
dethroned in folk imagination. He had, in fact, been dispossessed by
Christ. Lady Gregory deplored the fact that in the west of Ireland,
while the memory of Oisin and Finn was still alive, the name of
Cuchulain had virtually disappeared.

Her young friend Yeats was to perform for the lost Cuchulain an
even more impressive service than he had rendered the Fenians. In
passionate reveries inspired by the sagas he was to resurrect Cuchulain from centuries of neglect and transform him into a prime symbol of modern Ireland—an Ireland, he hoped, that would be free
equally from English and from clerical domination. For Yeats, Cuchulain came to symbolize not only the freedom of Ireland from any
trace of English influence, political or cultural, but also the spirit
of warlike aristocracy vanquished in modern times by the world of
stock exchange and counting house.

Even more surprising was the transformation of Cuchulain wrought
in the mind of Pearse. "I am Ireland," Pearse wrote of his native
land, "great my glory: I that bore Cuchulain the valiant." The future
president of the Irish Republic was not only an ardent nationalist
but a devout Catholic as well. Yet so great was his devotion to the
ancient sagas that he is said to have believed the Cuchulain epic to
have been divinely inspired. In Pearse's mind the images of Christ
and Cuchulain blended into one. Where others saw only the Irish
Achilles, he saw also the Crucified One. To the boys of St. Enda's
the Cuchulain extolled by Pearse was no longer the savage slayer,
hands reeking with the blood of foemen, but miraculously transformed into "a small dark sad boy, comeliest of all the boys of Eire,"
a hero with a childlike heart, none other than Pearse himself. Written
around the hall of St. Enda's, so that every boy in school should
know the words by heart, was a sentence attributed to Cuchulain:
"Though I live but a year and a day, I will live so that my name
goes sounding down the ages." AE, too, advised the youth of Ireland
to take Cuchulain as their model. He wrote: "Cuchulain represents,
as much as Prometheus, the heroic spirit of the redeemer in man."
Slieve Gullion, the mountain in Armagh connected by legend with
Cuchulain, should be as sacred to the Irish people, declared AE, as
Mount Sinai was to the Jews.

Whatever his romantic misconceptions about the past, Pearse did
actually reenact in life, in an Ireland that had grown sick of words
and phrases, tragedy as stark as any recorded in the sagas of old.
For the pastoral idyll of St. Enda's culminated in "a fiery epic be-

neath the burning ruins of the Dublin Post Office." Hence, with no sense of incongruity, Yeats could couple in verse the names of Pearse and Cuchulain, and identify the mild priestlike Catholic with the fierce pagan slayer.

> When Pearse summoned Cuchulain to his side
> What stalked through the Post Office?
> Who thought Cuchulain till, it seemed
> He stood where they had stood?

Today in Dublin's General Post Office, amid the ceaseless indifferent crowds that throng the building, Oliver Sheppard's beautiful *Pietà* of the dying Cuchulain, clasped by Erin in her arms, commemorates the sacrifice of Pearse and his comrades in the cause of Irish freedom.

BIBLIOGRAPHY

Colum, Padraic: *Treasury of Irish Folklore* (1954)
Flower, Robin: *The Irish Tradition* (1947)
Gregory, Lady Isabella:
_____: *Cuchulain of Muirthemne* (1902)
_____: *Gods and Fighting Men* (1904)
_____: *Poets and Dreamers* (1903)
Hyde, Douglas: *Songs of Connacht* (1893)
Macalister, R. A. S.: *The Archaeology of Ireland* (1949)
MacNeill, Eoin: *Phases of Irish History* (1937)
O'Grady, Standish: *The Coming of Cuchulain* (1894)
O'Rahilly, Thomas F.: *Early Irish History and Mythology* (1946)
O'Riordan, Sean P.: *Antiquities of the Irish Countryside* (1942)
O'Riordan, Sean P., and Glyn, Daniel: *Newgrange* (1965)
Powell, T. G. A.: *The Celts* (1958)
Raftery, Joseph: *Pre-Historic Ireland* (1951)
Yeats, W. B.: *The Celtic Twilight* (1893)

II

Ireland in the Dark Ages

St. Patrick

Gaelic Ireland was never incorporated into the Roman Empire. In A.D. 84, Julius Agricola, the ablest Roman governor of Britain, saw the mountains of Antrim from the Scottish coast and, according to Tacitus, meditated the conquest of Ireland with a single legion. When one recalls the failure of Caesar a century earlier to conquer Britain with two legions, it would seem that Agricola was fortunate in having changed his mind. No subsequent governor, so far as we know, ever set eyes on Ireland.

In Britain the destruction of Roman civilization in the fifth century was virtually total, so that Roman Britain bequeathed almost nothing to the future. Hence it may be surmised that Ireland, too, ultimately lost little in not having been brought under Roman rule. The one spiritual influence—Christianity—that did survive the collapse of Roman power in Britain was, however, transmitted to Ireland by a curious chance.

The gradual disintegration of the Roman Empire caused a political power vacuum that the barbarian tribes around its borders attempted to fill. Thus, at the end of the fourth century, the Roman province of Britain was simultaneously assailed from three directions—by the Saxons from Germany in the east, by the Picts from Scotland in the north, and by the Scots from Ireland in the west. The word "Scot" then meant "pirate" or "raider," and Ireland was known to the Romans not only as Hibernia, but as Scotia, the land of the sea raiders. (About the year A.D. 570, a number of these Scots migrated from

Ulster across the North Channel into the territory of the Picts, giving their name to the lands they now conquered—hence the northern half of Britain was in future to be known as Scotland.)

Early in the fifth century, one of these bands of Scots from Ireland, raiding along the shores of the Bristol Channel, captured the son of a Romano-British official, a boy named Sucat, and took him into slavery. After six years of captivity, the youth escaped to Gaul, became a convert to Christianity, and resolved to convert Ireland to the new religion. Sucat was to become St. Patrick, Apostle of Ireland. The conventionally accepted date of Patrick's conversion of Ireland is the year 432, and he is thought to have labored in that country until his death in 461—a date still open to question.

Modern scholars have found good grounds for doubting the truth of this familiar account. It is known, for example, that not Patrick but Palladius was the first Christian missionary to Ireland; and that Bede, the most learned historian of the Dark Ages, refers to Palladius but never mentions Patrick at all. The traditional account of Patrick's life is filled with stories of miracles—such as his magical victory over the Druid priesthood at Tara—but in his autobiography, the saint made no claim to have performed a single miracle. Since the earliest life of Patrick, written by Tirechan about 670, did not appear until two centuries after his death, there was ample time for the proliferation of pious legends.

In the *Confession,* which he composed in Latin, Patrick wrote in confident expectation of the imminent end of the world and Second Coming of Christ. With such an outlook he was naturally indifferent to facts and tells us tantalizingly little about actual persons and places. He was conscious of a lack of education ("rustic, exiled, unlearned," he calls himself) and tells us that he fought constantly against sexual temptation. Curiously enough, he seems at times not to have identified himself with Ireland or the Irish, a people he describes as "heathen barbarians," among whom he lived "daily expecting either slaughter, or to be defrauded, or reduced to slavery. . . ." As Professor Bury wrote, Patrick may have regarded Britain as his real home and himself as living in exile in his adopted land.

Yet whatever the reservations of scholars, the hold of Patrick upon the imagination of the Irish people has remained unshaken for more than fifteen hundred years. Other peoples have had their apostles, but it is doubtful whether any other nation has ever venerated a patron saint with the same fervor as that with which the Irish have exalted Patrick. Countless miracles have been attributed to his intercession. Innumerable cures have been wrought at dozens of Patrick's wells scattered throughout the land. Thousands of cottages in Ireland today are adorned with oleographs showing the Saint, arrayed in episcopal vestments, angrily banishing the serpents from Erin. Hissing and writhing, the snakes, according to Sean O'Casey, vanish over a cliff to reappear centuries later in America in the guise of Tammany politicians.

Patrick's alleged grave at Downpatrick and his Purgatory on an island in Lough Derg, County Donegal, have for centuries been places of pilgrimage. Even now, on the last Sunday in July, large numbers of pilgrims toil up the jagged, rock-strewn slopes of Croagh Patrick, the holy mountain of the West, upon whose crest Patrick is believed to have fasted for forty days and forty nights. The controversies of the learned have never perplexed the simple faith of those who climb the sacred mount on blistered, bleeding feet. "It is a pleasant journey compared to eternity," philosophized one aged pilgrim.

The unique character of Irish history—the long and tragic subjection to a foreign power, the many centuries of suffering and oppression—may help to explain this passionate attachment to a person whose reality one can but dimly glimpse across the gulf of centuries. Patrick became in course of time the supreme father figure of Irish history. The traditional day of his death—March 17—became the national feast day. The shamrock, reputedly his favorite plant, became the national emblem. It was believed by many that on the Day of Judgment, Patrick would stand at Christ's right hand to intercede personally on behalf of his chosen people. In the nineteenth century such beliefs were taken across the ocean by thousands upon thousands of Irish emigrants and transplanted to new lands—in America or the Antipodes.

In 1932 the fifteenth centenary of Patrick's mission to Ireland was commemorated by the holding of a Eucharistic Congress in Dublin, attended by pilgrims from many parts of the world. Throughout Ireland, candles were lighted in cottage windows, and bonfires blazed on the hills. The very Mass bell that Patrick had once used—apart from two manuscripts, the only object that can now definitely be connected with him—was used again at the High Mass celebrated by the Papal Legate, while Count McCormack sang "Panis Angelicus." Feeble, indeed, whatever the reveries of Yeats or Pearse, was the hold of the ancient pagan heroes—Finn or Cuchulain—compared to this overwhelming demonstration of popular belief.

Early Christianity in Ireland

Three leading characteristics distinguished Christianity in Ireland during the Dark Ages: the comparative weakness of the diocesan organization set up by Patrick, the dominance of monasticism, and the popular exaltation of the hermit.

Patrick is said to have established the center of his church at Armagh, the Canterbury of Ireland, in 444; and to this day, the Primates of Ireland, both Catholic and Protestant, each claiming descent from Patrick, maintain their sees in Armagh, the rival steeples confronting one another above the slate roofs of the small north Irish county town. But for many centuries in Ireland the power of the bishops remained weak compared to that of the abbots, the Pope himself being often referred to as "Abbot of Rome."

The Irish monasteries were usually founded and endowed upon a tribal basis, so that the lack of political unity among the Gaels was reflected also in the organization of the Irish Church. The abbots were generally chosen from the families of the chiefs, and their authority was greater than that of the heads of continental monasteries. The earliest important figure in Irish monasticism was St. Enda, who died about 530, having established several monasteries on the Aran Islands, to which students are said to have come from all parts of Ireland. Among the disciples of St. Enda were St. Ciaran, who in 548 founded Clonmacnois on the Shannon; St. Columba, who founded Derry, Durrow, and Kells, before going into exile at Iona in Scotland in 563; and St. Jarlath of Tuam.

Other leading monastic founders were St. Brendan at Clonfert, County Galway (583); St. Canice at Kilkenny (600); St. Kevin at Glendalough (622); and St. Colman at Inishbofin, an island off the coast of Mayo (651). Among women saints the most prominent was St. Brigid (452–523), in whose convent at Kildare a sacred fire was kept constantly burning (in continuance of a former pagan rite) until it was finally extinguished during the Reformation.

The discipline of Irish monasteries was far more severe than that of the Benedictine houses on the Continent. Its harshness rivaled that practiced by the Egyptian monks in the Thebaid. The Irish monasteries were not only houses of prayer and rigid penitential discipline; they were also schools and centers of art and learning. As previously Ireland had escaped conquest by the Romans, so now it escaped the ravages of the Teutonic barbarians pushing westward over Europe. The sixth century, which in Britain and Gaul was a time of ceaseless war and plunder, was in Ireland a period of peace, which witnessed what has been called the golden age of Irish monasticism. Seeking refuge from Saxon, Frank, or Goth, scholars migrated to Ireland, bringing with them precious manuscripts, often in Greek. So common in Irish monasteries did a knowledge of that language become, at a time when its use had died out in many parts of Western Europe, that in the sixth century, if a man knew Greek, it was frequently assumed that he had come from Ireland. Alcuin, the leading scholar at the court of Charlemagne in the eighth century, and Eriugena, the foremost philosopher of Europe in the tenth, both studied at Clonmacnois.

The Latin classics were also copied in the scriptoria of Irish monasteries like Clonfert and Bangor. St. Columbanus could quote Virgil, Horace, Ovid, Sallust, and other classical writers. His learning was said to rival that of his contemporary Pope Gregory the Great (590–604). Bede praised the hospitality of Ireland to foreign scholars, referring to the Irish as "that harmless nation which has always been so friendly to the English." Arnold Toynbee dates the predominance of Irish scholarship in Western Europe from the founding of Clonmacnois in 548 to the founding of Ratisbon in Bavaria by Irish monks in 1090. During these five centuries, he writes, it was "the Irish who imparted culture and the English and Continentals who received it." Even Sir Winston Churchill, never a friend of the Irish, in *The Birth of Britain* grudgingly allows that in the Dark Ages Ireland was distinguished by "missionary endeavours and monkish scholarship."

The intellectual vitality of Ireland during the Dark Ages was perhaps the result of a cultural cross-fertilization in which the spirit of Christianity breathed fresh life into the old Gaelic society. It was as if the coming of the Christian faith, with its novel emphasis on virtues spurned by the pagans—peace, gentleness, and order—developed in Ireland new potentialities and unlocked new sources of spiritual energy which had hitherto found no release. For the first time in many centuries the island was linked to Europe by a common faith and culture. It was St. Patrick who first brought the art of writing into Ireland, and this alone may well have been a powerful cultural catalyst. Christianity also introduced a knowledge of Latin, thus providing Ireland with a key to a literature of astonishing richness, both pagan and Christian.

Early Christian Art in Ireland

It was in the realm of art that this cultural efflorescence in Ireland produced its finest results. The outstanding artistic achievement of Irish monasteries was the perfection of their illuminated manuscripts. Unequaled in Europe in their day, these products of Irish scriptoria are still remarkable for the extraordinary intricacy and precision of their design with its innumerable interlacings and convolutions. The eighth century Book of Kells, now the chief treasure of Trinity College, Dublin, is undoubtedly the glory of Irish religious art during the Dark Ages. Never before or since, perhaps, have such loving care and decorative skill been lavished upon parchment—in this case upon what Françoise Henry terms a "very bad and careless translation of the Gospels." Even Giraldus Cambrensis, that veteran traducer of things Irish, was astonished, during his visit to Ireland in 1185, by the beauty of the Book of Kells.

The unknown calligraphers who created this exquisite work were ardent in their idealism and inspired by a quest for perfection which they themselves would have described as a desire to serve the greater glory of God. Modern scholars have traced Byzantine and even Coptic influences in the Book of Kells, but its main artistic inspiration derives from the nonrepresentational, curvilinear art of Gaelic Ireland, which, after centuries of usage, still proved sufficiently vital to adapt itself to Christian purposes and foreign themes. So great was the vigor of this ancient decorative art that its impulse was transmitted also to Britain, where it flowered in Northumbria in masterpieces such as the Lindisfarne Gospels.

It is perhaps an amusing illustration of the ingrained anticlericalism of the modern Irish Renaissance that its leading writers not only belittled the monastic learning of the Dark Ages but proved insensitive to its artistic achievement as well. Thus Standish O'Grady, one of the pioneers of the movement, once described the Book of Kells as "an appalling monument of misdirected labour and too ingenious toil."

Another art that flourished in Ireland in the Dark Ages, and especially in the eighth century, was metal work—as seen in chalices, reliquaries, and other objects associated with religious worship. In the National Museum of Dublin today are many splendid examples of the superb achievement of these early metal workers. Of such artistic treasures perhaps the best known are the Tara Brooch, found accidentally in County Meath in 1850, and the Ardagh Chalice, excavated in 1868 in County Limerick. The brooch is made of bronze covered with a tracery of gold, and the chalice is silver, decorated with gold filigree.

When in the ninth century the art of the illuminated manuscript began to decline in Ireland, its place was taken by the newer art of the sculptured Celtic cross. Since during this period Ireland was subjected to the terror of repeated Viking invasions during which the monasteries were burned or plundered, it is possible that the new emphasis on sculpture arose from a desire to seek in images carved on stone a measure of survival improbable for a material as easily destructible as parchment.

Be this as it may, there developed in Ireland during the ninth and tenth centuries another highly characteristic native art—that of the beautiful "wheel" crosses, of which about thirty are still standing today. Like the illuminated manuscripts, the Celtic crosses represent a blending of Christian belief with Gaelic decorative impulse; here, too, it seems likely that, in this case through the sculptor's chisel, Mediterranean and Oriental influences found their way into Ireland. A Syrian motif has been detected in the grapevine pattern that adorns some crosses, and others are topped by miters that seem oddly to anticipate the turbaned headstones of Moslem graves.

Usually, Biblical scenes were chosen to decorate the shaft and arms of the high cross, but sometimes, as on the great cross at Clonmacnois where St. Martin of Tours is shown giving the Celtic tonsure to St. Patrick, more recent history is depicted. The supreme example of the "wheel" cross with sculptured panels is, of course, the Cross of Muiredeach at Monasterboice, County Louth (c. 923), where scenes from the Old and New Testaments are represented. According to one authority, Professor Arthur Kingsley Porter, the Christ of the Monasterboice Last Judgment is clearly descended from Osiris. In the art of the sculptured cross, he writes, Ireland was "immeasurably in advance of the rest of Europe."

The Early Irish Hermits

Strong as was the impulse felt by some to settle in religious communities, the need felt by others to flee society and seek peace in solitude was no less urgent. The numerous rocky islands lying off the west coast of Ireland came to exert a powerful attraction upon those who desired a solitary existence. Such hermits sought out the most lonely and inaccessible places they could find, living there in solitude among the sea birds, the gray sea below, the gray sky above, and hearing always "the three oldest cries in the world, the cry of water, the cry of wind, and the cry of birds." One of the most striking examples of this desire to "wander the loud waters" is found in an entry of the Anglo-Saxon Chronicle for the year 891 which records how three Irishmen were cast up by the sea upon the coast of Cornwall. Taking with them a few provisions, they had put to sea in a boat—"because for love of God they would be on pilgrimage, they recked not where."

Using the stones that everywhere strew the ground, the solitary anchorite would build for himself one of those small, circular, unmortised beehive huts called cloghauns. The Oratory of Gallerus in Kerry shows that even the humble cloghaun could sometimes aspire to the dignity and beauty of a work of art. Today one may still see dozens of these cloghauns clustering like gray growths upon the bleak promontories of the West. A spring of fresh water and a patch of soil on which to grow barley sufficed for the material needs of their occupants, whose days were spent in contemplation and worship of God.

If the lives of such anchorites were harshly austere, they were not without moral grandeur. Contemporaries felt something heroic in this shunning of the world to face alone the elemental hazards of existence. Such hermits were popularly regarded with awe and were frequently canonized by the piety of later generations. Perhaps the most appealing feature of such lives was their constant, familiar association with the world of nature, and their knowledge of the ways of birds and animals, the rhythm of whose existence was so closely interwoven with their own. The fact that they were vegetarians and never killed for food led often to an intimacy between man and beast, of which many charming legends are told. Sometimes, anticipating the story of St. Francis and the Wolf of Gubbio, these anchorites shared their abode fraternally with animals and lived in mutual regard.

The least attractive side of this hermit existence is the extreme severity of its penitential self-discipline. For no matter where these early saints settled—by storm-bound cliff or in the depths of some secluded grove—there in the secret desires of their own flesh, Satan accompanied and pursued them. By prolonged fastings and scourgings, by incredible penances and austerities, they sought to drive him out. Some immersed themselves up to their necks in freezing water, others slept with corpses. Yet even on the scene of such deluded victories gained over self, Satan still manifested his presence, inspiring some with the spirit of pride in their perverse self-conquest and others with an unholy zeal to emulate and surpass the performance of rival hermits also seeking popular acclaim.

The Irish Missionaries

The prestige of Celtic Christianity spread through Europe till it seemed almost to challenge that of Rome. Irish missionaries, traveling on foot, traversed northern France, Switzerland, and southern Germany. They passed beyond the Rhine and the Danube and crossed the Alps into Italy. Half a continent was brought peacefully under the sway of their spiritual dominion. By the eighth century, Irish influence was dominant in at least fifty important religious centers stretching across Europe from Brittany to Austria. Four centuries later, the great St. Bernard was to pay tribute to the work of Irish missionaries. "Into foreign lands," he wrote, "these swarms of saints poured as though a flood had risen."

Wherever they penetrated, these Irish monks planted seeds of new culture in lands devastated by the barbarian invasions, and took with them the arts and crafts of the Celts. Everywhere they exhibited the same independence and the same distaste for organized authority which had marked their existence in Ireland. It was said of the great Columbanus, who began his missionary journeys in 590, that he "railed at bishops, upbraided kings, and scolded popes." He founded monasteries without having secured the permission of the bishops in whose dioceses the monasteries were located. The independent, even satirical, spirit of the Irish is aptly illustrated in the well-known gloss found on one Gaelic manuscript:

> To go to Rome,
> Great trouble, little profit
> The king whom you seek, you will not find
> Unless you bring him with you.

In 563, St. Columba, who had exiled himself from Ireland in expiation of a crime committed in early manhood, brought Christianity to Scotland by founding a monastery on the rocky island of Iona. As a result of Columba's mission, some three hundred monasteries are said to have been founded in Scotland, of which fifty-three survived until much later times. From Scotland, St. Aidan, a pupil of Columba, carried the Christian faith into northern England, founding the monastery of Lindisfarne in 635. A number of Irish monks, like Fursey in East Anglia, also established themselves in various parts of England and played a considerable part in the development of Anglo-Saxon culture.

One of Columbanus' personal friends was the Irish monk St. Fiacre, who in the seventeenth century was, by an extraordinary chance, to become the special patron of two kings of France—Louis XIII and Louis XIV—and in the nineteenth to give his name to that popular Parisian conveyance—the cab.

Undoubtedly the two leading figures of Irish missionary activity during the Dark Ages were St. Columba, or Columcille, who died at Iona in 597, and St. Columbanus, who died in 616 at Bobbio in the Apennines, where his tomb may still be seen. In the minds of contemporaries, Columbanus came to rival Gregory the Great as the dominant personality of the age. St. Gall in Switzerland, Würzburg in Germany, Vienna in Austria, possibly even Prague in Bohemia, owe their origins as cultural centers to the restless energy of Columbanus and his followers. At Bobbio he founded a library that in the Middle Ages was to become one of the finest in Europe. Plundered by Renaissance scholars, its treasures later found their way to the Vatican Library in Rome and to the Ambrosiana in Milan, as well as to other famous libraries in Naples, Vienna, and at the Escorial.

In Ireland, Columba inspired a love and devotion second only to the reverence already felt for Patrick. Himself a poet, as well as a descendant of ancient kings—he claimed descent from Cormac of Tara in the tenth generation—Columba impressed those who knew him by his gentleness and fortitude. In his fondness for birds and animals he suggests a northern St. Francis. His life by St. Adamnan, one of his pupils, was one of the most popular works of the Dark Ages. In exile on Iona, Columba bore always in his heart the image of Ireland. Thus in a Gaelic poem attributed to him, he exclaims that should death suddenly overtake him, it would be because of "the love I bear the Gael."

To such an extent did Columba in Ireland become the patron saint of exiles that thirteen centuries after his death emigrants about to go to America would spend their last night in Ireland praying and weeping at the shrine by Gartan Lake in Donegal where the saint had been born.

Nor were the writings of Columba soon forgotten. In the twelfth century a beautiful lament written in exile was still attributed to him:

> Delightful to be on the Hill of Howth before going across the white-haired sea; the dashing of the waves on its face, the bareness of its shores. . . .

I stretch my gaze across the salt sea to the plain of the plenteous oak trees; many are the tears of my clear grey eye as I look back on Ireland.

Beloved are Derry and Durrow, beloved is pure Raphoe . . . beloved are Swords and Kells . . .

In the twentieth century many Irishmen look back nostalgically to the Dark Ages as the most splendid period in Irish history—as a period in which Ireland, secure from foreign invasion, exerted a beneficent and civilizing influence upon the continent of Europe. "Island of Saints and Scholars": how readily the familiar phrase comes to Irish lips. Compared to the universal homage paid by the people to Patrick and Columba, the invocation by artists and scholars of the memory of Cuchulain and the Fenians—potent as it was to prove in literature and politics—seemed a relatively esoteric and artificial thing.

It is a commonplace in modern Ireland to seek an analogy between the role of Irish missionaries in the twentieth century in bringing Catholicism to Africa, Asia, and America and that of their predecessors in the Dark Ages who saved so much of Western Europe for the Faith; and indeed it would be difficult to overestimate the debt owed by the Catholic Church in modern times to the devotion of Irish nuns and monks and priests. Some enthusiasts, alarmed by the threat of communism, go so far as to envisage Ireland as once more assuming the role of savior of spiritual values in the West. To such fantasies, an awareness of the modest if useful part played by Eire in the United Nations will supply a needed corrective.

The Vikings in Ireland

In the ninth century out of the far North there began to fall upon Europe a pitiless rain of destruction. To Western Europe the Viking onslaught proved a scourge even more terrible than the barbarian invasions that had overthrown the Roman Empire. During the ninth and tenth centuries Christian civilization, which had raised itself with such difficulty out of the ruins of the ancient world, was itself in danger of destruction. From Paris to Byzantium, and from Iona to Seville, the Vikings loosed their murderous rage, burning and raping, sacking towns and monasteries, spreading desolation through many lands. On many corpse-strewn fields of battle they boasted of the warm meals they had given to the wolf or the raven. An agonized petition, wrung from terrorized Christians, was inserted in the Liturgy in an effort to secure divine protection. "From the fury of the Northmen, good Lord deliver us!" This was everywhere the prayer of Christian men—from Iona to the Pillars of Hercules.

From this new menace, Ireland, which had escaped both conquest by the Romans and plunder by the Saxons, was not immune. For more than a thousand years—since the first coming of the Gaels—Ireland had been secure against invasion, but now she shared the common fate of Europe. Command of the sea was the basis of Viking power; it enabled the Norsemen to sail with impunity up the great rivers of Europe—Rhine, Humber, Seine, Loire, Tagus, or Guadalquivir—and to ravage cities far inland. The raven banner streaming from the mast, the gaudy-colored sails and brightly burnished shields, the elaborately carved and proudly swelling prows of Viking ships—these for two centuries were the bane of Western seas—from the Shetlands to Gibraltar.

Ireland with her brimming rivers was peculiarly vulnerable to seaborne invaders. The Shannon, the Liffey, the Lee, the Barrow, the Nore, the Blackwater, and all the other streams that water the land so generously, returning its abundant rainfall to the sea—these became the highways of the Northmen. Without leaving their vessels, they could penetrate to the heart of the island. Hence Clonmacnois, situated on the Shannon almost in the geographical center of Ireland, was as vulnerable as seaports like Dublin or Waterford. The dense forests that in later centuries were to prove so formidable an obstacle to English armies—as Essex and other English generals would learn to their cost—were no security against an enemy who moved by water. Tempestuous wintry weather was welcomed for the brief security from invasion that it might bring. "Fierce is the wind tonight," begins a Gaelic poem of the eighth century,

> It ploughs up the wild hair of the sea.
> I have no fear that Viking hosts
> Will come over the water to me.

The Norwegians, coming down from the Hebrides, were the first to prey upon the coasts of Ireland. In 795, the monastic *Annals of the Four Masters* include the direful entry: "The burning of Rathlin by the foreigners; its shrines broken and plundered." In 802, Iona was sacked and the shrine of Columba left desolate. His bones are said to have been taken up by his followers and brought back to Ireland. By 812 the Norsemen had penetrated as far as Dingle in Kerry. In 819 they landed beneath Ben Eder, the headland that forms the northern arm of Dublin Bay, and named the little harbor

Howth. Nowhere in Ireland did the Vikings encounter organized opposition. Indeed, the petty kings of Ireland were more anxious to engage in local skirmishes than to unite against the foreigner. So the Vikings sailed unmolested up the rivers of Ireland. In 839, Armagh, the ecclesiastical capital, suffered its first thorough devastation. Two years later, the pirate Thorgils enthroned his wife, Aud, upon the high altar of Clonmacnois, whence she uttered direful heathen prophecies.

Not until about 841 did the Norwegians settle at Ath Cliath, by the Ford of the Hurdles near Liffey mouth, where the route from Tara to Wicklow crossed the river. From the black pool formed by the confluence of the Liffey and the Dodder they renamed the place "Dubh Linn," and thus at length Dublin came into existence.

The monopoly of plunder in Ireland held by the Norwegians remained unchallenged for half a century, but in 851 the raven banners and bright sails of their kinsmen, the Danes, appeared on the Irish Sea coming up from the south. In that year, after a great naval engagement in Carlingford Lough which is said to have lasted three days and nights, the Danes defeated the Norwegians and drove them out of Irish waters. The victors now took over the agreeable task of plunder and destruction.

Clonmacnois and Armagh were both sacked about a dozen times; Kildare sixteen or seventeen times; Kells five times; Glendalough four times, and other monastic centers suffered in similar fashion. Probably not a single monastery in Ireland escaped pillage, though not all were wiped out. The monastic schools were destroyed, and the art of illuminating manuscripts was virtually extinguished. Thistles grew and pigs rooted among the ruins of what had once been houses of prayer. Some places, like Clonmacnois, were destroyed so thoroughly that they remained but a memory—as the scholar-poet Thomas Rolleston wrote in the nineteenth century:

> In a quiet, watered land, a land of roses,
> Stands St. Ciaran's city fair,
> And the warriors of Erin
> In their generations slumber there.

The plunder ransacked from Irish monasteries may be seen today in the museums of Oslo, Bergen, and elsewhere in Norway.

The chronicles of the later Dark Ages in Ireland, as elsewhere in Europe, are little more than an endless, monotonous, dreary catalogue of horror—a record of unceasing violence and terror, rape and wrong, mutilation and murder: an episode in the long nightmare from which history has not yet awakened. As always, war brought in its wake disease and starvation. At times even cannibalism made its appearance. In 963 a chronicler recorded tersely that there was "intolerable famine, so that the father used to kill his son and daughter to get food."

In course of time all storms blow over, and after some two hundred years the storm of the Vikings began at length to subside. Warriors gradually turned into traders, the worship of Thor and Woden blended with that of Christ, and the Savior was transformed into a young warrior dying valiantly in his Father's cause. It is impossible to fix a precise date at which the Danes in Ireland accepted Christianity. Such acceptance was at first often nominal, a swapping of gods for the sake of some fancied advantage. Some thought the Cross to be sovereign on land, the hammer of Thor on sea. Christian baptism was often succeeded by a relapse into pagan ways. Confusion was compounded by the demoralization of Christianity itself, so that in their own internal feuds, Irish chieftains would sometimes call upon the Danes for aid against their Christian neighbors. The lines dividing Christian and heathen became blurred, especially when the two peoples began to intermarry—as for example, when Brian Boru, the first effective king of all Ireland, took for his queen a Danish princess, Gormlaith.

From the confused and shifting warfare of the petty Irish kings, fighting one another and the Danes, there emerged at length the first real secular hero in Irish history, Brian Boru. Brian was king of Munster for thirty-seven years (965–1002), and then High King of Ireland from 1002 to 1014. He was to Ireland what Charlemagne had been to France, and Alfred the Great to England. Like Alfred, Brian was not only a successful warrior but a patron of art and learning. He rebuilt churches and monastic schools and sent abroad for manuscripts and teachers. He restored Armagh as the ecclesiastical capital of Ireland. Again like Alfred, his good repute does not derive solely from native sources, for in the Icelandic sagas also he is described as a fair and honorable foeman, free from vindictiveness.

It was on Good Friday, April 23, 1014, that the long struggle between the Irish and the Danes reached its dramatic climax. The Leinstermen, regarding Brian as an upstart from Munster, formed an alliance against him with the Danes of Dublin and with Norsemen from the Orkneys. The issue was joined at Clontarf by the shore of Dublin Bay. The battle lasted from dawn to sunset on a cold and gusty day of spring. So closely were the warriors engaged that the "sharp cold wind" from the east blew drops of Danish blood into the faces of the Irish. From the ramparts of the city the Norsemen of Dublin watched the struggle. As the sun was setting, the Danes, still fighting furiously, were slowly "driven back upon their ships moored off the shore, and were drowned by hundreds because the tide was at flood." *

In the hour of victory, as he knelt in prayer, the seventy-three-year-old Brian was slaughtered by Brodir, leader of a band of Vikings who burst into his tent. His son and grandson were also killed that day. Their bodies were taken up and buried reverently with that of Brian in Armagh. The battle of Clontarf was long remembered by both peoples who took part in it. In faraway Iceland the Saga of Burnt Njal described how Odin himself, mounted on a gray horse, was seen riding to the fray, while Irish chroniclers related how on the fatal day King Brian heard the ominous wail of the banshee.

After the battle, Brian's court poet MacLiaig mourned the passing of his master and the subsequent decay of Kincora, the capital that Brian had established on the Shannon (near the modern Killaloe, County Clare). In the nineteenth century, James Clarence Mangan translated this Gaelic elegy in his famous "Lament for Kincora."

> Oh where, Kincora, is Brian the Great?
> Oh, where is the beauty that once was thine?
> Oh, where are the princes and nobles that sate
> At the feast in thy halls, and drank the red wine?
> Where, oh Kincora?

Gradually the Danes in Ireland, who remained in control of the chief ports, accepted Christianity and intermarried with the native Irish, adopting their dress, language, and customs. Thus Sitric, ruler of Dublin, married a daughter of Brian Boru and founded Christ Church Cathedral in 1040. The Ostmen—as the Danes in Ireland came to be called—soon became the most enterprising traders of the northern seas; and when the carnage of two centuries was ended, it became clear that the Vikings had performed one valuable service for Ireland: they were the first people ever to introduce town life into the island. Even today many of the leading Irish seaports bear the names the Vikings gave them—Cork, Limerick, Wexford, Waterford, Wicklow—as do three of the four provinces—Ulster, Leinster, and Munster. In their piratical raids the Danes had sundered Ireland from the Continent, but after the wars were over, in busy commercial intercourse they reforged the links they had severed and now began

---

*Modern research has established that there was in fact high tide in Dublin Bay at six o'clock on that fateful April evening.

to contribute positively to Ireland's wealth and prosperity. As early as the tenth century, it would appear, the wine trade was in their hands; and as late as the seventeenth century a majority of Dublin merchants could trace their names back to the Norsemen.

The Round Towers

Of Irish architecture in the Dark Ages very little has survived, because the Christians, like the pagan Celts before them, built usually in wood. Now, by a curious irony, the period of destruction inaugurated by the Vikings saw a new type of structure which was to prove more permanent than any other contemporary building—the Round Tower.

The Round Towers of Ireland constitute, as it were, a sort of mysterious and romantic signature of the Dark Ages themselves. No other buildings are so unmistakably indigenous to Ireland as they. Even now, as one catches an unexpected glimpse of one of those extraordinary stone cylinders—rising above the rook-filled treetops or by the still waters of a lake, dominating some ruined church or punctuating some melancholy reach of bogland—one experiences a sensation that no other country can yield.

The antiquarian George Petrie, who traveled through Ireland in the early nineteenth century, was one of the first to speculate seriously about the original purpose of those mysterious structures, which had fascinated him since boyhood. It seems clear now that they may have served a dual purpose—both religious and military: as belfries, but also as lookout towers, signal stations, and defensive strongholds. No weapons existed in the Dark Ages which could batter down the thickness of their walls. When marauders were scouring the countryside, killing and burning, it seems highly probable that whole local populations—with their poultry, pigs, and perhaps even livestock—would take refuge in the towers. Since it was impossible to set fire to these buildings, or to smoke their defenders out, starvation remained the only means of reducing them. But to invaders as restless as the Danes, this could hardly have seemed an eligible course of action—hence they probably departed in search of easier plunder elsewhere. One may imagine the gratitude and affection felt toward the Round Towers by those whom they had saved from possible torture or death.

Older authorities list about 120 Round Towers as having survived the Dark Ages. Today there are about eighty of them still standing in Ireland. Some—like those at Glendalough or at St. Canice's Cathedral in Kilkenny—are in an excellent state of preservation;

others are half in ruins. Some have lost their conical stone caps; others have kept them. The Round Towers are so distinctively Irish that outside that island only two have been discovered—both of them in Scotland (at Brechin and Abernathy) and both showing signs of Irish influence.

BIBLIOGRAPHY

Ashe, Geoffrey: *Land to the West* (1962)

Bieler, Ludwig: *The Life and Legend of Saint Patrick* (1949)

_____: *Ireland: Harbinger of the Middle Ages* (1963)

Carney, James: *The Problem of St. Patrick* (1963)

Daniel-Rops, Henri: *The Miracle of Ireland* (1959)

DePaor, Maire and Liam: *Early Christian Ireland* (1945)

Gougaud, Dom Louis: *Christianity in Celtic Lands* (1932)

Henry, Françoise: *Early Christian Irish Art* (1963)

_____: *Irish Art During the Viking Invasions, 800–1020* (1967)

_____: *Irish High Crosses* (1964)

Hughes, Kathleen: *The Church in Early Irish Society* (1966)

Kenney, James F.: *Sources for the Early History of Ireland* (1929)

McNally, Robert E.: *Old Ireland* (1965)

Mould, Daphne D. C. Pochin: *Ireland of the Saints* (1953)

Porter, Arthur Kingsley: *The Crosses and Culture of Ireland* (1931)

Ryan, Rev. John: *Irish Monasticism* (1931)

Sweeney, James, ed.: *Irish Illuminated MSS* (1965)

Walsh, A.: *Scandinavian Relations with Ireland in the Viking Period* (1922)

III

Ireland in the Middle Ages

The Bull of Adrian IV (1156)

The Norman Conquest of 1066 gave England a unity she had not known since Roman times, and the introduction of feudalism meant a social and political system almost identical with that which prevailed on the Continent. The Normans were also political allies of the Papacy and enforced in England the ecclesiastical reforms that popes like Gregory VII sought to impose everywhere in Europe. Dynastically, England's fortunes were now linked closely to those of France. The result was that England found herself closer to the Continent, both culturally and politically, than she had been since the days of ancient Rome.

These developments accentuated the social and cultural isolation of Ireland from the rest of Europe. Ireland had not yet achieved political unity: after the death of Brian Boru, his kingdom had collapsed. Ireland still clung to the unwritten customs of the old Brehon laws derived from the Gaelic past, with their stress upon communal ownership of land.

The failure of Ireland to participate in the Crusades not only demonstrated the degree of her isolation from the rest of Europe but confirmed the low opinion of her held by Continental nations. In the twelfth century, St. Bernard—despite his acquaintance with St. Malachy (1100–48), the most powerful personality in the Irish Church since Columbanus—denounced the Irish as "a barbarous people," Christians in name only, and strangers to Christian marriage. The recent failure of Ireland to join the Second Crusade, which Bernard preached so fanatically, may have been the immediate cause of his strictures against a country of which he knew only by report.

The Norman kings of England, who combined ruthless cruelty with superstitious piety, were not slow to see the possibilities of this situation or to exploit it for their own advantage. Parvenus themselves, and always greedy for land, they had good reason to exaggerate the backwardness of Ireland. Lanfranc and Anselm, the first two Norman Primates, both claimed jurisdiction for Canterbury over the Irish Church. Perhaps as the result of such claims, at the Synod of Kells in 1152 the Irish bishops at last reformed the Church in Ireland and strengthened its organization, establishing thirty-six dioceses and four provinces—Armagh, Dublin, Cashel, and Tuam—each under an archbishop. But neither such reforms nor even the universal respect accorded to St. Laurence O'Toole (1132-80), the last native Irish Archbishop of Dublin, could avert the subjection that menaced the Irish Church.

In 1156, by the famous Bull *Laudabiliter,* Adrian IV (Nicholas Brakespear) solemnly granted the lordship of Ireland to the king of England—in this case Henry II (1154-89), founder of the Plantagenet dynasty. In the Bull, Adrian—the only English pope in history—authorized Henry to conquer Ireland in order to teach "the truth of the Christian faith to the ignorant and rude." A secondary motive was that Peter's Pence should be transmitted more punctually to Rome. The authority cited for this extraordinary papal claim to dispose of a distant island was the Donation of Constantine of 325, finally proved in 1440 by the Renaissance scholar Lorenzo Vallo to have been a forgery of the Vatican Chancery in the late eighth century.

For the Irish who in later generations were to pride themselves upon their special loyalty to the Holy See, Adrian's Bull was a severe blow to national pride. It is not surprising, therefore, that in the nineteenth century, Cardinal Moran and other leading Irish clerics should denounce the document as a forgery. Their natural suspicions were reinforced because the original of the Bull had disappeared. Not even a copy could be found in the Vatican archives, the only extant versions coming from English sources. A generation that saw the exposure of the clumsy attempt by the *Times* to ruin Parnell by forgery was disposed to believe that this was not the first time England had employed such means to advance her interests in Ireland.

Unfortunately for the theory of forgery, throughout the Middle Ages and down to the Reformation the Irish unquestioningly accepted Adrian's Bull. They likewise accepted as authentic three letters of a later pope, Alexander III, all of which are still extant, confirming Henry II's right to conquer Ireland. Ultimately the matter was put beyond doubt by the scholarly investigations of Kate Norgate in 1893;

and today no reputable Irish scholar disputes the authenticity of the Bull, which thus provided moral justification for a conquest that was to inaugurate one of the great tragedies of Western history and subject Ireland to foreign rule for 750 years.

The Norman Conquest of Ireland (1170–71)

Fourteen years elapsed before the English—or to be more exact, the Anglo-Normans—acted on the authority contained in Adrian's Bull. The actual pretext for invasion was provided by the infidelity of a woman—a fact with which medieval chroniclers, a hardy race of misogynists, did not fail to make great play.

In 1152, Devorguilla, wife of O'Rourke, prince of Brefni, eloped with Diarmid, king of Leinster. The lady in question was forty-four, her husband sixty, while Diarmid himself was a mere forty-two. "Never, never," says the Young Man in Yeats's *Dreaming of the Bones*, "never, never shall Diarmid and Devorguilla be forgiven." Fourteen years passed before O'Rourke got his revenge, but in 1166, Diarmid—already hated by his subjects for numerous cruelties—was driven out of Ireland. He promptly sought help from Henry II of England in regaining his kingdom.

The person, however, who was at this moment best situated to aid Diarmid was Henry's vassal, Strongbow, Earl of Pembroke in Wales. After a small vanguard of Norman knights landed at Bannow, County Wexford, in May, 1169, Strongbow himself invaded Ireland in August, 1170, with two hundred Norman knights and about a thousand men-at-arms. He took Waterford by storm, and in Reginald's tower—which still stands on the quays by the Suir—he married Diarmid's daughter, Eva, with promise of succession to her father's throne. Then in September, the Normans took Dublin from the Ostmen. This news spurred Henry into action. Fearing that Strongbow might establish himself as an independent sovereign in Ireland, the English king came to Dublin in October, 1171, and received Strongbow's homage along with that of a number of Irish chieftains. Finally, in 1175, Rory O'Conor, last claimant to the ancient title "High King of Ireland," went to England in person and at the Treaty of Windsor swore allegiance to Henry as his lord. In return he was confirmed as king over those parts of Ireland that were not yet in Norman hands.

It is interesting to note that, in deference to the Pope's authority, Henry contented himself with the modest title "Lord of Ireland" and refrained from styling himself King. Not until England had broken with the Papacy at the Reformation did any English ruler arrogate to himself sovereignty over Ireland. In 1541, Henry VIII finally changed his title from "Lord" to the more imposing one of "King of Ireland."

Giraldus Cambrensis on Ireland

Ireland was overcome by a handful of ruthless adventurers whose violence and cruelty were masked by a façade of religiousness. Strongbow and his allies were true descendants of the band of robber barons who had conquered England on the field of Hastings. Strongbow himself, a barbarian with a squeaky voice, is said to have hewn his own son in half when the boy showed signs of fear in battle— a deed that, according to some, is commemorated in Christ Church cathedral in Dublin, where the earl lies in effigy with the truncated body of the boy beside him, carved in stone. As for Henry, the earl's liege lord, he came to Ireland fresh from the murder of Becket and condemned throughout Christendom for the sacrilege.

It is a principle of human nature, wrote Tacitus, to hate those whom we have injured. The conquest of Ireland was to provide a further illustration of this truth. In the eighth century, Bede had described the Irish in a kindly and charitable way. Four centuries later, the chronicler William of Malmesbury could still refer to them as "a race of men harmless in genuine simplicity and guiltless of every crime." During a conquest marked by extreme brutality, such friendly judgments could serve no useful purpose.

In 1185, Giraldus Cambrensis (Gerald of Wales), a dignitary of the Welsh Church, came to Dublin in the train of Prince John, youngest son of Henry II. In two works, the *Conquest of Ireland,* dedicated to the king, and the *Topography of Ireland,* dedicated to his son, Richard the Lion Heart, Giraldus justified the conquest and vilified the conquered people.

"For that we may not omit all mention of the perjury and treachery, the thefts and robberies in which this people with few exceptions so outrageously indulge, nor of their divers vices and most unnatural filthinesses," exclaimed Gerald bombastically, "this nation is the foulest, the most sunk in vice, the most uninstructed in the rudiments of faith of all nations upon earth. They shrink not from incest, nor do they frequent the Church of God with due reverence." While in Ireland, Giraldus had the pleasing opportunity of lecturing his hosts upon their vices. Preaching in Dublin, he scolded the Irish bishops for not having "rooted out some of the great enormities of the nation."

Reflecting on the great number of saints in the Irish calendar, Giraldus could not resist the taunt that Ireland had not yet produced a single martyr—an omission all the more unaccountable, he observed maliciously, in "a nation so exceedingly cruel and thirsty for blood." At this point, the Archbishop of Cashel was heard to whisper to his neighbor that Ireland's deficiency in this respect was likely soon to be remedied.

On returning to England, Giraldus repeated his forensic triumph in three successive lectures before appreciative audiences at Oxford. Throughout the Middle Ages the Archdeacon of Wales was to remain the chief, indeed almost the sole, interpreter of Ireland to the English people. In every century he was to serve as the model for later traducers of Ireland—from Edmund Spenser in the reign of Elizabeth down to James Anthony Froude in that of Victoria.

Characteristics of Norman Ireland

In a single year, 1170, two hundred knights, supported by about a thousand men-at-arms, conquered Leinster, the richest province of Ireland. The ease of the victory may be explained in terms of Norman superiority both in weapons and in military organization. The Irish, who fought on foot and wore almost no protective armor, were no match for heavily mailed knights fighting on horseback. Nor were their spears and light axes able to withstand the heavy battle-axes of the invaders. The Welsh infantry who protected the flanks of the Norman cavalry were armed with an even more deadly weapon—the longbow, the weapon that in later centuries would win England a series of brilliant victories over France in the Hundred Years' War. Stated in modern terms, the Normans had superiority over the Irish both in firepower and in mobility.

To subjugate Ireland effectively, the Normans constructed castles—originally of timber but later of stone, like those they had already built in Britain to overawe the Saxons and the Welsh. By means of almost impregnable strongholds such as those at Trim, County Meath, and Carrickfergus, County Antrim, they were able to hold down large areas with comparatively small forces and secure their communications from attack. By 1205, Dublin Castle—the Irish equivalent of the Tower of London—had been built. For seven and a half centuries it was to remain the most hated symbol of foreign domination in Ireland. In defiance of the Treaty of Windsor, large areas were taken from the Irish and granted to Norman lords like Hugo de Lacy in Meath or John de Courcy in Ulster.

As in England and in Wales, so in Ireland the castles of the Normans everywhere dominated town and countryside. Under the protective cover of their crenellated walls, the invaders introduced wholesale into Ireland the institutions they had already developed in the sister island: counties with sheriffs, assize courts with justices and juries, and the whole system of feudal land tenures. By 1260, some fourteen counties had been established. The Brehon laws based upon communal property in land were swept away, and feudal ownership was established in their place. This change involved a sudden, violent breach of customs that were well over a thousand years old. The Irish were either driven from the river valleys into the bogs and forests or else were suffered to remain as serfs—to till the lands of their conquerors.

Charters of incorporation modeled after those of English boroughs were granted to the Norman towns of Ireland. Thus Dublin, colonized by Bristol merchants, received a charter modeled on that of the city of Bristol. For the first time in Irish history, Irish administration was centralized in Dublin. A Council, modeled on the Norman Curia, was set up under a Justiciar, and three Courts of Common Law—King's Bench, Common Pleas, and Exchequer—were introduced precisely on the model of the famous Courts of Common Law in England. At the head of the Irish administration was a Lord Deputy, appointed by the Crown in London, to represent the person of the king. The liberties promised by John in Magna Carta (1215) were extended to Norman Ireland the following year. Finally, as the keystone of the governmental edifice, some thirty years after Parliament, the last great institution of the Middle Ages, had emerged at Westminster in 1265, a similar body, with two representatives elected from nine Irish counties, was summoned by royal writ to meet in Dublin. The Irish parliament, meeting first in 1297, came to be composed of two chambers—a House of Lords and a House of Commons. Representation in these bodies was, of course, confined to the Anglo-Normans, the native Irish being entirely excluded from them. Both towns and boroughs were represented in the Dublin parliament from 1300 onward.

Failure of the Normans in Ireland

Yet, however much the medieval institutions of England and Ireland might parallel one another, in one fateful respect the Norman conquest of Ireland differed entirely from the earlier conquest of England by the Normans. For whereas in England circumstances

fused the two peoples, Saxon and Norman, conquered and conquerors, into one, in Ireland, the two peoples remained tragically
divided, each hating and despising the other. Throughout the Middle
Ages in Ireland, there were really two nations, not one: Anglo-
Norman Ireland, based on town and castle, with its earls, barons, and
knights; and the old Gaelic Ireland whose social order was still
rooted in the tribal customs of the Celts. These two Irelands were
further sundered by the gulf of language, since Gaelic survived
down to the eighteenth century as the language of the people. Gaelic
Ireland, moreover, remained hopelessly divided against itself, since
not even the coming of a foreign invader could persuade the Celts
to unite and lay aside their ancient feuds.

The Anglo-Normans never succeeded in controlling much more than
half of Ireland; and during the fourteenth and fifteenth centuries the
area under their rule steadily contracted until by about 1450, outside
of the towns protected by the castles, it had shrunk to a coastal strip
of territory known as the Pale, which actually included little more
than the county of Dublin. The long strain of the Hundred Years'
War (1337–1453) waged by England against France was undoubtedly
a factor in diverting the attention of the English kings from the
lordship they claimed in Ireland.

In a vain attempt to arrest this territorial shrinkage, the Anglo-
Normans promulgated the famous Statute of Kilkenny in 1366. Its
object was to prevent further encroachments by the culture of the
native Irish upon that of the invaders. For the basic fact about the
Anglo-Norman occupation of Ireland was that it failed to attract
sufficient emigrants from England. Hence the English settlers were
constantly intermarrying with the Irish and even adopting their
language, their customs, their culture, and their dress. The Statute
of Kilkenny was designed to put an end to this process of assimilation by which the English settlers were constantly in danger of losing
their identity. By making marriage between English and Irish a capital
crime, it attempted to establish in Ireland a sort of fourteenth-century
apartheid. It likewise prohibited to Englishmen the use of the Irish
language, the singing of Irish airs, the playing of the Irish harp, and
the wearing of the kilt. Despite the savage penalties meted out by the
statute, it proved impossible to enforce and remained largely a dead
letter. The assimilation of the English into the native Irish population
proceeded just as before. Thus Gerald, third Earl of Desmond, one of
the leading Anglo-Norman noblemen in Ireland, became famous for
the excellence of the Gaelic poetry that he composed.

The power of the Anglo-Normans was still further weakened by their internecine feuds. In course of time, three great baronial families emerged—the FitzGeralds, who in 1328 became Earls of Kildare; a younger branch of the family, who about the same ume became Earls of Desmond; and the Butlers (from which family W. B. Yeats later liked to fancy himself descended), who became Earls of Ormonde in 1329, and who sixty years later acquired Kilkenny Castle as their seat. During the fourteenth and fifteenth centuries the history of southern Ireland was to a large extent the dismal story of the intrigues, marriages, assassinations, and wars that engrossed these three competing houses and their supporters. Lesser families carried on smaller feuds with their own neighbors. One feature of these baronial wars that proved especially injurious to the common people was the custom known as "coygne and livery," by which private armies claimed the right to live off the lands over which they fought.

In addition to the rivalry of the great Anglo-Norman families, there was also the constant hostility between these families and the merchants of the towns. The latter owed direct allegiance to the English Crown, which had granted them their charters and were at loggerheads with the neighboring territorial magnates who sought to encroach upon their liberties. Often, fear of the dispossessed Irish constituted the only bond between the merchants living by trade and the feudal lords who maintained themselves by exploiting the serf labor of the native Irish.

A further illustration of the pitiful state of medieval Ireland is provided by the fact that the Church, whose authority was nominally accepted by both Anglo-Normans and Irish, proved totally unable to control the savagery of either. Christian men now inflicted upon one another atrocities similar to those that they had once suffered from the Vikings. Norman barons—like the Crusaders, Vikings beneath a veneer of Christianity—plundered Irish monasteries without mercy. Thus the cathedral of Armagh was ravaged no less than three times in five years (between 1184 and 1189). "It is generally asserted," complained Donnell O'Neill, lord of Tyrone, in 1315, "that to kill an Irishman is no more than to kill a dog—and even monks have been known to say this and to make it good in arms." Doubtless there was little to choose between the barbarism of either party, despite their profession of a common faith.

Two events in particular, during the fourteenth century, brought greater horror to Ireland than anything she had suffered since the Dark Ages—the invasion of the Scots under Edward Bruce, between 1315 and 1318, and the coming of the Black Death in 1350–51. In 1315, in a desperate attempt to throw off English rule, a number of

Irish chieftains, led by the O'Neills of Ulster, offered the crown of Ireland to Edward Bruce, younger brother of Robert Bruce, king of Scotland. Since the English had just suffered at Bannockburn in 1314 the most severe defeat they had ever sustained at the hands of the Scots, it seemed an auspicious moment. Landing at Larne, in Antrim, the next year, Edward Bruce revealed his ruthlessness by destroying the town of Dundalk and burning a church at Ardee that was full of helpless refugees. In 1316, Bruce had himself crowned king of Ireland at Dundalk and destroyed the country as far south as Dublin and westward to the Shannon. Two years later he was killed in battle at Faughart, County Louth. For three and a half years the marauding Scots had proved themselves a worse scourge than even the Anglo-Normans. Large areas were reduced to desolation; acute famine appeared in 1316–17, and there were numerous deaths from starvation. The annalists record instances of cannibalism during these years.

A generation later, as the country was just beginning to recover from this disaster, there came the calamity of the Black Death, which ravaged Ireland in 1348 and 1349 and swept away, as elsewhere in Europe, perhaps a third of the population. In a single effortless stroke Nature thus surpassed the accumulated horrors of generations of man-made disaster in Ireland. John Clyn, a Franciscan friar in Kilkenny, has left a vivid account of the suffering caused by the Plague. In the last sentence of his work he expressed doubt whether a single member of the human race could survive it. He himself did not.

Despite the desolation wrought by disease and war, and notwithstanding the Statute of Kilkenny, the fourteenth century in Ireland saw a strong upsurge of Gaelic culture and a corresponding weakening in Anglo-Norman power. In the last decade of that century the rise of Art MacMurrough (1357–1417), who styled himself king of Leinster, alarmed the English so greatly that Richard II, taking advantage of a truce in the Hundred Years' War, came in person in 1394 to pacify Ireland—the first visit of a reigning sovereign since that of Henry II in 1171. Confronted with the largest army that had ever crossed the Irish Sea, MacMurrough prudently submitted; but no sooner had Richard departed than he revolted again. Richard's second visit to Ireland in 1399 proved the prelude to his own downfall, since in his absence from England his cousin Henry Bolingbroke seized the throne.

Two centuries later, referring to these unsuccessful forays of Richard II, Shakespeare was to perpetuate the anti-Irish prejudice voiced by the Elizabethan chronicler Raphael Holinshed:

We must supplant those rough rug-headed kerns,
Which live like venom where no venom else
But only they have privilege to live.

Aspects of Medieval Ireland

The Middle Ages often witnessed—at its highest intensity of contrast—
the immemorial conflict between the forces of life and death, of love
and hate, of creation and destruction, which constitutes the warp
and woof of every civilization. In medieval Ireland, too, despite the
continuous, inescapable presence of cruelty and violence, at least
three new creative influences can be discerned: the coming of a new
monastic order, the introduction of Gothic architecture, and the ad-
vent of the friars.

In 1150 the Cistercian monks made their earliest settlement in Ireland at Mellifont, County Meath, which became the motherhouse
of twenty-five Cistercian abbeys. The Cistercians were the first to introduce into Ireland the soaring forms of Gothic that were just then
arising everywhere in Western Europe; and from the meadows by the
Boyne there now arose the long tapering lancet windows, which were
the most characteristic feature of the new style. The new architecture
heralded the end of Irish Romanesque, of which the exquisite little
Chapel of Cormac, built on the Rock of Cashel between 1127 and
1134, may be considered the masterpiece.

Nearly a hundred years later arrived the mendicant friars—the
Dominicans in 1224 and the Franciscans in 1231—bringing with them
to Ireland the vitality of religious and social change that was stirring
throughout Europe in the thirteenth century. In Ireland, as elsewhere, by bringing succor to the poor, the Franciscans won immediate popularity; and soon there was scarcely a town of any size which
did not house one of their convents. Unfortunately, in the familiar
inevitable cycle their popularity gradually led to the usual wealth
and worldliness, so that in the fourteenth century they had become
as elsewhere a byword for selfishness and corruption.

Unlike the older monasteries, the friaries were located in towns
and hence shared in urban prosperity; for despite the endless feuding
of the times, there developed, especially in the fifteenth century, a
thriving commerce between Ireland and the Continent, especially with
Spain and France, and on this the prosperity of the towns was based.
The Cistercians proved to be excellent sheep-breeders. Irish wool, on
account of its fineness, was much in demand and commanded a good
price in Continental markets. Irish exports also included grain, salt,

meat, butter, cheese, fish, furs, hides, and timber. Wine was the chief article of import, together with coal, glass, salt, cloth from Flanders, and luxuries such as silks, satins, and spices. In some parts of Ireland, Spanish coins were almost the chief currency in use. Galway, especially, as the main port of entry for Spanish wine, achieved a degree of prosperity never equaled in later times. One curious feature of medieval Irish trade patterns was that the almost total dependence of Ireland upon England, which is the main characteristic of her economic life today, did not then exist, Irish commerce being far more bound up with Spain and France than with the sister island. As late as the mid-sixteenth century, a Spanish diplomat sent to Ireland by Philip II reported a brisk trade being carried on between Waterford and Lisbon, Galicia and Andalusia.

Despite the comparative prosperity of the seaports, Irish townsmen never came to play a part in the national life analogous to that of the English burghers in the House of Commons. This relative absence of a strong middle class may help to explain why throughout the Middle Ages Ireland remained one of the few European countries without a native university. We hear of a considerable number of Irish undergraduates as early as the thirteenth century, especially students of law, at Oxford; but in the early fifteenth century, Irish students were prohibited from entering either Oxford or Cambridge, and those who were then in residence were expelled. In view of this, the failure of Ireland to develop a native university is even more puzzling. Attempts were made at Dublin in 1320, and at Drogheda in 1468, to establish universities, but both attempts proved unsuccessful.

No doubt the failure of Ireland in the field of secular learning is accounted for partly by the strength of the old monastic schools and partly by the strong vitality of the Gaelic tradition of culture which had never become institutionalized in the form of the university. Yet it was a great modern Gaelic scholar, Douglas Hyde, who admitted that in the later Middle Ages "Ireland produced nothing in art, literature, or scholarship even faintly comparable to what she had achieved before."

Poynings' Law and Silken Thomas

In England, the accession of the Tudors in 1485 is conventionally regarded as ending the Middle Ages. In Ireland, two unrelated events may perhaps be regarded as terminating the medieval period: the passing of Poynings' Law in 1494, and the execution of Silken Thomas, Earl of Kildare, in 1537.

In 1494, an English Lord Deputy, Sir Edward Poynings, summoned a packed parliament to Drogheda and got it to pass a statute that limited the authority of the Irish parliament and greatly increased its dependence upon the English Crown. For the act provided that no business should be brought before the Irish parliament unless it had already been approved by the English Privy Council, and also that the consent of the Council was necessary to validate any measure that the Irish parliament might pass. The act was also construed as implying that all previous statutes enacted by English parliaments should apply equally in Ireland. Thus the Irish Lords and Commons were placed in leading strings controlled from Westminster and the vaunted legislative independence of Ireland became a fiction.

One must remember, however, that the claim of the Dublin parliament to represent Ireland was no less a fiction, because only the Anglo-Norman minority was represented in it, and its effective authority hardly extended beyond the narrow limits of the Pale. In later centuries the Protestant ascendancy in Ireland would strongly resent the subjection to which Poynings' Law had reduced the Dublin parliament. Such subjection was the more galling, since in 1409 and 1450 Irish statutes had declared the Irish parliament to be alone competent to legislate for Ireland.

The revolt of Silken Thomas in 1534 may be regarded as a protest against the resolve of the English Crown to humble the pride and degrade the authority of the Anglo-Norman minority in Ireland, and as the last defiance by that minority of the government in London. In the fifteenth century the Earls of Kildare had emerged as the most powerful family in Ireland. Between 1470 and 1536, four successive Geraldines had virtually ruled that part of Ireland that still professed allegiance to the Crown. The office of Lord Deputy had frequently been entrusted to them. They had even intervened in English politics, as when during the Wars of the Roses they had supported the House of York; and after the Lancastrian victory at Bosworth in 1485, which placed Henry VII on the throne, the Kildares continued to support Yorkist pretenders such as Lambert Simnel (who was actually crowned as Edward VI in Dublin) and Perkin Warbeck, the personable young Flemish Jew whom Bacon called that "little cockatrice of a king." Arrested by Henry VII for his part in these plots, Garrett FitzGerald, the eighth earl, known also as the "Great Earl," Lord Deputy from 1478 to 1513, was imprisoned in London but was soon released. If all Ireland could not rule the earl, Henry Tudor is reported to have said, then he should rule all Ireland.

The strong centralized despotism of the Tudors was the English version of the statecraft expounded in Machiavelli's handbook *The Prince* (1513). In England the Court of Star Chamber (1487) was the Crown's chief agency for enforcing its despotic will, and it was not long before its equivalent appeared in Ireland also—the Court of Castle Chamber, with its headquarters in Dublin Castle.

The new despotism was naturally hostile to the medieval loyalties that still survived in Ireland, regardless whether they were feudal or tribal in character. Cardinal Wolsey, therefore, who was completely subservient to his master Henry VIII and who dominated politics from 1513 to 1529, determined to eliminate the power of the Fitz-Geralds in Ireland. To a political upstart like Wolsey, wholly identified with the royal absolutism, the very existence of quasi-independent feudatories such as the Kildares was both an anomaly and an affront. Three times in fifteen years (1519, 1527, and 1534) the ninth earl was summoned to England to answer charges of treason. In 1534 he died grief-stricken in captivity in the Tower of London.

His son, Thomas FitzGerald, tenth Earl of Kildare, was then twenty-one—a handsome, impulsive, high-spirited, and ambitious young man. Although born in England of an English mother and married to an English wife, Silken Thomas (known by this sobriquet from the silken tassels worn by his knights upon their helmets) identified himself wholly with the fortunes of his family in Ireland. Angered by his father's fate, in 1534 he revolted and made common cause with the native Irish against the English Crown. Since this was also the moment at which Henry VIII had renounced the Pope's authority, Kildare seized the opportunity to proclaim that Henry was a "heretic," whereupon Paul III withdrew the excommunication that he had previously passed upon the earl for having instigated the murder of an aged Archbishop of Dublin, an Englishman named Allen.

For more than a year this "headlong Irish Hotspur" controlled the greater part of Leinster, though never Dublin itself. But though he had some seven thousand troops ("galloglasses") at his disposal, Silken Thomas lacked the vital new weapon that had recently transformed the art of war. His castle at Maynooth, which had been considered impregnable, was battered down by a train of siege artillery brought from England, and the earl was taken captive. Five of his uncles were also arrested, though three of them had not only taken no part in the rebellion but had counseled against it.

For sixteen months the young earl was imprisoned in the Tower of London, and for part of this time at least, he was left starving and half-naked. One may still see in the Beauchamp Tower the pathetic lettering incised upon the wall of a cell THOMAS FITZG— the name cut short no doubt by an abrupt summons to the scaffold. For in February, 1537, together with his uncles, Silken Thomas suffered death at Tyburn under the headsman's axe. This execution before the jeers and curses of an alien mob was perhaps the most ceremonious blood-letting that had yet taken place in Ireland's history. It would be the grim harbinger of many more in future. By a curious irony, while Silken Thomas thus suffered the ignominious and terrible fate of a traitor, his sister, the "fair Geraldine," whose beauty the Earl of Surrey praised in several sonnets, was to become a chief ornament in the society of Elizabethan England.

It is noteworthy that so young and glamorous a victim as Silken Thomas, whose life and death alike were so dramatic, should have failed to become a popular symbol in Ireland. Later generations never regarded him as a martyr in the struggle for independence. The Young Irelanders, the Fenians, and the men of 1916 made no use whatever of his name; the revolutionary canon established by Pearse in the Declaration of Easter Week likewise excluded him. The oblivion that fell upon the memory of Silken Thomas is no doubt testimony that in the early sixteenth century the sentiment of Irish nationality was still waiting to emerge.

BIBLIOGRAPHY

Curtis, Edmund: *History of Medieval Ireland* (1938)

Green, Mrs. Alice Stopford: *The Making of Ireland and Its Undoing, 1200–1600 (1908)*

Leask, H. G.: *Irish Churches and Monastic Buildings*, 3 vols. (1955–61)

Orpen, Goddard: *Ireland Under the Normans, 1169–1216*, 4 vols. (1911–20)

Richardson, Henry G.: *Parliaments and Councils of Medieval Ireland* (1947)

Richardson, Henry G., and Sayles, G. O.: *The Administration of Ireland, 1172–1377* (1962)

_____: *The Irish Parliament in the Middle Ages* (1952)

Seymour, Rev. St. J. D.: *Anglo-Irish Literature, 1200–1582* (1929)

Zimmer, Heinrich: *The Irish Element in Medieval Culture* (1891)

IRELAND SINCE 1500

- •   Towns
- △   Mountains (of historic interest)
- ✸   Battlefields

IV

Ireland in the Sixteenth Century

Characteristics of Tudor Ireland

The sixteenth century was decisive in Irish history, for it was under the Tudors, and especially in the reign of Elizabeth, that the tragedy of Ireland began to assume its specifically modern aspect. In that period there occurred four new developments that were to be crucial in the shaping of Irish destiny for the next three hundred years. The first was the coming of the Reformation, which added the new factor of religious intolerance to the existing sources of division between Ireland and England.

The second was the Elizabethan policy of the Plantations, continued under the Stuarts, by which millions of acres of Irish land were seized by English colonists, their previous owners being driven into the bogs or the mountains, or left to die of starvation—a fate that befell tens of thousands. For all their brutality, the original Anglo-Norman settlers had never indulged in the wholesale eviction of the native inhabitants, still less their extermination—a policy that was now to be advocated by Elizabethan statesmen and men of letters and justified upon grounds of religion.

The third new feature of the situation was Ireland's appeal for help to the Continent. From this time forward it was realized that England's danger was Ireland's opportunity. Irishmen, therefore, sought aid from whatever Continental power happened to be England's enemy at the moment. In the sixteenth century this naturally meant Spain. In later centuries it would involve successively France, whether Bourbon or Revolutionary, Imperial Germany, and even—on one brief occasion—Communist Russia.

The final characteristic of Irish history during the sixteenth century was the long-delayed emergence of a genuine feeling of nationality. The wholesale introduction of English settlers and the brutality of the attempt to colonize Ireland broke down the barriers between the native Irish and the Anglo-Irish (for so we may now term the descendants of the original Anglo-Normans) and thereby paved the way for joint action, based upon a new awareness of a common interest.

Hugh O'Neill, Earl of Tyrone, and his son-in-law, Red Hugh O'Donnell, Earl of Tyrconnell, are perhaps the first figures to fore-shadow the modern spirit of Irish nationalism; and it is interesting to note that at this very time—the opening years of the seventeenth century—occurs the earliest of those evocations of Ireland as a suf-fering woman, whose appeal was to involve so many future genera-tions of young men. It was about the year 1600 that Costello of Ballyhaunis, a bard attached to the O'Donnell family, first sang the praise and mourned the sorrows of Ireland under the haunting image of the Dark Rosaleen. Nearly three centuries later, Parnell would assert that of all who had died for Ireland, few would have done so had they not been able to picture her as a young and beautiful woman in distress, for whose sake, if necessary, they must lay down their lives. The same romantic dream consoled John Mitchel in the bitterness of Tasmanian exile after the failure of 1848.

The Reformation in Ireland (1537–60)

Alarmed perhaps by the Geraldine rebellion, the Tudors sought to win over the leading Irish families by conferring upon them for the first time titles of nobility. Thus, having himself assumed the title "King of Ireland" in 1541, Henry VIII in 1542 created the Ulster chieftain, Con O'Neill, Earl of Tyrone, while the Burkes of Galway became Earls of Clanricarde and the O'Briens of Clare, Earls of Thomond.

The rebellion of Shane O'Neill in 1562, made in the name of the old Gaelic order, showed how hollow such titular allegiance actually was. Nor did Shane the Proud's extraordinary personal visit to Elizabeth in 1562 diminish his fierce spirit of independence or increase his respect for the Crown. The presence of his galloglasses at the English court, wrote the historian William Camden, caused "as much wonderment as if they had come from China or America." Shane's career, however, was cut short by his enemies the Mac-Donnells of Antrim, who murdered him in 1567. His head was sold to the English and for the next four years graced the gate of Dublin Castle.

In 1585, by the Composition of Connacht, the tribal chiefs of that province were transformed into territorial magnates holding their land directly from the English Crown. This meant that the new nobility became by law absolute owners of the soil, and the feudal rule of primogeniture superseded the customary rules of inheritance sanctioned by the Brehon laws. Hence not only was the personal authority of the Crown extended, but the ancient Gaelic tradition disintegrated.

A further means of aggrandizement lay ready to hand. The English Crown had always used the Church in Ireland as an instrument by which to promote its own interests. Important sees, like those of Dublin and Kilkenny, were habitually reserved for Englishmen. Hence when the Reformation was forced upon Ireland, it was accepted with equal docility by the Irish bishops and by the Dublin parliament. In 1537, the Royal Supremacy was proclaimed and the Pope's authority denounced. Simultaneously the dissolution of Irish monasteries and friaries was decreed. The Irish conventual houses were ransacked with a thoroughness and brutality rivaling that practiced by Thomas Cromwell in England—yet no popular revolt took place in Ireland like the Pilgrimage of Grace in Yorkshire. Nevertheless, with few exceptions the Irish chieftains refused to share in the monastic spoils.

Under Edward VI (1547-53) Protestantism was first established in Ireland. Without even the pretense of consulting the Dublin parliament, the Mass was prohibited in 1549, and Cranmer's *Book of Common Prayer* forced upon the Irish Church. Next year the first printing press was set up in Ireland for the express purpose of issuing the *Prayer Book* in English. Undoubtedly the new worship was difficult to enforce in the country at large, a circumstance that may help to explain why there was still no Catholic revolt in Ireland, nor had there yet been any martyrs, such as St. Thomas More in England.

If there was no overt resistance to the Protestant legislation of Edward VI, neither was there any enthusiasm for his Catholic sister, Mary (1553-58). If she was a Catholic, she was also a Tudor. Although no Protestant martyrs were burned alive in Ireland during her reign, Mary began the odious policy of the "plantations" by evicting the Irish from the two counties of Offaly and Leix, replacing them with Englishmen, and renaming those areas the King's County and the Queen's County—names that were not abolished until 1922.

Under Elizabeth (1558-1603) the English Acts of Supremacy and Uniformity of 1559, which were the foundation of the Anglican Church, were applied next year in Ireland and were accepted tamely by the Dublin parliament. The Mass was again abolished, the English liturgy reintroduced, and the Thirty-Nine Articles proclaimed. Thus the Protestant Episcopal Church of Ireland came into existence, with full possession of tithes and endowments and of all existing sources of ecclesiastical revenue. Yet outside Dublin and the leading towns it was again impossible to enforce the new religion. The magistrates could not collect the recusancy fines levied on Catholics for non-attendance at church. The fact, moreover, that so much of Ireland was still Gaelic-speaking emphasized the absurdity of attempting to introduce a Prayer Book in English.

Cases of individual resistance, however, and even individual heroism, were not lacking. In June, 1584, Diarmid O'Hurley, Archbishop of Cashel, suffered a martyr's death. His legs were roasted so thoroughly that the flesh fell away from the bones. After this excruciating torture the archbishop, courageous to the end, was hanged from a gibbet in Dublin. Thus was fulfilled the prophecy of his predecessor in the see of Cashel replying to the taunts of Giraldus four centuries before—that in future Ireland should not lack for martyrs.

Ireland was the only country in Europe, observed Lord Acton, where Protestantism, though supported by the government, failed to establish itself as the popular religion. This was due, no doubt, partly to the absence in Ireland of a strong middle class such as was elsewhere in Europe the seeding ground of Protestantism, and partly to the fact that Irish Protestantism was not a native growth but had been forcibly imposed from outside. Hence, from the beginning, Irish national sentiment was united against it. An unforeseen consequence of the Reformation in Ireland was the gradual drawing together, in defense of the old religion, of the native Irish and their old adversaries, the Anglo-Irish.

One subsidiary result of the Reformation in Ireland was the establishment of the first Irish university. In 1592, Queen Elizabeth founded Trinity College, Dublin, in part to strengthen the Protestant interest in Ireland, in part to counteract the lure for young Irishmen of Catholic colleges in Spain, France, and Italy, where many of the wealthier Catholic families had been sending their sons to be educated. Since Trinity, however, limited its membership strictly to Protestants, it is hard to see how this part of its professed intention could possibly have been realized.

The Reformation immeasurably widened the gulf that divided the two islands. England and Ireland became as alien to one another as any two countries in Europe. From then on, political differences were inflamed by religious bitterness as well. The English, who had once prided themselves upon their Catholicism, now despised the Irish for remaining true to that religion. The Irish, on the other hand, seeing Catholicism rejected by their hereditary enemies, embraced it all the more ardently. From that time forward, therefore, emerged that passionate loyalty to the See of Rome which still characterizes Ireland in the twentieth century.

The Plantation of Munster (1584)

During the "plantations" of Offaly and Leix, carried out under Mary, Dowdall, the Catholic Archbishop of Armagh, had suggested that the solution to the Irish problem was to drive out or kill the native Irish, settling the island with Englishmen. Under Elizabeth, the revolt of the Desmonds in Munster (1579-83) afforded a pretext for the policy of wholesale confiscation and partial extermination.

In 1579, Sir James FitzMaurice, cousin to the Earl of Desmond, landed in Kerry with the Pope's blessing and six hundred men supplied with arms by Spain. After Sir James had been killed in a skirmish, the rebellion quickly collapsed. In 1580 an equal number of soldiers—Spaniards, Italians, and Irish—landed at Smerwick on a dangerous and rocky stretch of the Kerry coast. Lord Grey de Wilton, the Lord Deputy, stormed their fort and though quarter had been promised, put to the sword every single survivor. The massacre was carried out by his second-in-command, Sir Walter Raleigh. Finally, in 1583, the Earl of Desmond, two of whose brothers had already been hanged and quartered, was captured and the rebellion came to an end. The earl's head was sent as "a goodly gift" to Elizabeth, who caused it to be set up on London Bridge, while the headless trunk adorned the city walls of Cork.

The manner in which the Desmond rebellion was crushed was bluntly explained by the Elizabethan sea dog, Sir Humphrey Gilbert, half-brother to Sir Walter Raleigh. "I slew," he wrote, "all those from time to time that did belong to, feed, accompany or maintain any outlaws or traiters; and after my first summoning of a castle or fort, if they would not presently yield it, I would not take it afterwards of their gift, but won it perforce—how many lives soever it cost; putting man, woman, and child to the sword."

The war had turned the fertile valleys of Munster into a charred and desolate waste. Towns and villages were destroyed, churches burned to the ground, human beings and cattle slaughtered. Before the rebellion, wrote the Irish annalists known as the Four Masters, "there was no need to watch cattle or close doors from Dunquin in Kerry to the green-bordered meeting of the three waters." * After the rising was over, they continued: "The lowing of a cow or the voice of a ploughman, could scarcely be heard from Dunquin to Cashel in Munster."

The experience of Munster was not untypical of the Elizabethan wars in Ireland. Thus in 1567 Sir Henry Sidney reported to the Queen how his troops had passed through Mayo and Roscommon "leaving behind them as fruitful a country as was in England or Ireland utterly laid waste"; while in 1580, having marched from Dublin to Limerick, Sir William Pelham described how he had "passed through the rebel countries, consuming with fire all habitations and executing the people wherever we found them." Severed heads of rebels were often despatched to Dublin. Without warning, soldiers would descend at daybreak upon peaceful mountain glens and butcher the sleeping inhabitants. We "slew many churls, women and children," reported a Captain Agard laconically in 1572, after one such manhunt at Glenmalure in the Wicklow mountains. Sometimes, just for "amusement" as Froude put it, the soldiers would strip peasants naked and throw them into bogs so as to enjoy their convulsive struggles for life.

The few half-naked wretches that survived such raids were starving. Wrote Edmund Spenser, the poet, who was an eyewitness of such horrors:

Out of every corner of the woods and glens, they came creeping forth upon their hands, for their legs would not bear them. They looked like anatomies of death; they spake like ghosts crying out of their graves; they did eat of the dead carrions, happy were they if they could find them, yea, and one after another soon after, insomuch as the very carcasses they spared not to scrape out of their graves. And if they found a plot of watercresses or shamrocks, they flocked there as to a feast.

The plains were littered with corpses whose mouths were stained green from the nettles and other weeds they had devoured in a last effort to keep themselves alive. A few years later, Fynes Moryson, the English secretary of Lord Mountjoy, described how the fleeing Irish

*The "green-bordered meeting of the three waters" refers to the confluence, near Waterford, of the Suir, the Nore, and the Barrow.

would devour shamrock, "which as they run and are chased they snatch like beasts out of the ditches."

The suppression of Desmond's rebellion was followed in 1584 by the Plantation of Munster. Half a million acres of fertile land were confiscated to the Crown. No distinction was made between those who had revolted and those who had not. All were expelled or put to death. The land was parceled out among "undertakers," who undertook to bring in sufficient settlers from England to re-people the country. Among those who received grants of land were Raleigh, who got twelve thousand acres, chiefly in County Cork, where he settled at Youghal, and Spenser, who got three thousand acres in North Cork.

Perhaps the most rapacious of the new landlords was Richard Boyle (1566–1643), who at the age of twenty-one arrived in Ireland with a gold bracelet, a diamond ring, and twenty-seven pounds in cash. By judicious speculation in land (he bought Raleigh's estates cheaply when the latter left Ireland), Boyle amassed a huge fortune and in 1620 was created Earl of Cork. (Robert Boyle, the eminent scientist after whom "Boyle's law" was named, was his seventh son and fourteenth child.)

Notwithstanding the misery caused by the Plantation of Munster, it failed in its prime object, since not enough Englishmen could be persuaded to settle in what was regarded as so dangerous and savage a country as Ireland. (In the next century, many Englishmen preferred to brave the hazards of the North Atlantic and the hostility of the American Indians, rather than risk their lives and fortunes among the natives of Ireland.) The original inhabitants therefore soon drifted back, virtual serfs on the land they had once owned, and became "hewers of wood and drawers of water" for their new English masters. Occasionally their resentment flared savagely, as when in 1598 they burned Kilcolman Castle, the home of Spenser, one of whose children is said to have perished in the fire. The poet himself managed to flee to Cork and thence to London, where three months later he died, a broken man both in body and in spirit.

Some of the "undertakers" made enormous profits out of cutting down the forests with which, in earliest times, the hillsides of Ireland had been densely covered. The Irish forests had always been dreaded by the English, partly for the obstacles they put in the way of communication, and partly because they afforded such shelter to Irish rebels. Now they were turned into a profitable source of revenue for the intruders. A valuable market for Irish timber, especially useful for casks in the wine trade with Madeira and the Canaries, yielded quick profits for English adventurers like Raleigh, who made a fortune. Thousands of acres of Irish woodland were permanently denuded. When Spenser first welcomed Raleigh at Kilcolman, the castle was encircled by woods "of matchless height." A few years later, not a tree was left, but "only a few naked fields surrounding the bare and burned walls of the castle." In the nineteenth century the Oxford historian Froude was to blame the Irish for having thus squandered their natural resources.

In his famous tract the *View of the Present State of Ireland,* written in Ireland in 1596 but not printed till 1633, Spenser hinted at the desirability of eliminating the Irish altogether. What distressed him most was the degree to which the Anglo-Irish ("the old foreigners," as the Irish now called them in contrast to the new Protestant settlers) and the original inhabitants had intermingled. The descendants of the Anglo-Normans he found "much more lawless and licentious than the very wild Irish. . . . The most part of them are degenerated and growen allmost meere Irish, yea and more malicious to the English than the very Irish themselves." As for the latter, he stigmatized them, in terms that closely echo Giraldus, for "theyr savage brutishnesse and loathsome filthinesse." Reverting to ideas that had once inspired the Statute of Kilkenny, Spenser now urged again the absolute prohibition of marriage between the two peoples, as well as the abolition of the Gaelic language and of Irish customs such as the barbarous use in surnames of prefixes like "O" and "Mac."

The very existence of the Irish was felt as an affront by many Elizabethans. "For if we consider the nature of the Irish customs," wrote Sir John Davies, Attorney General of Ireland under James I, "we shall find that the people which doth use them must of necessity be rebels to all good government, destroy the commonwealth wherein they live, and bring barbarism and desolation upon the richest and most fruitful land in the world." Sir Francis Bacon added the support of his great legal authority. Ireland, he argued, was "the last of the daughters of Europe" to be "reclaimed from desolation—to population and plantation; and from savage and barbarous customs to humanity and civility." Sir George Wise was another who paid tribute to England's civilizing mission in Ireland. "To this time," he explained, "this poor country had in manner no feeling of good order, neither knew the poor fools God nor their prince, but as brute beasts lived under the miserable yoke of their ungodly Irish lords."

Others saw in the tragedy of Ireland God's judgment on a sinful people. "The vengeance of Heaven," declared the chronicler Holinshed, "was heavy on the land." Sophisticated observers probed more deeply. "The real explanation of the mischief," wrote Wise, "was the devil who would not have Ireland reformed." Sir Geoffrey Fenton suggested the abundance of witches in Ireland as an alternate explanation for the recalcitrance of the Irish. Some Englishmen frankly despaired of any rational explanation. "There lieth some secret mystery," observed a Lord Deputy, Sir William FitzWilliam, "in this universal rebellious disposition." The famous antiquarian William Leland was impatient with the Irish for not allowing themselves to die out. Even when driven into the bogs and the mountains, he complained, "they increased to infinite numbers by promiscuous generation." Even religious antagonism among Englishmen made no difference where the Irish were concerned. Thus John Stow, a fanatical Protestant chronicler, denounced "the fury of the wild and savage people" who lived in Ireland; while Edmund Campion, the Catholic martyr and contemporary of Stow, condemned the Irish as being "for the most part infidels, wild and furious." Rare indeed was the common sense of a man like Sir William Cecil, Elizabeth's Secretary of State, who remarked in 1582 that "the Flemings had not such cause to rebel against the oppression of the Spaniards as the Irish against the tyranny of England."

The Revolt of Hugh O'Neill (1595–1603)

So little sense of unity was to be found at this time among the Irish that during the rebellion of the Desmonds the rest of Ireland had not rallied to their help. Even their kinsmen, the FitzGeralds of Kildare, remained neutral in the struggle that laid waste Munster; and the Ormondes at Kilkenny sided with the government against their fellow countrymen. Not until the great rebellion in Ulster in 1595 did the first glimmerings of a national spirit of resistance begin to appear in Ireland.

The Ulster revolt was led by Hugh O'Neill, Earl of Tyrone (1540–1616), and his son-in-law, Red Hugh O'Donnell (1571–1602), who between them managed to lift the revolt out of the sphere of tribal loyalties and infuse it with a truly national feeling. O'Neill had been brought up at the English court and had there learned something of the latest methods of war. He equipped his troops with modern arms, transforming the kernes who had fought with bows and arrows into musketeers, and the galloglasses who had fought with axes into pikemen. He also maintained a force of native mercenaries called "bonnachts." Although he purchased ammunition from Scotland, he lacked cannon and was unable to capture any walled city held by the English.

Red Hugh O'Donnell, who was thirty years younger than his father-

Hugh O'Neill (1540?-1616). Earl of Tyrone, leader of the Nine Years War (1595-1603) against Elizabeth; buried in Rome.

in-law, had a personal grievance against the English, who in 1588 had kidnaped him from a ship in Lough Swilly and kept him prisoner for six years in a dungeon of Dublin Castle. On Christmas night, 1594, Red Hugh, who had been put in irons after a previous escape, got away a second time. Snow had fallen and so bitter was the cold that he almost perished during his flight. Both his feet were frozen, and his great toes had to be amputated. Painfully he made his way north to Ulster, where O'Neill gave him protection and joined him in rebellion. Thus began the Nine Years' War (1595-1603).

After three years of desultory fighting, the combined forces of the two Irish chiefs gained a complete victory over Sir Henry Bagenal, the English commander, in 1598 at the battle of the Yellow Ford on the Blackwater, County Armagh. Bagenal was killed and his army of four thousand men destroyed in the most decisive victory that the Irish had ever gained against an organized English force. The following year, Red Hugh defeated and killed Sir Conyers Clifford, Governor of Connacht, in a battle in the Curlew Mountains, near Boyle, County Roscommon. As a result of these victories, revolt broke out in many parts of Ireland, including the one that destroyed Kilcolman and forced Spenser to flee for his life.

To crush the spreading revolt, Elizabeth in 1599 sent over her favorite, the young Earl of Essex, hero of the Spanish war, with sixteen thousand foot soldiers and thirteen hundred horsemen—the largest English force that had yet appeared in Ireland. The queen had always detested O'Neill personally and was shocked that chance "should make a base Irish kerne to be accounted so famous a rebel." She sternly admonished Essex not to return without victory. To her intense chagrin, after spending six months in Ireland the earl became so disgusted with the country, its inhabitants, and its climate that he threw up his command and returned to London—to die on the scaffold.

To replace Essex, Elizabeth sent out Sir Charles Blount, later Lord Mountjoy, whom Professor A. L. Rowse calls "perhaps the greatest English soldier of the period." Mountjoy brought with him, as his secretary, Fynes Moryson, whose sensational account of the contemporary degradation of Irish life made him the Giraldus of his age and an authority on Ireland who was still being quoted in Victorian times.

With the arrival of Mountjoy, the Spaniards realized that the crisis of the rebellion was at hand. Already, in 1595, Philip II had sent a fleet of ninety-eight ships, carrying eleven thousand soldiers, to help O'Neill; but storms at sea had dispersed this armada, which never reached Ireland. Now, in 1601, one of the ablest soldiers in Europe, Don Juan del Aguilar, landed at Kinsale with some four thousand men. From O'Neill's point of view, the Spaniards could hardly have chosen a worse base of operations since it was separated from Ulster by the whole length of Ireland, a country still almost without roads. The O'Neill and the O'Donnell nevertheless traversed this great distance, only to be routed by Mountjoy's horsemen on Christmas Eve at the battle of Kinsale (1601). The Spanish army was allowed to reembark for Spain, Del Aguilar praising the generosity of Mountjoy while condemning his late allies for being treacherous, useless, and barbarous.

After the disaster at Kinsale, which proved that the Irish levies were still no match for seasoned English troops, Red Hugh took ship for Spain, hoping to prevail upon the Spaniards to send another force to Ireland. In 1602, however, he was poisoned at Simancas by one James Blake, a renegade Irishman and agent of the English Crown. He was buried in the church of San Francisco in Valladolid, but the exact site of his grave is now unknown.

As for Hugh O'Neill, almost at the moment of Elizabeth's death in 1603, by the Treaty of Mellifont he made formal submission to the Crown. That same year, accompanied by Rory O'Donnell (1575–1608), younger brother of Red Hugh, he was invited to London by James I. There, to the disgust of many, they were received ceremoniously at court, where the king bestowed on Rory the title Earl of Tyrconnell. "How did I labour after that knave's destruction," growled Sir John Harington as he beheld O'Neill in the king's presence. "I adventured perils by land and sea, was near starving, ate horse-flesh in Munster, and all to quell that man who now smileth in peace with those what did hazard their lives to destroy him."

While the war had brought famine and desolation to many parts of Ireland, it had also cost England dear. "The Irish action," wrote a contemporary of Elizabeth, "we may call a malady and consumption of her times, for it accompanied her to her end; and it was of so profuse and vast an expense that it drew near a distemperature of state." The historian Clarendon was later to term Ireland "a sponge to draw and a gulph to swallow all that could be spared and all that could be got from England." Modern historians have put the cost of Elizabeth's Irish wars at more than two million pounds—a huge sum in Tudor money and perhaps near the equivalent in modern purchasing power of some $150 million. Not only money disappeared in Ireland but also reputations—for the failure of Essex was but the first in a long line that was to extend down to Augustine Birrell and Sir Hamar Greenwood in the twentieth century.

O'Sullivan Beare (1602–3)

Out of the ignominy and confusion attending the failure of O'Neill's rebellion, one remarkable episode deserves remembrance. Donnell O'Sullivan Beare, Lord of Dunboy (1562–1618), had been appointed by Tyrone to command the Irish forces in Munster. After the disaster at Kinsale and the subsequent retreat of O'Neill back to Ulster, O'Sullivan refused to surrender. Retiring to his castle at Dunboy, he declared himself for Philip II of Spain, and with 143 men held out against a besieging force of about 4,000, led by Sir George Carew, the President of Munster, till June, 1602. Of the valiant garrison, all but 50 were killed during the siege. Carew declared that Dunboy had been defended more obstinately than any other stronghold he had known. The bravery of the defenders, however, did not prevent him from hanging every one of the survivors he could lay his hands on.

O'Sullivan himself managed to escape. He promptly raised fresh forces and made his way to Glengariff, where, hoping for Spanish aid, he held out for some months longer. By January, 1603, his supplies were exhausted, and he realized that no help was to be expected from abroad. Determined not to surrender, he resolved to leave his wife and children in concealment and set out with a thousand followers on his famous winter march across Ireland. The sick and the wounded were perforce left behind, and all were killed by the English.

Of the motley band that accompanied O'Sullivan, only four hundred were men-at-arms, the rest being noncombatants, including a number of women and children. The terrible journey was made in freezing weather, with snow lying on the mountains. When the party reached the Shannon, a formidable obstacle, they managed to cross it by constructing eleven curraghs out of osiers and covered with the raw hides of their slaughtered horses. During the march they were continually attacked, both by the native Irish and by the Anglo-Irish. After an agonizing journey of two hundred miles, accomplished in the astonishing time of two weeks, a handful of survivors crossed the Curlew mountains into Leitrim and safety. Of the thousand who had originally set out, only thirty-five were still alive—eighteen soldiers, sixteen horseboys, and one woman. The corpses of those who had perished were said to have marked the way they had come.

The intrepid O'Sullivan finally arrived safely at the headquarters of O'Neill, whom he accompanied on his mission to London later that year. In 1604, taking his wife and children with him, he sailed for Spain, where Philip III created him Count of Berehaven and granted him a pension. On July 16, 1618, returning from Mass one morning in Madrid, he was murdered by a servant, John Bathe. Besides his extraordinary courage, O'Sullivan was remembered for his tall, graceful, handsome presence. His son, Donnell, fell a generation later fighting the Turks at Belgrade.

Though the name of O'Sullivan Beare is never mentioned in English textbooks, in Ireland his memory is still cherished. Thus during the Black and Tan war in 1920, as his flying column crossed the boggy pass between the mountains separating the counties of Cork and Kerry, Commandant Tom Barry recalled with pride how, more than three hundred years before, O'Sullivan Beare had traversed that identical route.

The epitaph of O'Sullivan Beare was written in the nineteenth century by James Clarence Mangan in the stirring poem that begins with the grandiloquent line:

Here lies the great O'Sullivan where thunder cannot rouse . . .

The Flight of the Earls (1607)

In 1607 there took place an unprecedented event that symbolically brought one long chapter of Irish history to a close, while opening a new one that introduced an element of discord and bitterness that has lasted to the present day.

After Mountjoy's death in 1606, his place as Lord Deputy was taken by Sir Arthur Chichester, who from the first was suspicious of Hugh O'Neill, Earl of Tyrone, and set spies upon him. Believing himself in imminent danger of arrest, O'Neill decided to flee Ireland and persuaded his young relative, Rory O'Donnell, to accompany him. They may conceivably have hoped to obtain Spanish aid and to return to Ireland with a Spanish army.

On September 3, 1607, the two earls, with ninety-nine followers, took ship at Rathmullen on Lough Swilly. It is said that O'Neill wept at being compelled in old age to go into exile. Their families had held power in Ulster since the twelfth century. The Four Masters, who were still recording Irish history in the monastery of Donegal, plangently expressed their grief over the Flight of the Earls. "It is certain that the sea has not borne nor the wind wafted from Ireland," they lamented, "a party in any one ship more eminent, illustrious and noble than they were. . . . Woe to the heart that meditated, woe to the mind that planned, woe to the counsel that decided on the project of their setting out on that voyage. . . ."

The two earls traveled slowly across France and Flanders, where they were lavishly entertained by the Spanish authorities, and finally reached Rome, where they took up residence and were received by the Pope in 1608. Not long after, O'Donnell died; but O'Neill lived on till 1616. The earls were interred side by side, beneath elaborately carved and crested tombstones, in the little church of San Pietro in Montorio on the slope of the Janiculum, with its incomparable view eastward over the domes and palaces of Rome.

Buried with the two earls in San Montorio were the last hopes of Gaelic Ireland. Twenty years later, the chronicle of the Four Masters came likewise to an end. Michael O'Clery, the last of the four authors and a lay Franciscan, died in Louvain in 1645. For him the Flight of the Earls must have meant the extinction of all prospect of an independent Gaelic Ireland. He had devoted himself all his life to history, wrote O'Clery, "for the glory of God and the honour of Ireland, and because the race of the Gael has passed under a cloud of darkness."

After the departure of O'Neill and O'Donnell, they were accused of treason and their lands declared forfeit to the Crown. The way was thus prepared for the Plantation of Ulster in 1608, in which thousands of Scottish Presbyterians and Englishmen were introduced into northern Ireland to settle on the territories from which thousands of Catholic peasants had been evicted. The Flight of the Earls proved a stroke of fortune for the Protestant interest in Ireland. Wrote Sir John Davies, the Irish Attorney General, in great jubilation:

> As for us that are here, we are glad to see the day wherein the countenance and majesty of the civil law and government hath banished Tyrone out of Ireland, which the best army in Europe and the expense of two millions of sterling pounds did not bring to pass. And we hope His Majesty's Government will work a greater miracle in this kingdom than ever St. Patrick did; for St. Patrick did only banish the poisonous worms, but suffered the men full of poison to inhabit the land still; but His Majesty's blessed genius will banish all those generations of vipers out of it, and make it, ere it be long, a right fortunate island.

Never was prophecy more deluded, for the century that was just opening was to be even more calamitous for Ireland, if that were possible, than the one that had just ended. The policy of extermination on which the poet Spenser had allowed himself to speculate was soon to be enacted in grim reality by the sword of Cromwell.

By a curious irony, from this period of despair there rose a song of hope—of hope indomitable, tinged with melancholy, longing, and defiance; for it was at this very time that Costello of Ballyhaunis conceived of the Dark Rosaleen.

Two centuries later a waif of the Dublin slums, James Clarence Mangan, would turn Costello's Gaelic into passionate English verse, and fuse inseparably the sorrows of his own life with the misfortunes of his country. In the nineteenth century, Lionel Johnson was to praise the "adoring, flashing, flying, laughing rapture of patriotic passion" which to him characterized Mangan's poem; but this rapture has been set to a music whose mournful cadences belie the sanguine message of the poem. From the tension thereby created arises an effect that is somber and haunting.

> O my Dark Rosaleen!
>   Do not sigh, do not weep!
> The priests are on the ocean green,
>   They march along the deep.

There's wine from the royal Pope
   Upon the ocean green,
And Spanish ale shall give you hope,
   My dark Rosaleen!
   My own Rosaleen!
Shall glad your heart, shall give you hope,
Shall give you health, and help, and hope,
   My dark Rosaleen!

BIBLIOGRAPHY

Bagwell, Richard: *Ireland Under the Tudors,* 3 vols. (1885–90)
Edwards, R. Dudley: *Church and State in Tudor Ireland* (1935)
Falls, Sir Cyril: *Elizabeth's Irish Wars* (1950)
_____: *Mountjoy, Elizabethan General* (1955)
Holloway, Henry: *The Reformation in Ireland* (1919)
Longfield, Ada K.: *Anglo-Irish Trade in the Sixteenth Century* (1929)
MacManus, M. J.: *Irish Cavalcade: 1550–1850* (1939)
Maxwell, Constantia: *Irish History from Contemporary Sources, 1509–1610* (1923)
_____: *The Stranger in Ireland, From the Reign of Elizabeth to the Great Famine* (1954)
Morley, Henry, ed.: *Ireland Under Elizabeth and James I* (1890)
Quinn, David S.: *The Elizabethans and the Irish* (1966)
Ronan, Myles V.: *The Reformation in Dublin, 1536–58* (1926)
_____: *The Reformation in Ireland Under Elizabeth* (1930)
Seymour, St. John D.: *Irish Witchcraft and Demonology* (1913)
Spenser, Edmund: *View of the Present State of Ireland* (1596, 1633)

V

Ireland in the Seventeenth Century

The Plantation of Ulster (1608)

The Plantation of Ulster in 1608, carried out under Sir Arthur Chichester as Lord Deputy, theoretically involved the annexation of six entire counties, comprising some two million acres.* Of this huge area, about a quarter was cultivable land, the greater part of which was allotted to new settlers from England and Scotland.

The Privy Council in London divided the territory into lots of from 1,000 to 2,000 acres, to be held at rents varying from a penny to twopence an acre per annum. The largest lots went to "undertakers," who bound themselves to build castles and maintain troops and not to sublet their land to Irishmen. More than 200,000 acres were allotted to these "undertakers," while 100,000 more were reserved for the Protestant Church of Ireland. The city of London received the whole county and town of Derry, now renamed Londonderry, which was parceled out among the twelve city companies. The native Irish inhabitants were left with some 50,000 acres—less than one-fortieth of the whole area involved, and consisting of the poorest soil.

The hopes of the government were disappointed, for by 1630 only 8,000 Scots and English had settled on the confiscated lands, and only 13,000 in the whole of Ulster. Hence much of the unoccupied land was bought up by speculators who, contrary to the intention of

*The six counties, not to be confused with the Six Counties of Northern Ireland today, were Donegal (Tyrconnell), Tyrone, Fermanagh, Cavan, Armagh and Derry (Coleraine). The counties of Antrim, and Down, being already settled to a considerable degree by Scots who had emigrated to Ireland during the sixteenth century, were not included in the Plantation. Many of these Scots, settled in the Glens of Antrim and elsewhere, had remained Catholic in religion and Gaelic in speech.

the government, rented it back to its original owners. The latter now found themselves living without any security of tenure—they could be evicted at any time—on lands that their ancestors had owned for centuries. The new settlers from Scotland and England, however, were protected against eviction by what came to be known as "Ulster tenant right." Such was the beginning of the Ulster Scots—the Scotch-Irish as they became known in America; and thus began a new and more serious religious division than any that had yet appeared in Ireland and whose results, unfortunately, are still evident today.

James I took a keen personal interest in the Plantation "merely for the goodness and morality of it, esteeming the settling of religion, the introducing of civility, order and government among a barbarous and unsubjected people to be an act of piety and glory and worthy also of a christian prince to endeavour." The furtherance of true religion was held to be a prime motive for the Plantation since a commission of enquiry had established that there was no more religion in Ireland "than among Tartars and cannibals." Chichester, who carried out the annexation, affirmed that Irish Catholics were "the most treacherous infidels in the world, and we have too mild spirits and good consciences to be their masters. He is a well-governed and wary gentleman," solemnly warned Sir Arthur, "whom their villainy doth not deceive."

To cast a cloak of legality over the whole proceeding, James caused the Dublin Parliament to be summoned in 1613—for the first time in nearly thirty years. This parliament, which was packed as no parliament had ever been packed before, formally attainted Tyrone and Tyrconnell as guilty of treason, thereby justifying retroactively the seizure of their lands. The same parliament abolished the Brehon laws—those last vestiges of ancient custom that still prevailed in the west of Ireland after two thousand years. In their place was introduced the common law of England with its tenures, assize courts, and grand juries. The purpose of the change was not to do justice but to legalize injustice. The Brehon laws were popular; they were cheap; and they were readily understood by the people. The new law was foreign, expensive, and incomprehensible. All that the people knew was that it was designed to rob them of their immemorial rights.

Strafford in Ireland (1633–40)

In 1632, James's successor, Charles I, appointed a new Lord Deputy—Thomas Wentworth, Earl of Strafford (1632–40). Strafford established in Ireland a despotism more ruthless and more efficient than any that unhappy country had yet known. Previous administrations at Dublin Castle had often acted with cruelty and dispatch, but without system and continuity. By means of a well-disciplined, mercenary army of about 10,000 men, Strafford secured a base of power against all rivals. Secure also in the support of the Crown, he feared no man and cared not whom he offended. He boasted that his rule was "thorough," and it was as merciless as thorough.

The sole object of Strafford's policy was the aggrandizement of the Crown in Ireland and the increase of its revenues. In pursuit of these ends, the earl bore down with equal severity on the Anglo-Irish nobility and on the Catholic peasantry, on the Presbyterians of the north and on the Catholics of the south. "Ireland was a conquered country," he boasted, "and the King could do with it what he liked."

Typical of Strafford's financial exactions was his harassment of the city of London, one of the king's chief enemies in England. Discovering that the merchants of London had not lived up to the agreement by which they had acquired land in Ulster, the Lord Deputy instituted proceedings against them. When the merchants offered £40,000 to clear themselves, Strafford fined them £70,000 and in addition confiscated the lands in question. For such imprudence, he was to pay dearly in 1641 when his turn came to stand trial for treason in Westminster Hall.

In similar fashion, Strafford showed his contempt for the great lords who had in effect ruled Ireland before his arrival. The greediest and most insolent of them all was perhaps Richard Boyle, Earl of Cork, who controlled eight seats in the Dublin House of Commons and who was now perhaps the richest man in the country. For a breach of law which no Deputy in the past had questioned, Strafford fined Cork £40,000 and ordered him to remove from before the altar of St. Patrick's Cathedral in Dublin the enormous marble monument to himself and his family that the upstart earl had erected. In 1641, Lord Cork was to be one of the most voluble and malignant witnesses in Westminster Hall at the trial of the fallen Deputy.

Strafford showed equal harshness to Catholics. In Connacht he rejected titles to land for which no royal warrant could be produced, and refused to accept evidence of sixty years' possession as constituting a valid title. About a quarter of that province was annexed and sold to English settlers. As for the Protestants of the North, to punish them for their strong sympathy with their Presbyterian kinsmen in Scotland whom Charles was now persecuting, Strafford forced on them the hated "Black Oath," by which they forswore their coreligionists and promised absolute loyalty to the king.

On the credit side of Strafford's rule was his suppression of piracy on the high seas—in 1630, Algerian corsairs had burned the town of Baltimore in Cork and carried its inhabitants into slavery—and his encouragement of the linen industry, on which Ulster's prosperity for the next three hundred years was so largely to depend. It is at this time that Belfast began to develop from a fishing village by the mud flats of the Lagan into a town of some importance and ultimately the capital of Northern Ireland. Yet if Strafford stimulated the linen industry, he also attempted to destroy the long-established manufacture of woolen goods in Ireland. His object was to make that country an economic colony of England—selling her raw wool to English merchants and being dependent on them for manufactured cloth. Thus one of Ireland's basic industries would be ruined and the yield of her customs duties increased.

So entirely dependent was Strafford on the favor of the Crown that when in 1640 the Long Parliament in England put an end to Charles's despotism, the power of his Deputy in Ireland crumbled on the instant; and when in May, 1641, a hundred thousand Londoners shouted themselves hoarse with joy over the execution of Strafford, "Black Tom, the tyrant," they undoubtedly expressed—by an unprecedented coincidence—the sentiment of the Irish as well. The sudden termination, however, of Strafford's harsh rule in Ireland resulted in an equally sharp reaction against it—the rebellion of 1641.

The Rebellion of 1641

In retrospect it seems strange that the Plantation of Ulster had not been followed by a revolt on the part of the dispossessed. No doubt the Flight of the Earls had demoralized their followers. In 1630 the Earl of Cork remarked on the general peacefulness of Ireland. "The rebellious spirits," he wrote, "are not to be seen and have no armies. There is no barbarism and plunder.... Contentment is in fact general." Since the rebellion of 1641 was to be the most formidable that had yet occurred in Irish history, Cork's optimism was as misplaced as that of Augustine Birrell on the eve of a later revolt—the Easter Rising of 1916.

The Irish Catholic clergy took a leading part in organizing the rebellion. October 23, 1641, had been decided on, months in advance, as the date for the rising; and on that day it broke out simultaneously in a number of places. The rebels had intended to seize Dublin Castle, where Strafford had stored arms and ammunition for 10,000 men. Had they been able to do so, English rule in Ireland would have been gravely jeopardized. Though the rebels did not know it, the castle at that moment was guarded by only forty-eight men; but the plot was betrayed, and the nerve center of English power remained intact. (A similar failure, it may be remarked, was later to ruin what small chance of victory the Rising of 1916 might have had.)

The insurrection met with its greatest success in Ulster, where the Protestant settlers were taken completely by surprise. Thousands were evicted from their holdings. Towns and villages were sacked and burned. Lisburn and Lurgan were wiped out. Individual atrocities took place—notably the drowning of a hundred Protestants in the Bann at Portadown—but the majority of deaths occurred in the panic-stricken flight of refugees that choked the roads to Dublin. Many died along the way from hunger and fatigue. Others succumbed to exposure in a period of intense cold.

There can be no doubt that terrible hardships were suffered by unarmed helpless people in what Sir Philip Warwick, a young English royalist, called "that dismal, inhuman, and bloody rebellion of the Irish," which he attributed to "jesuitical secrecy and cruelty." Yet the horrors of 1641 were no different in kind, though they were smaller in scale, from innumerable instances of cruelty perpetrated during the previous four centuries, and especially under Elizabeth, by the conquerors.

As soon as the news reached England, the number of Protestants slain was exaggerated in the wildest fashion. Warwick reported calmly that "very near a hundred thousand had been massacred" during the first week. Mrs. Lucy Hutchinson, wife of a well-known Puritan colonel, maintained that "in that cursed rebellion—above 200,000 were massacred in two months space—many of them most inhumanly butchered and tormented." In his *History of the Rebellion* written in 1646, Sir John Temple estimated the number slain at 300,000. A generation later, as passions began to subside, the royalist historian Lord Clarendon was content to accept from forty to fifty thousand as a reasonable estimate of the number that had lost their lives.

The absurdity of such exaggerations is evident when one remembers that in 1641 the total number of English and Scottish settlers in Ulster, where most of the horrors took place, could not have been much above 20,000. The most reliable contemporary estimate for the population of Ireland as a whole is that of the statistician Sir William Petty, who put the total number of inhabitants at 1,400,000, among whom he reckoned about 210,000 Protestants. The first English writer to expose the fiction of a general massacre was Sir Fernando

Warner who in the eighteenth century suggested the figure of 4,000 as approximately the number of those who had perished—a figure that modern scholars accept as somewhere near the truth.

The hysterical hyperbole concerning the numbers killed was accompanied by the usual atrocity stories related by the survivors, whose depositions fill more than thirty stout volumes in Trinity library. When, however, the Catholic Confederation in Kilkenny forthwith challenged the authorities to submit these depositions to impartial scrutiny, the challenge was refused. Nearly thirty years later when George Fox, the founder of the Quakers, came to Ireland, he imagined that he could almost smell the stench of blood still impregnating the atmosphere over a hundred miles away. "When we came before Dublin," he wrote in his journal for 1669, "the earth and air smelt methought of the corruption of the nation, so that it yielded another smell to me than England did; which I imputed to be Popish massacres that had been committed, and the blood that had been spilt— from which a foulness ascended."

Perhaps, in conclusion, one may quote the verdict of a distinguished historian—a conservative in politics, and a Protestant in religion. "The Irish massacre of 1641," wrote W. E. H. Lecky in 1876, "seems to me one of the great fictions of history, though a great number of murders were committed. The consensus of modern English historians, however, about it is so great that it is hardly possible to shake the belief in the English mind."

Belief rooted in emotion is impervious to reason, and numerous Orangemen today justify their aversion to Catholicism and their hostility to the South by the cherished memory of the atrocities of 1641, a year that was, in fact, traumatic for the Protestants of the North. Even now in the twentieth century, in times of political or religious crisis, Ulster leaders like Lord Carson and Lord Ernest Hamilton have not scrupled to inflame the emotions of their compatriots by demagogic appeals to the passions easily roused by invoking the memory of "1641."

Owen Roe O'Neill (1642-49)

The leaders of the rebellion had two main objects in view—to secure freedom for Catholicism in Ireland and to win the support of the Anglo-Irish gentry and nobility, many of whom had remained Catholic despite sixty years of harassment by the government in Dublin. The Catholic bishops, led by O'Reilly, the Primate, now took the lead in organizing a national opposition. The result was the establish-

Owen Roe O'Neill (1590-1649).
First Irish hero of modern times.

ment in 1642 of the Catholic Confederation. Ignoring the Dublin parliament, the Confederation fixed its headquarters at Kilkenny. The temper of the parliament that met there may be judged from Patrick Darcy's declaration that Ireland owed allegiance not to the English parliament but only to the Crown—a statement that anticipated those of Grattan in 1782, Arthur Griffith in 1905, and the Statute of Westminster in 1931.

In Kilkenny some of the ablest lawyers in Ireland drafted a new constitution. The legislature was to consist of a single Assembly, peers and commoners sitting together. The executive power was to be vested in a Supreme Council of twenty-four, to be elected by the Assembly. Each of the four provinces was to have six members on the Council, each province to have a general commanding its own forces. Thus essential military unity was sacrificed in an attempt to avoid provincial jealousies. Apart from this limitation, the chief defect of the new constitution was that it confined political freedom to Catholics, both the Protestant Anglo-Irish and the Presbyterian Scots being excluded from parliament.

In 1643, Charles I, hard pressed by the Puritan armies in England, authorized the Earl of Ormonde, his commander in Ireland, to conclude a truce with the Confederation—a plan that the Long Parliament in London at once denounced as "an impious design—to sell for naught the crying blood of many hundreds of thousands of British Protestants by a dishonourable truce with the rebels." Next year the Confederation sent envoys to the king at Oxford, demanding the abolition of the penal laws against Catholics in Ireland and the canceling of Strafford's land confiscations. Faced by these demands, Charles temporized as usual.

In 1645 the situation altered with the arrival of a Papal Nuncio, Cardinal Rinuccini, who came well supplied with arms and money. The Kilkenny Confederation had vainly appealed for help to France and Spain, but Father Luke Wadding, an able and learned Irish Franciscan in Rome, had got the Papacy to realize the value of Ireland as a forward base for the Counter-Reformation. A rift, however, soon developed between the Kilkenny Assembly and the Nuncio, for whereas the former desired a favorable accommodation with Charles I, Rinuccini wanted a total breach with England.

Matters were not helped by the arbitrary conduct of the imperious Cardinal. His manners were haughty and formal, and he behaved like a dictator. He scarcely troubled to conceal his contempt for the barbarians among whom, by the chances of war, his lot had now been cast. Possessed of ample funds, he intervened in military matters and intrigued against the Supreme Council. When in 1646 this body negotiated a peace with Ormonde, the Nuncio imprisoned its members, laid Kilkenny under interdict, and threatened excommunication against any who accepted the peace. Even the Catholic bishops resented Rinuccini's interference in politics, and in 1649 he finally quit Ireland in disgust.

In the 1640s, three interests contended for power in Ireland. Dublin and the Pale were held by Ormonde for the king; the North was held by an army composed of Puritans and Scots Presbyterians, commanded by General Munro and loyal to the English parliament; while the Kilkenny Confederation, linked with Charles I in an uneasy alliance, represented the Irish Catholics. As these three forces struggled against each other, armies marched and countermarched across the country, which suffered the usual devastation that accompanies such hostilities. Towns were plundered and the countryside laid waste.

During this dreary period of plots, intrigues, and skirmishes, one figure of real stature emerged. Born in 1590, Owen Roe O'Neill was a nephew of Hugh O'Neill and had sailed with him from Ireland in 1607. Since then he had served for more than thirty years in the armies of Spain and had become one of the best-known professional soldiers in Europe. He had married an Irish wife and throughout long years of exile had never lost interest in his native land. Though not the eldest member of the O'Neills, he was regarded as the most illustrious living member of that ancient clan. In 1642, Owen Roe landed at Sheephaven in Donegal to put his sword at the service of the rebellion.

Since each province had its own general, O'Neill—by far the ablest soldier then in Ireland—was denied national command and given control only of the Catholic forces in the north. The Leinstermen were jealous of Ulster, and the Kilkenny Assembly grudgingly doled out the supplies it made available to Owen Roe. Despite these handicaps, he welded together a disciplined army out of the raw levies entrusted to him, and at Benburb, County Tyrone, on June 6, 1646, won a smashing victory over the veterans of Munro. Against the Anglo-Scottish army of nine thousand, O'Neill had five thousand pikemen and five hundred horse. Munro alone possessed artillery. Nevertheless, he was outmaneuvered, and a rout like that of Agincourt ensued. With a loss of only seventy men, the Irish killed more than three thousand of the enemy. Benburb was a far more decisive victory than the Yellow Ford had been in 1598. "At the news of this astounding success," wrote J. F. Taylor, "breaking the long spell of national disaster, Celtic Ireland went wild with delight." Throughout the land, Owen Roe was greeted as "the Liberator."

Unfortunately for Ireland, O'Neill's victory was negated by political bickering and intrigue. Some charged, without evidence, that Owen Roe aimed to make himself King of Ireland. The feud between Rinuccini and the Confederation became more rancorous than ever, and O'Neill could not avoid being drawn into the quarrel. Worse still, at this point Ormonde—who, though Irish by descent, boasted of being "an Englishman by birth, extraction, and choice"—surrendered Dublin to the English Parliament. The loss of the capital offset the victory of Benburb and proved to be the turning point of the war. Early in August, 1649, an English Puritan army under Michael Jones defeated Ormonde at Rathmines, just outside the walls of Dublin. Two weeks later, Oliver Cromwell landed on the quays of the Liffey.

The stage was now set for the personal encounter of the two foremost generals thrown up by the Civil War. O'Neill's plan was to avoid pitched battle, to lure Cromwell into the interior and wait for winter. "The defending of passes and the season," he wrote, "must beat Cromwell." But before winter came, Owen Roe himself was dead—possibly of the plague, though it was widely believed that he had died of poison. In November, 1649, he was buried in Cavan in the robes of a lay Franciscan. He had lived just long enough to hear of Cromwell's massacres at Drogheda and Wexford but not long enough to avenge them.

The death of Owen Roe ended whatever chance Ireland might have had of defeating Cromwell, for O'Neill—the Irish Fabius, as he has been called—was the only soldier of the first rank that Ireland had yet produced. At his death, wrote a contemporary, all Ireland was turned into "a dowager of moan and grief by day and night renewed."

Two centuries later, Young Ireland still drew inspiration from the memory of O'Neill. Thomas Davis' romantic "Lament for the Death of Owen Roe O'Neill" was a response to a loss that was felt both as immediate and personal:

> We thought you would not die—we were sure you would not go
> And leave us in our utmost need to Cromwell's cruel blow—
> Sheep without a shepherd when the snow shuts out the sky—
> Oh, why did you leave us, Owen? Why did you die?*

Owen Roe was perhaps the only Irishman of his time who had a vision of the nation as transcending personal interests and provincial loyalties. In his eyes all Irishmen—whether Gaels or Anglo-Irish, whether from Connacht or the Pale—were equal. "I hold him to be no better than a devil," he once broke out vehemently to his nephew, "who will make these distinctions, but call all Irish alike." In forty years of military service, he was never charged with inhumanity or wanton cruelty. Owen's magnanimity in war was shortly to be thrown into high relief by the vindictiveness of the enemy. Within a year of his death, Owen's son, Henry, captured by the Puritan commander, Sir Charles Coote, was put to death though quarter had been promised.

Cromwell in Ireland (1649)

Cromwell stayed in Ireland for a little over nine months—from August, 1649 to May, 1650. His siege of Drogheda lasted ten days (September 2-11), and its successful conclusion was followed by four days of general massacre directed by Cromwell himself, during which period some four thousand people were murdered. When on October 1, Wexford too was stormed, the same vengeance was exacted, and two thousand people more—men, women, and children, priests, nuns, and laymen—were put to death.

The Bishop of Ferns was an eyewitness to the slaughter. Having made his escape to Antwerp, twenty years later he set down his recollections of that terrible first of October. "On that most lamentable day," he wrote, "my native city of Wexford . . . was destroyed by the sword, and given a prey to the infuriated soldiers by Cromwell, that English pest of hell. There, before God's altar fell many sacred vic-

---

*This lament by Thomas Davis was a favorite poem of the late Senator Robert F. Kennedy.

Oliver Cromwell (1559–1658). Lord Protector of England (1653–58).

tims . . . others, who were seized outside the church, were scourged with whips; others were hanged; and others were put to death by most cruel tortures."

Having given this grim warning, Cromwell refrained from further atrocities in Ireland. When he captured New Ross, Kilkenny, and Clonmel, the defenders were granted honorable terms of surrender, and these were observed. Nevertheless, on account of Drogheda and Wexford, Cromwell left behind him in Ireland a name for cruelty such as the passage of three hundred years has scarcely erased from memory.

After his departure for England, Cromwell turned over the command to his son-in-law, General Ireton. The capitulation of Galway in May, 1652, brought the fighting to an end. By the terms of surrender, many Catholic soldiers—according to Sir William Petty, some 34,000—were permitted to embark for the Continent. Cromwell was no doubt glad to be rid so easily of the best fighting men in Ireland; in any case, France and Spain were now bidding against each other for the services of the Irish, and the latter would be well employed killing other Catholics abroad. Hence at many a harbor, leaving their womenfolk behind, whole companies of Irish soldiers marched into exile to the mournful sound of pipes, seeking—and sometimes finding—glory in the armies of France or Spain.

The most terrible aspect of the Cromwellian conquest of Ireland was not the savage bloodletting at Drogheda and Wexford but its effect on the population as a whole. Sir William Petty, the most reliable contemporary population expert, estimated that between 1641 and 1652, more than half the population of Ireland died—mostly of starvation or disease. If even approximately true, this figure would mean that within a single decade, some three quarters of a million people had perished. Compared to this monstrous, stark, unrealizable statistic, the number of the slain at Drogheda and Wexford pales into insignificance.

The details of the massacres are in fact appalling. At Drogheda, an orgy of murder, rape, sacrilege, and arson lasted incredibly for four successive days and nights. Convents, churches, houses, schools—all were looted and given to the flames. Old men and women, little children, as well as nuns, monks, and priests, were indiscriminately put to the sword. The steep streets of the city reeked with the stench of corpses beneath a low-lying pall of smoke. Yet what shocks the modern conscience nearly as much as the actual details of the carnage is the complacency and sanctimoniousness with which Cromwell contemplated the massacres and sought to justify them in the sight of God and man.

The day after the slaughter at Drogheda, Cromwell sat down and told his friend James Bradshaw, President of the Council of State in London: "I believe we put to the sword the whole number of the defendants. . . . This hath been a marvellous great mercy. . . . I wish that all honest hearts may give the glory of this to God alone, to whom indeed the praise of this mercy belongs." The next day he returned to the subject. "I am persuaded," he wrote solemnly, "that this is a righteous judgment of God upon these barbarous wretches, who have imbrued their hands in so much innocent blood; and that it will tend to prevent the effusion of blood for the future, which are the satisfactory grounds to such actions, which otherwise cannot but work remorse and regret." The possible suggestion here of guilt was belied in fact by the slaughter at Wexford, which took place only two weeks later.

After Wexford, Cromwell was at pains to emphasize that this massacre, unlike the previous one at Drogheda, had been unpremeditated —"yet God would not have it so; but by an unexpected providence, in his righteous justice, brought a just judgment upon them, causing them to become a prey to the soldier." Thus Deity was made an accomplice in murder.

Shortly before his death in 1658, Cromwell still felt the need to justify what he had done. "Your covenant is with death and hell," he stormed against the Irish bishops in the last months of his life. "Remember, ye hypocrites, Ireland was once united to England. You broke this union! You, unprovoked, put the English to the most unheard-of and most barbarous massacre (without respect of age or sex) that ever the sun beheld. . . . Is God, will God, be with you? I am confident that he will not!" That Ireland had been united to England by physical force, and against the will of the Irish people, seems never to have entered Cromwell's consciousness.

It is hardly surprising that in the somber record of Irish history, Oliver Cromwell should have come to signify to the Irish evil incarnate, or that down through successive generations the curse of his name should have been regarded as the most fearful malediction one person could call down upon another. Yet Raleigh and Gilbert had been guilty of similar frightfulness, and a poet as gentle as Spenser had justified such actions. In England, Cromwell was often moderate and just; where the Jews, for example, were concerned, he was far in advance of his age in the humanity he showed. In England, Cromwell's invincible Ironsides were a model of deportment and strict military discipline: there they committed few atrocities against their fellow countrymen.

What then is the explanation of Cromwell's cruel and compulsive behavior in Ireland? From childhood he had been raised in an atmosphere of paranoiac hatred for Catholicism. When he was only six, a group of desperate English Catholics had tried to blow king, Lords, and Commons sky-high: after the Gunpowder Plot of 1605, a fear and loathing of Catholicism that was to last for many years swept England and formed the background of Cromwell's childhood education. Later came the inevitable immersion in Foxe's sadistic *Book of Martyrs,* a work second only to the Bible in those days as preferred reading for Protestant youth. In the pages of Foxe, an impressionable child would learn what indeed had actually happened —how at Smithfield under Mary Tudor, heroic Protestant men and women had been roasted alive because of their religious belief. Foxe spared his readers none of the gory details; rather, he reveled in them. Under Cromwell the Irish paid dearly for crimes they had never committed, till the fires of Smithfield were quenched by the waters of the Boyne. Finally in Cromwell's adult years came the reports of the unspeakable atrocities committed by Irish Catholics in 1641—reports that, as we have seen, were grossly overstated but that seemed to establish irrefutably the unchanging nature of the evil that was Catholicism. In the background all this time, there lurked in the minds of Englishmen the lurid and sinister image of the Spanish Inquisition, which was in fact busy burning heretics at the stake for love of God.

Hence when at length Cromwell set foot in Ireland, he felt it a solemn duty to avenge a series of monstrous crimes committed by Catholics against Protestants in the past. On all other subjects save Catholicism he was eminently sane; on that subject alone he was demented, and Ireland paid the penalty for his madness. For him, Catholics—especially Irish Catholics—were simply wolves, vermin to be exterminated. Such is the nature of paranoia, as we have since learned from Hitler's persecution of the Jews, from the blood purges carried out by Stalin, and from the obsessive anticommunism of respectable citizens in our own time. Cromwell, too, was in his own country a very respectable man.

The Cromwellian Settlement (1652–54)

More tragic for the future of Ireland than the vengeance of Cromwell was the land settlement decreed by the Rump Parliament in London in 1652. This "Act of Settlement" went far beyond the earlier confiscations carried out under Elizabeth and James I, for whereas the Munster Plantation had involved half a million acres, and that of Ulster nearly two million, the Cromwellian settlement now envisaged the annexation of almost eight million acres of Irish soil—about half the cultivable land in the island.

The entire native population was to be forcibly evicted from the three most fertile provinces and herded beyond the Shannon into the poorest province of all—Connacht. Those to whom the act applied (the immense majority of the population) were given until May 1, 1654, to remove themselves across the Shannon or face the penalty of death. In the vivid phase that was to become proverbial among future generations of Irishmen, they were offered the choice of—Hell or Connacht.

As in the case of the earlier Plantations, however, an annexation on such a scale, involving the physical coercion of a whole population, was impossible to enforce. Not only that, the new owners desired the customary supply of cheap servile labor with which to till their lands.

The underlying motive for what was in fact robbery on a gigantic scale was twofold. One object was to compensate with Irish land Cromwell's soldiers, who had long been in arrears of pay; the other was to repay the sum of about a million pounds which had been advanced to the Long Parliament by various Englishmen in 1641. The security given for this immense loan was two and a half million acres of promised Irish land. After the war was over, in lieu of the principal sum, the security was handed over to the creditors of the government. Thus Ireland helped to underwrite the cost of the English Civil War.

It was felt that some excuse was necessary to justify this unparalleled act of spoliation. The confiscations were therefore represented as just retribution for the losses suffered by the Protestants in 1641, although in fact the chief sufferers in the Cromwellian land settlement had been the Anglo-Irish gentry of Leinster and Munster, who had taken little part in the 1641 rebellion. The sanction of religion was also invoked to justify the wholesale theft of land. As Robert Dunlop, a modern English historian, comments: "For a long time afterwards hardly a letter left Ireland without containing some reflection on the blood-guiltiness of the nation, and the necessity there was of propitiating the Divine wrath for the innocent blood spilt, by bringing the authors of the massacres to justice."

Theoretically, under the Act of 1652 some eighty thousand persons were liable to the death penalty. About two hundred of the most prominent leaders of the rising were actually executed; but thousands of young Irish men and women were shipped out as slaves to the sugar plantations in Barbados and to Jamaica, which had recently been conquered from Spain.

A graphic picture of the cost in human terms of the Cromwellian settlement was given more than a hundred years ago by the Irish historian John P. Prendergast. "The bodies of many wandering orphans whose fathers had embarked for Spain," he wrote in a well-known passage, "and whose mothers had died of famine, were preyed upon by wolves. In the years 1652 and 1653 a man might travel twenty or thirty miles and not see a living creature. Man, beast, and bird were all dead or had quit those desolate places. The troopers would tell stories of the places they saw smoke, it was so rare to see either smoke by day or fire of candle by night."

A political corollary to the land settlement was the abolition of the Irish parliament after an existence of some three and a half centuries. By the Instrument of Government of 1654—the written constitution devised for England by Cromwell's officers—Ireland received instead the right to send thirty representatives to the House of Commons at Westminster. These Irish members of parliament were of course to be elected by the new Cromwellian landlords from among their own number. The abolition of the Irish Parliament, however, proved to be temporary, since at the Restoration in 1660 the Lords and Commons were reestablished in Dublin.

The chief permanent result of the Cromwellian occupation of Ireland was the creation of a new landlord class—drawn partly from

Cromwell's officers and partly from English speculators who had bought land cheaply from the soldiers, the latter being in many cases loath to settle in Ireland and only too willing to sell the estates they had been allotted. In course of time this new Protestant aristocracy, like the old Anglo-Norman baronage before it, would come to feel itself less and less English and more and more Irish. For the next 250 years, with one brief interruption in 1689, this class would govern Ireland—but only with the support of English bayonets.

As for the rest of the population, from now on the native Irish and the Catholic Anglo-Irish were confounded in one common, overwhelming mass of misery and degradation. Out of their suffering, and out of the bitterness bred by that suffering, the consciousness of the modern Irish nation was born. For England had at last succeeded in accomplishing what no Irish leader, however gifted, had yet been able to achieve—the unity of the oppressed people of Ireland.

The Reign of Charles II (1660-85)

The restoration of the monarchy in 1660 ended, amid universal rejoicing, the rule of the Puritans in England. For the Irish, however, the reign of Charles II, which followed (1660-85), brought only new burdens and restrictions while preserving the old ones intact. Under the "Merry Monarch," Ireland suffered under three kinds of discrimination—affecting land, commerce, and religion.

The general theory of the Restoration was, of course, that all Cromwellian legislation had always been invalid. In Ireland, however, the land settlement of 1652 remained substantially in force. Not only that, but fresh grants of land were made to royal favorites clamoring to be rewarded for a decade of exile. Thus the Earl of Ormonde received 100,000 acres in addition to the huge ancestral estates that were now restored to him. The king's brother, the Duke of York (later James II), received 77,000 acres. It has been estimated that whereas in 1640, Catholics still owned three-quarters of the cultivable land in Ireland, twenty years later they owned only one-quarter of it and this chiefly in the barren province of Connacht.

In desperation many of the former Catholic landowners, cheated of all hope of recovering their estates on the return of a king whose title they had never repudiated, now resorted to violence. They took to the woods and mountains, and harassed the new landlords incessantly. Denounced as "tories" or "rapparees," they gained great popularity among the Catholic peasantry. Some were declared outlaws, and a price was put on their heads. Many, like Count Redmond

O'Hanlon of Armagh, who had been educated in France, were captured and executed. The Slieve Bloom mountains were especially famous as the resort of these Irish counterparts of Robin Hood. While they lacked the strength to wage regular guerrilla war, in the twentieth century the I.R.A. did not disdain to study their tactics.

Although the royalist parliament at Westminster endorsed the Cromwellian settlement, it was determined that the new Protestant masters of Ireland should in no way compete with English interests. In 1663 a Navigation Act forbade Irish merchants to export any commodities to the American Colonies; seven years later a similar prohibition was extended to most imports into Ireland from America.

Another series of statutes, enacted at Westminster between 1663 and 1667, prohibited the export to England of Irish cattle, sheep, and pigs. This legislation was particularly injurious to the new owners of Irish soil because, as a result of the depopulation that had occurred under the Commonwealth, in many areas pasture had displaced agriculture as the mainstay of rural life. In response to the new legal prohibitions, many Protestant landlords now shifted from cattle raising to wool growing, thereby stimulating the native Irish cloth industry. This development was furthered by the arrival of numerous Huguenots, fleeing from a terrible Catholic persecution in France after the revocation of the Edict of Nantes in 1685. This new Protestant prosperity was likewise discriminated against—by an act of 1699, which prohibited the export of Irish woolen goods to England. Ireland, it was clear, though under the rule of a Protestant ascendancy, was still no more than a colony of the larger island.

Since Charles II was known to be partial to Catholicism (the faith of his mother, and in which he was to die), it might have been expected that at least in matters of religion, Ireland would be granted toleration. In fact, the ordinary Catholic population was not actively persecuted; but in 1672 the Dublin parliament passed for the first time a statute prohibiting the election of Catholic members to parliament.

When in 1678 the venom of the Popish Plot was unloosed in England—the last savage outburst there of anti-Catholicism on a national scale—Charles II, well knowing that the accusations of Titus Oates were based on fraud and perjury, nevertheless allowed numbers of innocent Catholics to die upon the scaffold. To these victims Ireland naturally furnished her quota, the most illustrious—and saintly—being the venerable Primate, Oliver Plunket, Archbishop of Armagh (1629-81). Educated at the Irish College in Rome, Plunket spent twenty-five years in that city before being nominated Primate of

Ireland in 1669. During his ten years' subsequent ministry in Ireland, the Archbishop frequently led the life of a fugitive hunted through the forests and the mountains and finding refuge in the cabins and hovels of the common people. Everywhere he went, Plunket found among the peasantry a universal desire to receive the consolations of religion. "People," he wrote, "swarm to confirmations like flies."

Accused of treason, the Archbishop was denied trial in Ireland, where, on account of the respect that was universally felt for him, it was doubtful that even a Protestant jury would convict him. At his trial in London he was denied counsel. On the perjured testimony of paid informers he was found guilty and duly hanged at Tyburn, his heart and entrails being plucked from his body to be burned by the public hangman. In 1920, Oliver Plunket was at length beatified by the Church. The severed head of the martyr is still preserved, and exhibited, in St. Peter's Church in Drogheda. By a singular chance, however, to this very day no Irish martyr has yet been canonized by Rome.

James II and Ireland (1685-91)

James II, who succeeded his brother Charles as king in 1685, was an ardent convert to Catholicism, determined at all costs to restore the old faith in Ireland. As may well be imagined, James's adopted religion made him as popular in Ireland as it made him detested in England. He promptly sent over to Dublin as Lord Lieutenant (a title that had replaced the older title of Lord Deputy) a Catholic Anglo-Irishman, Richard Talbot, Earl of Tyrconnell. The laws against Catholicism in Ireland were now suspended, and Catholics were appointed to high office in that country. In addition, some five thousand Irish Catholic soldiers were brought over to England to bolster James's despotism there. This folly—satirized in the ballad "Lillibulero," which had an enormous popularity in England—contributed much to James's sudden overthrow at the hands of his Calvinist son-in-law, William of Orange, in November, 1688. Fleeing from London, James was captured by William but immediately released and allowed to proceed to France.

During the following winter, while William was master of England and James an exile in France, Tyrconnell held Ireland for James with a Catholic army. In March, 1689, James himself landed in Ireland, bringing with him French arms and money. Two months later he summoned to Dublin a parliament that passed a Declaratory Act asserting its independence of Westminster; but James refused to allow the formal repeal of Poynings' Law (1494), which had given the Crown a degree of control over the Dublin assembly. This "patriot parliament" also swept away all existing legislation against Catholicism in Ireland. Freedom of worship was promised to all religions. Finally, the Cromwellian land settlement was undone. Some two thousand Protestants were deemed to have forfeited their estates, and many Catholics were restored to their lands.

Foreseeing what was coming, the Protestant gentry had already taken alarm. Thousands fled across the sea to England. Those that remained gathered their forces at two strongholds in the North—Londonderry and Enniskillen. James appeared with an army before the former city but failed to press the siege with sufficient vigor. After a heroic defense of 105 days, during which time the city was reduced almost to starvation, Londonderry was relieved on August 13, 1689, as the food ship *Mountjoy* broke the boom across the mouth of the River Foyle. During the siege, the thirty thousand defenders of the city had been greatly inspired by the courage and devotion of a Presbyterian minister, the Reverend George Walker, whose statue today rises high above the town, the walls and ramparts of which are still intact.

The relief of Londonderry was not only a serious military reverse for James but an immense moral stimulus to the Protestant cause—perhaps the first example in Irish history of sheer heroism against great odds exerted on behalf of the reformed religion. Even now the thirteenth of August is celebrated every year in Londonderry as a great Protestant festival with much beating of the Orange drum. On the same day that Londonderry was saved, the defenders of Enniskillen raised the siege of that town also and won a decisive victory at Newtown Butler. Shortly after, William's Dutch general Schomberg landed near Belfast with ten thousand Protestant veterans, and by September all Ulster was in his hands.

Early next year, alarmed by these Protestant victories, Louis XIV sent over a French army of seven thousand men commanded by Lauzun, a general who proved to be incompetent. In reply to this intervention, in June, 1690, William of Orange—his power now secure in England, where he had been crowned William III—crossed over to Ireland, landing at Carrickfergus on Belfast Lough. The exact spot where William disembarked is still held sacred by many Orangemen today.

Marching on Dublin, William found his way barred by James along the line of the Boyne. On July 1, 1690, there took place the decisive battle that was to settle the fate of Ireland for more than

Patrick Sarsfield (?–1693). Earl of Lucan, defender of Limerick (1691) and head of the Irish Brigade; killed in battle.

two centuries. An Anglo-Dutch army of 36,000 routed a Franco-Irish force of 23,000.* Even before the issue had finally been decided, James (having no mind to be captured the second time by William) fled from battle and a week later took ship from Ireland. Schomberg was killed on the field and was buried in St. Patrick's in Dublin.

From his asylum in France, the poltroon James abused the Irish for their cowardice. In Ireland his ignominious flight was long remembered, and for generations he was known derisively as "Jim Dung." The scorn for James felt by the Irish extended to the whole House of Stuart and was to have important consequences in the eighteenth century. For when in 1715 and 1745 the Catholic Highlanders of Scotland rose on behalf of the Jacobite cause, Ireland refused to stir. Blind Raftery, the famous Gaelic poet of the eighteenth century, never a friend to the Stuarts, assailed them in songs and ballads. Two hundred years after the Boyne, Lady Gregory noted that disgust for James's memory was still to be encountered among the peasants of the west of Ireland.

Notwithstanding James's desertion, the Irish continued to carry on the war. In Patrick Sarsfield, Earl of Lucan, they found their ablest military commander since Owen Roe O'Neill. Like him, Sarsfield, familiar with the campaigns of Owen Roe, wished to avoid pitched battles, but his superior, the French commander, St. Ruth, who had

*When the news of the Protestant victory at the Boyne reached the Vatican, Pope Innocent XI ordered a solemn *Te Deum* to be sung in honor of the event. The explanation of this remarkable occurrence is that, not for the first time, political considerations took precedence over religious ones in the calculation of the Papacy. For Louis XIV, with his championship of the Gallican Church, seemed to Rome a potential Henry VIII of France, and as such an even greater menace than William of Orange, the Calvinist.

replaced Lauzun, determined to stake all on a decisive victory. Instead, at Aughrim, County Galway, on July 12, 1691, St. Ruth met with overwhelming defeat and was himself killed in the battle. Aughrim put an end to the hopes of Catholic Ireland in the seventeenth century as effectively as Kinsale had ended those of Gaelic Ireland in the sixteenth. So great was the slaughter at Aughrim that for generations the peasantry were known to avoid the battlefield, strewn thickly as it was by the melancholy grave mounds of the dead. Such burial places were reputed to be haunted by the Danaans of old.

Even after Aughrim, Sarsfield held out in Limerick, where the courage of the Catholic defenders equaled that of the Protestants two years before—at Londonderry. When in October, 1691, Limerick finally capitulated to the Dutch general, Ginkel, it was upon honorable terms. Sarsfield and eleven thousand of his men were allowed to keep their arms and to embark for France with full honors of war. Basing his narrative upon contemporary sources, Macaulay gives a vivid picture of the scenes that occurred as the Irish soldiers, forced to leave behind their wives and children, sailed from the quays along the Shannon.

> Some women caught hold of the ropes, were dragged out of their depth, clung till their fingers were cut through and perished in the waves. The vessels began to move. A wild and terrible wail rose from the shore, and excited unwonted compassion in hearts steeled by hatred of the Irish race and of the Romish faith.

By the agreement signed with Ginkel on the "treaty stone," toleration for the Catholic religion in Ireland was promised. On no other terms would Sarsfield have laid down his arms.

Patrick Sarsfield (c. 1641–93) became the first national hero of modern Ireland. He was to live in Irish history as no other leader—not even Owen Roe—had done since Brian Boru in the eleventh century. Though worshiped by his troops, he lacked the military genius of O'Neill. His courageous defense of Limerick, followed by his deliberate choice of exile in preference to submission at home, made him the idol of his Catholic fellow countrymen. The manner of his death made him almost a martyr in their sight. For having taken service under Louis XIV, who created him Marshal of France, Sarsfield died on July 23, 1693, at the battle of Landen in Flanders from wounds received in fighting the English. "Oh, that this was shed for Ireland," he is said to have exclaimed, trying in vain to staunch the blood from his wounds.

A Gaelic poem, "Farewell to Sarsfield," popular in Ireland in the eighteenth century, has been translated in modern times by Frank O'Connor.

> Good luck, Patrick Sarsfield wherever you may roam
> You crossed the seas to France and left empty camps at home
> To plead our cause before many a foreign throne,
> Though you left ourselves and poor Ireland overthrown,
>   Och, ochone!
> Patrick Sarsfield, 'tis yourself that was sent to us by God
> And holy is the earth that your feet ever trod;
> May the sun and the white moon light your way,
> You trounced King Billy and won the day
>   Och, ochone!

The Irish Brigade who followed Sarsfield into exile, taking service with him under the King of France, were remembered with intense devotion by their countrymen under the nickname of the "Wild Geese." To inspire young Ireland in the nineteenth century, Thomas Davis was to invoke their memory in a number of romantic ballads; while in our own time, in a famous poem, William Butler Yeats was to remind his fellow countrymen how the "Wild Geese" had "spread the grey wing on every tide."

Yet, since it removed the last disciplined force that might have compelled the observance of the Treaty of Limerick, the flight of the "Wild Geese" was a calamity for the Irish. Hardly had the Brigade departed when the Protestant Parliament in Dublin revoked the religious concessions made by the treaty—an action confirmed by William III in London in 1695. Instead of the promised toleration, Sarsfield's valor gained only the Penal Laws—a system of religious persecution worse than any Ireland had yet known.

If in Ireland the name of Cromwell came to symbolize wanton cruelty, the name of Limerick was to symbolize deliberate perfidy. Whenever the Irish Brigade—as at Blenheim (1704) or Fontenoy (1745) —found themselves facing the English in battle, they charged with the hoarse cry, "Revenge, remember Limerick." Today the actual treaty stone, raised high on a pedestal above the banks of the Shannon, affords an emphatic visual reminder of a betrayal whose religious and social consequences were to be felt in Ireland for many years to come.*

---

*It is an extraordinary fact that when Sir Winston Churchill, in the third volume of his *History of the English-Speaking Peoples,* reaches this period, although he describes the siege of Derry, the battle of the Boyne and the flight of James, he omits all mention of the Treaty of Limerick. In his narrative, the Anglo-Irish war of 1689-91 never comes to an end—an amusing example of purposeful forgetting.

BIBLIOGRAPHY

Bagwell, Richard: *Ireland Under the Stuarts,* 3 vols. (1909–16)

Colles, Ramsey: *History of Ulster,* 4 vols. (1919–20)

Curtis, Emmanuel: *Blessed Oliver Plunket* (1963)

Dunlop, Robert: *Ireland Under the Commonwealth,* 2 vols. (1926)

Kearney, Hugh F.: *Strafford in Ireland, 1633–40* (1959)

Lee, G. L.: *Huguenot Settlements in Ireland* (1936)

MacLysaght, E.: *Irish Life in the Seventeenth Century after Cromwell* (1939)

MacManus, M. J.: *Irish Cavalcade, 1550–1850* (1939)

Maxwell, Constantia: *The Stranger in Ireland, from the Reign of Elizabeth to the Great Famine* (1954)

Milligan, Cecil D.: *The Siege of Londonderry* (1951)

Moody, Theodore W.: *The Londonderry Plantation, 1609–41* (1939)

Morley, Henry, ed.: *Ireland Under Elizabeth and James I* (1890)

Murray, Robert H.: *Ireland, 1603–1714* (1920)

O'Brien, George: *Economic History of Ireland in the 17th Century* (1919)

Petty, Sir William: *The Political Anatomy of Ireland* (1691)

Prendergast, John P.: *The Cromwellian Settlement of Ireland* (1865)

Ronan, Rev. Myles W.: *The Irish Martyrs of the Penal Laws* (1935)

Seymour, Rev. St. John D.: *Puritans in Ireland, 1647–61* (1921)

Simms, John G.: *The Williamite Confiscations in Ireland, 1690–1703* (1956)

————: *The Treaty of Limerick* (1691)

Taylor, John Francis: *Owen Roe O'Neill* (1896)

VI

Ireland in the Eighteenth Century

The Penal Laws

In the seventeenth century the misfortunes of Ireland seemed to have reached their tragic and terrible climax: national disaster could go no further. In the eighteenth century, however, before the crisis of the French Revolution, the wave of horror which had so long inundated the past appeared at last to have receded from the shores of Ireland. As the name of Grattan suggests, the Anglo-Irish aristocracy was not untouched by the liberal ideas of the Enlightenment that were gradually humanizing Western Europe. In the latter part of the century, Dublin attained a degree of prosperity as well as a measure of civic dignity and pride such as it had never known before.

Yet if in the Augustan Age the surface of Irish life seemed calm, the appearance was deceptive, for the calm was not that of the tranquillity that is promoted by a vigorous and conscious sense of well-being so much as the torpor that follows exhaustion or the lethargy that is bred by despair. On several occasions, as in 1729 and again in 1740, there was famine in Ireland and hundreds of thousands of human beings starved to death. Twice in the previous century the nation had revolted and twice it had failed. Now for three successive generations the peasantry of Ireland, helpless and prostrate, were incapable of serious attempt at national revolt. Not even the romantic risings in the Scottish Highlands—the Fifteen and the Forty-five—could strike a spark from their devitalized spirit.

The defeat of the Catholics in 1691 was followed by a fresh series of land confiscations. This time about a million more acres were annexed to the Crown. Out of these lands William of Orange rewarded his favorites—many of them Dutch—just as Charles II had rewarded his courtiers in 1660. The new forfeitures brought the amount of land legally confiscated since the reign of Elizabeth to the astonishing figure of nearly twelve million acres—out of a total of fifteen million acres of cultivable land in Ireland. By 1700 the Catholics, who constituted four-fifths of the population, owned only one-seventh of the soil.

This territorial plunder—carried out on a scale almost unmatched in modern European history—was accompanied by legal measures designed to rob the conquered people of its sense of historic identity. In an often-quoted indictment, couched in terms of scathing irony, Edmund Burke, who as much as any may be regarded as the conscience of Protestant Ireland during the eighteenth century, called the Penal Laws "a system of wise and elaborate contrivance, as well fitted for the oppression, impoverishment and degradation of a people, and the debasement in them of human nature itself, as ever proceeded from the perverted ingenuity of man." Another Protestant Irishman, Wolfe Tone, who was to die in an attempt to secure justice for his countrymen, stigmatized the Penal Laws more briefly and more harshly as "that execrable and infamous code, framed with the art and the malice of demons, to plunder and degrade and brutalize the Catholics."

One peculiar feature of the Penal Laws is that, from a formal point of view, they were not devised by one nation for the subjection of another but by a nation for its own self-humiliation. For these laws were not fastened upon Ireland by the parliament at Westminster but were the work of the parliament in Dublin. This body, though it claimed to legislate for the whole of Ireland, actually represented only the Protestant ascendancy, which numbered not more than a fifth of the population and whose power rested on the twin pillars of the landlord interest and the Episcopal Church.

The Penal Laws certainly did not aim at the conversion of the Catholic peasantry, since this would have meant that the ascendancy would have been forced to share its privileges with the rest of the nation. On the contrary, their object was to reduce the majority of the population forever to the status of a despised and servile minority. In the memorable phrase of Lecky, the outstanding historian of Protestant Ireland, the Penal Laws were intended to achieve "not the persecution of a sect, but the degradation of a nation."

The origin of the Penal Laws may be traced to 1692, when William III's first Irish parliament refused to ratify the treaty signed the previous year at Limerick. Then, in 1695, a second Dublin parliament formally denounced that treaty and began the enactment of a new penal code. To these proceedings the English parliament gave its unqualified assent.

In 1703, in the reign of Queen Anne (1702-14), the Irish parliament ordered all priests, under penalty of being branded on the cheek with a red-hot iron, to register their names and the names of their parishes: more than a thousand priests complied with the statute. Twenty pounds were offered as reward for information leading to the arrest of any who failed to register. Another statute that year required all priests to swear allegiance to the Protestant Succession and to renounce the House of Stuart. Almost the entire priesthood refused to subscribe to this act, thereby incurring the penalty of banishment—which was, however, impossible to enforce.

In its persecuting zeal the Irish Privy Council outdid even that of the Dublin parliament: it proposed in addition not only to brand unregistered priests but to castrate them. The government in London refused to countenance so barbarous a measure. Steps were also taken against the hierarchy. An act of 1719 banished all bishops from Ireland, under penalty of their being hanged, drawn, and quartered if discovered in the country; and a reward was offered for the apprehension of any offending prelate. Friars and monks were also banished from the land. These statutes, too, were impossible to enforce.

An Act of 1704 ordered the destruction of the public crosses venerated in Ireland by the peasantry. No Catholic chapel might be adorned with belfry, tower, or steeple. Pilgrimages and resort to holy wells—immemorial popular practices—were prohibited on the ground that they constituted riotous assemblies. Breach of this statute was to be punished by flogging.

Catholics were also excluded from Irish political life. In 1692 they were forbidden to sit in parliament and in 1727 to vote for members of parliament. In 1704 they were excluded from grand juries, bodies that were all-important in local government. Attempts were also made to deny them all education. Thus in 1704 they were forbidden under heavy penalties to send their children abroad to be educated; six years later they were forbidden to keep schools of their own. Ten pounds' reward was offered for the apprehension of Catholic schoolmasters. Education at Trinity College, Dublin, was of course reserved to Protestants. The result was that education in Ireland became at all levels a Protestant monopoly. Such statutes, too, inevitably defeated their own purpose.

Everywhere there sprang up "hedge schools"—so-called because they were held in the open air when weather permitted—in which devoted teachers risked their freedom, while their pupils made up for the lack of buildings and equipment by an extraordinary devotion to learning. In 1731 the Irish House of Lords reported the existence of 549 "Popish schools." Some of these continued even into the nineteenth century, when they numbered among their pupils such well-known public figures as William Carleton, the novelist, and John MacHale, Archbishop of Tuam. Wrote Judge John O'Hagan in a familiar verse about such schooling:

Still crouching 'neath the sheltering hedge
Or stretched on mountain fern,
The teacher and his pupils met feloniously to learn.

Poor people contributed out of their pitifully meager resources to support the "poor scholars" who taught in such schools. Young children sometimes learned their alphabet by copying in chalk the inscriptions from their parents' tombstones. Wandering poets and harpists like Carolan or Blind Raftery passed on to rapt audiences the Gaelic songs and traditions of the past. By a blazing turf fire of a winter's evening, children might even be taught the rudiments of the classics. "Thus Greek and Latin," wrote the historian Mrs. Green, "still found their way into the laborers' cottage." Owen Roe O'Sullivan of Kerry, prince of Gaelic-speaking poets in the Ireland of the Penal Laws, was a common laborer who first became known through his construing a passage in Greek for the son of his employer who had just returned from a college in France. O'Sullivan kept a hedge school at Charleville, County Cork.

Other laws aimed at the complete social degradation of Catholics. A statute of 1697 prohibited them from marrying Protestants. Another act in 1710 decreed the death penalty for any priest who should perform such a marriage. In 1752 all marriages were invalidated in civil law unless performed by a minister of the Church of Ireland. Especially in later years, when the Penal Laws were breaking down, a couple would be married first by a priest, then by a parson—as were the parents of Daniel O'Connell.

The legal profession was wholly barred to Catholics: they were forbidden to practice either as barristers or as solicitors or to sit as magistrates or judges. Membership in municipal corporations was denied to them. They could not hold commissions in the army or navy. They could neither own nor carry arms. The wearing of a sword on ceremonial occasions—the mark of the eighteenth-century gentleman—was prohibited to them. They were forbidden even to own a horse worth more than five pounds: by offering such a sum any Protestant might immediately compel a Catholic to sell him the animal, as happened to the grandfather of the eminent classical scholar Gilbert Murray.

No Catholic might acquire land from a Protestant—whether by gift, purchase, inheritance, or will. A Catholic landowner could not bequeath his estate as a whole but must divide it among his male heirs. A premium was put upon apostasy by the provision that if the eldest son of a Catholic landowner should turn Protestant, he would then inherit his father's whole estate. No Catholic, finally, might hold a lease for longer than thirty-one years.

The Penal Laws degraded four-fifths of the population to the status of helots. Lord Chancellor Bowes, who held office from 1758 to 1767, once ruled in Dublin "that the law does not suppose any such person to exist as an Irish Roman Catholic." Another Lord Chancellor, John Fitzgibbon, Earl of Clare, referred to his Catholic fellow subjects as "the scum of the earth." In his travels in Ireland in the 1770s, the English agricultural expert Arthur Young found that Protestants exercised at will the right to knock down, cane, or horsewhip any Catholic whose conduct appeared to them disrespectful. Even so staunch a Tory as Dr. Samuel Johnson once admitted: "The Irish are in a most unnatural state, for we there see the minority prevailing over the majority. There is no instance . . . of such severity as that which the Protestants of Ireland have exercised against the Catholics." As the French observer Gustave de Beaumont, friend of De Tocqueville, later commented on the Anglo-Irish gentry: "They said that they were Ireland and they ended by believing it."

The unintended but predictable result of the Penal Laws was to attach the Irish people more ardently than ever to the proscribed religion of their ancestors. Denied all other outlet for the expression of their feelings, love of country and devotion to Catholicism became indistinguishable for most of the Irish. Perhaps only in Poland after the Partitions could a parallel be found: indeed, De Tocqueville once termed Ireland the "Poland of the West." Nothing but a knowledge of the state of Ireland under the Penal Laws can explain the extraordinary power still wielded by the Catholic Church over Irishmen today—whether in Ireland or abroad.

Although the intolerance of the Anglo-Irish ascendancy was directed primarily at the Catholic body, the Presbyterians and other Protestant Dissenters did not escape harassment by the Dublin parliament. In the previous century, save for an interlude in the reign of Charles II, the Episcopal Church of Ireland had gladly cooperated with the Presbyterians against the Catholic majority. Now, with equal folly and arrogance, the Protestant gentry set out to alienate and degrade their former allies.

In 1704 the Dublin parliament passed a statute excluding Protestant dissenters from all public employment, whether civil or military. Presbyterian schools were closed and Presbyterian ministers denied the right to solemnize marriages. Such was the reward of the Scotch-Irish for the stouthearted help they had formerly given the Protestant cause in Ireland. One result of this foolish and vindictive persecution of the Presbyterians was that many of them emigrated to America, where naturally they became the most determined enemies of English government. In 1727 alone, to the alarm of Hugh Boulter (1671–1742), the English Primate of the Established Church, 3,000 Presbyterians left Ulster for America, filled with anger against England. Between 1769 and 1774 no less than 44,000 people left Northern Ireland, many for North America. "The Presbyterians in the North," wrote the Lord Lieutenant, Harcourt, in 1775, "are in their hearts Americans." In due course the Scotch-Irish were to provide some of the ablest leaders of the American Revolution and to furnish no less than ten future Presidents to the United States: Andrew Jackson, James K. Polk, James Buchanan, Andrew Johnson, Ulysses S. Grant, Chester A. Arthur, Grover Cleveland, Benjamin Harrison, William McKinley, and Woodrow Wilson were all descended from Scotch-Irish stock. So were five signatories of the Declaration of Independence: Thomas McKean, Edward Rutledge, James Smith, George Taylor, and Matthew Thornton, as well as Charles Thomson, secretary of the Congress that adopted the Declaration. The Declaration itself was first printed by John Dunlap, an Ulsterman born at Strabane, County Tyrone. Henry Knox, one of the four members of Washington's first Cabinet, came from Ulster; and John Rutledge, one of the earliest justices of the Supreme Court, was the son of an Ulsterman.

From such names as these, it is evident that the contribution of the Scotch-Irish to the making of the United States was a remarkable one, especially for so small a minority. They likewise made their mark on the battlefields of the Revolution. George Washington is reported to have declared: "If defeated everywhere else, I will make my last stand for liberty among the Scotch-Irish of my native Virginia." Professor James G. Leyburn, the foremost contemporary authority on the Ulster Scots in America, wrote that "they provided some of the best fighters in the American army. Indeed, there were those who held the Scotch-Irish responsible for the war itself." Sam Houston, Davy Crockett, and Stonewall Jackson were among the Scotch-Irishmen who distinguished themselves in American history at a later date.

The Presbyterian Church in the United States owes nearly as much to the Ulster Scots as does the Catholic Church in that country to Catholic Irishmen. The emigrants from Ulster and their descendants likewise had a marked effect on the ethos of American life. Professor Leyburn suggests that the stern, uncompromising conscience that is characteristic of one aspect of the American character derives not only from the New England Puritans but also from the Scotch-Irish immigrants from Ulster.

In a well-known passage from the *Winning of the West,* Theodore Roosevelt praised the contribution of the Scotch-Irish to pioneer life in the wilderness. He depicted them as being

> a grim, stern people, strong and simple, powerful for good and evil, swayed by gusts of stormy passion, the love of freedom rooted in their very hearts' core. . . . They suffered terrible injuries at the hands of the red men, and on their foes they waged a terrible warfare in return. They were relentless, revengeful, suspicious, knowing neither ruth nor pity; they were also upright, resolute and fearless, loyal to their friends, and devoted to their country. In spite of their many failings, they were of all men the best fitted to conquer the wilderness and hold it against all comers.

Political Subjection of Eighteenth-Century Ireland

If the Anglo-Irish ascendancy behaved arrogantly toward their own countrymen, they were compelled to accept a situation of galling inferiority toward Great Britain.* For during the eighteenth century, Britain maintained in Ireland a permanent military establishment of about fifteen thousand men—as compared with a peacetime army of about eighteen thousand stationed on British soil. Without such military help, the Protestant minority could never have maintained itself in power in Ireland. But as the price of such support, heavy penalties—both political and economic—were exacted.

In the political realm, Britain pulled more tightly than ever the strings whereby it controlled the Dublin parliament. In 1719 the British parliament passed the Declaratory Act by which for the first time it claimed the right to legislate directly for Ireland—though not the right to levy taxation there—without even going through the formality of consulting the Irish Lords and Commons.

*The Act of Union of 1707 had united the kingdoms and parliaments of England and Scotland to form the new political entity of Great Britain.

In economic matters also, the Westminster parliament subordinated the interests of Protestant Ireland to those of the sister country. In 1695 it prohibited the import into Ireland of sugar, tobacco, and cotton from Jamaica and the British West Indies. In 1698 it imposed a crippling duty upon the export of raw wool from Ireland. Next year it placed a similar duty upon Irish manufactured cloth, at the same time prohibiting its export anywhere except to England. Less independent than the American colonists, the Anglo-Irish submitted meekly to such treatment and saw their woolen manufacture, on which 42,000 Protestant families depended, almost ruined. Twenty thousand persons were forced upon charity, while thousands emigrated. One inevitable result of these restrictive measures was the development of large-scale smuggling between Ireland and the ports of France.

Similar measures were taken to injure the prosperous Irish glass industry, established at Waterford and elsewhere partly through the skill of Huguenot refugees. The export of Irish glass was forbidden by Westminster in 1746. Fifteen years earlier an attempt had been made to ruin the flourishing brewing industry, by banning the import of hops into Ireland. Only in the case of linen, which competed with English interests to a much lesser degree, was an Irish industry allowed to develop—and even here the colonial market was closed to Irish linen, while certain duties were imposed on its import into England. Irish merchants were also excluded altogether from the flourishing British trade with India.

The government of eighteenth-century Ireland was a model of all that a government ought not to be. Its head, the Lord Lieutenant—now often called the Viceroy—was appointed by the Crown and was directly responsible to it. He was almost invariably an English peer, and often an absentee. Although he had an absolute veto over all Irish legislation, the Dublin parliament had no control over his actions. This was the century that saw the growth in England of the power of the Prime Minister and the evolution of the Cabinet, together with the vital development of parliamentary control over taxation. The Dublin parliament never developed either a Cabinet or a Prime Minister, nor yet the power of the purse. Dublin Castle controlled everything.

The Viceroy, usually appointed for a term of two years, received the huge salary of £30,000, the use of two mansions, and lavish sums for official expenses. Few Viceroys spent more than six months in Ireland, and some never appeared at all. The Viceroy controlled a Civil List, the money for which came wholly out of Irish funds. The Irish Civil List was used largely as a means of providing ·pensions for Englishmen who had no connection with Ireland or her government. It might even be called upon to sustain the king's amours, as when George I granted his German mistress, the Duchess of Kendal, a pension of £3000 a year on the Irish establishment. Irish pensions often amounted to one-tenth the total cost of Irish government. These sums, of course, were wrung ultimately from a poverty-stricken peasantry living often in abject want and sometimes in actual destitution.

The Civil List was also used to furnish the Viceroy with money for political bribery, since in the eighteenth century, government in Ireland, as in England, was usually carried on by purchasing the support of sufficient members of parliament. In Dublin there arose a recognized class of professionals called "undertakers," whose business was to secure votes for the Viceroy through the judicious distribution of patronage and bribes.

Not only the viceroyalty, but many of the chief offices in church and state in Ireland, were customarily reserved for Englishmen. In this respect, the Protestant minority suffered discrimination as much as their Catholic fellow countrymen. Throughout the eighteenth century no Irishman was ever Primate of the Church of Ireland; nor, until the very end of that century, was an Irishman ever Lord Chancellor. The Chief Secretary, who was the real power in government in Dublin Castle and upon whose advice the Viceroy wholly depended, was invariably an Englishman. So completely was Ireland under the control of English politicians that in 1731, when Walpole was Prime Minister, the Earl of Egmont observed: "The welfare of that poor Kingdom lies in the breath of one Minister's nostrils." Many of the chief officers of state in Ireland were in fact foreigners in what was to them an alien land they detested and whose people they despised.

The eighteenth-century House of Commons in Britain was notorious for its corruption; that of the Irish Commons was even worse. Out of a total of 300 seats, no less than 212 were "pocket" boroughs, often controlled by a single peer. Two-thirds of the seats in the House were controlled by about a hundred persons. Where in England there were two absolutely "rotten" boroughs—that is to say, towns without a single voter—Ireland could boast of seventeen. Sixteen other Irish boroughs had one voter apiece, and ninety more had an average of thirteen voters.

Ireland also lacked some of the basic safeguards of individual freedom which in course of time had been evolved in England. Not until 1781, for example, had Irishmen the right to habeas corpus in criminal cases; and not until the following year were Irish judges at last granted the security of tenure essential to judicial independence.

Protests of the Protestant Ascendancy

It would be hard to imagine any people as completely subject as the Anglo-Irish to the dominance of another nation enduring such bondage without protesting their thralldom. In this unhappy period four Protestant leaders are memorable as having asserted publicly the rights of Ireland as a nation.

The first was William Molyneux (1656-98), member of parliament for Trinity and a friend of John Locke. Shortly before his death Molyneux caused a sensation by publishing his *Case for Ireland,* in which, anticipating Grattan, he argued that England and Ireland were separate kingdoms though under a common sovereign. He inveighed against the restrictions that curtailed the freedom of the Dublin parliament. "I have no other notion of slavery," he wrote, "but being bound by a law to which I do not consent." Molyneux's book was condemned by the English parliament and burned by the common hangman. It was reprinted, however, at least eleven times during the eighteenth century and was widely quoted as a declaration against colonialism by American lawyers at the time of the American Revolution. In 1782, Henry Grattan paid a moving tribute to the memory of Molyneux as a pioneer in the struggle for Irish freedom.

A generation later, by means of a vitriolic pen, a man of letters endowed with genius came to establish a unique personal ascendancy over Dublin. In 1723 appeared the famous *Drapier's Letters.* Although the anonymous author claimed to be only a simple Dublin shopkeeper, it was well known that the work had in fact been written by Jonathan Swift, Dean of St. Patrick's (1667-1745). The letters were written to protest the issuance to Ireland, without the consent of the Dublin parliament, of a new copper coinage, popularly known as Wood's Halfpence, which was expected to cause an inflation in Ireland while realizing a fortune for its English projectors. Swift used the occasion not only to denounce the new coinage but also to assert the claims of Ireland as a free nation.* "All government without the consent of the governed," wrote Swift, in words that directly echoed Molyneux, "is the very definition of slavery. . . . By the laws of GOD, of NA-TURE, of NATIONS, and of your own COUNTRY, you ARE and OUGHT to be as FREE a people as your brethren in England." "Before this time," Lecky commented on this intervention of Swift, "rebellion was the natural issue of every patriotic effort in Ireland.

---

*It must be remembered that in writing thus of Ireland, Swift, like Molyneux before him, was pleading the claims only of the Anglo-Irish minority, not of the Irish people as a whole.

. . . The age of Desmond and O'Neill had passed. The age of Grattan and O'Connell had begun."

When the *Drapier's Letters* appeared, Charles Lucas (1713-71) was a boy of ten. He grew up in the atmosphere of political ferment which was generated by them. Though a doctor, and a fellow of the Royal College of Surgeons in London, Lucas took an ardent interest in politics and in 1748 published a series of letters in which he declared Poynings' Act unconstitutional and the Declaratory Act of 1719 a measure passed by a "strange, foreign parliament," which inflicted on Ireland a bondage worse than that suffered under the Pharaohs by the Jews of old. A servile Dublin Corporation condemned this language as seditious, and the writings of Lucas, too, were burned by the common hangman. The doctor went over to London, where he became acquainted with, among others, Dr. Johnson, who, though no lover of Ireland, praised Lucas as "the friend of his country" and a "confessor of liberty."

The first voice to be raised actually within the Irish House of Commons on behalf of political freedom was that of Anthony Malone (1700-76), a fiery orator who quoted Molyneux and his successors and echoed their denunciations of "slavery." Malone, who had been educated at Oxford, succeeded in creating the nucleus of a genuine opposition within the Commons that foreshadowed the legislative independence achieved by Grattan in 1782.

Agrarian Conditions in Eighteenth-Century Ireland

The most appalling aspect of life in eighteenth-century Ireland was of course the condition of the peasantry—that is to say, of the great bulk of the population. The ruin of the native woolen industry was paralleled by the slow decay of Irish agriculture. During the violence and confusion of the Cromwellian and Williamite wars and confiscations, much land had gone out of cultivation. Since pasture, as distinct from arable land, needed relatively little capital for its development and yielded a quicker return, the new Protestant landlords tended to stock their new estates with cattle and horses. The effect of the short leases, which alone were legally available to Catholics, likewise encouraged pasture at the expense of tillage, since the former was more likely to secure quick profits in a shorter space of time. Since pasture land necessarily supports fewer people than land under agriculture, the inevitable result was that less land was available for people to live on.

In traveling through Ireland, John Wesley noted in his journal how thousands of peasants had been evicted from their holdings so that their land might be enclosed for pasture. The classic instance of the social effects of these enclosures is Oliver Goldsmith's poem, "The Deserted Village," wherein he movingly describes the fate that overtook sweet Auburn (Lissoy, County West Meath), the "sweetest village of the plain."*

So far from attempting to arrest the shrinkage of land under tillage, the Dublin parliament, in which breeders of cattle and horses were influential, actually encouraged the process. In 1736 a statute was passed exempting pasture land from tithes, thereby throwing the major burden of support for the established Church upon the cultivators of the soil—who, incidentally, belonged to the proscribed religion.

Despite the efforts made by enlightened bodies such as the Royal Dublin Society, founded in 1731, to improve the state of agriculture, there were few signs in Ireland of that interest in scientific agriculture that was beginning to bring prosperity to parts of rural England. For the profits from Irish farming were seldom put back into the soil. Instead, they served to enrich the merchants of Dublin or London who supplied the luxuries that the landlords desired. One unfortunate result of the neglect of Irish agriculture was that the majority of the population had been forced more and more to subsist upon a single crop, the potato—a development that had been evident even in the early part of the seventeenth century. Now, in the eighteenth century, partly because of the respite from constant war that had previously ravaged the country, the population began rapidly to multiply. This increased pressure upon the food supply, at a time when more and more land was going out of cultivation, began to pose a new and urgent problem. In a country known since early times for the fertility of its soil, food was scarce and hunger universal. In years of harvest failure, as in 1729 and 1740, actual famine appeared. In two years alone—1740 and 1741—it is estimated that 400,000 people died of starvation. For several decades the peasants were to refer to 1741 as "the year of the slaughter." Only a still greater catastrophe, a century later, would blot out from the memory of future generations those earlier famines that, to those who endured them, no doubt represented the ultimate in human suffering.

The misery caused by an inadequate amount of land devoted to the maintenance of an increasing population was aggravated by a vicious social system inherited from Cromwellian times. The peasantry

*Goldsmith, of course, might also have had in mind the distressing results of enclosures which he had witnessed in contemporary England.

of Ireland was victimized especially by two gross abuses—excessive rents and unjust tithes.

There was no legal restraint upon the landlord's power to exact the highest rents he could get; and since, on account of the population growth, the peasants' hunger for land was acute, rents tended constantly to rise. This exploitation by unscrupulous landlords of the helplessness of their tenants was known as "rack-renting." The evils of rack-renting, vividly depicted by Maria Edgeworth in her novel, *Castle Rackrent* (1800), were made still worse because the tenant had no security of tenure. Even though he paid his rent punctually, he might any moment be evicted without notice to make way for another tenant willing, or at least promising, to pay a higher rent. In the eyes of most peasants, their landlords could hardly have appeared otherwise than as they did to George Berkeley, the philosopher, who called them "vultures with iron bowels."

Another deplorable feature of Irish rural life at this time was the increase of absenteeism. As Dublin grew in prosperity toward the end of the eighteenth century, territorial magnates like the Duke of Leinster built themselves sumptuous town houses in the capital. Other noblemen and gentlemen began to imitate them, living in Dublin and spending their rents there for at least part of every year. It was estimated that 270 Irish peers spent £6000 annually in Dublin, while the 300 gentlemen who formed the House of Commons spent nearly half as much again.

The psychological result of absenteeism was that the landlord who removed himself from the scene of his exploitation could not possibly be moved by the spectacle of the misery endured by his tenants. What the eye hath not seen, the heart doth not grieve over. The springs of pity dried up at the source. The benevolent and patriarchal relationship that in England often characterized the dealings of the squire with his tenants and that tended to ameliorate social differences was almost unknown in Ireland. There the social situation took on the aspect of an undeclared, relentless, and unending war.

Strongly as the Irish peasants resented rack-renting, their chief hatred was reserved for the tithe. Payment of tithe meant that in addition to supporting their own church, the great majority of the Irish people were compelled by law to contribute to the support of a religion they deemed heretical. The Protestant Church of Ireland was in fact the moral arm of a nationwide system of oppression whose center was Dublin Castle. Not only was it a foreign establishment; in the country districts it was often an absentee one. No doubt it was an extreme case, but in 1763, out of seventy-six Protestant parishes in County Clare, sixty-two had no Protestant church and most had no resident parson or even curate to take his place. Whether the "black dragoon in every parish" was resented more for his absence or for his presence might be hard to determine.

Swift and Berkeley on the Peasantry: The Whiteboys

When in 1710 his friends the Tories had come into power in England under Queen Anne, Jonathan Swift had left Dublin for London, hoping no doubt that he would never have to return to the miserable island in which he had had the misfortune to be born. Four years later, involved in the ruin of Oxford and Bolingbroke, his hopes of a bishopric blasted, he returned to Ireland a deeply frustrated and embittered man. He detested Catholicism and despised the Catholic population, not only for what he regarded as its superstition but also for its poverty, dirt, and drunkenness. Circumstances made him a patriot in his own despite. The *Drapier's Letters* and the ensuing victory over Wood's Halfpence—which Brian FitzGerald calls "Ireland's first constitutional victory over England"—transformed Swift into a national hero almost overnight. Not unmoved by this sudden popularity, he began to develop a sense of national consciousness.

On a tour through Ireland in 1727, Swift was moved to indignation by the sight of the constant distress whose scenes unfolded daily before him. "No strangers from other countries," he wrote, "make this a part of their travels; where they can expect to see nothing but scenes of misery and desolation." In his *Short View of the Present State of Ireland* (1727) he aimed to give Englishmen a picture of conditions in the sister island for which they were responsible but concerning the details of which they preferred to remain in ignorance. "One third part of the rents of Ireland," Swift declared, "is spent in England, which, with the profits of employments, pensions, appeals, . . . and other incidents, will amount to a full half of the income of the whole kingdom, all clear profit to England."

The result of this continued seepage of wealth out of Ireland was evident in the condition of the peasantry which had both angered and repelled him. "The rise of our rents," he protested, "is squeezed out of the very blood, and vitals, and clothes, and dwellings of the tenants, who live worse than English beggars. . . . The miserable dress and diet . . . of the people; the general desolation in most parts of the kingdom; the old seats of the gentry and nobility all in ruins, and no new ones in their stead; the families of farmers, who pay great rents, living in filth and nastiness without . . . a house so convenient as an English hog-sty to receive them."

From the depths of this revulsion came that masterpiece of savage and inhuman irony the *Modest Proposal* (1729), which stands alone in the literature of political indignation in English—or perhaps in any other language.

If Swift was powerless to save Ireland, his new-found political concern enabled him to redeem his own life and conferred a new dignity on his few remaining years. The nature of this achievement is admirably summarized by the two biographers of Swift in the famous eleventh edition of the *Encyclopaedia Britannica:*

> He had fled to Ireland a broken man, to all appearance politically extinct; a few years were to raise him once more to the summit of popularity, though power was for ever denied him. Consciously or unconsciously he first taught the Irish to rely upon themselves and for many generations his name was the most universally popular in the country. With his fierce hatred of what he recognized as injustice, it was impossible that he should not feel exasperated at the gross misgovernment of Ireland for the supposed benefit of England, the systematic exclusion of Irishmen from places of honour and profit, the spoliation of the country by absentee landlords, the deliberate discouragement of Irish trade and manufactures.

A decade later another dignitary of the Protestant Church in Ireland echoed the concern expressed by Swift. In his journal, *The Querist* (1735-37). George Berkeley, the mild and amiable Bishop of Cloyne, posed a series of searching questions about the misery he observed daily around him. "Whether there be upon earth any Christian or civilized people as beggarly, wretched and destitute as the common Irish?" he asked. "Whether, nevertheless there is any other people whose wants may be more easily supplied from home? . . . whether a foreigner could imagine that one half of the people were starving in a country which sent out such plenty of provisions? . . . Whether it be not a vain attempt to project the flourishing of our Protestant gentry, exclusive of the bulk of the natives?" By such pointed rhetorical enquiries, the bishop attempted to prick the conscience of his neighbors among the Protestant gentry in County Cork.

Scattered through Berkeley's writings, as through those of Swift, are graphic descriptions of contemporary conditions. He wrote:

> The house of the Irish peasant is the cave of poverty. Within you see a pot and a little straw, without, a heap of children tumbling on the dunghill. . . . In every road the ragged ensigns of poverty are displayed; you often meet caravans of the poor, whole families

in a drove, without clothes to cover, or bread to feed them. . . .
They are encouraged in this vagabond life by the miserable hospitality they meet with in every cottage, whose inhabitants expect
the same kind reception in turn when they become beggars
themselves.

Berkeley had lived three years in Rhode Island, where he had
owned Negro slaves. Comparing their condition with that of Irish
peasants, he found the latter to be "more destitute than savages, and
more abject than negroes. The negroes in our Plantations have a
saying: 'If a negro was not negro, Irishman would be negro.' And it
may be affirmed with truth," Berkeley added, "that the very savages
of America are better clad and better lodged than the Irish cottagers
throughout the fertile counties of Limerick and Tipperary."

A generation later, in 1780 Arthur Young, whose *Travels in Ireland*
Maria Edgeworth called "the first faithful portrait of the Irish,"
described similar scenes:

> The cottages of the Irish, which are all called cabbins, are the most
> miserable looking hovels that can well be conceived. . . . A land-
> lord in Ireland can scarcely invent an order which a servant,
> labourer, or cottier dares to refuse to execute. . . . Disrespect,
> or anything tending towards sauciness, he may punish with his
> cane or his horsewhip with the most perfect security. A poor man
> would have his bones broken if he offered to lift a hand in his
> own defense.

One day in 1809, while at the Carlow races, Edward Gibbon Wakefield, later a pioneer in promoting emigration to Australia, saw a
poor man's cheek laid open by a whip because the man had failed
to get out of a gentleman's way.

Wakefield and Young were both shocked by the servility of the
Irish peasant. "Landlords of consequence," wrote the latter, "have
assured me that many of their cottier's would think themselves
honoured to have their wives and daughters sent for to the bed of
their master—a mark of slavery which proves the oppression under
which such people must live." Young's comment might have come
from a page out of the Old South.

Yet the human love of independence is hard to extinguish, and
even in eighteenth-century Ireland among a broken and famished
people it had not completely died out. After 1760 it began to revive
in the form of violent agrarian revolt. Usually in protest against
some intolerable local grievance—perhaps an outrageous increase

in rent or some unwonted brutality of the tithe proctor—peasant organizations arose spontaneously in different parts of the country. The Whiteboys in Munster in 1760 were the earliest of these agrarian societies. Three years later they were followed by the Oakboys in Ulster. In 1771 came the Steelboys, and in 1772 the Peep o'Day Boys. Many others followed in due course—Rightboys, Thrashers, Carders, Caravats, Shanavests, Rockites, Ribbonmen, Defenders.

Whatever the immediate occasion for the formation of such societies, their basic object was always the same—to secure that justice that the law denied them. The Whiteboys began as a protest against excessive tithes, the Oakboys against forced labor on the roads, the Steelboys against a sudden flood of evictions. Resort to violence was the common characteristic of all such groups; and of necessity all were local or regional—since because of the poverty and want of education of their leaders, they lacked a disciplined national organization. Hence none of them ever attained the status, or the dignity, of national rebellion.

Both Catholic and Presbyterian laborers took part in these sporadic outbursts. Tyrannical Catholic landlords were attacked as well as Protestant ones. Few people were killed, but much damage was done to property—houses destroyed, hayricks burned, or cattle houghed. In self-protection these societies exacted secret oaths from their members and imposed the death penalty upon informers. In consequence they were condemned by the Catholic Church and those who belonged to them were excommunicated. Outbreaks of savagery were crushed by methods that were no less savage. Meanwhile, nothing whatever was done to redress the grievances that had produced such violence, and as soon as one outburst was subdued, another erupted. "The gentlemen of Ireland," wrote Arthur Young, "never thought of a radical cure, from overlooking the real cause of the disease, which in fact lay in themselves, and not in the wretches they doomed to the gallows."

A further result of agrarian discontent was the emigration to the New World, especially from Ulster, of thousands of embittered farmers, who later were to be among the most implacable enemies of British rule in America. In the Shenandoah Valley today, may still be seen a typical tombstone of one of these Scotch-Irish exiles, containing a brief and pointed summary of his career: "Here lie the remains of John Lewis, who slew the Irish lord, settled August County, located the town of Stanton, and furnished five sons to fight the battle of the American Revolution."

Emigration from Ireland in the Eighteenth Century

During the eighteenth century three separate streams of emigration drained Ireland of her manhood: that of the Catholics to the Continent, seeking service in the armies of France, Spain, or the Empire; that of the Presbyterians to the American Colonies; and that of individuals from the Anglo-Irish minority seeking—and often finding— in London a more glittering success than Dublin could hope to offer, as the careers of Congreve, Farquhar, Goldsmith, Burke, Sheridan, and Tom Moore, among others, remind us.

Of these three emigrant groups, the first was of course numerically the most important and the only one to impress itself deeply upon the national consciousness. The Protestant historian Lecky went as far as to suggest that the real history of Catholic Ireland in the eighteenth century must be sought upon the Continent rather than at home. Prudence led Lecky to reject the incredible figure of nearly half a million Irishmen as having died in the French service between 1691 and 1745—a figure derived from the Abbé MacGeoghegan's researches in the French archives and later accepted as reliable by Mrs. Alice Stopford Green. Yet the fact remains that tens of thousands of Catholic Irishmen did join the "Wild Geese" on the Continent, where not a few won fame in the annals of their adopted countries.

> On far, foreign fields from Dunkirk to Belgrade
> Lie the soldiers and chiefs of the Irish Brigade.

These soldiers abroad did much to redeem the name of Ireland from reproach in contemporary Europe. As Swift, no admirer of Catholics, wrote in 1732:

> I cannot but highly esteem those gentlemen of Ireland who with all the disadvantages of being exiles and strangers, have been able to distinguish themselves by their valour and conduct in so many parts of Europe, I think above all other nations, which ought to make the English ashamed of the reproaches they cast on the ignorance, the dullness and the want of courage of the Irish natives; those defects, wherever they happen, arising only from the poverty and slavery they suffer from their inhuman neighbours, and from the base, corrupt spirit of too many of the chief gentry.

This phenomenon of the feckless and slothful Irishman at home being transformed abroad into the spirited and enterprising citizen of his adopted country was of course to be repeated in the nineteenth century on a much larger scale—above all in America.

In the wars of Louis XIV, the Irish Brigade fought under the French flag in Flanders, in Spain, and in Italy. It was in the course of these wars that Sarsfield had lost his life. The Irish opposed Marlborough on every one of his famous battlegrounds. At Blenheim in 1704, amid the confusion of the French retreat, they alone retired in perfect order and discipline. Along with numerous others the French Marshal Vendôme paid tribute to their repeated acts of reckless courage. A passionate desire for revenge was, no doubt, the special stimulus that preserved always fresh the incomparable *élan* of the Brigade.

The battle of Fontenoy (May 11, 1745) was the crowning triumph of the "Wild Geese." Led by Lord Clare, whose father had commanded at Blenheim and been killed at Ramillies, the Irish intervened at a critical moment of the engagement, turning almost certain defeat into victory by routing the Coldstream Guards, one of the élite regiments of the British army, who were justifiably astonished to hear English words of command issuing from the enemy ranks.

More than forty years later, on the eve of the French Revolution, veterans of the Brigade could still be seen in Paris sitting in the gardens of the Luxembourg, reliving—like Uncle Toby in *Tristram Shandy*—their recollections of Fontenoy and other campaigns; and fifty years after that, in a stirring ballad that quickened the pulse of Young Ireland, Thomas Davis commemorated the most important victory won by Irish arms upon the Continent.

On Fontenoy, on Fontenoy, hark to that fierce huzzah,
"Revenge! remember Limerick! dash down the Sasanach!"
                    .   .   .   .   .

And Fontenoy, famed Fontenoy, had been a Waterloo,
Were not these exiles ready then, fresh, vehement, and true.
                    .   .   .   .   .

How fierce the look these exiles wear, who're wont to be so gay,
The treasured wrongs of fifty years are in their hearts to-day,
The treaty broken, ere the ink wherewith 'twas writ could dry,
Their plundered homes, their ruined shrines, their women's parting cry,
Their priesthood hunted down like wolves, their country overthrown . . .

In 1762, in the hope of weakening the hold of the Irish Brigade upon the imagination of young Irishmen, the British Government proposed to raise seven Irish Catholic regiments for the service of Portugal, England's oldest ally on the Continent. The proposal, however, was defeated by the determined opposition of the Irish Protestants at home.

The service of Irish soldiers in France was so resented in England that in 1756 an act was passed condemning to death any native-born Irishman who, having fought in the French army, should thereafter return to Ireland. Notwithstanding this, young Irishmen continued to get smuggled across the sea, County Clare taking pride of place as a recruiting ground for the Brigade. Some families, like that of Daniel O'Connell in Kerry, supplied recruits in each successive generation. French officers in disguise would tramp the roads of Ireland seeking likely prospects. In 1732, Sir Charles Wogan told Dean Swift that during the forty years since Limerick, 120,000 Irishmen had left Ireland to serve in the French armies; and as late as 1773, Arthur Young declared that Irishmen were still being smuggled over to France: 4,000 had gone from Belfast alone, he reported, during that single year.

At one time there were no less than seven Irish regiments in the French service. One, commanded by Count Dillon, fought with the French in the War of the American Revolution and saw action at Savannah and in the West Indies.

The outbreak of the French Revolution, however, with its fierce anticlerical zeal, meant the dissolution of the Irish Brigade—which was formally disbanded in 1791. One of the last acts of Louis XVI is said to have been the presentation to the Brigade of a flag inscribed with the words: "1692-1792. *Semper et ubique fidelis.*" Being devout Catholics, many of the Irish threw in their lot with the royalist emigrés and left France. Count Dillon was guillotined. Others, like General Daniel O'Connell, uncle of the future "Liberator," hated the Revolution so much that they volunteered for service under George III. The Revolution naturally forced the closure also of the Irish colleges and seminaries in France.

Spain was second only to France in popularity with Irishmen seeking a military career abroad. The oldest Irish regiment in the Spanish service dated back to the early seventeenth century; and within fifty years twelve thousand members of it had lost their lives—some fighting against the French in Flanders, others in warfare with the Turks. By the end of the century, nine Irish regiments were enrolled under the Spanish flag. In 1701, and again in 1791, the unique privilege of equal status with Spanish subjects was confirmed to the Irish serving in Spain. Among Spanish generals of the eighteenth century were found such names as O'Mahony, O'Donnell, O'Gara, O'Reilly, and O'Neill. Under Charles III, Richard Wall, born in County Waterford, became first minister of Spain (1754-63). General Don Carlos Felix O'Neile, whose father had been killed at the Boyne, became governor of Havana; Field Marshal Arthur O'Neil, governor of Yucatán; and General John O'Donoghue, viceroy of Mexico. An Irishman named Lacy was Spanish ambassador to Stockholm; an O'Farrell to Berlin, an O'Mahony to Vienna. On one occasion during the 1770s, during a crisis in Spanish-Portuguese relations, the armies of the two countries faced each other across the border, the Spaniards being commanded by an O'Reilly and the Portuguese by an O'Hara. In the early nineteenth century Bernardo O'Higgins became Liberator of Chile and that country's national hero. He was known also for his enlightened political and social ideas, which included such diverse things as freedom of the press, concessions to Protestants, and the abolition of bullfighting. Admiral William Brown, born in Foxford, County Mayo and buried in Buenos Aires, became the founder of the Argentine navy and today ranks second only to San Martín in the list of Argentinian patriots.*

Fighting under Maria Theresa in the Seven Years' War (1756-63) were generals with names such as Browne, Lacy, Maguire, Nugent, and O'Donnell. A cousin of Browne became governor of Riga and a Russian field marshal. Another field marshal, Count Peter Lacy, who as a boy of thirteen had embarked from Limerick with Sarsfield, was to reorganize the army of Peter the Great and command the Russians against the Turks in the Crimea. In India, at the battle of Wandewash (1760)—the turning point in the struggle for empire between Britain and France—the victorious English forces were commanded by Sir Eyre Coote, a Protestant Irishman from County Limerick, and the defeated French by the Catholic Count Lally, whose father had sailed from Limerick with Sarsfield.

An account of Irishmen who distinguished themselves in foreign service during the eighteenth century would scarcely be complete without mention of those who took a prominent part in the American Revolution. As summarized by Mrs. Alice Stopford Green, "Charles Thompson of Strabane was secretary of the Continental Congress. Eight Irishmen, passionate organizers of the revolt, signed the Declaration of Independence. After the war, an Irishman prepared the

---

*It is interesting to note that Che Guevara also was partly of Irish descent, his paternal grandmother being a Lynch.

Declaration for publication from Jefferson's rough draft; an Irishman's son first publicly read it, an Irishman first printed it and published it."

Richard Montgomery (1739–75), a native of Donegal, who as a young man had served under Wolfe at the siege of Quebec, was appointed by Congress in 1775 to the joint command of American forces aimed at capturing that city, but like Wolfe was killed in action beneath the Heights of Abraham. Montgomery had reluctantly left civil life to accept the rank of brigadier general, declaring that "the will of an oppressed people, compelled to choose between liberty and slavery, must be obeyed." Twice in his short life Montgomery had proof of the truth of this maxim—first in Ireland, then in America. When in the House of Commons, Burke and Chatham praised the valor of Montgomery and even the Tory premier, Lord North conceded that he had been "a brave, able, humane, and generous rebel," the youthful Fox made the spirited reply: "The name of rebel is no certain mask of disgrace; all the great assertors of liberty, the saviors of their country, the benefactors of mankind in all ages, have been called rebels."

Another native of Ireland whose services to the Revolution were handsomely acknowledged by George Washington was Commodore John Barry of Rosslare in Wexford (1745–1803). At the age of ten Barry had gone to sea as a cabin boy on a merchantman and already at twenty-five was one of the most successful merchant seamen sailing between London and Philadelphia, his adopted home. During the war and afterwards, Barry distinguished himself by his organization of the infant American fleet. When in 1963, shortly before his death, President John Fitzgerald Kennedy went to Wexford—the county of his own ancestors—he paid tribute, amid enthusiastic public acclaim, to the memory of Commodore John Barry as a founder of the American Navy.

BIBLIOGRAPHY

Berkeley, George: *The Querist* (1735–37)

Burke, Edmund: *Letters, Speeches, and Tracts on Irish Affairs,* ed. M. Arnold (1881)

Craig, Maurice: *Dublin, 1660–1860* (1952)

————: *The Volunteer Earl* (1948)

Edgeworth, Maria: *Castle Rackrent* (1800)

Hayes, Richard J.: *Biographical Dictionary of Irishmen in France* (1949)

Lecky, W. E. H.: *History of Ireland in the 18th Century,* 5 vols. (1892)

McDowell, Robert B.: *Irish Public Opinion,* 1750–1800 (1944)

McManus, M. J.: *Irish Cavalcade,* 1550–1850 (1939)

Mahoney, Thomas A. D.: *Edmund Burke and Ireland* (1959)

Maxwell, Constantia: *Dublin under the Georges,· 1714–1830* (1937)

_____: *The Stranger in Ireland, from the Reign of Elizabeth to the Great Famine* (1954)

_____: *Town and Country Life in Ireland under the Georges* (1940)

Munter, Robert: *History of the Irish Newspaper, 1685–1760* (1967)

Murray, Alice: *History of the Commercial Relations between England and Ireland from 1660* (1903)

O'Brien, George: *Economic History of Ireland in the 18th Century* (1918)

O'Brien, William: *Edmund Burke as an Irishman* (1926)

O'Connell, Maurice: *Irish Politics and Social Conflict in the Age of the American Revolution* (1965)

Swift, Jonathan: *The Drapier's Letters* (1724)

_____: *A Modest Proposal* (1729)

_____: *Short View of the State of Ireland* (1727)

Wall, Maureen: *The Penal Laws, 1691–1760* (1961)

Young, Arthur: *Tour in Ireland* (1780)

VII

Ireland in the Age of Revolution

Ireland and the American Revolution

When the American Revolution broke out, public opinion in Ireland was generally sympathetic to the American cause. To numerous Irish children such as Daniel O'Connell, John Paul Jones at once became a popular hero. All his life O'Connell was to remember the excitement when American warships appeared off the coast of Kerry.

The Irish parliament at first rallied to the cause of the mother country. However, the additional taxation necessitated by the war caused resentment; this was increased when France and Spain declared war on Britain in 1778 and 1779 respectively—and Ireland found herself cut off from Continental markets. At the same time, most of the garrison was removed from Ireland in order to take part in the American war, thereby weakening England's control over that country.

Strong protests from Irish merchants against the galling restrictions on their commerce caused Lord North, the British premier, to yield; and in 1779, many of the duties that fettered Irish trade were removed. England's military weakness convinced the Dublin parliament that it would be well-advised to appease some of the religious grievances from which both Catholics and Presbyterians in Ireland suffered. Hence in 1779 came the first considerable relaxation of the Penal Laws. Catholics were at last allowed to acquire property in land. In 1780 the disqualifications that prevented Presbyterians from taking part in politics were removed: the Test Act ceased to apply to Protestant dissenters.

These economic and religious concessions resulted indirectly from the American war, which quickened the demand for freedom in Ireland at the same time it increased England's naval and military difficulties. The Dublin parliament was not slow to perceive that the war had benefited its political situation *vis-à-vis* Westminster. "What you trample on in America," Grattan warned, "will sting you in Europe." Three outstanding Protestants—Henry Grattan (1746–1820), Henry Flood (1732–91), and James Caulfield, Earl of Charlemont (1728–99)—now arose to demand the restoration of Ireland's legislative independence, much as Molyneux and Swift had advocated it in the past.

In 1779 these three leaders put themselves at the head of a volunteer force, organized nominally to defend Ireland against the possibility of French invasion but also to bring pressure to bear on the British government. "There arose," wrote Lecky, "one of those movements of enthusiasm that occur two or three times in the history of a nation." By 1780 the Irish volunteers, clothed in uniforms of Irish wool, numbered 100,000 men, all of them Protestants. Under the command of Lord Charlemont, they armed and drilled throughout the country. The Catholics, denied active participation in the movement, nevertheless helped it with contributions.

What Grattan called "the armed property of the nation" posed a serious threat to England's power. "The English have sowed their laws like dragons' teeth," exulted Hussey Burgh in a dramatic speech in the Irish House of Commons, "they have sprung up armed men." The climax came on February 15, 1782, when the volunteers, meeting in the parish church at Dungannon, County Tyrone, under the presidency of Lord Charlemont, asserted that only parliament in Dublin had the power to legislate for Ireland. The volunteers also recommended freedom of religious worship, and a further relaxation of the Penal Laws.

Lord Carlisle, the Viceroy, urged the British government to accede to these demands. Cornwallis' surrender at Yorktown in 1781 was the final blow to British prestige and led to the fall of North. The new Prime Minister, Lord Rockingham, had been influenced favorably toward Ireland by his friend Edmund Burke. The result was the repeal by the British parliament both of Poynings' Act and of the Declaratory Act of 1719. Thus after nearly three centuries the Irish parliament regained its legislative freedom.

"I found Ireland on her knees," exclaimed Grattan in an often-quoted speech in 1782, as he reviewed the volunteers on College Green in Dublin. "I watched over her with an eternal solicitude; I have traced her progress from injuries to arms and from arms to liberty. Spirit of Swift! Spirit of Molyneux! Your genius has prevailed!

Ireland is now a nation. In that new character I hail her! and bowing in her august presence, I say *Esto perpetua!*"

Despite the glitter of Grattan's rhetoric, the Irish parliament failed to use its newly won freedom to develop a system of responsible cabinet government such as had evolved in England. Equally respected for his character and admired for his eloquence, Grattan—"that most pure and eminent of my countrymen," as Sir Jonah Barrington called him—was now the first man in the Irish House of Commons. His voice was thin and sharp, and his speeches were devoid of wit and humor, yet he had the power of inspiring his hearers with enthusiasm. Though small in size and undistinguished in appearance, more than any other man Grattan had become the embodiment of Ireland's national aspirations.

Yet when Dublin Castle offered him a post in the new administration, Grattan at once refused it. Because of past corruption, office holding in Ireland had deservedly fallen into bad repute, and Grattan himself had frequently criticized others for accepting places of profit under the Viceroy. The result of this self-denial based on principle was that the government passed instead under the control of a reactionary clique headed by John Fitzgibbon, Earl of Clare—the evil genius of Ireland in the years ahead—who was restrained by no such scruples.

In 1783, on account of the quarrels among its leaders, the Volunteer movement came to an ignominious end. Grattan favored complete freedom of worship and the admission of propertied Catholics to parliament. "The Irish Protestant," he declared, "could never be free till the Irish Catholic had ceased to be a slave." Charlemont and Flood, however, were opposed to further concessions. Nevertheless, a Catholic Relief Bill passed the Dublin parliament in 1793. It gave Catholic forty-shilling freeholders the right to vote for members of parliament, though not to sit in the House. It granted Catholics the right to belong to grand juries and municipal corporations. It also allowed them to hold commissions in the army—up to the rank of colonel—and to study at Trinity College.

Grattan's liberalism concerning religion did not extend to agrarian reform. As a landowner he believed that the right way to deal with agrarian discontent was not to remove its causes but to quell it by means of coercion. Hence there was a continuance of the outrages perpetrated throughout the country by the secret agrarian societies. Hence, also, the severity with which James Connolly was later to attack the memory of Grattan, and to endorse Marx's scorn of him as a "parliamentary rogue." In fairness to Grattan, however, it should be remembered that he urged the commutation of tithes and that where agrarian matters were concerned, probably no member of the Dublin parliament was any more farsighted than he.

The one useful economic measure of this period was Foster's Act of 1784. John Foster, later Speaker of the Irish House of Commons, persuaded parliament to adopt a protectionist policy of encouraging agriculture by granting bounties on the' export of Irish corn and by putting high duties on the import of foreign corn as long as grain remained reasonably cheap in Ireland. The result of Foster's Act was an increase in the amount of arable land, and with it a consequent increase in the food supply, in rural employment, and in population.

Foster also secured bounties for such Irish industries as glass-making and the spinning and weaving of cotton. Belfast in particular benefited from the new protective duties. Employment was plentiful and wages began to rise. Not only the towns but even the country-side began to experience some degree of prosperity.

It was in Dublin above all, however, that a new vitality manifested itself—in the building of great mansions and the laying out of public squares, in the decorative skill of artists and craftsmen, in the construction of handsome edifices such as the Customs House, the Four Courts, and the King's Inns—all of them designed by James Gandon (1742–1823)—which gave the capital a dignity comparable to that of any city of its size in Europe. No doubt the revived independence of the Irish parliament was partly responsible for the air of well-being with which certain quarters of Dublin, despite the encompassing misery of the slums, now began to be invested.

The United Irishmen

The American Revolution had liberated the Protestant ascendancy from economic and political bondage to England. It even brought a measure of relief to the persecuted Catholic population. Yet of necessity the American Revolution remained a distant influence. Incomparably more profound in its effects—whether in the enthusiasm it generated, the hopes it raised, or the fervor of the faith it inspired—was the immense upheaval of the French Revolution. "All Europe," wrote De Quincey, "moved under the breath of that inspiration." Ireland was no exception.

The French Revolution was not merely a political revolt but also a social upheaval. In the full flush of its first enthusiasm and in the unsullied fervor of its original idealism, it seemed to many like the birth of a new religion as well. The French Declaration of the Rights of Man was the credo of the new faith. Anticipated by the ideas of Rousseau and other philosophers, it was a call for the regeneration of mankind. "Liberty, Equality and Fraternity" was not yet a tarnished cliché but a deeply felt aspiration capable of stirring men to sacrifice and even death. The Revolution was a challenge not merely to the power of existing governments but also to the fundamental principles on which they were based.

The Society of the United Irishmen, founded in Belfast in 1791 by Wolfe Tone (1763-98), was the form taken in Ireland by the revolutionary spirit that was then sweeping through Western Europe. Sympathy for the French Revolution first appeared in Ireland among the Protestant Dissenters of the north, who were already disposed to republicanism by virtue of their admiration of the United States. Belfast, in fact, had come to be known as "Little Boston." In his autobiography, Tone recalled the joy with which the Belfast radicals had greeted the fall of the Bastille on July 14, 1789. Every year after 1791, the United Irishmen in Belfast met on July 14 to celebrate the anniversary of that great event. They invoked with equal enthusiasm the names of Washington and Franklin, of Mirabeau and Lafayette. The American flag graced their banquets; the oratory of Patrick Henry and Samuel Adams was their inspiration. In 1792, four flags were flown in Belfast—those of the United States, France, Poland, and Ireland.

In January, 1792, there appeared in Belfast* a militant radical paper, the *Northern Whig,* founded by Wolfe Tone and others. Its first number identified the cause of Ireland with the revolutionary cause throughout Europe.

> Although Ireland will be the great object of the paper, yet *America* and *France* shall not be forgotten—America and Ireland long suffered under the arbitrary supremacy of Britain, and with a generous concern did Irishmen anxiously attend to the conflict that established American freedom: nor were they merely idle spectators; numbers of them supported her cause with their blood; and it may be truly said that *their* victories eminently contributed to establish the independence of Ireland. France, a country lately enthralled beyond even the hope of Freedom, has recently burst her chains, demolished the stronghold of despotism—and laid the foundations of a noble pile—the Temple of Universal Liberty.

At this time also Tom Paine's attack on Burke, *The Rights of Man,*

---

*It is interesting to remember that the population of Belfast at this time was less than twenty thousand.

was widely distributed and eagerly read in Belfast as well as in other parts of Ireland. A contemporary observer called it the Koran of the United Irishmen. Paine's controversy with Burke, wrote Lecky, "and the gigantic event which gave rise to it changed in an instant the politics of Ireland. . . . In a little time the French Revolution became the test of every man's political creed."

The appearance of the United Irishmen marks a new epoch in Irish history. Including Catholics and Protestants on equal terms, and transcending social differences as well, the United Irishmen aimed at a truly national representation. Democratic in spirit, they embodied not only the fervor of the French Revolution but also the liberal principles and the intellectual scope of the Enlightenment. As Gustave de Beaumont later remarked, they imparted to the cause of Irish reform "a philosophical character" that it had never had before. With the United Irishmen, the aspiration for national freedom ceased to be provincial in character, and linked itself with such aspirations everywhere in Europe.

The political program of Wolfe Tone and the United Irishmen aimed at four goals: the independence of Ireland; a democratic franchise; the purification of the whole corrupt system of Irish politics, including the abolition of the pocket and rotten boroughs; and Catholic Emancipation. This program anticipated no less than four of the six points of the People's Charter of 1838 in England—the first political manifesto of the English working class. While the United Irishmen had no agrarian proposals, some of their leaders used language that could not but alarm the landlords. "If the men of property will not support us," Wolfe Tone proclaimed defiantly, "they must fall; we can support ourselves by the aid of that numerous and respectable class of the community, *the men of no property.*"

While the United Irishmen hoped originally to secure reform by peaceful parliamentary means, they were at no pains to conceal their contempt for the aristocracy that monopolized power in the Dublin parliament. Tone, the son of a coachmaker, poured scorn on the pretentions of the Anglo-Irish landlords to represent the Irish people. "The Revolution of 1782," he wrote, attacking Grattan directly, "was the most bungling, imperfect business that ever threw ridicule on a lofty epithet, by assuming it unworthily. . . . The Revolution of 1782," he went on indignantly, "was a Revolution which enabled Irishmen to sell at a much higher price their honour, their integrity and the interests of their country; it was a Revolution which . . . left three fourths of our countrymen slaves as it found them, and the government of Ireland in the base and wicked, and contemptible hands of those who had spent their lives in degrading and plundering her." "Beyond all comparison the most shamelessly profligate and abandoned by all sense of virtue, principle or even common decency," Tone wrote in his autobiography, "was the legislature of my own country."

It is not difficult to imagine the fear with which the appearance of the United Irishmen filled the Irish governing class. A typical representative of that class was Sir Jonah Barrington, whose *Recollections* give us a vivid insight into the habits, thoughts and feelings of the Protestant ascendancy at this time. "I profess to be a sound Protestant without bigotry," Sir Jonah proudly declared, "and an hereditary royalist without ultraism. Liberty I love, democracy I hate, fanaticism I denounce." As for the United Irishmen, he professed himself ready to risk his life "to put down that spirit of mad democracy which sought to subvert all legal institutions." *"Radical Reform,"* he pontificated, "is in reality proximate revolution; *Universal Suffrage* appears to me inextinguishable uproar; *Annual Parliaments* nothing less than periodical bloodshed."

While Sir Jonah thus raged privately among his friends, a far greater figure than he now entered the lists against the United Irishmen to challenge them by the equal force of argument and eloquence. The *Reflections on the French Revolution* (1790) had made Burke the most respected political philosopher in England and the leading champion of counterrevolution throughout Europe. "The United Irishmen," wrote Burke, denouncing his fellow countrymen, "without any regard for religion, club all kinds of discontents together, in order to produce all kinds of discontents. That unwise body, the United Irishmen, have had the folly to represent those evils as owing to this country [Britain], when in truth its chief guilt is its total neglect and its entire ignorance of Ireland."

To this accusation Wolfe Tone replied sharply that Burke, "in an eloquent publication which flattered so many of their prejudices," had misrepresented the nature of the French Revolution to the people of England. The Irish, however, Tone went on to say, "feeling themselves to be an oppressed, insulted and plundered nation," were not in the same position as the English. "We had not, like the English, a prejudice rooted deep in our very nature against France. As the Revolution advanced . . . the public spirit of Ireland rose with a rapid acceleration. It became the test of everyman's political creed."

The basic incompatibility between the aristocratic government of Britain and the egalitarian spirit of revolutionary France could not be resolved but by war; and in 1793 war broke out between the two countries. Automatically, sympathy with the Revolution became

treason in England and, officially, in Ireland too. In 1794 the British
Prime Minister, William Pitt, ordered the suppression of the United
Irishmen. From this point onward, therefore, the latter were driven
underground. They entered into virtual alliance with the French and
began to plan the overthrow of the Irish government by force of
arms.

Lord Fitzwilliam (1795)

In 1795, Pitt sought to thwart these developments by a double counter-
stroke: by granting Catholic emancipation and simultaneously en-
listing the support of the Irish Catholic bishops on behalf of the
government. Early in 1795, Lord Fitzwilliam, an enlightened Whig
aristocrat and friend of Pitt, arrived in Dublin as Lord Lieutenant,
with instructions to sound out the Anglo-Irish ascendancy with regard
to the possibility of further Catholic relief.

The new Viceroy decided to break the stranglehold of Dublin
Castle upon Irish politics. He moved at once to dismiss the Lord
Chancellor, John Fitzgibbon, Earl of Clare, the son of a Catholic
turned Protestant, and a man notorious for the contempt and hatred
that he felt for Catholics. Pressure on behalf of Clare was brought
to bear on Pitt in London, and Fitzwilliam had to be content with
purging some of the worst Castle officials—foremost among them
John Beresford, who controlled the largest share of patronage in
Ireland, where his name was soon to be execrated for the floggings
and tortures that he was to supervise in 1798.

The ascendancy persuaded Pitt that Fitzwilliam's liberal policies
were conducive to revolt in Ireland, and the Prime Minister, already
in a state approaching panic because of the military successes of
the French, lost his nerve. To the consternation of Dublin, which
went into mourning over the event, the popular Lord Lieutenant
was suddenly recalled—after a stay of only six weeks. The mature
judgment of Lecky, some eighty years later, was that had Fitzwilliam
been allowed to remain, he might have been able to persuade the
Irish parliament to grant Catholic emancipation, thereby averting
the horrors of 1798. The departure of Fitzwilliam meant the triumph
of Clare, the most cynical and corrupt official in the Irish government. It also guaranteed that rebellion, should it come, would be
crushed with savage cruelty. The stage was set for the bloodiest
tragedy in Ireland since the time of Cromwell.

Pitt's second line of defense against the possibility of revolt in
Ireland—a working alliance with the Catholic hierarchy—was facili-

tated by their joint hostility to the French Revolution. The English minister soon realized that the Irish bishops, alarmed by the anti-religious fervor of the French, might be transformed from a suspect and persecuted body into a bulwark of the established order. With this end in view Pitt—in a maneuver that would have been incredible in prerevolutionary days—persuaded the Dublin parliament to sub-sidize the new seminary at Maynooth for the training of a Catholic priesthood; and when, in 1800, the Act of Union abolished that parliament, the British government assumed direct responsibility for the annual subvention of £9,000 to Maynooth. Thus the bishops, who under the penal laws had been proscribed and hunted down, now found themselves treated by the government with the respect due to trusted allies.

It is not surprising that soon afterwards Maynooth condemned the United Irishmen—even though one of their avowed objects was Catho-lic emancipation—as "a set of desperate and profligate men." From the steps of the altar Dr. Troy, Archbishop of Dublin, denounced their "horrid principles"; while in the West, Dr. Dillon, Bishop of Kilmacduagh, warned his flock against "the machinations of dangerous and designing men."

The Beginning of the Orange Lodges (1795)

In the same year, 1795, another event occurred that at the time seemed insignificant but that was to exert a baleful influence on the future of Ireland down to the present time. Despite the efforts of the United Irishmen to harmonize religious differences, friction between Catholi-cism and Presbyterianism arose in Ulster, where Catholic peasants, in their desperate hunger for land, were willing to pay higher rents to rack-renting landlords than Protestant tenants, with the result that some of the latter began to be dispossessed in favor of Catholics.

The result was the skirmish known as the "Battle of the Diamond" in County Armagh (September 21, 1795), in which a small group of impoverished Presbyterians routed a small group of equally poor Catholics. That very same evening the victors founded a new secret society—the Grand Orange Lodge of Ulster. From this tiny seed was to proliferate the anti-Catholic Masonic organizations that are still powerful today in the north of Ireland. Orange lodges sprang up in many parts of Ulster, and as Lecky admits: "A terrible persecution of the Catholics immediately followed." Their chapels were burned and their hovels attacked by howling mobs. The old Cromwellian cry—"To Hell or Connacht"—was revived, and—reversing 1641—

thousands of homeless Catholics were driven out of Ulster to take refuge beyond the Shannon. "It is no secret," reported the Earl of Gosford, Lord Lieutenant of Armagh, in 1796 "that a persecution, accompanied with all the circumstances of ferocious cruelty which have in all ages distinguished that dreadful calamity, is now raging in this country. . . . The only crime which the wretched objects of this merciless persecution are charged with, is a crime of easy proof. It is simply a profession of the Roman Catholic faith."

"I see the Orange boys are playing the devil in Ireland," chafed Wolfe Tone in exile in 1796. "I have no doubt it is the work of the Government." At the very least it was a stroke of good fortune for Pitt that the generous hopes of the United Irishmen were destroyed in this sudden, unexpected recrudescence of the old religious fanaticism. Thus the political liberalism that had characterized dissent in Ulster throughout the eighteenth century was now supplanted by the new Orange spirit of religious and political reaction that was to dominate Ulster thenceforward. The "Battle of the Diamond" is a tragic landmark in the history of religious intolerance in Ireland. While its immediate effect was to shatter the ideals of the United Irishmen, its ultimate result was to perpetuate a religious discord that has divided Ireland down to the present day.

The Attempted Invasion of Ireland by Hoche (1796)

After 1795 the main hope of the United Irishmen was to effect a union between its middle-class and largely Protestant leadership, which had developed in Belfast, Dublin, and other towns, and the mass of poor, discontented Catholic peasants who were now enrolling in secret agrarian societies calling themselves the "Defenders." Under the leadership of a young Protestant nobleman, Lord Edward Fitzgerald, son of the Duke of Leinster, premier peer of Ireland, the United Irishmen established a Supreme Executive of five members, with a local executive in each of the four provinces responsible to it. Its aim was to organize the peasantry on a nationwide scale for revolt.

The United Irishmen, therefore, now began to drill and organize the rural population while at the same time seeking military aid from France, where Tone, after a brief sojourn in the United States, had arrived in 1797. The revolutionaries claimed some 110,000 supporters in Ulster, 100,000 in Munster, and 68,000 in Leinster. Tone, ever sanguine, believed that a landing in Ireland of some five or ten thousand French soldiers would guarantee the success of the rebellion

—a hope that was not perhaps too unreasonable, considering that by this time the youthful veterans of the French revolutionary armies had become the finest soldiers in Europe.

Toward the close of 1796 the French Directory fitted out an army of fifteen thousand men for the invasion of Ireland, placing it under the command of a brilliant and youthful general, Lazare Hoche, whose chief object in life, Wolfe Tone observed with joy, was "the destruction of the power of England." Neither Philip II of Spain nor Louis XIV had ever devoted a force of such size to the liberation of Ireland.

In December, 1796, Hoche sailed from Brest with a fleet of forty-three vessels, Tone accompanying him with the rank of Adjutant-General in the French Army. The fleet was scattered in a gale, and part of it was dispersed by fog. Just before Christmas, nevertheless, six thousand French soldiers under General Grouchy—later to lose Waterloo for Napoleon—anchored in Bantry Bay in County Cork. After five days Grouchy weighed anchor and departed. Tone, who was on the spot, was beside himself with chagrin. "I am so near the shore," he wrote, "that I can in a manner touch the sides of Bantry Bay with my right and left hand. In an enterprise like ours, everything depends upon the promptitude and audacity of our first movements and we are here . . . most pitifully languid. . . . I could tear my flesh with rage and vexation." "England has not had such an escape since the Spanish Armada," he complained. "That expedition, like ours, was defeated by the weather."*

On account of the mutinies in the British Navy which took place in 1797, that year, too, seemed favorable for the liberation of Ireland. This time the French, having overrun the Dutch Republic, planned to use Holland as a base against the British Isles. Tone accordingly went to Amsterdam. Contrary winds during most of the summer kept the invasion fleet from putting out to sea, and once again the impetuous Irish leader saw the ruin of his hopes. "It is most terrible," he fumed impotently in his journal. "Twice within nine months has England been saved by the wind. It seems as if the very elements had conspired against us. It seems as if the very elements had conspired to perpetuate our slavery and protect the insolence and oppression of our tyrants." At this point chance was to deal Ireland another blow, for before the year was out, Lazare Hoche, the chief hope of Ireland, was dead at the age of thirty-three.

Hoche's successor, a young general named Bonaparte, was little

---

*The Spanish Armada in 1588 had been defeated by the English navy long before part of it was shipwrecked in the equinoctial gales of September.

interested in invading Ireland—some felt, through jealousy of his brilliant predecessor. The future emperor was already dazzled by the exploits of Alexander the Great and anxious to emulate his conquests in the East. When on May 19, 1798, a French army of fifty thousand with Bonaparte himself on board sailed from Toulon for Egypt in a fleet of 250 transports, it was the end of all hope for Irish independence. Such an army, had it ever landed in Ireland, must almost certainly have gained that country's freedom. Twenty years later, in exile at St. Helena, Napoleon told Las Cases that he regretted not having sailed for Ireland in 1798, in which case he would have avoided the fiasco of the Egyptian campaign. It was in fact one of the few serious strategical blunders of Napoleon's career.

The Rebellion of 1798

Even though not a single French soldier had landed in Ireland in 1796, the mere appearance of the French fleet at Bantry Bay aroused the nation. It convinced the peasants that the hour of deliverance for which they had waited so long was at hand. Reported one of Pitt's informers, Leonard MacNally:

> The whole body of the peasantry would join the French in case of an invasion. . . . The sufferings of the common people from high rents and low wages, from oppressions of their landlords . . . and tithes are not the only causes of disaffection to Government, and hatred to England; for though these have long kept the Irish peasant in a state of slavery and indigence, yet another cause, more dangerous, pervaded them all. . . . This cause is an attachment to French principles in politics and religion . . . and an ardent desire for a republican Government.

But while the peasants, encouraged by the United Irishmen, were drilling and arming, Dublin Castle and Downing Street were concerting countermeasures. By far the largest army that had ever been stationed in Ireland was now quartered there. It consisted of seventy thousand British regulars and an equal number of troops raised in Ireland, including both militia and yeomanry. The militia was composed of pauperized Catholics who had enlisted for pay, the yeomanry of Protestant farmers led by Protestant landlords. These forces raised to hold Ireland in subjection were larger than any British army that ever fought against Napoleon on the Continent.

Already in 1797, General Gerald Lake (1744–1807), who was to leave behind him in Ireland a reputation for cruelty second only to that of Cromwell, had taken steps to crush incipient revolt. As a warning to others, a popular young Presbyterian farmer, William Orr (1766-97), a member of the United Irishmen, was arrested on a trumped-up charge and hanged at Carrickfergus in Antrim, leaving a wife and five small children. Orr's last words were said to have been: "I die at peace and charity with all mankind." What was generally regarded as a judicial murder gave rise to widespread resentment. A poem, "The Wake of William Orr," by Dr. William Drennan (1754-1826), a member of the United Irishmen and a Belfast Unitarian minister, in which personal grief for the death of a brave young man was mingled with sorrow for the fate of Ireland, became immensely popular throughout the country.

> There our murdered brother lies,
> Wake him not with women's cries,
> Mourn the way that manhood ought—
> Sit in silent trance of thought
>
> Hapless nation, rent and torn!
> Thou wert early taught to mourn;
> Warfare for six hundred years!
> Epoch marked with blood and tears.
>
> Hunted through thy native grounds,
> Or flung reward to human hounds,
> Each one pulled and tore his share,
> Reckless of thy deep despair.
>
> God of mercy! God of peace!
> Make this mad confusion cease!
> O'er the mental chaos move,
> Let it speak the light of love.

By burning, looting, and flogging, Lake's regulars spread terror through the countryside, especially in the north. Even Sir Ralph Abercromby, the British commander-in-chief in Ireland, declared in February, 1798, that the conduct of Lake's troops "proved the army to be in a state of licentiousness which must render it formidable to everyone but the enemy." Two months later Abercromby resigned in protest against the virtual breakdown of military discipline. "Every crime, every cruelty," he wrote, "that could be committed by Cossacks and Calmucks, has been transacted here." Abercromby's second-in-command, Sir John Moore—later to die heroically at Corunna—endorsed this judgment. "The officers are in general profligate and idle," Moore protested. "If a man of sufficient character and talent was to be found . . . he might still save Ireland."

Wearied of waiting for help from France that never came, the

United Irishmen, under the leadership of Lord Edward Fitzgerald, finally chose May 23, 1798, as the date for a national uprising. Unfortunately for them, their ranks were riddled with informers in the pay of Pitt. Many of their leaders were betrayed by government spies before the plans for insurrection were complete, and were subsequently executed. At least thirty-four of the original members of the Society died on the gallows.

Four days before the appointed date for the rebellion, Lord Edward himself was betrayed and on June 4 died of wounds received while resisting arrest at the hands of Major Sirr. Wolfe Tone being still in France, the death of Lord Edward deprived the rebels of the one professional soldier whose leadership was available to them.

Nevertheless, on the appointed day, rebellion broke out at different places in Leinster. That May morning, goaded by present wrongs and stirred by ancestral memories, 4,000 peasants armed with scythes and pitchforks assembled on the hill of Tara. Routed by the firearms of the militia under Lord Fingall and Lord Dunsany, by nightfall some 350 peasants lay dead upon the sacred hill. They were buried *en masse,* in what came to be known as the "Croppies' grave." *

On May 26, Father John Murphy of Boolavogue, County Wexford, himself an opponent of the United Irishmen, instigated his parishioners to ambush a small detachment of yeomanry, whom they killed with pitchforks. That same evening—it was the eve of Pentecost—Father John noted laconically in his diary: "Began the Republic of Ireland in Boolavogue." On the news of this unexpected victory over the hated yeomanry, the whole county of Wexford rose in arms. The rebels seized the towns of Wexford and Enniscorthy but on June 13 were overwhelmed at Vinegar Hill by thirteen thousand seasoned troops under General Lake. The leaders, including Father Murphy, were promptly hanged.

The Wexford rebellion was a spontaneous peasant uprising provoked by long memories of intolerable injustice. Though the United Irishmen had not instigated this particular revolt, the Catholic bishops at once condemned the rebellion, rallying public opinion to the support of the government—a fact that no doubt explains the failure of the rest of Ireland to rise in support of the men of Wexford.

Brief as was the rising, it was savagely fought. As in most peasant revolts, terrible atrocities were committed. Protestant gentry who fell into the hands of the rebels were executed in batches, many being spitted upon pikes. Ninety-seven Protestants were thrown into the

---

*As a protest against the aristocratic custom of wearing wigs, sympathizers with the French Revolution cut their hair extremely short. In Ireland they were nicknamed "croppies" by the English.

Slaney from a bridge in Wexford and drowned. At Scullabogue, near New Ross, 184 defenseless Protestants—men, women, and children—were trapped in a barn and slaughtered by the peasants.

Atrocities, however, were not committed only—or chiefly—by the rebels. The authorities, panic-striken by the unexpected defiance of those whom they so thoroughly despised, took a savage revenge. Order was reestablished throughout Wexford by a veritable reign of terror, with floggings in the villages and gallows in the towns. The terror spread to parts of Ireland that had not even been implicated in the revolt. In Dublin, which had remained inert, the infamous John Beresford used his riding school as a torture chamber to demoralize the capital. His example was imitated by lesser sadists in many an Irish town and village. The pitchcap—a device by which scalding pitch was poured on peasants' heads—was widely used. Lord Charlemont's memoirs are filled with references to hangings, floggings, and tortures inflicted throughout the country. In the opinion of Lord Morley, the excesses committed by the British authorities in Ireland in 1798 exceeded in horror the September massacres in Paris in 1792, which had so revolted and alarmed the people of England.

A new Lord Lieutenant, the Marquis Cornwallis*—a humane and amiable man—arrived in Ireland just after the rebellion was over and was appalled by the brutality of the vengeance which he saw everywhere enacted. The militia, he observed, "were totally without discipline" but "ferocious and cruel in the extreme when any poor wretches, either with or without arms, come into their power: in short, murder appears to be their favorite pastime." Two months later he reported: "Numberless murders are committed hourly by our people without any process or examination whatever. . . . The yeomanry are in the style of the Loyalists in America, only much more numerous and powerful, and a thousand times more ferocious." Unless such excesses were stopped, Cornwallis prophesied "the extirpation of the greater number of the inhabitants and the utter destruction of the country."

The thirst for blood was not confined to soldiers in the field. The same mood of sadism prevailed at the dinner tables of the gentry, who were "in such a state," wrote Cornwallis, "that nothing but blood will satisfy them. . . . Even at my table, where you may suppose I do all I can to prevent it, the conversation always turns on hanging, shooting, burning and so forth; and if a priest has been put to death, the greatest joy is expressed by the whole company."

Although the rebellion of 1798 lasted but a month and was virtually

---

*This was the Cornwallis (1738–1805) who had surrendered at Yorktown in 1781.

confined to a single county, no event since the time of Cromwell—
not even the battle of the Boyne or the defense of Limerick—impressed itself so deeply on the consciousness of the Irish people. Many
a local hero, like Gunner Magee in Mayo, survived long in folk
memory. "When the English," wrote Frank O'Connor, "put the rope
round his neck, he threw back his head and laughed." The Croppies'
grave at Tara was believed to be haunted forever.

One reason for the unrelenting hatred later felt for England by the
Irish leader Charles Stewart Parnell was his vivid childhood recollection of terrible tales told him by servants about the Wicklow
floggings inflicted in ninety-eight on the backs of the peasantry.
From her tenantry in Galway, Lady Gregory heard similar stories;
while William Butler Yeats chose Mayo as the setting for *Cathleen
ni Houlihan* because he had met peasants in that county who still
spoke about children spitted upon bayonets and other atrocities
committed in 1798.

"The story of those days," wrote Sir James Sexton, a twentieth-
century member of the British Labour party descended from Irish
emigrants, "was handed on to the children of all who endured their
agony; it spread all over the world and engendered in the mind of
every Irishman and Irishwoman who heard it, hatred—bitter and
boundless hatred—of everything connected with Britain and the
British. That, so far as my mind was concerned, is my principal
political and spiritual inheritance."

A ballad literature grew out of "ninety-eight" ensuring that its memory should always be kept green. "Croppies Lie Down," "Kelly the Boy
from Killane," "The Boys of Wexford," and "The Shan Van Vocht"
were some of the songs that animated the sentiment of revolt and
passed it on from mouth to mouth in each succeeding generation.
Dion Boucicault's poem, "The Wearing of the Green," despite its
bathos, was to become as popular as any song ever sung in Ireland.

> She's the most distressful country that ever yet was seen,
> They are hanging men and women for the Wearing of the Green.
> Then since the colour we must wear is England's cruel red,
> Sure Ireland's sons will ne'er forget the blood that they have shed.

Such simple verses, reported George Petrie, the archaeologist, who
traveled throughout Ireland in the nineteenth century, were sung in
every peasant's cottage. On the eve of executions in Dublin, when the
thoughts of all were turned toward the condemned cell in Mountjoy
or Kilmainham, the effect in the theater of such references to hanging
was electrifying—even in the twentieth century.

Despite Daniel O'Connell's contempt for the men of ninety-eight, the Young Irelanders triumphantly revived their memory. "The red rain," wrote Thomas Davis, "made Wexford's harvest grow." In the columns of *The Nation,* the magazine that Davis founded, there appeared a sentimental poem by a retiring young Trinity don, John Kells Ingram, "Who Fears to Speak of Ninety-Eight?," whose popularity came almost to rival that of "The Wearing of the Green."

> Some lie far off beyond the wave,
> Some sleep in Ireland, too;
> All, all are gone, but still lives on
> The fame of those who died;
> All true men, like you men,
> Remember them with pride.
>
> They rose in dark and evil days
> To right their native land;
> They kindled here a living blaze
> That nothing shall withstand.

Remembering the popular appeal of ballads such as these, and disregarding their evident bathos, Yeats, like Shelley before him, believed that in the shaping of a nation's consciousness, poets were more important than legislators. When in 1963 John Fitzgerald Kennedy visited his ancestral home in Wexford, he received overwhelming proof that ballad literature had indeed preserved the memory of ninety-eight intact into the twentieth century.

Wolfe Tone and 1798

Never again did so favorable an opportunity present itself for the liberation of Ireland by a foreign army. In 1798 there had been universal discontent, and though ill-armed, large numbers of peasants were prepared to rise. On the Continent the French had proved themselves invincible, and there can be no doubt that had a sizable French force landed in Ireland, it would have defeated any British troops that might have been sent against it. In addition, the British Navy had been in a state of mutiny for several months in 1797—mutinies in which numerous United Irishmen were involved, since many poverty-stricken Irish had enlisted in the British armed forces for the sake of pay.

Through a combination of political bungling and adverse weather, the golden opportunity of these years had been lost. Well might

Wolfe Tone (1763–98). Leader of the United Irishmen; committed suicide while awaiting execution in 1798.

Wolfe Tone, a helpless and anguished spectator of these events, fret and chafe and seek relief in drink. The departure in 1798 of a large French armada for Egypt, coupled with the ensuing failure of the Wexford revolt, seemed to terminate the single bright period of hope.

Then, suddenly, like a bolt from the blue, on August 22, 1798, a French army of a thousand men under General Humbert landed at Killala in Mayo. The smallness of the force and the failure to synchronize the landing with the Wexford rising foredoomed the effort to failure, but not before Humbert had badly jolted British pride. General Lake, fresh from his campaign of terror against helpless peasants, was sent against Humbert. Though his forces outnumbered the French by nearly three to one, they were now facing not raw country levies but battle-hardened veterans from the armies of Italy and the Rhine. The result was not a fight but a flight. After a brief engagement called in derision by the Irish "the races of Castlebar," Lake's looters broke ranks and scarcely stopped till they reached the shelter of Athlone, some sixty miles away.

The discipline of Humbert's revolutionaries was admirable: no pillage or plunder took place. The Irish people marveled to see the endurance and *élan* of such sallow-faced, undersized warriors, able if necessary to sustain themselves on bread and water. The orderly army of atheists was no less astonished by the extreme piety of the Connacht peasantry.

Notwithstanding the victory of Castlebar, it was only a matter of time before the English assembled large forces, which soon outnumbered the French by twenty to one. They were compelled to surrender at Ballinamuck, County Longford, after a march inland of a 150 miles. Though Humbert was granted honorable release—he later fought with Andrew Jackson at New Orleans, where he died in 1823 —Wolfe Tone's brother, Matthew, who had fought with Humbert, was taken to Dublin and hanged at Arbour Hill barracks. Though the French had behaved chivalrously and the men of Connacht had held aloof from the conflict—perhaps because their spirit had been broken by Lake's floggings the previous year—General Lake now avenged his humiliation at Castlebar by fresh atrocities.

The ludicrous anticlimax to the tragicomedy of French aid came with the departure for Ireland, just twelve days after Humbert's surrender, of Admiral Bompard with nine ships and three thousand men. With the admiral on his flagship, the *Hoche,* sailed Wolfe Tone. In Lough Swilly on October 12, after a fierce six hours' battle, a superior British naval force captured the *Hoche.* Tone was court-martialed in Dublin. Denied his request to be shot as a prisoner of war instead of being hanged as a felon, he cut his throat in prison and died on November 19, 1798. Thus perished the ablest of the United Irishmen —the most spirited and nimble-witted, the most implacable and resourceful of them all.

A liberal Englishman, Goldwin Smith, who taught at Oxford and Cornell in the latter half of the nineteenth century, paid a handsome tribute to Wolfe Tone. Regretting that his name was "little known amongst Englishmen"—an observation the truth of which applies to many Irish patriots besides Tone—Professor Smith characterized him as "brave, adventurous, sanguine, fertile in resource, buoyant under misfortune, warm-hearted," and in a striking analogy, "almost as fatal an enemy to England as Hannibal was to Rome."

In his autobiography, Wolfe Tone gives one an unforgettable picture of a personality that was at once gay and volatile, ardent and impetuous, audacious and high-spirited, full of humor and self-mockery. Unlike Patrick Pearse, Tone was not one of those revolutionary idealists who have wholly sublimated their natural impulses in the cause of freedom. He was a devoted husband and father, with three children he adored (his elder son grew up to take part in Napoleon's last desperate campaigns). Lord Edward Fitzgerald, too, had had a wife and three children to whom he was deeply attached, and whom he left to hazard all for Ireland—in what Yeats terms "that delirium of the brave."

The French Revolution was the decisive influence in the life of

Tone. Neither Stendhal nor Heine nor Pushkin were more truly its children. The revolution taught Tone to see Irish history in a new light. It gave his life a meaning and a purpose it had never had before. It gave him a new religion and made him a democrat as well as a patriot. It found him provincial and left him cosmopolitan. While it deepened his love for Ireland, it enlarged his sympathies to include other oppressed peoples such as the Poles and the Italians. It created in him a burning hatred of tyranny wherever encountered but above all when the victim was his native land.

"From my earliest youth," Wolfe Tone told the military judges at his court-martial, "I have regarded the connection between Ireland and Great Britain as the curse of the Irish nation; and felt that while it lasted, this country could never be free nor happy. . . . That Ireland was not able of herself to throw off the yoke I knew, I therefore sought for aid wherever it was to be found . . . I remained faithful to what I thought the cause of my country and sought in the French Republic an ally to rescue three millions of my countrymen." "I was led by a hatred of England," Tone noted in his journal, "so deeply rooted in my nature that it was rather an instinct than a principle. . . . The truth is, I hate the very name of England. I hated her before my exile and I will hate her always."

Wolfe Tone and Edward Fitzgerald were the first martyrs of modern Ireland. Patrick Sarsfield had been the last survivor of an elder aristocratic world, not the precursor of a new democratic one; but the United Irishmen anticipated Young Ireland, the Fenians, and Sinn Fein. They foreshadowed, as they were to inspire, Thomas Davis and John Mitchel, John O'Leary and Michael Davitt, Patrick Pearse and James Connolly—and Roger Casement. Tone's *Autobiography,* together with Mitchel's *Jail Journal,* furnish as complete a portrait of a revolutionary as can be found in Irish literature.

As long as Daniel O'Connell had influence over his countrymen, the United Irishmen stood condemned; but with the repudiation of O'Connell by Young Ireland after 1843, the way was open for a more just, as well as a more generous, appreciation of Wolfe Tone— "the clearest, boldest spirit sprung from Irish soil," as Thomas Francis Meagher was to call him. The modern devotion to his memory begins with the visit paid in 1843 by Thomas Davis, the founder of Young Ireland, to the half-ruined ivy-covered country graveyard at Bodenstown, County Kildare, where Tone lies buried. There Davis erected a monument the artless verse of whose inscription generations of Irish children were to know by heart.

> In Bodenstown churchyard there is a green grave
> And freely around it let winter winds rave,
> Far better they suit him—the ruin, the gloom—
> Till Ireland, a nation, shall build him a tomb.

All subsequent attempts to win freedom for Ireland by force invoked the name of Tone. The annual pilgrimage to Bodenstown in June came to rival in appeal that to Croagh Patrick in July. Brendan Behan, who was brought up to regard Wolfe Tone as "the greatest Irishman that ever lived" and to revere him as a patriot "held in the utmost affection by every Irishman," made the annual pilgrimage as a boy in the Fianna, and as an adult in the I.R.A. Thousands of others still do the same today.

"We have come to the holiest place in Ireland," Pearse proclaimed at Bodenstown in 1913, "holier to us than the place where Patrick sleeps in Down. Patrick brought us life, but this man died for us." "Wolfe Tone," he asserted, "is the Irish nation in action, gay and heroic and terrible." It was said of Pearse that he carried with him Tone's *Autobiography* as others might carry a Bible.

In Pearse's judgment, while John Mitchel was the chief literary genius of revolutionary Ireland, Tone surpassed him as a human being and as a leader of men. "Tone's was a broader humanity, with as intense a nationality," Pearse affirmed. "Tone's was as sunny a nature with as stubborn a soul. But Mitchel stands next to Tone: and these two shall teach and lead you unto the path of national salvation. For this I will answer on the Judgment Day." The seed planted by the United Irishmen blossomed ultimately in Easter Week, and with his life Pearse was to vindicate his fervent profession of faith.

The Act of Union (1800)

As a result of the alarm caused by the Wexford rebellion and Humbert's invasion, Pitt determined in the interests of Britain to destroy the Irish parliament and bring Ireland under direct English control. Since 1782 every Viceroy had privately recommended such a measure to the British Cabinet. The difficulty was how to persuade the Irish Lords and Commons to put an end to their own existence and tamely accept union with Westminster. Apart from the loss of political power, a degree of pride and dignity was necessarily invested in an institution that was over five hundred years old. There was also the question of public opinion in Dublin, and throughout Ireland. Even in the cynical atmosphere of eighteenth-century politics, there was felt to be a certain awkwardness—illustrated by the Partitions of Poland—about extinguishing the independence of a nation.

The Viceroy, Cornwallis, soon realized that sufficient pecuniary inducement would make the Irish parliament amenable to reason, but he advised Pitt that a grant of Catholic emancipation should accompany the Union. The Prime Minister, however, gave way before the obdurate refusal of Lord Clare, the Chancellor of Ireland, to countenance any further relief to Irish Catholics. There was also the difficulty of persuading George III, whose sentiments on the subject might be judged from an announcement he had once made: "I would rather give up my throne and beg my bread from door to door throughout Europe than consent to such a measure." Pitt nevertheless let the Irish Catholic leaders know that he would support emancipation once the Union had been accomplished.

The sordid business of "managing" the Dublin parliament was entrusted by Pitt to Lord Castlereagh, Chief Secretary of Ireland and the first Irishman to hold that office in the eighteenth century. One and a quarter million pounds—perhaps the equivalent of $50 million today—was spent in bribing those who controlled seats in the House of Commons. Fifteen thousand pounds was the average price paid for a "rotten" borough. The government's task, wrote Castlereagh, was nothing less than "to buy out and secure to the Crown for ever the fee simple of Irish corruption." Sir Jonah Barrington called it "one of the most flagrant acts of public corruption on the records of history." In addition to the money that changed hands, the transaction was facilitated by the bestowal in Ireland of six English peerages, twenty-eight Irish peerages, and twenty promotions in the Irish peerage.

The bill passed the Irish Commons by 158 votes to 115, and the Lords (a body of 180 peers) by 75 to 26. Grattan asserted that of all who voted for the Union, only seven were unbribed. Cornwallis observed that half of those voting for the measure in the Commons detested it in their hearts. The Lord Lieutenant was a man of sensibility, who was revolted by what he called "this most cursed of all situations, most repugnant to my feelings." In his private correspondence Cornwallis relieved his pent-up feelings. "I despise and hate myself every hour," he confessed, "for engaging in such corrupt work, and am supported only by the reflection that without a Union the British Empire must be dissolved. . . . Nothing but a conviction that the Union is absolutely necessary could make me endure the shocking task which is imposed upon me."

The chief opposition to the Union came from John Foster, the

Speaker of the House, from Sir John Parnell, Chancellor of the Exchequer and great-grandfather of the future Home Rule leader, and from Henry Grattan, who emerged from retirement to startle the House by appearing at dawn in Volunteer uniform, "deathly pale and hardly able to walk," to speak against the bill. "Thou art not conquered yet," he apostrophized the Irish parliament.

> Beauty's ensign yet
> Is crimson in thy cheeks and on thy lips
> And Death's pale flag is not advanced there.

Shakesperian rhetoric, however, could not save the legislative body that was being eliminated by Castlereagh, pilloried for his part in this nefarious transaction by Byron in the opening lines of *Don Juan* as a "smooth-faced miscreant dabbling his sleek young hands in Erin's gore."

By the Act of Union of 1800, Ireland got a hundred seats in the British House of Commons and thirty-two seats in the British House of Lords, four of them allotted to bishops of the Church of Ireland. Since at this time there were already 558 members in the Lower House at Westminster, and about 400 in the Upper House, it was clear that in any division of opinion between Great Britain and Ireland, the Irish members would be hopelessly outvoted. The act gave Ireland about fifteen percent of the seats at Westminster, whereas on a population basis she would have been entitled to more than forty-five percent, there being at that time about five million people living in Ireland, as compared to eleven million in Great Britain. Although the act abolished the Irish legislature, it left intact the offices of Viceroy and Chief Secretary. It also preserved the Irish Courts of Common Law and Chancery, and the Irish bar. The Episcopal Church of Ireland was formally united to the Church of England but remained in complete control of its own government, lands, and revenues. Virtual free trade was established between Ireland and Britain.

As for public opinion concerning the Union, the majority of the nation—always ragged and hungry, and now sullen and embittered after the floggings of ninety-eight—responded with indifference. "The mass of the people of Ireland," reported the Viceroy, "do not care one farthing about Union." To a famished peasant in danger of eviction, it could matter little whether the power ultimately responsible for his misery was located in Dublin Castle or in Whitehall.

The Anglo-Irish minority, however, felt otherwise. It is significant that the government never dared hold a general election to test the opinion of the Protestant electorate upon the question of Union. One hundred and seven thousand persons throughout Ireland signed petitions against the Union, as opposed to 3,000 in favor of it. The Dublin bar voted against it by 168 votes to 32. The Irish bar in general reflected a similar overwhelming opposition. Nearly all the boroughs of Ireland were opposed to the Union—with the notable exception of Cork, whose Corporation had been bribed by the promise of a great British naval arsenal. Even the Orange Lodges of the North, whose members, if they were Protestant, were still Irish, protested against the extinction of the native parliament.

Only one influence, apart from that of the government, was exerted on behalf of the Union. Beguiled by the hope of emancipation, the Irish Catholic peers, led by Lord Kenmare and Lord Fingall, supported Pitt and Castlereagh. Still more powerful help came from the Catholic hierarchy, who, with the exception of the Bishop of Limerick, endorsed the Union unanimously. Dr. Moylan, Bishop of Cork, with one eye on the arsenal, the other on Catholic relief, was one of the leaders of the campaign against the Dublin parliament. Another was Dr. Hussey, Bishop of Waterford, who proclaimed that he would rather live under the Mamelukes of Egypt than under "the iron rod of the Mamelukes of Ireland." Hence Grattan condemned the Catholic bishops as "a band of prostituted men." In addition to the hope of Catholic relief promised as an accompaniment of Union, fear of the free-thinking principles of the French Revolution was no doubt a potent factor in bringing about the improbable alliance of the Catholic hierarchy and the British government, the bishops calculating that subversive ideas would be more sternly repressed by the British Prime Minister than by the indolent gentry of Ireland.

That the support of the episcopate was decisive in passing the Union was the opinion of Castlereagh, who now repeated to Pitt what he had already maintained in 1799—"that the measure could not be carried if the Catholics were in opposition to it." In 1823, reviewing the whole history of the Union, Sir John Parnell told the British House of Commons that but for the help given by the leaders of the Catholic body in Ireland, "it is now universally admitted that the measure could not have been carried."

It was one thing for Pitt to hint that Catholic emancipation would be the reward for supporting Union; it was quite another to fulfill the implied pledge. The immovable prejudices of George III stood squarely in the way. "What is this?" the King broke out indignantly when Castlereagh first broached the delicate subject to him, "what is this that the young lord from Ireland has brought over to throw at my head? Its the most jacobinical thing I ever heard of." The king's confusion of Catholicism and Jacobinism was the result of the implacable hostility he felt toward both, not a symptom of incipient insanity—such as would later manifest itself.

Finding himself unable to get George III to accept Catholic emancipation, Pitt resigned office in 1801—an act that most English historians have regarded as vindicating his personal honor. Three weeks after his resignation, however, Pitt resisted a motion for emancipation in the Commons; and in 1804, when he became premier again, he opposed a motion on that subject introduced by his rival, Fox. Whatever the morality of Pitt's personal conduct, it is certain that the mass of the Irish people felt themselves once more betrayed—as in fact they had been. Nearly thirty weary years—seemingly interminable—would have to elapse, and the specter of revolution be invoked, before Pitt's promise would be redeemed. But by the time Daniel O'Connell took his seat in the British House of Commons, Pitt himself had been dead for nearly a quarter of a century.

The results of the Union were almost wholly disastrous for Ireland. "Do not unite with us," Dr. Johnson had told an Irishman in a moment of candor in 1779. "We should unite with you only to rob you." After the British and Irish Exchequers were united in 1817, Ireland was taxed as though she were part of the English county system. She was now burdened with the responsibility for one-fifteenth of the British national debt, which in 1815, because of the cost of financing the Napoleonic Wars, had reached the staggering figure of £880 million. This meant that, whereas in 1793 the Irish national debt had stood at £2,250,000, a generation later her share in the British National Debt exceeded £50 million. Ireland had, in fact, borne a considerable share of the cost of defending Britain against Napoleon. "The first result of the Union," wrote Stephen Gwynn, "was to render Ireland bankrupt by committing the country to a scale of expenditure wholly beyond its means." Throughout the nineteenth century, more money was raised by taxation in Ireland than was spent on that country's own needs. Thus the poorer nation was drained of wealth to support its richer neighbor.

Pitt had forecast that after the Union, English capital would flow into Ireland to revitalize her industries. Precisely the opposite took place. During the nineteenth century, the profits from Irish land were continually invested in English industry and manufactures; whereas

English capital, though invested all over the world—in Europe and India, in North and South America, in Africa and China—was seldom invested in Ireland.

Even free trade, which in the eighteenth century Irish merchants had so eagerly desired, proved ruinous to the manufacture of Irish woolens and cottons (which had begun to prosper after 1782), because they could not compete with the gigantic growth of British industry made possible by the Industrial Revolution. Only the linen industry of the North was able to survive the overwhelming competition of imported British goods.

Dublin, of course, suffered from the Union more than any other city in Ireland. From being the capital of a nation, it was now degraded to the status of a provincial town. The wealthier members of the Irish nobility and gentry moved to London to be near the center of political life. As a result, the value of houses in Dublin fell by thirty percent within two decades. The great architectural tradition of the eighteenth century came to an abrupt end, and little by little the splendid mansions of the aristocracy were transformed into the swarming tenements of the poor. The chief buildings of nineteenth-century Dublin were to be, not mansions, but prisons, barracks, and lunatic asylums.

The Act of Union of 1800—"the union of a shark with its prey," as Byron called it—constitutes a melancholy climax in Irish history. A century of misery, want, and persecution preceded it. A century of famine, emigration, and hopelessness followed. However much the Union might have benefited Britain, to Ireland it seemed like the prelude to the slow bleeding to death of a nation.

The awakening of England's conscience was long delayed. John Stuart Mill was one of the first to emphasize the injustice that Ireland had suffered under the Union. At last in 1886, a Liberal Prime Minister had the courage to speak out against it. The Act of 1800, Gladstone solemnly told the House of Commons in advocating Home Rule for Ireland, was nothing but "a paper Union obtained by force and fraud, and never sanctioned or accepted by the Irish nation." Three years later he attacked it still more scathingly as "the offspring of tyranny, of bribery and fraud." At Oxford, the leading authority on constitutional law, Professor Albert Venn Dicey, himself opposed to Home Rule, characterized the Union as "an agreement which, could it have been referred to a court of law, must at once have been cancelled as a contract hopelessly tainted with fraud and corruption."

Robert Emmet (1778–1803). Leader of the rebellion of 1803, and executed for his part in it.

Robert Emmet's Rebellion (1803)

The dreadful events of 1798 and the infamous betrayal of 1800 were followed by a generation sunk in torpor and listlessness, a generation only too conscious of its own failure and ignominy. Yet even in this degraded period, the gleam of revolt flickered across the darkening scene. In Emmet's rebellion of 1803, the torch that the United Irishmen had kindled from the blaze of the French Revolution flamed for a single incandescent moment before it was quenched in the Dublin slums. If Emmet's rising was the briefest in Irish history, it was by no means the least memorable.

Born in 1778, the eighteenth and youngest son of the State Physician of Ireland, Robert Emmet was brought up as a Protestant and educated at Trinity College. Tom Moore, the poet, his senior by one year in college, remembered him "not only for his learning and eloquence, but also for the blamelessness of his life, and the grave suavity of his manners." At Trinity, Emmet became a deist and a democrat and publicly praised "the grand and perilous example of the young Republic of France." Wolfe Tone had been a visitor at his father's house on Stephen's Green. In 1798, Emmet was expelled from Trinity for subversive nationalist activities and fled to France, thereby missing the rebellion that broke out in Ireland soon afterward.

Like Tone, Emmet sought to interest the French on behalf of Irish freedom; on one occasion he even procured an interview with Bonaparte himself. But not unnaturally, after the failure of 1798, the French were inclined to leave Ireland alone. By 1803, Emmet was back in Dublin, without French aid but actively preparing for revolt. He had a proclamation printed announcing a "Provisional Government" and urging the men of Dublin to rally to "the sacred though long degraded green." He fixed the date of the rising for the evening of Saturday, July 23. At nine o'clock, clad in a general's uniform with gold epaulettes and white jacket faced with green, and wearing a cocked hat with a long green feather, Emmet exhorted the slum dwellers in the teeming warrens near St. Patrick's. "Turn out, .my boys," the self-appointed general, aged twenty-five, was heard to rally them. "Now is your time for liberty. Liberty, my boys. Turn out, turn out." Only forty or fifty men followed him. Soon troops arrived, and it was all over in two hours. Then the redcoats went to work, looting, burning, and attacking women. Three hundred persons were arrested and thrown into Kilmainham Jail, then but recently completed.

In the confusion and darkness Emmet managed to get away and might have escaped to America but for his refusal to leave the neighborhood of Sarah Curran, to whom he was engaged. "I would rather have the affections of your daughter in the backwoods of America," he had written her father, John Philpot Curran, the eminent advocate, "than the first situation this country could offer without them." In the vain hope of seeing Sarah once more, he lingered in the foothills of the Dublin mountains and was arrested at Harold's Cross on August 25 by Major Sirr, the same officer who had apprehended Lord Edward Fitzgerald.

So far the rebellion had been a ludicrous fiasco, but the government, having learned nothing from centuries of misrule in Ireland, determined to make Emmet a martyr. It transformed him from a laughing stock into a hero. By his noble bearing at his trial, which took place in Green Street courthouse on September 19, by the constancy and courage that he there exhibited, and by his fearless and eloquent defiance of his captors, Emmet effaced the memory of folly and atoned for failure. Foreshadowing the events of 1916, the city that in July had rejected Emmet with scorn, in September took him to her heart.

The trial lasted for twelve hours, during which time Emmet, weighed down with manacles on hands and feet, and faint from lack of food, stood in the dock before Lord Norbury, a vindictive and sadistic judge, who taunted and derided the defenseless prisoner. "I wished to procure for my country," Emmet told the court, "the guarantee which Washington procured for America." When Norbury interrupted him, Emmet rebuked him gravely: "My Lord, you are impatient for the sacrifice."

Exactly what were Emmet's last words we do not know, since there are some twenty extant versions of what he is supposed to have said. According to the generally accepted account, he concluded: "My ministry is ended. I am going to my cold and silent grave. My lamp of life is nearly extinguished. . . . The grave opens to receive me and I sink into its bosom. I am ready to die. . . . Let there be no inscription on my tomb. Let no man write my epitaph. . . . When my country takes her place among the nations of the world, then, and not till then, let my epitaph be written. I have done."

Early next morning, September 20, in the presence of an enormous crowd, he was executed outside St. Catherine's Church, which still stands in Thomas Street, Dublin. Refusing the proferred orthodox religious consolation, he died a deist, his last words being: "My friends I die in peace, and with sentiments of universal love and kindness towards all men." Having hanged him by the neck, the executioner cut down the slim, still-writhing body and chopped off the head with a knife. As the blood spurted, the hangman grasped the hair and held up the severed head for all to see. The decapitated body was taken to Kilmainham and buried no man knows where. To the grave of Emmet there can be no pilgrimage.

To devote so much space to a scuffle in the Dublin slums may seem excessive. Historical events, however, must be judged not only with regard to their contemporary importance but even more for the impact they make upon posterity. It is doubtful whether any death has ever moved the Irish people as much as that of Robert Emmet. "Life is very sweet, brother, who would wish to die," said the gypsy Petulengro in George Borrow's *Lavengro*. Emmet had died at twenty-five—for Ireland. "Greater men died in the struggle," wrote Thomas Davis, "but none was so warmly loved or so passionately lamented." Generations of children learned Emmet's last speech from the dock. In 1916, Michael Collins is said to have recited the peroration to his comrades on the eve of the Easter Rising. In New York the numerous children of O'Donovan Rossa, the Fenian exile, had learned those words by heart. Abraham Lincoln, as a self-taught youth, had read them by the firelight of a Kentucky cabin. Copies of the speech were to be found on the walls of Irish slum boardinghouses in Boston or New York, and many an Irish child born in the New World was named after Robert Emmet.

When Patrick Pearse taught at St. Enda's School at Rathfarnham, Emmet joined Cuchulain there in the pantheon of national heroes. It is reported that after the first two hours in the post office on Easter Monday, 1916, Pearse pulled out his watch and reminded Connolly that they had already outlasted Emmet. In Kilmainham as he too lay awaiting execution, it may be supposed that Pearse identified himself with the young man who had preceded him in the condemned cell—under circumstances at once so similar and so tragic.

James Connolly was not a romantic like Pearse, but he was equally devoted to the memory of Emmet. Rightly or wrongly, he saw in Emmet's attempt to rouse the weavers and tanners of the Dublin slums evidence of a genuinely proletarian concern. Connolly was especially proud that working-class men and women, knowing Emmet's dangerous secret, had not betrayed him: the government spies and informers had all come from classes higher in the social scale.

Not until many years after Emmet's death was it discovered that Leonard MacNally, whose passionate defense of Emmet in Green Street courthouse had made his hearers weep, and who had kissed Emmet as he left the dock, had been all along a paid informer—and had betrayed many of the United Irishmen as well as Emmet. Since 1794, Dublin had been, in fact, honeycombed with spies in the pay of the Castle. Hence the curse called down for generations upon the informer: May the hearthstone of hell be his bed rest for ever!

BIBLIOGRAPHY

Barrington, Sir Jonah: *Recollections* (1835)

Bolton, G. C.: *The Passing of the Irish Act of Union* (1961)

Burke, Edmund: *Letters, Speeches, and Tracts on Irish Affairs,* ed. M. Arnold (1881)

Fisher, Joseph: *The End of the Irish Parliament* (1911)

Gwynn, Stephen: *Henry Grattan and His Times* (1949)

————: *Thomas Moore* (1905)

Jacob, Rosamund: *The Rise of the United Irishmen* (1937)

Johnston, Edith: *Great Britain and Ireland, 1760–1800* (1964)

Lecky, W. E. H.: *History of Ireland in the 18th Century,* 5 vols. (1892)

————: *Leaders of Public Opinion in Ireland,* 2 vols. (1903)

McDowell, Robert B.: *Irish Public Opinion, 1750–1800* (1944)

McHugh, Roger: *Carlow in '98* (1949)

McManus, M. J.: *Irish Cavalcade, 1550–1850* (1939)

Madden, R. R.: *Lives and Times of the United Irishmen,* 4 vols. (1857–60)

Mahoney, Thomas A. D.: *Edmund Burke and Ireland* (1959)

Maxwell, Constantia: *Dublin Under the Georges 1714–1830* (1937)

————: *The Stranger in Ireland, from the Reign of Elizabeth to the Great Famine* (1954)

————: *Town and Country Life in Ireland Under the Georges* (1940)

Moore, Thomas: *Irish Melodies* (1849)

———: *Life of Lord Edward Fitzgerald* (1838)

O'Brien, William: *Edmund Burke as an Irishman* (1926)

O'Connell, Maurice: *Irish Politics and Social Conflict in the Age of the American Revolution* (1965)

Sayles, G. O.: *The Irish Parliament in 1782* (1954)

Tone, Theobald Wolfe: *Autobiography,* ed. Sean O'Faolain (1937)

VIII

Emancipation and Repeal

Daniel O'Connell and Catholic Emancipation (1823-29)

Following the Union of 1800 and the denial of Catholic emancipation, a sense of impotence and shame pervaded Ireland. Hitherto, although the Catholics had been degraded, the ascendancy had been exalted, but now—with very few exceptions—all alike, Protestant and Catholic, gentry and peasantry—felt humiliated and sullenly resented their country's disgrace. Sir Jonah Barrington spoke for many of his class, when after the Union he observed: "Ireland lost all charms for me; the Parliament—source of all my pride, ambition and gratification as a public man—had been bought and sold; I felt myself nobody. I became languid, careless and indifferent to everything." Nowhere was the atmosphere of depression more heavy, the sense of demoralization more complete than in Dublin, the erstwhile capital of a sovereign nation, now reduced to the status of an unimportant provincial city of the United Kingdom.

As if to ensure that the prostrate land should never rise, England proceeded to govern Ireland with frequent applications of military rule. Nearly sixty Coercion Acts were passed during as many years. The press was gagged, public meetings harassed, and habeas corpus repeatedly suspended—for example, in 1804-5, 1807-10, 1824-25, 1833-34 and 1847-48.

From a state of lethargy bordering on despair, Ireland was roused by the perfervid oratory and almost superhuman energy of a single individual—Daniel O'Connell (1775-1847). No man was ever more completely than he the incarnation of the aspirations of his people. For more than thirty years O'Connell, unlike Tone or Emmet before him, or Young Ireland and the Fenians after him, was not ahead of

Daniel O'Connell (1775–1847). Champion of Catholic emancipation.

his own generation but exactly abreast of it. More than any other man, he was able to articulate in words the wrongs felt by his countrymen and to make their tormentors wince under the lash of his fierce invective. Even Sir Robert Peel, an unrelenting enemy of O'Connell, acknowledged that he had "inspired the serf of Clare with the resolution and energy of a freeman"—and what O'Connell did for the peasants of Clare he did for the peasants of all Ireland. Even those who justly reprobate O'Connell for his grossness, mendacity, and unscrupulousness must recognize that he lifted Ireland out of the stupor of things past into a hope of better things to come.

Descended from an ancient Kerry family, O'Connell was sent to be educated at the Irish College at St. Omer in France. Fleeing from the revolution in 1792, he completed his education in London and was called to the bar at Lincoln's Inn. At this time he was far from being the professional patriot he later became. "I knew that the victories of the French would be attended by bad consequences," he wrote of Hoche's attempted invasion in 1796. "The Irish people," he added sententiously, "are not yet sufficiently enlightened to bear the sun of freedom. Freedom would soon dwindle into licentiousness. They would rob; they would murder."

As a devout Catholic he criticized the United Irishmen for their deism; as a large landowner in Kerry he abhorred their disregard for the rights of property. He denounced the Wexford rebels of 1798 as "miscreants," "cut-throats," and blunderers who had paved the way for the Union. "Oh, Liberty," he gasped, "what horrors are perpetrated in thy name!" When Emmet made his forlorn attempt at rebellion, O'Connell turned out with a Dublin yeomanry corps to put to rout the last remnant of the rising.

The passing of the Act of Union, however, did not leave him unmoved. He liked to recall how "his blood had boiled" when he heard the bells of St. Patrick's ring out his country's shame. "I vowed," he wrote, "that the foul national dishonour should not last, if ever I could put an end to it." His pride as a Catholic was equally galled by the denial of emancipation. He now formed the ambition to lead his countrymen in a dual crusade—for Catholic emancipation and for the repeal of the Union. In pursuit of the first of these goals, O'Connell was to achieve a brilliant success; in pursuit of the second, to know abysmal failure.

It was at the Dublin bar that O'Connell made his name and fortune. In 1800 he was still an unknown barrister; by 1815 he had become the outstanding advocate in Ireland and one of the richest men in the country. His unrivaled success was due not to any deep knowledge of the law but to a keen intuitive understanding of human nature and an unerring skill in exploiting its weaknesses. O'Connell also possessed unique forensic gifts. First the Dublin courts, and presently the whole nation, were to become familiar with that overpowering torrent of rhetoric—declamation, invective, vituperation, humor, satire, and bombast—that poured from him unceasingly. Past the cold, disdainful glare of judges, he appealed not to abstract reason but to the emotions and prejudices of the juries whom he alternately flattered, entreated, cajoled, wheedled, or bullied. He knew that he held them in the hollow of his hand and that, whenever he wished, he could sweep them away on an irresistible surge of feeling. From a boisterous humor that verged upon buffoonery to an effusive and lachrymose sentimentality, he dominated his audiences and made them laugh or cry as he saw fit.

O'Connell's voice was a flexible instrument whose compass he had learned to control. It was by turns suave and melodious, sonorous and commanding, soft and beguiling. "His language," Lecky remarked, "was clear, nervous and fluent, but often incorrect, and scarcely ever polished." What perhaps impressed his hearers most was the overwhelming sense of personal involvement that O'Connell conveyed, by means of which he held them all in thrall. "I know of no living orator," wrote M. Duvergier, a French visitor to Ireland, "who communicates so thoroughly to his audience the sense of the most profound and absolute conviction." O'Connell himself "used to say that his most carefully prepared speeches were always the least successful."

Many years later, Francis Jeffery, the editor of the *Edinburgh Review* and a man who knew almost everyone in the political, legal, and literary world of his time, heard O'Connell speak at Westminster and declared him to be "indisputably the greatest orator in the House —nervous, passionate, without art or ornament; concise, intrepid, terrible, far more in the style of the Old Demosthenic directness than anything I have ever heard in this modern world, yet often coarse and sometimes tiresome." Charles Dickens, too, as a young reporter in the Commons, paid tribute to the power of O'Connell's eloquence.

Aggressive and unscrupulous, lacking in taste and sensibility, O'Connell specialized in scurrility and personal abuse of his opponents, whose names and appearance he delighted to ridicule. Speaking of Sugden, one of the foremost barristers of his time, O'Connell roguishly demanded: "Would you call a pig, now, by the name of Sugden?" At other times he would convulse the court by casting doubt on the paternity of a troublesome adversary. At the Dublin bar O'Connell was long remembered as a most formidable bully.

Those whom he lampooned were usually advocates for the government and enemies of the people, as in the sensational case of the Dublin editor John Magee, whom O'Connell defended against a charge of seditious libel in 1813. John Mitchel, the Young Irelander and later one of O'Connell's chief foes, called his defense of Magee "the most powerful forensic achievement since Demosthenes." Under O'Connell's savage onslaught it appeared that the government, rather than Magee, was on trial. His violent indictment of the attorney general became legendary in Dublin. Its choicest passages were passed on by word of mouth. Hawked about the streets as a pamphlet, it sold thousands of copies. Not since the time of Swift had the conquered people so boldly defied its conqueror. It mattered little, except to the unfortunate Magee, that a packed jury should have brought in a verdict of guilty.

Sir Robert Peel (1788–1850), who was to clash repeatedly with O'Connell in the years to come, had just arrived in Ireland as Chief Secretary and was present in court. He confessed himself dumbfounded by what he saw and heard that day. "O'Connell spoke for four hours," he recalled. "His abuse of the Attorney-General was more scurrilous and more vulgar than was ever permitted within the walls of a court of justice. He insulted the jury, both collectively and individually, accused the Chief Justice of corruption and prejudice against his client and avowed himself a traitor, if not to Ireland, to the British Empire." As for Peel, the son of a wealthy cotton manufacturer, O'Connell derided him as "a raw youth squeezed out of the workings of I know not what factory in England."

Meanwhile the cause of Catholic emancipation was not dead but sleeping. After Waterloo and the defeat of Napoleon it was obvious that the Papacy had become the ally of the reactionary Metternich and a main bulwark against revolutionary ideas in Europe. In England, in consequence, Catholicism was no longer regarded as a dreadful menace except by the most bigoted Tories. George Canning, for example, a former disciple of Pitt and now leader of the liberal Tories, was openly in favor of emancipation.

Taking advantage of this altered religious atmosphere, O'Connell launched the Catholic Association in Ireland in 1823. He was now to prove himself as adept at politics as he had previously been successful at the bar. He transformed Irish political life by making use of two new forces he summoned into existence—an organized Catholic priesthood and an organized Catholic peasantry. By fixing the dues for the Catholic Association at the very low rate of a farthing a week, O'Connell achieved two important ends: he gave the peasants a sense of personal participation in a national movement—since even the poorest tenant could afford a penny a month—while at the same time he raised immense sums from the contribution of the half-million peasants who joined the Association.

The levy was collected in every parish at the chapel door on Sunday by the priest after Mass. This "Catholic rent," as it came to be called, soon yielded nearly £2000 a week. When in 1824 the British government banned the Catholic Association, O'Connell promptly reestablished it under another name. As the Irish historian Sir James O'Connor wrote, O'Connell had "created a vast and well-equipped army, officered by the priests and comprising almost every adult Catholic in Ireland within its ranks." So well organized was this body that on a given Sunday (January 18, 1828) O'Connell was able to arrange for two thousand protest meetings to be held simultaneously throughout the land. Nothing like this had ever occurred before in Ireland—or, for that matter, in England.

In 1828 the Clare election provided a decisive test of strength between O'Connell and the government. Though legally debarred as a Catholic from sitting in parliament, O'Connell offered himself as a candidate in Clare against a popular Protestant landowner, Vesey

Fitzgerald. Hitherto, the Catholic forty-shilling freeholders who had been enfranchised in 1793 had timidly voted for their Protestant landlords, but since 1826 O'Connell had inspired in them sufficient courage to throw off that subjection.

The Clare election engrossed the attention of all Ireland. "A fever of religious and political excitement" swept the nation, wrote Peel. When O'Connell was declared the victor at the polls in Ennis, candles were lit in cottage windows throughout the land, and bonfires blazed on the hilltops. In Clare that night it was said that the barren mountains looked like a single sheet of flame. To celebrate the greatest victory won by Catholicism in Ireland since the Reformation, the peasants went in solemn procession to country churchyards in order to lay wreaths on the graves of ancestors who had suffered in penal times. There they embraced and swore eternal friendship with one another.

A die-hard Tory government, however, was in power in England, with the Duke of Wellington as Prime Minister and Peel as Home Secretary—Peel, who years before had observed that what Ireland really needed was "an honest despotic Government." When O'Connell, having gone to London to claim his seat, was denied membership in the Commons, Ireland was in a ferment of excitement. Huge protest meetings were held all over the country, and for the first time in a generation, a mass rising seemed imminent. There were at that moment 25,000 British regulars in Ireland, but Wellington believed that at least 70,000 would be necessary to hold revolt in check. Convinced that Ireland was on the verge of civil war, the Iron Duke yielded and in 1829 allowed the passage of the Catholic Emancipation Act (1829), which opened all offices in Ireland, save only those of Viceroy and Lord Chancellor, to Catholics, while at the same time admitting Catholics to parliament. George IV, who had inherited the obstinate prejudices of his father, signed the bill into law, "weeping, raging and protesting."

Sir James O'Connor rightly terms the Catholic Association "the greatest constitutional movement" that had hitherto been known in Ireland. For the energies of the peasantry that had once found futile outlet in secret societies and agrarian outrages had been mobilized by O'Connell into a single, disciplined, national movement.

O'Connell, on whom his countrymen now bestowed the proud title of "Liberator," was the first Catholic since penal times to take his seat in parliament. Single-handed, he had defied the most powerful empire in the world and had emerged victorious. It was a triumph that aroused interest throughout Europe. France was delighted to see the conqueror of Napoleon defeated in peaceful combat by the "uncrowned king of Ireland." Montalembert wrote that to many Frenchmen the Clare election seemed like a victory over the hereditary foe—as if Crecy as well as Waterloo had been avenged. Victor Hugo and Freiligrath both wrote poems sympathizing with the wrongs of Ireland. There were some, however, who already saw through the glamor of the public hero to the pathetic weakness of the man. "The Chateaubriand of Ireland," Duvergier called O'Connell, "bigoted and intoxicated with his own words, especially with his sentimental romanticism. He weeps," the Frenchman noted satirically, "at the name of Brian Boru, the great prince who defended the Emerald Isle against the Danes."

The people of Belgium, newly liberated from Dutch rule in 1830, actually offered O'Connell the crown of their new kingdom, which, however, he had the wisdom to decline. Catholic countries naturally rejoiced most in the victory O'Connell had won. The French novelist Balzac ranked him along with Napoleon and Cuvier, the founder of paleontology, as the three greatest men of the epoch. Goethe, then in extreme old age at Weimar, was another enthusiastic admirer of that "wonderful man," Daniel O'Connell. In Germany, travelers like Count Pückler-Muskau were lionized merely because they had seen O'Connell and had heard him speak. Unusually adventurous spirits, like Duvergier or Montalembert, would brave both the English Channel and the Irish Sea to journey to the remote headlands of Kerry, where, at Derrynane, surrounded by his ragged, half-starving peasantry, O'Connell might be found dispensing hospitality in almost feudal style.

From Vienna in the 1840s, the British Ambassador, Sir Robert Gordon, reported that "O'Connell is usually looked upon as a Saint and Martyr." When Richard Cobden in 1847 was acclaimed in Venice as the champion of free trade, he found his name coupled with that of O'Connell. During the year of revolution of 1848, the name of the Liberator was taken up by liberals as a symbol of freedom—by Havlitchek in Prague and by Brofferio in Turin.

The Liberator himself was not one to hide his light under a bushel. "Grattan," he proclaimed, "sat by the cradle of his country and followed her hearse; it was left for me to sound the resurrection trumpet, and to show that she was not dead, but sleeping." "Can we wonder," asked Lecky, "at the proud exultation which he felt?" Nor could anything, as Desmond Ryan later observed, ever cancel the gratitude of Irish Catholics towards the man "whose savage tongue and titanic energy had blasted away the Penal Code forever."

O'Connell and the Failure of Repeal (1830–40)

In 1829, at the climax of his career, O'Connell was fifty-four. No one could then foresee that in his remaining eighteen years he would fail in nearly everything he attempted and experience the humiliation of being scornfully repudiated by a younger generation—that of Young Ireland.

In the very hour of victory, O'Connell sustained in fact a serious defeat. For the price of emancipation decreed by the British government was the abolition of the forty-shilling freehold vote in Ireland —though not in England. In a move to destroy the mass support that O'Connell had built up, the property qualification in Ireland was raised fivefold—from forty shillings to ten pounds. The result was a reduction in the number of Catholic freeholders from 200,000 to about 19,000. With his usual bombast O'Connell had declared that should such a restriction ever take place, he "would conceive it just to resist by force, and in such resistance," he added menacingly, he "would be ready to perish in the field or on the scaffold." When the measure, however, became law, the lion that roared submitted as meekly as a lamb.

O'Connell's subsequent efforts to repeal the Union also met with failure. "Catholic emancipation," scornfully declared Thomas Francis Meagher, an ardent Young Irelander, had only "enabled a few Catholic gentlemen to sit in Parliament, and there concur in the degradation of their country." In fairness to O'Connell, however, it should be pointed out that repeal had never the remotest chance of passing the House of Commons. For whereas Catholic emancipation had enjoyed considerable public support in England—led by the Duke of Norfolk, the premier peer of the realm; Lord Grey, the leader of the Whig party; and prominent politicians of both parties such as George Canning, a Tory, and Henry Brougham, a Radical—repeal of the Union was almost universally regarded in Britain as dangerous and subversive and could command scarcely a single vote in parliament. With the danger from Napoleon still fresh in everyone's mind, it was certain that England would never again allow the possibility that Ireland would be used as a base for enemy invasion in case of war.

The hopelessness of the task facing O'Connell is evident from the failure of Parnell's Home Rule movement half a century later. During the intervening period, two important political developments, both potentially favorable to the granting of Ireland's legislative freedom, had taken place—the growth of democracy in Britain, as illustrated by the Reform Acts of 1867 and 1885, and the gift of self-government to the English-speaking colonies abroad. Despite such hopeful developments, and notwithstanding the political genius of Parnell himself, Home Rule foundered. If Parnell was to fail in the age of Gladstone, what chance could O'Connell have had in the age of Wellington and Peel?

There were three phases in O'Connell's attempt to secure a parliamentary Repeal of the Union: the first, from 1830 to 1834, in which he loyally cooperated with the Whigs under Lord Grey and supported progressive measures such as the Reform Act of 1832 and the abolition of slavery in 1833; the second, from 1835 to 1839, inaugurated by the Lichfield House Compact, in which the Irish leader pledged support to the new Whig government under Lord Melbourne; the third, from 1840 to 1843, marked by O'Connell's realization that he had been duped by the Whigs, who would never countenance repeal, no matter what help O'Connell might give them in parliament. Hence the founding by the Liberator in 1840 of the Repeal Association and the adoption of a new political militancy.

During the 1830s O'Connell was known as a radical democrat. He supported not only parliamentary reform but also manhood suffrage, vote by ballot, and the abolition of the property qualification for M.P.s—all future Chartist proposals. He also championed an elective House of Lords. He urged the abolition of capital punishment, of flogging in the army, and of the Game Laws. He defended freedom of the press and freedom for the Negro. Especially was he known for his abhorrence of slavery. Harriet Martineau mentions that on meeting an American, O'Connell would refuse to shake hands with him unless he was an abolitionist. This anti-American bias on account of slavery was so pronounced that in the 1840s, O'Connell even urged Britain to annex Texas and Oregon. It was in this connection that James Connolly later alluded to him as having joined England to "bring down the American eagle in its highest pride of flight."

The Liberator was in fact a phenomenon nearly unique in Europe as representing an almost unheard of alliance between Catholicism and democracy. The leader of the English Catholics, Lord Shrewsbury, derided O'Connell as being no more than "king of the beggars." John Henry Newman, in his *Apologia* written thirty years later, went so far as to say that his own "unspeakable aversion" to Daniel O'Connell had been one of the factors impeding his conversion to Catholicism. In the Rome of Gregory XVI the Liberator's progressive political views were greeted with similar distrust. To such ultramontane hostility O'Connell was impervious, declaring on one occasion that he would as soon take his politics from Constantinople as from Rome.

During the 1830s, while O'Connell at Westminster was working with the Whigs for reform, Ireland found itself convulsed by a recrudescence of agrarian strife. For Catholic emancipation had not been accompanied by the abolition of the tithe, even though Grattan had urged such a measure as long before as 1783, in which year, speaking in the Irish parliament, he had poured scorn upon any parson callous enough to take tithes from a starving peasantry. Such a man, he declared, "exacts contribution from a pauper, gleans from wretchedness, leases from poverty; he fattens on hunger, raggedness and destitution." It was at that time, too, that Arthur Young was describing tithe proctors as "vultures ready to strip and skin the peasant."

Fifty years later the tithe was still being everywhere exacted. Many peasants, however, flushed by their victory in the Clare election, began to withhold payment. Police and troops were called in to seize their property, and in several places, as at Newtownbarry, County Wexford, and Carrickshock, County Kilkenny, fighting occurred and a number of people were killed (1831). In 1833, habeas corpus was suspended and a harsh Coercion Act passed. Resistance to tithes became almost nationwide, and for five years Ireland was racked once more by violence and disorder.

The tithe now amounted to an annual charge of £600,000—an immense sum to be wrung from an impoverished peasantry. Such extortion apart, the Church of Ireland owned five million acres of land, from which it derived a revenue of a million pounds a year. Many Protestant bishops in Ireland were richer than their episcopal counterparts in England, for whereas no Irish bishop received less than £4000 per annum, and some got as much as £15,000, in England the revenue of several bishops was still below £3000 a year. In Ireland, too, the old evils of absenteeism and pluralism still remained. So rare were Protestants in some districts of the south and west that in 151 parishes, the parson had not a single parishioner—yet tithes were levied against the crops or property of Catholic peasants. Now as at any time in the past, the tithe was economically burdensome, politically dangerous, and morally indefensible.

In 1838 a virtual civil war of seven years' duration was ended by the compromise embodied in the Tithe Commutation Act. The amount of the tithe was reduced by twenty-five percent, while in the future the charge was to be levied against the owner and not against the occupier of land—against the landlord and not against the tenant. Since rack-renting, however, still prevailed, the justice intended toward the peasantry by the act of 1838 failed to materialize. In many cases landlords simply raised rents, thereby painlessly absorbing the extra cost of the tithe, which the peasant went on paying as before—now, however, in a disguised form.

While the Tithe War raged in Ireland, one constructive statute affecting that country was passed at Westminster—the Education Act of 1831. This act established in Ireland a state-supported system of secular elementary education controlled by a national board. Teachers were to be appointed locally but could be dismissed by the board. Although a government commission in 1825 had reported that a million and a half people still spoke Gaelic, that language was not allowed in the new schools, English being the sole medium of instruction. English history and literature were to be taught—to the total exclusion of the native history and literature of Ireland. Richard Whately, Archbishop of Dublin and sometime Commissioner of Irish Education, even struck out from all poetry books used in the National Schools the familiar lines from Scott's "Lay of the Last Minstrel":

> Breathes there the man, with soul so dead,
> Who never to himself hath said,
> This is my own, my native land?

Instead of voicing such dangerous sentiments as these, ragged little Irish boys and girls were taught to chant unexceptionable verses:

> I thank the goodness and the grace
> That on my life hath smiled,
> And made me in this Christian age
> A happy English child.

Daniel O'Connell, who spoke Gaelic himself, supported the exclusion of Irish from the National Schools on purely utilitarian grounds. He declared:

A diversity of tongues is no benefit. It was first imposed on mankind as a curse at the building of Babel. It would be of vast advantage to mankind if all the inhabitants of earth spoke the same language. Therefore, though the Irish language is connected with many recollections that twine around the hearts of Irishmen, yet the superior utility of the English tongue, as the medium of all modern communication, is so great that I can witness without a sigh the gradual disuse of the Irish.

For his lack of interest in the ancient language, the Liberator was later to be censured by the patriots of the Gaelic League. Desmond Ryan regretted that as a young man O'Connell had read more Bentham than Ossian, and even went so far as to maintain that O'Connell had done more to destroy Gaelic than any other man in history, including Cromwell and Whately.

The Gaelic League believed that the role of the Education Act of 1831 was second only to the Famine in the destruction of the ancient language. This, doubtless, helps to explain why the English government chose to confer upon Ireland the boon of universal elementary education, which it was to withhold from its own people for another forty years. The Education Act was a propaganda weapon, the object of which was to destroy in the Irish people any awareness of their own national identity. *Timeo Danaos et dona ferentes.*

By 1840, O'Connell had become convinced that repeal would never be granted by the Whigs in England—still less, of course, by the Tories. In that year, therefore, he launched the Repeal Association, with its headquarters in Conciliation Hall, Dublin, hoping to repeat once more the brilliant victory he had gained in the cause of Catholic emancipation. By this time, however, O'Connell was a man of sixty-five. Self-indulgent, corpulent, and ageing, he was no longer the tireless worker he had been twenty years before. After his ten years at Westminster, repeal was obviously as far from fulfillment as ever. Criticism began to be heard that O'Connell was living on his past laurels and not exerting sufficient leadership in the present.

Such criticism became still more pointed with the founding in 1842 in Dublin of a magazine called *The Nation,* behind which was a group of young men who adopted a new name, Young Ireland. Their leaders were Thomas Davis, a Protestant man of letters; Charles Gavan Duffy, a Catholic barrister and journalist; and John Blake Dillon, a Catholic landowner from Mayo. Young Ireland attacked O'Connell's leadership as flaccid and ineffectual, hinting that he should make way for a new and more vigorous generation. The Liberator sought to drown such attacks in ridicule, proclaiming that if his opponents represented Young Ireland, he represented "Auld Ireland." The time for jokes such as this, however, was over.

Nevertheless the challenge of younger patriots stimulated O'Connell to greater activity than he had shown for a dozen years. In 1843 he organized a series of huge repeal meetings and traveled throughout the country to address them. He displayed once more his old knowledge of mob psychology, exhibiting again the same recklessness of speech, the same defiance of authority, and the same scurrility toward opponents. Since he had given up his practice at the bar to devote himself wholly to the cause of repeal, a grateful public had established a fund of £20,000 per annum, putting it entirely at his disposal. No accounting of this large sum was ever asked or given.

Sir Robert Peel, Prime Minister since 1841, fearing that the success of the Catholic Association was about to be repeated, took alarm and hinted at using force against repeal. "There is no alternative," he warned, "which I do not think preferable to the dismemberment of this empire." O'Connell was not slow to respond to such a challenge. During a period of ten days in May, 1843, he addressed mass meetings at Charleville, Cork, Cashel, Nenagh, and Longford, at which the press estimated perhaps a million people had been present. On Tara Hill, on the feast of the Assumption, the London *Times* reported that 100,000 people had heard him. Numerous priests graced O'Connell's platform with their presence and celebrated Mass on the hill once sacred to Druid deities. Forty-two brass bands were in attendance.

Knowing that he could take whatever liberties he pleased, O'Connell would sometimes taunt his audiences for being "slaves." "You are seven million," he would bellow. "Know your own strength. . . . Call for freedom . . . let seven million call for it together. . . . You may have the alternative to live as slaves or die as freemen." He represented repeal as a panacea for all the ills of Ireland; yet, as a large landowner, he seldom referred to agrarian problems. Within twelve months' time he told a ragged audience that hung on his every word that old Ireland should have her parliament again on College Green. If not, he added melodramatically amid intense excitement, he would "offer his head on the block."

While professing to be a man of peace, O'Connell would sometimes incite his hearers to the verge of violence. "A country's freedom," he told the Corporation of Dublin, "was not worth a drop of blood"; yet at Clonmel he referred to the military as "men of blood" and proclaimed that "with a hundred thousand of my brave Tipperary boys I'd soon drive them into the sea before me." At Kilkenny in 1843 he had the effrontery to tell his peasant audience that with military discipline they would surpass Wellington's troops at Waterloo and be capable of conquering Europe.

For the climax of his campaign, O'Connell chose the site of the most famous victory in Irish history—Clontarf, where Brian Boru in *his* day had broken foreign rule in Ireland. The date fixed for the monster meeting was Sunday, October 5, 1843. A vast multitude was expected—Irish emigrants from England and Scotland, as well as people from all parts of Ireland. Almost at the last, Peel prohibited the assembly. O'Connell could have defied the ban and gone to jail. Instead, he bowed to authority and canceled the meeting. This failure of nerve, coming as an anticlimax to months of frenzied oratory, destroyed the Liberator's reputation. The bubble had been pricked at last. In 1844 the government followed up its advantage and for the first time jailed O'Connell—for a year. The judgment of Count Cavour seemed amply justified by events—that O'Connell had been "audacious only in proportion to the patience of his adversaries."

The Place of O'Connell in Irish History

For nearly forty years Daniel O'Connell had so dominated the Irish nation that he seemed the incarnation of Ireland herself—the epitome of her virtues and vices, the embodiment of her strength and her weakness. One would have to go back fourteen centuries—to St. Patrick—to find a father figure of equal power over the imagination of a people; and many believed in fact that O'Connell, like Patrick, had delivered a whole nation from bondage.

Worshiped in Ireland, the Liberator was universally vilified in England—not only because he had humbled English pride but because of the coarseness and scurrility of his language. O'Connell was fond of informing Irish audiences that "so dishonest and besotted a people as the English never lived," and that nineteen out of twenty English-women had borne children before marriage. Few prominent Englishmen escaped his irresponsible tongue. Disraeli he called the heir-at-law to the impenitent thief who had died on the Cross; the Duke of Wellington was "a doting corporal" and "a screaming liar"; Lord Grey was "an insane dotard," full of "childish hatred and maniac contempt for the people of Ireland"; Grey's colleague Lord Brougham was "the greatest miscreant that ever breathed"; the king's close friend Lord Alvanley was "a bloated buffoon"; Peel's smile was like the silver plate on the lid of a coffin. The Whigs, as soon as he had broken with them, became "the base, brutal and bloody Whigs, with brains of lead, hearts of stone and fangs of iron."

The English naturally gave as good as they got. The London *Times* bespattered O'Connell in some three hundred editorials, calling him among other things "a long-tailed Irish baboon" and "a foul creature of the mud and slime." It also alluded to the broods of bastards al-legedly sired by O'Connell who were said to be roaming both the slums of Dublin and the bogs of Kerry.

Scum condensed of Irish bog,
Ruffian, coward, demagogue,
Boundless liar, base detractor.
Nurse of murders, treason's factor.
Of pope and priest the crouching slave
While thy lips of freedom rave.

The *Times* was not alone in its abuse of O'Connell. Peel thought him "a shabby scoundrel"; Grey termed him "an unprincipled ruffian" whose villainy equaled that of the worst revolutionaries in France; Disraeli called him "the hired instrument of the papacy . . . a systematic liar . . . a beggarly cheat, swindler and poltroon." O'Connell, said Disraeli, had "committed every crime that did not require courage." Charles Greville, the well-known diarist, spoke for Victorian England when he described O'Connell as being "utterly lost to all sense of shame and decency, trampling truth and honour under his feet, cast off by all respectable men. . . . He cares not whom he insults, because having covered his cowardice with the cloak of religious prejudice, he is invulnerable." Thomas Carlyle once heard O'Connell speak in Ireland and thought him "the hugest palpable Humbug I ever set eyes on . . . the chief quack in the world . . . the Demosthenes of blarney."

Even in Ireland, O'Connell did not lack critics—chiefly, of course, among the Protestants. Not long before his death in 1820, Henry Grattan scathingly characterized the future Liberator. "He makes politics a trade," wrote Grattan, "to serve his desperate and interested purpose. This man can bring forth nothing good; in abortion he is the most fertile." The triumph of Catholic emancipation gave the lie to much of this, but there is no denying the base demagoguery that animated many of O'Connell's tirades. According to Grattan, O'Connell had vented "against Great Britain the most disgusting calumny, falsehoods, and treachery, equalled only by his impudence; describing Great Britain as the most stupid, the most dishonest and the most besotted nation that ever existed." Anticipating the fiasco of Clontarf, Grattan observed that O'Connell first seduced people into mischief and then abandoned them through fear.

Deep as was the gulf separating the Enlightenment from the fervor of romantic nationalism, Young Ireland echoed Grattan in repudiating O'Connell and his methods. Both were shocked by his vulgarity and braggadocio, and both resented the strain of insincerity they detected in his oratory. While paying tribute to the services rendered to emancipation by the Liberator, Gavan Duffy nevertheless deplored "the language of insufferable coarseness which he constantly used." "If anything," wrote Thomas Davis, "could change my mixed admiration and censure of O'Connell into genuine hostility, it would be the vicious adulation and lying incentives proferred to him by the little stupid mercenary devils about him; and his patronage of the vilest and weakest of them." The Young Irelanders stressed the importance of recovering national self-respect. They deplored O'Connell's rant and buffoonery and his outrageous flattery of his illiterate and sometimes inebriated audiences, one of whom, at Mullaghmast, County Kildare, he termed "the finest people on the face of God's earth, the most moral, the most temperate, the most orderly, the most religious people in the world exceeding in religion, in morality, in temperance any nation under the sun."

The left wing of Young Ireland, led by James Fintan Lalor and John Mitchel, was indignant at O'Connell's neglect of the agrarian problem and apparent indifference to the misery of the peasantry. In the course of his double career, first at the bar and then in politics, the Liberator had amassed enormous wealth and for years had maintained three expensive establishments simultaneously—one in Kerry, one in Dublin, and one in London; yet his own tenants lived in the same want and wretchedness that prevailed everywhere in Ireland. "Not a pane of glass in the parish," wrote one visitor to Derrynane, "not a window of any kind in half the cottages. . . . On the estate of Daniel O'Connell are to be found the most wretched tenants that are to be seen in Ireland; there was a frightful state of overpopulation on an estate that brought in £3000 a year." William Howard Russell, the distinguished correspondent of the *Times,* corroborated this account.

A passionate idealist like Lalor could not help detesting O'Connell as a fraud and a sham. He found his politics "essentially vile and base," declaring that he himself had refrained from joining the Repeal Association by the same instinct that made one refrain from eating carrion. At Conciliation Hall he found nothing but "a craven crew, with a sworn dastard and a foresworn traitor at the helm."

In his last years O'Connell knew that he had been repudiated by a generation that was sick of bombast and weary of words, a generation that was willing to face sacrifice and suffering—the generation of Young Ireland. It was John Mitchel who pronounced upon O'Connell the final crushing verdict, and no one had a better right to speak than he, since Mitchel had risked all, and lost all, for Ireland, and was now writing as a convict in Tasmania. "Poor old Dan!" wrote Mitchel in his *Jail Journal.*

Wonderful, mighty, jovial, mean old man with silver tongue and smile of witchery, and heart of melting ruth! lying tongue! smile of treachery! heart of unfathomable fraud! What a royal, yet vulgar soul! with the keen eye and the potent swoop of a generous eagle of Cairn Tual—with the base servility of a hound and the cold cruelty of a spider. . . . A man of giant proportions in body and in mind with no profound learning, indeed, even in his own profession of the law, but with a vast and varied knowledge of human nature, in all its strength, and especially in all its weakness; with a voice like thunder and earthquake, yet musical and soft at will, as the song of birds; with a genius and fancy, tempestuous, playful, cloudy, fiery, mournful, merry, lofty and mean by turns, as the mood was on him . . . hating and loving heartily, outrageous in his merriment, and passionate in his lamentation, he had the power to make other men love or hate, laugh or weep, at his good pleasure—in so much that Daniel O'Connell, by virtue of being more intensely Irish, carrying to a more extravagant pitch all Irish strength and passion and weakness than other Irishmen, led and swayed his people by a kind of divine, or else diabolic gift.

The Fenians echoed the judgment of Young Ireland on O'Connell, and Sinn Fein echoed that of the Fenians. All alike, taking for granted the triumph of emancipation, were revolted by the rant and bluster that had failed to win repeal. Arthur Griffith, the founder of Sinn Fein, contrasted the quiet resolution of Thomas Davis with the demagoguery of the Liberator, and concluded correctly that "the giant figure of O'Connell inspired no generation but his own." Sinn Fein joined with the Gaelic League to condemn O'Connell on another ground—his betrayal of the Irish language.

Pearse and the men of 1916, intent on action and resolved if necessary to die, never invoked the name of O'Connell, passing over it in scornful silence. James Connolly, however, recalled O'Connell's hostility to the Irish working-class movement of his day—how he had opposed the abolition of child labor, ridiculing the 1833 Factory Act, which aimed to accomplish this end, as being "against the nature of things," and how in 1838 O'Connell had rejected the proposal for a minimum wage. Remembering these facts, Connolly was moved to describe the Liberator as "the most bitter and unscrupulous enemy of Trade Unionism" that Ireland had yet produced—the William Michael Murphy of his day.* Liam O'Flaherty, perhaps, sums

*William Michael Murphy was the man who did most to defeat the Dublin General Strike of 1913.

up the attitude to O'Connell of Labor in modern Ireland when he dismisses him contemptuously as "this hapless Cleon of the nineteenth century."

The memory of the Liberator was no less offensive to the writers of the Irish Literary Renaissance. Standish O'Grady stigmatized O'Connell's Repeal Association as "an example of colossal lying and public fraud which brought disgrace on the Irish name." What Yeats objected to chiefly in O'Connell was that he was so largely responsible for the caricature of the Irishman which came to be accepted in England as an authentic portrait of the Irish in general—alternately bullying and cringing, blustering and wheedling, full of blarney and deceit—the "stage Irishman," in fact, as portrayed in Samuel Lover's *Handy Andy* (1842). Yeats blamed the violence of O'Connell's invective for what was worst in Irish political manners and contrasted it with the noble self-discipline of Thomas Davis. Praising Parnell and John O'Leary, the Fenian, for exemplifying what Blake had called "naked beauty displayed," Yeats demanded rhetorically to know what "was O'Connell and all his seed, breed and generation but a roaring machine?" "He debauched the Irish people morally and mentally," wrote Sir James O'Connor of the Liberator.

In one quarter, however, the fame of O'Connell has suffered no diminution: the Catholic Church in Ireland has never forgotten that it owed him its freedom. In proportion to the degree of their orthodoxy, Catholic writers have lavished unstinting praise on the Liberator, turning a blind eye to his faults. On the fiftieth anniversary of his death, Canon Sheehan, the novelist, affirmed that O'Connell's name was "beyond cavil or criticism." The Canon's only regret was that after his death, as well as during life, the Liberator had had to face "the treachery of small minds that could never rise to the lofty stature of his genius or nobility." Another clerical writer, the historian Canon d'Alton, refers obliquely and bathetically to O'Connell's notorious moral lapses: "Of course, like.the rest of us, he had his faults."

This indulgence toward the frailties of O'Connell is in marked contrast to the savage clerical condemnation of Parnell's later lapse from conventional morality, redeemed though this was by a deep and unalterable devotion to the woman he loved. Desmond Ryan and other writers have commented on the "half-humorous tradition" that has allowed O'Connell a freedom in morals denied to Parnell. The Liberator has become in fact, as Sean O'Faolain says, "a rascal to whom one forgives everything." In view of this indulgence toward the memory of O'Connell, it is ironic to recall that the eulogy of the

Liberator delivered after his death by the popular Italian preacher, the Reverend Gioachino Ventura, had been immediately condemned by the Vatican and placed upon the Index. In his sermon the preacher had imprudently defended the right of oppressed peoples, such as the Irish, to rise against their oppressors.

O'Connell's end was pitiful. His physical vitality ruined, his reputation gone, he had the misfortune to outlive his fame. In 1826, Duvergier de Hauranne had noted acutely of O'Connell: "An inordinate love of popularity is his ruling passion; he is its absolute slave: if he were to lose it he would die instantly." In this sense O'Connell had already died, but his personal tragedy was eclipsed by the greater tragedy of the Famine. Lecky has described the Liberator's last appearance in parliament: "an old, feeble, broken-hearted man, murmuring amid the deep silence of the House a few pathetic words which were only audible to those who were near him: 'Ireland is in your hands, in your power. If you do not save her, she cannot save herself. I solemnly call on you to recollect that I predict with the sincerest conviction that a quarter of her population will perish unless you come to her relief.'" Even Disraeli could now afford to patronize him as being no more than "a feeble old man muttering before a table."

Obsessed with feelings of guilt, afraid of eternal punishment, and scarcely to be parted from his confessor, in the spring of 1847 O'Connell set out on pilgrimage to Rome. His last urgent desire was denied him: he never reached the Holy City. He died in Genoa. His heart was forwarded to Rome, where it now lies in an urn in the Church of St. Agatha, his body having been sent home to Ireland for a national funeral in Glasnevin. The plain iron bedstead whereon the Liberator had died was preserved as a relic by the Irish College in Rome.

Despite his virtual repudiation by romantic and revolutionary nationalism, O'Connell still occupies a unique place in popular esteem in Ireland. Like the Church, the common people have remained faithful to his memory. The largest statue in Dublin commemorates his person; the broadest street in Dublin commemorates his name; the tallest monument in Glasnevin commemorates his resting place.

Thomas Drummond and Ireland (1835–40)

While O'Connell was still at the height of his power, one attempt had been made to redress the agrarian grievances of Ireland that

O'Connell had ignored. With the possible exception of Lord Fitzwilliam in 1795, Thomas Drummond, Under Secretary at Dublin Castle from 1835 to 1840, was the most popular British official that had ever arrived in Dublin. Drummond was born in Edinburgh in 1797, and Scottish upbringing might well have been responsible for his sympathy with Ireland, "the land of my adoption" as he called it, and for his freedom from the usual Castle prejudices. A contemporary Irish historian observed that Drummond gave Ireland "the first real attempt at good government she had known in a century and a half." When he died prematurely in 1840, Drummond was given a great public funeral through the streets of the capital.

For the first time since the Union, Drummond enforced the law impartially against Protestants and Catholics alike. Discovering that, despite emancipation, Catholics were still discriminated against in the holding of public office, Drummond, himself a Protestant, compelled local authorities to accept Catholics in positions of public trust. When in 1838 he learned that 20,000 peasants in Tipperary had been evicted from their holdings over a period of five years, he pointedly reminded the magistrates of that county that "property has its duties as well as its rights." Utilitarian in outlook, he had the insight—rare in that age—to perceive that crime resulted from bad social conditions and that the way to eliminate it was not by the infliction of cruel punishments but by improving the deplorable conditions that had produced it. Not without reason did John O'Leary later refer to Thomas Drummond as "probably the greatest non-Irish ruler we have ever had."

In 1835 Drummond created the first efficient police forces in Irish history—the Dublin Metropolitan Police and the Irish Constabulary*—modeled partly on the police force recently established by Sir Robert Peel in London. The new constabulary consisted of about ten thousand men, Catholics being recruited on equal terms with Protestants.

The new Under Secretary was also the first Castle official to take measures against the militant Orange Lodges of the north, which were now reported to have 200,000 men under arms and to be contemplating violence. An Orange plot in 1837 to dethrone Victoria, the young queen of England, in order to install as king her uncle, the Duke of Cumberland, the leading reactionary in England and Grand Master of the Orange Order, gave Drummond his opportunity to act. He dissolved the central structure of the Order, while allowing the individual lodges to remain in existence.

---

*Later given the title "Royal" for their part in quelling the Fenian disturbances. Hence the name "R.I.C."

Thanks to Drummond's reforming zeal, a number of commissions were set up to inquire into the social and economic life of Ireland, with a view to redressing inequities and injustices. In contrast to England, Ireland had never had a Poor Law, and consequently the indigent there had never known relief, except through private charity. Drummond now forced parliament to take cognizance of the problem —one that O'Connell had entirely neglected.

The Poor Law Commission of 1836 drew up an appalling report. It estimated that for about thirty weeks out of every year no less than 585,000 people—with 1,800,000 dependents—were "out of work and in distress." Many of them kept alive only through the money they made working at harvest time in England for a few weeks every summer. The number of people found to be in urgent need of relief was between a third and a quarter of the total population. To alleviate such misery, Drummond made a suggestion that was both farsighted and revolutionary. He urged the development of public works at state expense, including the building of railways and the construction of hospitals, as well as the granting of outdoor relief. Because of the enormous number of the poor in Ireland, Drummond was convinced that a workhouse system, on the model of that established in England by the New Poor Law of 1834, could not possibly function. Nevertheless, this was what Ireland got.

The Irish Poor Law, passed by parliament on the recommendation of an English official who had been only six weeks in Ireland, ignored Drummond's recommendations. Against the opposition of all shades of opinion in Ireland, it established the workhouse system whose brutality in England Charles Dickens was at that very time exposing in the novel *Oliver Twist*. One hundred and thirty Poor Law unions were set up in Ireland. The buildings themselves, huge in size and bleak in aspect, suggesting penal institutions rather than agencies of social welfare, struck a chill into the hearts of those who beheld them. Men and women, husbands and wives, parents and children, were rigidly segregated under an inhuman regimen that seemed designed primarily to demoralize the inmates and deter them from remaining as objects of public support. Outdoor relief—relief, that is to say, granted to people still living in their own homes—was prohibited.

While traveling in Ireland in the 1830s, Alexis de Tocqueville visited a poor house in Dublin. He described its condition as presenting "the most hideous and disgustful aspect of wretchedness." This particular establishment consisted of a very long room full of women and children whose age or infirmity prevents them from working. On the floor the poor are seated pell-mell like pigs in the mud of their sty. It is difficult to avoid treading on a half-naked body. In the left wing, a smaller room full of old or disabled men. They sit on wooden benches crowded close together and all looking in the same direction, as if in the pit of a theatre. They do not appear to be thinking. They neither expect, fear, nor hope for anything from life. I am mistaken: they are waiting for supper which is due in three hours. It is the only pleasure that remains to them; apart from that they would have nothing to do but die. . . . On leaving we came across a small covered barrow pushed by two paupers. This barrow was going to the doors of the houses of the rich. They throw the leftover of their meals into the barrow and this débris is taken to the Poorhouse to make the soup.

What might be termed the classic description of the average union as set up by the Act of 1838 is that of Mrs. Cecil Woodham-Smith in her moving book, *The Great Hunger.*

Huge and forbidding, the Castlebar Union had opened its doors in 1841. Built from blocks of grey stone, surrounded by high walls, standing outside the town on bare and treeless land, and appearing half fortress and half prison, it was regarded by the people of Mayo with dread. Within were stone walls of great thickness, immense wards with wooden platforms where the paupers lay on straw. . . . But there was food, however revolting, however meagre; and the Union was besieged. Starving mothers dragged their children to the Union doors and besought that they at least should be taken in; whole families made their painful way from the wild lands and collapsed moaning in the courtyard when they were refused.

Such buildings, however, constituted almost the sole protection afforded to the majority of the population against the disaster that was now about to befall Ireland.

BIBLIOGRAPHY

Gwynn, Denis Rolleston: *Daniel O'Connèll* (1947)
MacIntyre, Angus: *The Liberator* (1965)

Nowlan, Kevin B.: *The Politics of Repeal, 1841-50* (1964)

O'Brien, R. Barry: *Thomas Drummond* (1889)

O'Connell, Daniel: *A Memoir on Ireland, Native & Saxon,* Vol. I, *1172-1660* (1843)

O'Connell, John: *Life and Speeches of Daniel O'Connell* (1846)

O'Connor, Sir James: *History of Ireland, 1801-1924,* 2 vols. (1926)

O'Faolain, Sean: *The King of the Beggars: a Life of Daniel O'Connell* (1938)

O'Hegarty, Patrick Sarsfield: *History of Ireland Under the Union, 1801-1922* (1952)

Reynolds, James: *The Catholic Emancipation Crisis in Ireland, 1824-29* (1954)

Senior, Hereward: *Orangeism in England and Ireland, 1795-1836* (1966)

Strauss, Emil: *Irish Nationalism and British Democracy* (1951)

IX

The Famine

Ireland on the Eve of the Famine

Through the high prices that they had made possible to the English farmer, the Napoleonic Wars had put a premium upon agriculture in England. Napoleon's blockade had caused a shortage of grain; there were also large armies on the Continent that had to be fed. Both landlords and tenants in Ireland shared in this artificial wartime prosperity. After 1815, tens of thousands of soldiers from Wellington's armies—more than a third of them Irish—were suddenly demobilized and thrown on the labor market. At the same time, despite the high tariff of the Corn Laws, foreign grain began to compete once more in the British market. Faced by this competition the price of Irish corn began to fall. It was no longer so profitable to raise wheat, oats, or rye. Hence the amount of land under tillage in Ireland, which had increased considerably since Foster's Act of 1784, now began once more to diminish, while pasturage gained. Since this occurred during a period of intense population growth, the result was an increased pressure on land, and the subdivision of the existing peasant holdings into ever smaller and smaller lots.

In 1800 the population of Ireland was approaching 5 million—somewhat larger than that of the United States at that date. The first Irish census, taken in 1821, showed a population of 6,801,827; a figure that had risen to 8,196,597 by 1841. The precise reasons for this extraordinary increase are both obscure and complex, though they have been ably analyzed in Dr. K. H. Connell's *Population of Ireland, 1750-1845* (1950). The inevitable result of rapid population growth accompanied by a decrease in the amount of land under cultivation was a recurrence of acute rural distress. This intensification of the old agrarian troubles took place at a time when, as has been pointed out, Ireland's industries were being ruined by the competition from cheap mass-produced goods in England. Irish manufactures, as well as Irish agriculture, were woefully undercapitalized.

So backward was the state of Irish agriculture that evidence laid before the Poor Law Commission in 1836–37 revealed that while in Ireland four times as many people were employed on the land as in England, Ireland's yield was only half as large. Yet in 1779, Arthur Young, England's foremost agricultural expert, had considered Ireland to be more fertile than England; and in 1834, when William Cobbett, that sturdy English farmer, visited Ireland, he corroborated Young by observing that "one acre of land here is worth four acres in Surrey." (Surrey was his own home, and one of the most fertile counties in England.)

The period from 1815 to 1826 was one of extreme agrarian distress in Ireland, actual famine—as distinct from chronic semistarvation—appearing in 1817. "What can we say of the misery of Ireland?" asked Mrs. Richard Trench, the charitable mother of a future Archbishop of Dublin, in that very year. "At first it created watchful nights, cheerless days, and a sort of reluctant shame at sitting down to a table amply spread. But the awful continuance of famine," she noted with equal honesty and realism, "had blunted the edge of these feelings."

When William Carleton, the Irish novelist, called his country "one vast lazar-house, filled with famine, disease and death," he was not speaking of the major tragedy of 1845–46, but of the minor one of 1817; and when in 1846, he came to write his novel *The Black Prophet,* Carleton explained that the appalling scenes therein described not only reflected the condition of contemporary Ireland but had been graven indelibly upon his memory by the horrors that he remembered from 1817.

The inevitable result of worsening social conditions was a recrudescence in the 1820s and '30s of the secret societies and agrarian outrages of the late eighteenth century. In 1825 appeared the Ribbonmen who were, as James Connolly later remarked, a sort of secret agricultural trade union. As in South Africa today, because of intense misery and frustration the oppressed fought not only their oppressors but also one another. When they were not destroying landlords' property, rival factions were at one another's throats. In the wake of the Ribbonmen, numerous ragged gangs proliferated through the countryside: Shanavests and Caravats, Caffees and Ruskavallas, Dingens and Dawsons, Bootashees and Tubbers; Gumminses and Darrigs,

Whitefeet and Blackfeet, Blackhens and Magpies, Terryalts and Rocka-fellers. These fought one another and their own landlords indis-criminately. A hunger for land, reported the Devon Commission in 1845, "stifled all other feelings and extinguished the plainest feelings of humanity."

Such faction fights were often the result of heavy drinking—that last resort of the wretched. Monsignor Nolan, Bishop of Carlow, told De Tocqueville in 1835 that his people were "gentle, polite and hos-pitable. But," he added, "when the chance of a drunken orgy offers, they do not know how to resist it. They become turbulent and often violent and disorderly." The Bishop of Kilkenny observed of his flock: "They have the virtues dear to God, but they are ignorant, violent, intemperate and as incapable of resisting the first impulse as savages."

A few weeks later, attending the Waterford Assizes, De Tocqueville gained ample confirmation of such observations. "These Assizes," he wrote, "gave us the strong impression that the lower classes in this county are very prone to quarrels and fights, and that almost every village forms a faction with a code name. . . . When men of different factions meet, at a fair, a wedding or elsewhere, it is ex-ceptional if they do not come to blows . . . generally speaking, human life seems of little value here."

Besides De Tocqueville, a generation of English and European writers have left graphic accounts of the state of Ireland during these years of peace. In 1812 Lord Byron told his fellow peers that nowhere in his travels through the Ottoman Empire had he seen such wretched-ness as in Ireland. In that year, too, the youthful idealist Shelley came to Dublin to spread the gospel of reason. After a few shocking days spent in the Irish capital he was forced to admit that he had had "no conception of the depth of human misery till now. . . . The poor of Dublin are assuredly the meanest and most miserable of all . . . thousands are huddled together—one mass of animated filth. The rich grind the poor into abjectness, then complain that they are ab-ject. They goad them to famine, and hang them if they steal a loaf." During the three days he spent on foot in northern Ireland in 1818, John Keats, too, was appalled by "the worse than nakedness, the rags, the dirt and the misery of the poor common Irish. A Scotch cottage," he wrote, "is a palace to the Irish one."

A generation later, the Victorian novelist William Makepeace Thackeray was revolted by the universal filth and delapidation that he had seen in Ireland in 1842. A Hottentot kraal, he declared, was more comfortable than many an Irish cabin. The half-ruined villages were full of epileptic idiots, drunken old men, and filthy women suckling their infants in public. Everywhere the streets were swarming with the most repulsive beggars, fawning and wheedling in expectation of a penny, abusive and snarling if refused. Thackeray could not resist the temptation of contrasting these forlorn outcasts with his own self-respecting fellow countrymen and lecturing the Irish upon the deplorable weakness of their character.

Two years after Thackeray, a German visitor, Johann Georg Kohl, who like Byron had traveled in the Balkans, came to Ireland. When in Bosnia and Servia, he had thought the peasants "among the poorest and most pitiable people in Europe"; but having seen Ireland in 1844, he considered them better off than the Irish.

The most discerning, however, of foreign visitors to Ireland was Gustave de Beaumont, the friend of Alexis de Tocqueville, with whom he had traveled in America. De Beaumont, indeed, not only described carefully what he saw but also made a penetrating analysis of the factors underlying Ireland's social and economic plight. Like De Tocqueville, De Beaumont had a keen interest in history and politics, and his *Ireland* (1839), though on a smaller scale, may not unjustly be compared to De Tocqueville's classic *Democracy in America* (1835). Two generations later, Albert Venn Dicey, the eminent Oxford constitutional authority, paid tribute to De Beaumont from whose "profound wisdom," he said, he had learned more about Ireland than from any other writer of the nineteenth century.

"I have seen the Indian in his forests," wrote De Beaumont, echoing Berkeley, who had also traveled in America, "and the Negro in his chains, and thought, as I contemplated their pitiable condition, that I saw the very extreme of human wretchedness; but I did not then know the condition of unfortunate Ireland." Every nation had its poor, but not till now had he seen a whole nation of paupers. "There is no doubt," he wrote, "that the most miserable of English paupers is better fed and clothed than the most prosperous of Irish laborers." Visitors to Ireland were shocked to see pigs and human beings sharing the same hovel; but actually, as De Beaumont pointed out, to possess a pig was "a sign of comparative comfort" and raised a man above the level of many of his neighbors. Three million human beings were reported at this time to be subject periodically to "absolute destitution."

"Almost the only splendid buildings in Ireland," De Beaumont observed, were the prisons and the barracks. Nearly all else was in ruins—medieval ruins of monastery and castle, modern débris of house and hovel. "The number of ruins encountered in travel through

Ireland," he noted, "is perfectly amazing." It was as though the remains of all the centuries had collapsed, like some dreadful jerry-
built tenement, into a single monstrous ruin. This macabre landscape,
furthermore, was peopled with *walking* ruins—tattered and derelict
wrecks of humanity, deformed or diseased, half-naked or clad in
stinking rags: the repulsive flotsam and jetsam of a decaying social
order.

De Beaumont described accurately and in detail the rack-renting
and absenteeism of Irish landlords, the lack of security and want of
initiative among the peasants, as well as the inhumanity of evictions.
He also observed the injustice of the law as it was administered in
Ireland. "I have been present," he wrote, "at many criminal trials
in Ireland, and it is impossible to describe the painful feelings with
which such spectacles filled my mind." The law was "a lie of forms,"
and justice "a preparation of vengeance." Judge and magistrates usually treated the accused "as a kind of idolatrous savage . . . as an
enemy that must be destroyed. . . . It is difficult," De Beaumont
added, "to form an idea of the tone of contempt and insolence in
which the members of the Irish Bar speak of the people and the
lower classes." The result of this alienation of the people from justice
was the sympathy felt everywhere in Ireland for the criminal and
fugitive. "Hatred of the law," wrote De Beaumont, "is almost universal." More than half a century later, Synge would encounter this
identical sentiment among the Aran Islanders.

Like Disraeli in contemporary England, De Beaumont found in
Ireland not one nation but two—the rich and the poor. In Ireland,
however, the two nations were separated not only by politics and
economics but by religion as well—and by the tenacity and bitterness
of the memories of the past. "Nearly two centuries afterward," wrote
De Beaumont, "I passed through the country once traversed by Cromwell, and found it still full of the terror of his name." De Tocqueville,
traveling about the same time, was reminded in Clare of ancient
wrongs "with a terrifying exactitude of local memory. Whatever
one does," he added, "the memory of the great persecutions is not
forgotten. Who sows injustice must sooner or later reap the fruits."
The great French writer emphasized especially the ill-will generated
in Ireland by religious differences. "All the rich Protestants whom I
saw in Dublin," he noted in his journal, "speak of the Catholics
with extraordinary hatred and scorn. The latter, they say, are savages
. . . and fanatics led into all sorts of disorders by their priests."

Another French observer, Duvergier de Hauranne, who was in
Ireland in 1826, made the same point about two peoples living to-

gether in one country yet total strangers to each other. There were in Ireland, wrote Duvergier, "two nations, the conquerors and the conquered. . . . There is nothing between the master and the slave, between the cabin and the palace. There is nothing between all the luxuries of existence and the last degree of human wretchedness."

A distinguished Italian statesman, Count Camillo de Cavour, made a similar diagnosis of the conditions of Irish life. "Ireland has been divided into two hostile classes," wrote the future Prime Minister of Italy in 1844, "one which possesses, the other which tills the soil. Its population is composed of Protestants, intolerant, haughty, treating with contempt those whom they have conquered; and of tenants, Catholic, poor, ignorant, superstitious, animated by a violent hatred of the despoilers of their country. Such a social state has no parallel in Europe."

The observations of these foreign visitors were confirmed by official government sources. No part of the empire, no country in Europe, was ever more thoroughly investigated than Ireland in the years before the Famine. Between 1800 and 1845, no less than 114 royal commissions and 61 special committees inquired into conditions in what was already known as "the most distressful country." (These parliamentary inquiries were accompanied by eighteen Coercion Acts enacted during the same period.)

Perhaps the most important of these investigating bodies was the Devon Commission established by Peel in 1843. Two years later, it reported on the state of the peasantry of Ireland. "It would be impossible," the commission stated in its findings, "adequately to describe the privations which they habitually and silently endure . . . in many districts their only food is the potato, their only beverage water . . . their cabins are seldom a protection against the weather . . . a bed or a blanket is a rare luxury . . . and nearly in all, their pig and a manure heap constitute their only property." The commissioners expressed their "strong sense of the patient endurance which the labouring classes have exhibited under sufferings greater, we believe, than the people of any other country in Europe have to sustain."

Like the Poor Law Commission in 1836, the Devon Commission urged that a large-scale program of public works be undertaken in Ireland to relieve poverty and unemployment. It reported that, should capital be provided, nearly 4 million acres of waste land could be made productive: of these, 2,330,000 could be brought under pasture, while 1,425,000 would yield food crops. Incredible as it may seem, despite these revealing statistics, the Peel government did nothing whatever to implement the findings of the Devon Commission.

Effects of the Famine on Irish History

Unusually wet summers in 1845 and 1846 caused poor harvests everywhere in Western Europe from Norway to Spain, but only in Ireland did actual famine occur. What distinguished Ireland from the rest of Europe was not its bad weather but its appalling social system, the roots of which, as we have seen, go back through the eighteenth century to the Cromwellian land confiscations of the seventeenth. One unique result of rural poverty in Ireland was the sinking of the bulk of the population into dependence upon a single crop—the potato. "Its greedy acceptance by the people," writes Professor Salaman, the foremost modern authority on the history of the potato, "was no mere accident, for it satisfied their needs as efficiently as it symbolized their helpless degradation. . . . The fall of manna in the desert was not more opportune than the coming of the potato to Ireland."

Although there is apparently no foundation for the legend that Sir Walter Raleigh introduced the potato from Virginia into Ireland in 1586, it seems probable nevertheless that during the first four decades of the seventeenth century the cultivation of the potato spread throughout Ireland and assumed a degree of importance in the national economy unparalleled in the experience of any other country in Europe. From the native Irish the Cromwellian settlers acquired a liking for the new root. By 1691 we find Sir William Petty in his *Political Anatomy of Ireland* referring to the potato as an article of almost universal consumption in Ireland. "All the Irish," he writes, "live in a brutish nasty condition, as in Cabins with neither chimney, door, stairs nor window; feed chiefly upon milk and potatoes whereby their spirits are not disposed to war."

Since the crop needed little labor to harvest, while a small acreage furnished a large yield, it was ideally suited to the turbulent conditions of Ireland in the seventeenth century; by 1700 it had largely displaced grain as the staple food of the majority of the people. In 1779, Arthur Young estimated that a given acreage under potatoes would support four times the population of a similar acreage under wheat.

In the Victorian Era, three-quarters of the cultivable soil was under corn, with the result that three-fourths of the people were forced to subsist on a crop produced by the remaining quarter of the land.

Most Irish peasants seldom ate bread, let alone meat; while milk, though in common consumption during the eighteenth century, had practically disappeared from their diet, its place having been taken by cheap, heavily adulterated tea. In the world of the potato, moreover, as in other realms, there were gradations of value, and the Irish peasant subsisted on the lowest and coarsest member of the potato family. He lived on "lumpers"—grey, indigestible tubers, which had originally been introduced as fodder for pigs, and which were regarded by most people, not only on account of their repulsive appearance, as unfit for human consumption.

As the potato had originally come from America, so did the blight that ruined it in 1845. In Ireland this blight appeared that year with extreme suddenness. In many places the promise of an abundant yield was converted overnight into the certainty of ruin. Father Mathew, the renowned temperance preacher, described how that summer, as he traveled from Cork to Dublin, he saw everywhere fields of healthy looking plants. Returning the same way a few days later, he found a scene of universal desolation: the leaves had curled up and shriveled; black spots had appeared on the potatoes, while a curious stench lay over the ground. Weeping and lamenting, the peasants beheld the ruin of the crop on which their lives depended. Some attributed it to the wrath of God, poured forth once again upon a long-suffering but devoted people. For the five years from 1846 through 1850, the total loss incurred through failure of the potato crop was put at £16 million—the equivalent perhaps of $500 million today.

One of the most remarkable circumstances connected with the Famine is that while tens of thousands were dying of hunger, Irish grain was being exported to England, where, under the protection of the Corn Laws, it still commanded high prices. As George O'Brien, the Irish economic historian, observes, people daily starved in the midst of plenty. The English historian G. M. Young estimates that during these years an average of two million quarters of wheat was annually shipped out of Ireland, an amount that Gavan Duffy claimed was sufficient to have fed the whole population. Thus even in the famine years Irish agriculture continued to yield profit both to Irish landlords and to English merchants.

Under such circumstances the resignation of the peasantry to their fate is remarkable. Relatively few food riots took place. Attacks on property seldom occurred. Crimes of violence were infrequent. To be sure there was an army of occupation of fifty thousand in the country, backed up in every town and village by an armed constabulary. "The forbearance of the Irish peasantry," declared the Census Commission of 1851, "and the calm submission with which they bore the deadliest ills that can fall on man can scarcely be paralleled in the annals of any nation."

The enormity of the disaster caused by the Famine eludes our comprehension. The statistics are both stark and terrible, yet their power over our imagination is limited. Within five years, about a million human beings perished in Ireland. Most of these, debilitated by long starvation, succumbed finally to typhus or typhoid fever. These two major killers were aided notably by cholera, dysentery, and scurvy. During the famine years there was also a great increase in the number of certified lunatics in Ireland.

In this ghastly period, more than a million persons fled the stricken island to seek their living in foreign lands. Hitherto, despite the flight of the "Wild Geese" to the Continent and the stream of Scotch-Irish emigration to the New World during the eighteenth century, the Catholic peasantry of Ireland had clung tenaciously to their own hearths and hovels. No matter what the degree of their misery, they had shown small disposition to leave their native land. Fearing the effect upon their religious beliefs of absorption into the predominantly Anglo-Saxon and Protestant world of America, the Catholic Church had also discouraged emigration to the New World. Even during the first few terrible months of the Famine, few peasants left Ireland.

Then suddenly, as if a giant dam had collapsed, a wave of panic swept the country and a huge tide of emigration set in. At first it flowed to Britain, where tens of thousands of destitute Irishmen and -women were dumped in the cellars and slums of Liverpool, Glasgow, and other industrial towns; then, gaining momentum, it surged across the Atlantic and flung hordes of derelicts upon the wharves of Boston and New York. Until 1845 an average of 61,000 persons had left Ireland every year; in 1846 the figure rose to 106,000; in 1847, it swelled to 212,000; in 1848, 178,000; in 1849, 212,000; in 1850, 209,000; and in 1851, the last year of the great migration, it reached 250,000.

Thus, within five years, through the combined effects of death and emigration, Ireland lost more than two million of her people—more than a quarter of her whole population. By 1900, two and a half million more had left Irish ports to cross the Atlantic; tens of thousands of others, still more venturous, had sailed to the Antipodes. During the nineteenth century throughout the Western World, population was rapidly increasing: in Ireland, it was halved. Among

European nations only Norway can show a similar record of demographic loss.

After the inevitable initial period of intense homesickness, loneliness, and frequent humiliation, many of the emigrants—generally employed as menials, the boys and men in the hardest manual labor, the girls and women in domestic service—gradually reconciled themselves to life abroad and found opportunities for success that in their own homeland they had never known. Henry Ford was the grandson of one such emigrant from Ireland; Grace Kelly, Princess of Monaco, the granddaughter of another. The most conspicuous example, of course, of such transatlantic success is that which awaited the descendants of a family of small farmers called Kennedy, who in 1848 sailed for America from the little fishing port of New Ross, County Wexford, center of some of the most savage fighting in 'ninety-eight. A great-grandson of these poverty-stricken emigrants was destined to become the first Catholic President of the United States.

Contemporary Accounts of Famine Conditions

Two and a half centuries after Edmund Spenser, the dreadful scenes he had so vividly described were once again reenacted in Ireland. Once more the ditches were filled with dead and dying, the streets littered with swollen corpses, their mouths stained green from the nettles and weeds with which in their last hours they had sought to appease their hunger. Along the coasts, people were known to exist on seaweed. Cases of cannibalism were again reported. Two contemporary descriptions of the tragedy may be quoted—one by John Mitchel, written in exile in Tasmania, the other by William Carleton, remembering 1817 as well as 1846. In his *Jail Journal*, Mitchel recalled:

> A calm, still horror was over all the land. Go where you would, in the heart of the town or in the church, on the mountain side or on the level plain, there was the stillness and heavy pall-like feeling of the chamber of death. You stood in the presence of a dread, silent, vast dissolution. An unseen ruin was creeping round you. . . . You could weep, but the rising curse died unspoken within your heart, like a profanity. Human passion there was none, but inhuman and unearthly quiet. Children met you, toiling heavily on stoneheaps, but their burning eyes were senseless, and their faces cramped and weasened like stunted old men. Gangs worked, but without a murmur, or a whistle, or a laugh, ghostly, like

voiceless shadows to the eye. . . . The very dogs, hairless . . . the vertebrae of the back protruding like the saw of a bone, glared at you from the ditchside with a wolfish avid eye, and then slunk away scowling and cowardly. Nay, the sky of heaven, the blue mountains, the still lake stretching far away westward, looked not as their wont. Between them and you rose up a streaming agony, a film of suffering, impervious and dim. It seemed as if the "anima mundi," the soul of the land, was faint and dying, and that the faintness and the death had crept into all things of earth and heaven.

Carleton, too, transcribed in exact and graphic detail the horrors that still haunted his memory:

Go where you might, every object reminded you of the fearful desolation that was progressing around you. The features of the people were gaunt, their eyes wild and hollow, their gait feeble and tottering. Pass through the fields, and you were met by little groups bearing home on their shoulders, and that with difficulty, a coffin, or perhaps two of them. The roads were literally black with funerals, and as you passed from parish to parish, the deathbells were pealing forth in slow but gloomy tones the triumph which pestilence was achieving over the face of our devoted country—a country that was every day filled with darker desolation and deeper mourning.

In *The Black Prophet,* Carleton described a famine graveyard where coffins were sometimes buried only a foot beneath the ground. He wrote:

One horrific remnant of humanity, whose nearly black features retained the frightful and spasmodic contortions of cholera, was being thrown, coffinless and half-naked, into what was rather a shallow trench than a grave. Gaunt starving dogs ravenously howled their hunger and waited . . . for the moment when the graves were unguarded. In one place, lay a mangled arm, in another a half-eaten head, in another a leg that had been partially pulled from the earth. In a corner by the wall a wolfish hound lay undisturbed making his meal off the features of a head held calmly between his paws.

How much of such a narrative is fiction, how much fact, is hard to say, but what is not to be doubted is that it bears the stamp of verisimilitude.

For a literal transcript from reality one might quote the appeal made in 1846 by a Justice of the Peace in County Cork, imploring the Duke of Wellington to intercede on behalf of the land of his birth. The magistrate had just returned from Skibbereen, haunted by the suffering he had seen. In one miserable hovel, he told the Duke, he had found "six famished and ghastly skeletons, to all appearances dead, huddled in a corner, their sole covering what appeared to be a ragged horse-cloth—I approached in horror, and found by a low moaning that they were alive—they were in fever—four children, a woman and what had once been a man. . . . In a few minutes I was surrounded by at least two hundred of such phantoms." The dispensary doctor in Skibbereen had found seven bodies under a cloak—"one had been dead many hours, but the others were unable to move either themselves or the corpse." "My Lord Duke," begged the magistrate, "in the name of starving thousands I implore you to break the frigid and flimsy chain of office, and save the land of your birth." There is no evidence that the Duke ever responded to this appeal for help.

Only by recalling scenes such as these can one hope to glimpse the terrible reality that lies buried in the moldering pages of state papers. One concrete example carries more weight than all the generalizations in the world. No matter what insight one may derive from reading, and no matter how powerful its impact may be, it still falls far short of reality.

When Carlyle made his tour in 1849, he found in Ireland the dank atmosphere of a charnel house. A pall of death lay over the land. The population, as Carlyle noted tersely, had "gone to the work-house, to England, to the grave." The living, not yet recovered from the catastrophe they had survived, were still in a state of trauma. People sang no longer in the fields or at their daily work. Silence lay over the country and heavy on the town. Oranmore, in Galway, was typical of many small towns. Carlyle found it "silent as a tomb . . . not a hammer stirring in it, or a footfall heard; stagnant at the head of its sleeping tide-water."

"This awful, unwonted silence," wrote George Petrie, the archaeologist, "which during the famine and subsequent years almost everywhere prevailed, struck more fearfully on their imaginations, as many Irish gentlemen informed me, and gave them a deeper feeling of the desolation with which the country had been visited, than any other circumstance which forced itself on their attention."

Ruins, beggars, silence—such was Ireland in 1849. Mendicancy,

Carlyle believed, was the country's chief industry. "Never saw such begging in the world," he noted. "Often get in a rage at it." At Killarney, beggars were "storming round you, like ravenous dogs round carrion." At Millstreet, County Cork, when tourists threw halfpennies from the coach, "the population ran at them like rabid dogs." Kildare was "one of the wretchedest wild villages I ever saw; full of ragged beggars . . . exotic altogether 'like a village in Dahomey.' " Outside the monastery at Mount Melleray, "squalid hordes of beggars" sat hoping for charity all day long. In country places beggars would wait for hours at crossroads and run after passing carriages for a mile or two till at length they collapsed from exhaustion. "Poor wretches," commented Carlyle. "But human pity dies away into stony misery and disgust at the excess of such scenes." Before leaving, he recorded his final impression of Ireland: ". . . the whole country figures in my mind like a ragged coat; one huge beggar's gabardine, not patched or patchable any longer."

Inadequacy of Famine Relief

The measures for the relief of starvation taken by the British government were both halfhearted and inadequate. Because of a pedantic adherence to doctrinaire economics, much that might have been done to alleviate distress was never even attempted. The Tory government of Sir Robert Peel was in office till June, 1846; after that date, the Whig government of Lord John Russell. Both failed to grasp the nature of the tragedy being enacted just across the Irish Sea—a tragedy whose effects they were careful to avoid seeing with their own eyes. Both insisted on regarding the Famine as a local and temporary failure of the harvest, to deal with which hasty and improvised measures would be sufficient, rather than as the worst disaster to visit any portion of the British Isles since the Black Death five centuries before. After a year of extreme scarcity in Ireland, the Famine did indeed force Peel to abolish the Corn Laws, but the expected inundation of England by cheap foreign corn did not take place. The result was that corn grown in Ireland continued to be exported to the English market and was not available in any appreciable amount to relieve starvation at home.

In all, the government spent some seven million pounds in direct relief, and some eight million more in the purchase of maize from America. (By way of comparison, in 1833 the British parliament had voted twenty million pounds to buy out a relatively small number of slave owners in the West Indies and South Africa.) Private charity, much of it due to Quakers like W. E. Forster, raised another million to feed the starving poor.

By the Poor Law Amendment Act of 1847, no peasant with a holding of a quarter of an acre or more was eligible for relief. The result was that, in order to obtain such aid, tens of thousands of peasants felt compelled to part with their last shred of security—the miserable plot of land on which they had grown their potatoes.

At the beginning of the Famine, many months passed—and many thousands died—before the government could bring itself to admit the necessity of direct financial help to Ireland. When at last in 1847 such aid was given, it took the form chiefly of free soup kitchens and of public works that were designed to be useless so that they would not interfere with private enterprise.

By 1847 more than three million people in Ireland—not far short of half the population—were being fed at public expense. Absolute want usually annihilates the sense of individual personality, reducing human beings to the level of animals: at the soup kitchens in Ireland, scenes of degradation took place not unlike those that occurred nearly a century later at Auschwitz, Buchenwald, and other concentration camps. "Here were wild crowds," wrote William Carleton, "ragged, sickly, and wasted away to skin and bone, struggling for the dole of charity like so many hungry vultures about the remnant of some carcase which they were tearing, amid noise, and screams, and strife, into very shreds . . . all sense of becoming restraint or shame was now abandoned."

As for public works, hundreds of thousands of men were set to work constructing roads in places where there was no need for them. Sometimes the roads terminated in the middle of a bog, since the government, against the repeated recommendations of parliamentary commissions, deliberately established the principle that public works must not be productive. Another example of the same principle was the construction of the great demesne walls, which are still a unique feature of many Irish country roads.

There was an urgent need to build railways and harbors in Ireland, and to develop fisheries: off the continental shelf west of the island, the seas were teeming with fish that could not be caught for lack of trawlers ·and heavy equipment. Almost nothing was spent on such projects. Thomas Drummond, in particular, had urged the state to build railways in Ireland, yet in 1846 that country had only 164 miles of railway, as compared with 6621 miles in England in 1850; and none were built in Ireland during the famine years.

Realizing that nothing was more demoralizing than deliberately unproductive labor, John Stuart Mill condemned the whole system of Irish relief. He proposed that the state should buy up waste land in Ireland, in order to bring it under cultivation and divide it up under peasant proprietorship—a procedure that Gustave de Beaumont had earlier suggested. Needless to say, such constructive proposals were never acted on.

Like Catholic emancipation in 1829, the repeal of the Corn Laws split the Conservative party in England and again forced Peel from office. A generation later the Irish question was to split the Liberal party also—this time on the question of Home Rule—and put Gladstone out of office. There was thus a sort of nemesis in this power of Ireland to bedevil English politics and confound English parties. During the nineteenth century many an English politician must have rued the day when Pitt had forced the Union upon Ireland, instead of leaving a people so impossible as the Irish to their own unintelligible devices. Sir Winston Churchill in the twentieth century was to voice similar sentiments.

Effect of the Famine on Agrarian Conditions

Despite relief, tens of thousands of peasants fell in arrears of rent and were evicted during the Famine years. Thus further suffering was added to that already caused by disease and starvation. A humane English visitor, Josephine Butler, later one of the pioneers in the movement for women's freedom, was living in Ireland at this time and described some of the ejections that she had personally witnessed. She wrote:

> Sick and aged, little children, and women with child were alike thrust forth into the snows of winter, for the winters of 1846 and 1847 were exceptionally severe, and to prevent their return their cabins were levelled to the ground . . . the few remaining tenants were forbidden to receive the outcasts . . . the majority rendered penniless by the years of famine, wandered aimlessly about the roads or bogs till they found refuge in the workhouse or the grave.

Traveling in Clare in 1849, an English member of parliament, Poulett Scrope, noted everywhere the remains of hovels that had been destroyed following the eviction of their inhabitants. Sometimes a wisp of smoke arising from one corner would reveal the presence of a family still crouching by a few turf sods propped up against a ruined wall. In Mayo, the Earl of Lucan—soon to be notorious for his part in the blunder known as the Charge of the Light Brigade—evicted some forty thousand peasants, for which he became known as the "great exterminator." Mrs. Woodham-Smith doubts whether Lord Lucan considered the Irish peasantry to be fully human. Not surprisingly, Lucan's name is still hated as much in Mayo as Cromwell's elsewhere in Ireland.

The tendency toward evictions was accelerated by other factors. Having lost their preferential position in the English market, Irish landlords often took their land out of cultivation and returned it to pasture as it had been before Foster's Act in 1784. In many parts of the country the death or flight of the tenantry led to the consolidation of their holdings in fewer hands.

Numerous landlords also suffered hardship during the Famine and found themselves encumbered by debt. It has been estimated that one third of the Irish landlords were ruined in the Famine years. In 1849, in order to facilitate the sale of land by distressed landowners, Parliament passed the Encumbered Estates Act as a result of which, property worth £23 million was acquired by new owners, many of them speculators from England anxious to make quick profits. The result was a further conversion of arable to pasture and a sharp increase in the number of evictions. During the twenty years from 1846 to 1866, no less than 300,000 evictions took place— a proceeding that may have involved as many as two million people. In the House of Commons, John Stuart Mill called attention to the suffering occasioned by this inhuman policy but was unable to persuade the government to introduce legislation designed to mitigate the harshness of the peasants' lot.

The last years of William Carleton's life were darkened by the evictions he witnessed during the 1850s and '60s. In a typical passage he exhibits the mingled pity and indignation aroused by such scenes.

On the roadside there were the humble traces of two or three cabins, whose little hearths had been extinguished, and whose walls were levelled to the earth. The black fungus, the burdock, the nettle, and all those offensive weeds that follow in the train of oppression and ruin were here; and as the dreary wind stirred them into sluggish motion, and piped its melancholy wail through these desolate mounds, I could not help asking myself, if those who do these things ever think that there is a reckoning in after life, where power, insolence and wealth misapplied, and rapacity, and persecution, and revenge, and sensuality, and gluttony, will be placed face to face with those humble beings, on whose rights and privileges of simple existence they have trampled with such a selfish and exterminating tread.

English Attitudes Toward the Famine

In any study of English opinion concerning the Famine, a striking difference emerges between the attitude of officials resident in Ireland—from Lord Clarendon, the Viceroy, on down—and that of the government in London, whose members, no matter whether they were Whigs or Tories, seldom if ever crossed the Irish Sea to see things for themselves.

"A great social revolution is now going on in Ireland," the Viceroy wrote Lord John Russell, the Prime Minister, in October, 1847. "The accumulated evils of misgovernment and mismanagement are now coming to a crisis." This accurate diagnosis, made after twenty-four months of famine conditions, was ignored in London. "Ireland cannot be left to her own resources, they are manifestly insufficient," warned Lord Clarendon. "We are not to let the people die of starvation, we must not believe that rebellion is impossible." To this urgent appeal, the Prime Minister responded heartlessly enough: "The state of Ireland for the next few months must be one of great suffering. Unhappily the agitation for Repeal has contrived to destroy nearly all sympathy in this country." Eighteen months later, in April, 1849, Clarendon expressed himself as still dissatisfied with the relief measures that had been adopted in Ireland. "I don't think there is another legislature in Europe," he frankly told Russell, "that would disregard such suffering as now exists in the west of Ireland, or coldly persist in the policy of extermination."

Another English official, Twistleton, Chief Poor Law Commissioner in Ireland, resigned in 1849 in protest against what he regarded as the callousness of the government at Westminster. "He thinks that the destitution here is so horrible," Clarendon reported to the Prime Minister, "and the indifference of the House of Commons to it is so manifest, that he is an unfit agent of a policy which must be one of extermination. . . . Twistleton feels that . . . he is placed in a position . . . which no man of honour and humanity can endure."

The Treasury was adamant against proposals to increase the amount of money allotted to famine relief. Its permanent head, Sir Charles Trevelyan, a leading Whig and grandfather of the distinguished historian, George Macaulay Trevelyan, viewed conditions in Ireland with equanimity. In September, 1846, when starvation had been widespread for more than a year without direct state relief, Sir Charles expressed himself apparently without the least consciousness of irony: "The poorest and most ignorant Irish peasant must, I think, by this time have become sensible of the advantage of belonging to a powerful community like that of the United Kingdom, the establishments and pecuniary resources of which are at all times ready to be employed for his benefit."

Three months later, contrary to the wishful hopes cherished in London, the Famine had still not disappeared and measures for relief were more and more strongly being urged in some quarters. "Feeling in London is so strong against the Irish," Trevelyan commented coolly on one of these proposals, "that I doubt if much progress will be made in subscription until further horrifying accounts are received." Sometimes in moments of irritation Sir Charles felt inclined to shift responsibility for the whole affair to supernatural forces. The Irish problem, he wrote in October, 1846, referring to overpopulation, "being altogether beyond the power of man, the cure had been applied by the direct stroke of an all-wise Providence in a manner as unexpected and as unthought of as it is likely to be effectual." Two years, and perhaps half a million deaths later, Sir Charles conceded: "The matter is awfully serious, but we are in the hands of Providence, without a possibility of averting the catastrophe if it is to happen [!]. We can only await the result." He even pitied the Irish for not realizing their situation *vis-à-vis* Providence. "It is hard upon the poor people," he wrote on one occasion, "that they should be deprived of knowing that they are suffering from an affliction of God's providence." Could Olympian detachment go further?

Trevelyan's political chief, Sir Charles Wood, Chancellor of the Exchequer and grandfather of the Halifax of appeasement in the 1930s, held similar opinions. "I am not at all appalled by your tenantry going," he wrote an Irish landlord in 1848. "That seems to me a necessary part of the process. . . . We must not complain of what we really want to obtain." This attitude of what one might call nonsqueamishness was also considered to have a Providential justification. There was no escape for the Irish people, Wood noted philosophically, except "through a purgatory of misery and starvation." All that the Treasury could do was to further, in a modest way, the plain designs of Providence. As the Victorian diarist Charles Greville noted in 1849, the Chancellor of the Exchequer "had all along set his face against giving or lending money [to Ireland] . . . he contemplates (with what seems like cruelty, though he is not really cruel) that misery and distress should run their course." A million dead and a million exiles were evidence enough that the Chancellor had got his wish. When the worst was over, Sir Robert Peel observed: "The time is come when it is not any longer necessary to pet Ireland. We can only spoil her by undeserved flattery, and by treating her to every thing for which she herself ought to pay." Peel's lifelong friend, John Wilson Croker, an Irishman by birth, visited Ireland in his old age and assured Peel that the reports of famine need not be taken seriously.

Nassau Senior, Professor of Political Economy at Oxford, sanctioned the views of the Treasury with the authority of the academic world. It was in reference to Senior that Benjamin Jowett, later Master of Balliol College, Oxford, once remarked: "I have always felt a certain horror of political economists, since I heard one of them say that he feared the famine of 1848 in Ireland would not kill more than a million people, and that would scarcely be enough to do much good." In contemplating with equanimity the possible extermination of a people, Professor Senior was by no means alone. All that distinguished him from numerous government officials was the complete candor with which he avowed such views. Even so he had a competitor in the London *Times,* which exulted editorially at the prospect of an era when a native Irishman would be "as rare on the banks of the Liffey as a red man on the banks of the Manhattan" [*sic*].

The Tacitean maxim about the human need to hate where we have injured is relevant to Anglo-Irish relations in the nineteenth century no less than in the twelfth. The slanders on the Irish national character once uttered by Giraldus Cambrensis were now repeated in the pages of *Punch,* which, in the words of Mrs. Woodham-Smith, "published cartoons week after week depicting the Irishman as a filthy, brutal creature, an assassin and a murderer, begging for money, under a pretence of buying food, to spend on weapons."

Some English observers traced the genesis of the ills that afflicted Ireland in the famine years to defects inherent in the character of the Irish people themselves. "The great evil with which we have to contend," declared Sir Charles Trevelyan in 1846, was "not the physical evil of the famine, but the moral evil of the selfish, perverse and turbulent character of the people."

A slightly more sophisticated version of the theory that the Irish were primarily responsible for the disaster that had befallen them involved their habits of reproduction. The root cause of the Famine, it was held, was overpopulation, itself the result of improvident and reckless breeding. This was the view taken by the well-known Victorian philanthropist, the Reverend Sidney Godolphin Osborne, whom the *Times* sent out to Mayo as its special correspondent in 1849. So convinced was Osborne of the fact of overpopulation that he even endorsed the brutal mass-eviction of the Mayo peasantry by Lord Lucan.*

The real trouble in Ireland, of course, lay in the primitive condition of her agriculture and in the appalling social system that it supported. Robert Owen and Thomas Drummond in the 1830s, the Devon Commission in 1845 and John Stuart Mill in the 1850s, all perceived that what Ireland really needed was capital investment in agriculture, the reclamation of large areas of waste land that could be brought under cultivation, and a system of public works. Mill was almost alone in foreseeing the ultimate necessity of peasant proprietorship in Ireland.

In the meantime it was more gratifying to lecture and scold the Irish. To go from England to Ireland, wrote Poulett Scrope in 1849, was to pass "from an age of civilization and science to one of ignorance and barbarism." No doubt the observation was correct—but not the implication that the Irish themselves were responsible for this state of affairs. Macaulay was another who could not help expressing his irritation at so obstinate an exception as Ireland to contemporary evidence of Progress—"a marsh," he termed the island contemptuously, "saturated with the vapours of the Atlantic."

In 1844 Disraeli had summed up the situation in Ireland with devastating accuracy: "a starving population, an absentee aristocracy, an alien church and the weakest executive in the world." But when it came to finding a remedy for this intolerable state of affairs, he merely shrugged his shoulders. "One day the Pope, the next day potatoes." With this sardonic quip, Disraeli turned away from the boring problem of an incorrigible people, nor did he thereafter in the course of his long political career devote any serious attention to the affairs of Ireland.

By the end of the century Lord Salisbury, then Prime Minister, could declare publicly that the Irish were no more fit for self-government than the Hottentots; while Tennyson could fulminate: "Kelts are all made furious fools. They live in a horrible island and have no history of their own worth the least notice." A recent invention of Alfred Nobel suggested a possible solution. "Could not

*This Malthusian view of Ireland during the Famine is still held by contemporary English economic historians such as T. S. Ashton. The Oxford historian James Anthony Froude, in a masterpiece of understatement, admitted that "thousands" had died during the Famine in Ireland. As for Sir Winston Churchill, he passes over the Famine almost as lightly as he passed over the Treaty of Limerick.

anyone," asked the poet laureate, "blow up that horrible island with dynamite and carry it off in pieces—a long way off ?"

The Famine and Emigration

The Famine had momentous consequences both for Ireland herself and for the world. The most immediate, and perhaps the most important, of these was the transplanting of two and a half million Irishmen and Irishwomen to the New World and the Antipodes. In the new lands of America or Australia, these emigrants—even those of the first generation like Thomas Francis Meagher in the United States, Thomas d'Arcy McGee in Canada, or Sir Charles Gavan Duffy in Australia—sometimes rose to positions of power and influence, thus belying the widespread Victorian belief in the innate inferiority of the Irish.

Not unnaturally the emigrants took with them across the ocean, and passed on to their children and their children's children, a burning hatred of the country that had been the cause of their misfortunes and their exile. Idealization of the "auld country" was for many inseparably connected with unrelenting animosity to Britain.

At Grosse Island, near Detroit, the Ancient Order of Hibernians in 1909 unveiled a plaque that reads: "In this secluded spot lie the mortal remains of 5,294 persons who, flying from pestilence and famine in Ireland in the year 1847, found in America but a grave." It is recorded that the husband of one of those who died at Grosse Island—four thousand miles away from the fever-ridden homeland—placed two shovels in the form of a cross over his wife's grave, and swore a solemn oath: "By that cross, Mary, I swear to avenge your death. As soon as I earn the price of my passage home, I'll go back and shoot the man that murdered you—and that's the landlord." This spirit—of implacable resentment mingled with a desire for revenge—was to embitter Anglo-American relations during the next century.

One result of Irish emigration to the United States—and to other English-speaking countries—was the immense strengthening of the power of the Catholic Church. At the time of the Famine the British government and the Irish episcopate had been, each from the point of view of its own self-interest, equally shortsighted. For while the British cabinet could view America as a convenient dumping ground for refuse from Ireland—using the New World as a large-scale northern Botany Bay—and rejoiced to see the Irish depart in hundreds of thousands across the Atlantic, so too the Catholic hierarchy failed initially to comprehend that the United States would open up an enormous area for the extension of Catholic influence within a world that hitherto had been almost exclusively Protestant and Anglo-Saxon.

An ancillary effect of the emigration to America was that henceforward Irish nationalist politics would have a base in the New World, as well as a source of indispensable financial aid. From now on, all movements for the liberation of Ireland—the Fenian Brotherhood, Home Rule, Sinn Fein—regardless whether their methods were peaceful or violent, would find powerful financial support from America. Irish-American hostility to Britain was reinforced by the latent Anglophobia—an unfortunate legacy of the American Revolution and the War of 1812—that was widespread in America during the nineteenth century and the early part of the twentieth. Indeed it may be said, without disparagement to the valor of Sinn Fein, that the establishment in 1922 of the Irish Free State was due largely to the pressure exerted on the British government by outraged public opinion in America. Thus the emigration caused by the Famine had very important, if indirect, results for the future of Anglo-American relations and for the future of Ireland herself.

The psychological effects of the Famine upon Ireland were no less profound and lasted through three succeeding generations. Nearly a hundred years later, Paul Henry, the painter, maintained in his autobiography that the Irish people had still not forgotten the Famine, and he believed that they never would. Everywhere, deep in the minds of simple people, was the fear that one day the tragedy might repeat itself. In our own time, Professor Roger McHugh has illustrated how widely and how poignantly this elemental fear has embedded itself in popular consciousness.

The Famine still further weakened the declining hold of the Gaelic language upon the Irish people. For its ravages had been most severe, the emigration most concentrated, in those areas of the west and southwest where the majority of Gaelic speakers had lived. As Douglas Hyde put it, in the years after the Famine, the language "just wilted off the face of Ireland." Between 1861 and 1891, except in certain districts of the Gaelteacht,* the old language died out almost completely. In 1891, according to Dr. Hyde, there were fewer Gaelic speakers in all Ireland than there had been before the Famine in the single province of Connacht.

The Young Ireland movement, aiming at complete separation from Britain, had been launched before the Famine began, but indignation caused by the sight of universal suffering—and still more by the ap-

*The name for the Gaelic-speaking part of Ireland.

parent callousness of the British government in the face of such suffering—caused many of the Young Ireland leaders to contemplate once more resorting to arms to break the connection with Britain. In 1848, Charles Gavan Duffy called the Famine "a fearful murder committed on the mass of the people." John Mitchel believed that the tragedy was the result of a diabolical plot to exterminate the Irish nation. "A million and a half human beings," he later asserted in his *History of Ireland* (1869),

> were carefully, prudently and peacefully slain by the British Gov-
> ernment. They died of hunger in the midst of abundance which
> their own hands created. . . . This was a strictly artificial famine—
> that is to say, it was a famine which desolated a rich and fertile
> island, that produced every year abundance and super-abundance
> to sustain all her people and many more. The English, indeed,
> call that famine a dispensation of Providence; and ascribe it en-
> tirely to the blight of the potatoes. But potatoes failed in like
> manner all over Europe, and there was no famine save in Ireland.
> The British account of the matter, then, is, first a fraud; second,
> a blasphemy. The Almighty, indeed, sent the potato blight, but
> the English created the famine.

The belief in Ireland that the Famine was the result of a deliberate conspiracy on the part of the British government was no doubt as mistaken and as oversimplified as the English belief that the Famine was due to overpopulation. The theory of conspiracy has long been abandoned by serious Irish historians. Yet in all conscience it is not difficult to sympathize with the sense of outrage felt by men like Mitchel and Duffy, as they beheld the long-protracted agony of a whole nation.

Had the British government ever realized the full immensity of the misery, had statesmen like Peel and Russell seen for themselves the appalling spectacle of a whole people reduced to rags and beggary, the fever-haunted poorhouses, the mud-huts full of skeletons, the ditches choked with corpses, the mass graves, they might have been less bound by abstract economic theories and more willing to give generous relief. English statesmen showed themselves not so much wicked as unfeeling and unimaginative. Even among educated people in England there were few who possessed the disinterested intelli-gence of John Stuart Mill and were able to realize with him that the fundamental cause of the Famine had been the rottenness and ob-solescence of the social order that had been riveted upon Ireland as the result of centuries of past oppression.

BIBLIOGRAPHY

Adams, William Forbes: *Ireland and Irish Emigration to the New World from 1815 to the Famine* (1932)

Carleton, William: *The Black Prophet* (1847)

Carlyle, Thomas: *Reminiscences of My Irish Journey in 1849* (1882)

Connell, K. H.: *The Population of Ireland, 1750–1845* (1950)

De Beaumont, Gustave: *Ireland* (1839)

Edwards, R. Dudley, and Williams, Desmond: *The Great Famine* (1957)

Freeman, Thomas Walter: *Pre-Famine Ireland* (1957)

McDowell, Robert B.: *Social Life in Ireland, 1800–45* (1957)

O'Brien, George: *Economic History of Ireland from the Union to the Famine* (1921)

O'Connor, Sir James: *History of Ireland, 1801–1924*, 2 vols. (1926)

O'Flaherty, Liam: *Famine* (1937)

O'Hegarty, Patrick Sarsfield: *History of Ireland Under the Union, 1801–1922* (1952)

Pomfret, John Edwin: *The Struggle for Land in Ireland, 1800–1923* (1930)

Salaman, Redcliffe N.: *The History and Social Influence of the Potato* (1949)

Smith, Goldwin: *Irish Life and Character* (1861)

Strauss, Emil: *Irish Nationalism and British Democracy* (1951)

Thackeray, William Makepeace: *Irish Sketch Book* (1844)

De Tocqueville, Alexis: *Journeys in England and Ireland in 1835* (1958)

Woodham-Smith, Cecil: *The Great Hunger: Ireland, 1845–49* (1962)

X

Young Ireland and the Fenians

Thomas Davis and The Nation *(1842)*

The Young Ireland movement, whose earliest leader was Thomas Davis (1814–45), a brilliant young Protestant graduate of Trinity, was founded in Dublin in 1842. It was the Irish version of the romantic nationalism which, inspired by Mazzini's Young Italy, was just then revitalizing Europe with an idealism such as that continent had not known since the French Revolution. If in Europe that spirit was bound to come into conflict with the repressive policies of Metternich, in Ireland it was no less bound to challenge the forcible subjection of that country to British rule.

Young Ireland, however, was compelled to fight a war on two fronts, for while it rejected British domination, it rejected equally the claim of Daniel O'Connell to continue any longer as spokesman for the Irish people. Especially after the Clontarf fiasco in 1843, Young Ireland realized the hopelessness of working with the Repeal Association, and the folly of expecting anything from the flatulent oratory of the Liberator. Young Ireland was wearied by O'Connell's endless flow of words and disgusted by his rant and bombast. Like Sinn Fein after the fall of Parnell, it sought relief in action.

The organ of Young Ireland was *The Nation,* a weekly journal edited by Thomas Davis, the first number of which appeared on October 15, 1842. Along with Davis, the founders of *The Nation* were Charles Gavan Duffy (1816–1903), an able Dublin journalist, and John Blake Dillon (1814–66), a landowner from Mayo. *The Nation* aimed at restoring to Ireland a sense of dignity and pride in her inheritance. It was inspired by an ardent nationalism and glori-

Thomas Davis (1814–45). Founder of The Nation *(1842), and first leader of Young Ireland.*

James Clarence Mangan (1803–49). Poet of Young Ireland and author of "Dark Rosaleen."

fied the heroes of Irish history. In effect, it hoped to do for that country what Sir Walter Scott had already done for Scotland.

Capably edited and brilliantly written, *The Nation* was an immediate success. Its first issue sold twelve thousand copies. Published in Dublin, it was the first magazine in Irish history to circulate throughout the country. In the provinces it had a larger circulation than that of any provincial paper. Like Cobbett's *Political Register* in England, it was read by tens of thousands, being passed from hand to hand until it almost literally fell to pieces. One of the poets who made his reputation in the columns of *The Nation* was James Clarence Mangan (1803–49), that astonishing self-taught prodigy-waif of the Dublin slums, whose "Dark Rosaleen" had appeared in 1840 in the *Dublin Penny Journal.* Both John Mitchel and John O'Leary regarded Mangan as the finest poet that Ireland had yet produced.

A selection of patriotic ballads from *The Nation,* many of them written by Davis, went through no less than sixty editions. Artless as such poems might be, the old Fenian, O'Leary, spoke no doubt for many of his generation when in his *Recollections* he wrote that in reading Davis' poems as a young man he had undergone the equivalent of a religious "conversion."

Thomas Davis ranged over centuries of Irish history, from the coming of the Normans, down through Elizabethan and Cromwellian times, to Owen Roe, Sarsfield, and the "Wild Geese." In every period he found justification for patriotic pride and fresh reason for resenting the yoke of the foreigner. By concentrating on Irish history,

Davis was able to counteract the effects of the Education Act of 1831, aimed, as it was, at eradicating among Irish boys and girls any sense of their own national identity.

The Nation reawakened memories of "ninety-eight" and held the United Irishmen in high regard. It rescued Wolfe Tone and Robert Emmet from the scorn of O'Connell, who had dismissed them as "miscreants." Thomas Davis' visit in 1843 to Tone's grave at Bodenstown was destined to inaugurate a pilgrimage that would become an annual consecration of the principle of Irish nationality.

Not only did Davis rekindle in his hearers a love of Irish history, he also inspired a profound feeling for the old land itself. He had visited almost every county in Ireland and was familiar with the details of its local history. Long after Davis' death, John Mitchel was to recall his "passionate and deep love not only for the people but for the very soil, rocks, woods, waters and skies of his native land." Like Spenser, Davis was enchanted with the foliage that was mirrored in the Nore and the Blackwater, and judged those rivers not inferior in beauty to the Rhine. In the bays and headlands of Kerry, he found "the boldness of Norway united with the colouring of Naples." He advised his countrymen, when they went abroad, to forsake the tourist round—what he termed "the weary tale of the Louvre and Munich"—and seek instead places linked forever with Ireland by historic associations. Thus he urged them to dwell upon the memory of Columba at Iona, of Columbanus in Bobbio, of O'Neill and O'Donnell in Rome, and of the Irish Brigade on the fields of Blenheim or Fontenoy.

But most of all, anticipating writers such as Synge and Yeats, Thomas Davis turned for inspiration to the west of Ireland. For him the wildness of Connemara came to symbolize Ireland's unquenchable love of freedom.

> When all beside a vigil keep,
> The West's asleep, the West's asleep—
> Alas! and well may Erin weep
> While Connacht lies in slumber deep.
> There lake and plain smile fair and free
> 'Mid rocks—their guardian chivalry—
> Sing, oh! let man learn liberty
> From crashing wave and lashing sea.
>
> . . . . .
>
> Sing, oh! they died their land to save,
> At Aughrim's slopes and Shannon's wave.

Despite his strong nationalism Davis, having traveled on the Continent, was far more cosmopolitan in outlook than most contemporary Irishmen, being familiar with French, Italian, and German literature. Heinrich Heine was one of his favorite poets.

Curiously enough, the literary sources of Davis' ardently romantic nationalism were almost wholly English. Though he had the usual uncritical belief in Ireland's mythological past—disparaging the Firbolgs as "rude people," and praising the Danaans as "a refined and noble race"—he knew little or no Gaelic and had small interest in Gaelic history. Ignoring Cuchulain and the Fenians, he found his literary models in the contemporary ballad literature of Britain—in poets like Walter Scott, Thomas Campbell, and Lord Macaulay. Davis had a high regard for the language of the conquerors, and praised its purity in former times—as exhibited, for example, in Shakespeare, Spenser, and the King James Bible.

Intellectually, Thomas Davis bridged two worlds—those of Irish nationalism and English literature. The scholar who valued Trinity and its traditions and was proud to be a Trinity man, was nevertheless willing to assail that Protestant citadel for its inveterate hostility to the land of which it was a part, and for its classical pedantry, indifference to modern languages, and disdain for contemporary thought.

Conscious of how much he owed England in respect of his own mental culture, Davis could write with an objectivity of which few other Young Irelanders were capable:

> We repeat, again and again—no hatred of the English. For much that England did in literature, politics and war, we are, as men, grateful. Her oppression we would not even avenge. We would, were she eternally dethroned from us, rejoice in her prosperity; but we cannot, and will not try to forget her long, cursing, merciless tyranny to Ireland; and we do not desire to share her gains, her responsibility or her glory.

In personality Thomas Davis was modest, gentle, and selfless—beloved by all who knew him. He seemed to have submerged himself completely in the country he idealized. "The sorrows of the people," declared Patrick Pearse, "affected Davis like a personal sorrow." Yeats praised his magnanimity, finding it refreshing after the jealous egotism of O'Connell. Discouraged by literary feuds and rivalries, Yeats would remind himself of Davis' freedom from pettiness and malice. "I remember this man," he wrote, "who was so destitute of peacock talent, having neither wit nor oratory, who put money into no man's pocket." Like the chivalrous John O'Leary,

Thomas Davis also deprecated violence and deplored assassination as a political weapon.

A victim of scarlet fever at the age of thirty-one, Davis died just before his intended marriage to Annie Hutton and did not live to see the Famine. He was thus spared the pain of sharing in the suffering that was to fall upon the land he loved. "The greatest of the Young Irelanders," John O'Leary termed him, "the poet who holds first place in the hearts of all good Irishmen." What the old Fenian especially admired in Davis was his strong moral sense and his instinctive aversion from anything cheap or mean. "In so far as you feel with Davis," O'Leary once told the working men of Newcastle-on-Tyne, "you can never go astray and in thinking with him you are safer than with any Irishman I know."

John Mitchel (1815–75). One of the leaders of Young Ireland, he was sent to Tasmania as a convict for his part in the movement.

John Mitchel and James Fintan Lalor (1847–48)

Already before the death of Davis, the breach between Young Ireland and O'Connell had widened irreparably. The parting of the ways came with Peel's proposal in 1845 to satisfy an increasing demand for higher education in Ireland by establishing three undenominational "Queen's Colleges"—in Belfast, Cork, and Galway. Because no faculties of theology were included in the scheme, the Catholic hierarchy strongly opposed the measure; and when the Young Irelanders declared their willingness to accept the colleges,

O'Connell joined with the bishops in damning them as "godless." The colleges survived none the less.

Dr. MacHale, Archbishop of Tuam, hysterically denounced the bill as "a scheme of mercenary infidels," attempting "to bribe Catholic youths into abandoning their religion." Dr. Dewy, Bishop of Clonfert, condemned it as "a Satanic scheme for the ruin of faith in the rising generations," while one of O'Connell's sons called it "an abominable attempt to undermine religion and morality in Ireland." Dr. Higgins, Bishop of Meath, went still further and indicted *The Nation* as a "voltairean newspaper," "the most dangerous publication that ever appeared in Ireland." The Young Irelanders were incensed by the base demagoguery displayed on this occasion by the aged Liberator and his sons.

The disaster of the Famine, and the government's failure to take adequate steps to cope with that disaster, drove the Young Irelanders to more desperate courses than Davis himself had ever contemplated. In any estimate of the motives that led to the ill-timed revolt of 1848, pride of place must be assigned to the sense of outrage that possessed men so different in temperament as Smith O'Brien, Thomas Francis Meagher, John Mitchel, and Charles Gavan Duffy. In July, 1846, these Young Ireland leaders broke with O'Connell and his Repeal Association and founded a new political group, which they named the Irish Confederation.

On July 28, 1846, Meagher launched the passionate appeal to arms that gained him the famous sobriquet, "Meagher of the Sword." "Abhor the sword? Stigmatize the sword?" he asked rhetorically. "No—for at its blow a great nation started from the waters of the Atlantic; and by its redeeming magic, and in the quivering of its crimson light, the crippled colony sprang into the altitude of a proud Republic." Such praise of the United States was, of course, above all effective at a time when so many young Irishmen were seeking a new life in America.

In 1847, Mitchel, who had edited *The Nation* since the death of Davis, broke with the writers of that magazine and founded a still more radical journal, the *United Irishman,* in whose columns he urged a "holy war to sweep this island clear of the English name and nation." So outspoken was Mitchel—he described the Viceroy as "Her Majesty's Executioner-General and General Butcher of Ireland"—that he was soon arrested and charged with the new crime of treason-felony. Found guilty in May, 1848, by a packed jury in Dublin, he was sentenced to fourteen years' transportation. Loaded down with chains, Mitchel was not even allowed to take leave of his wife and children but was shipped out forthwith to a convict station in Tasmania. In his *History of Ireland,* written some twenty years later, Mitchel referred to the fate that had befallen him, passing over in silence the passion of rage and frustration that had reduced him, for the first and only time, to tears. "Mr. Mitchel," he wrote tersely, "was carried off and never saw his country any more." * The rebellion, therefore, when it broke out in July, was deprived of Mitchel's powers of organization and leadership.

Vehement and uncompromising though Mitchel was, during his last months in Ireland he had come under the influence of a thinker even more audacious and more radical than he. James Fintan Lalor (1810–49) was a self-educated recluse who had grown up in a village in the boglands of Leix. In the frail, misshapen body of a hunchback was lodged an original and powerful intellect. Notwithstanding his utter isolation in Leix, Lalor, a voracious reader, had come in contact with the ideas of contemporary socialism and had embraced them.

While Mitchel had echoed Wolfe Tone's appeal to "that most respectable class of the nation—the men of no property," Lalor went further, assuring the rural proletariat that they were "the true owners of the soil." He advocated the expropriation of the landlord class and the nationalization of land. As a first step toward this goal, anticipating Michael Davitt by thirty years, Lalor urged the peasants to refuse to pay rent. "Mankind will yet be masters of the earth," he prophesied. Along with this revolutionary program, Lalor, like Mitchel, boldly demanded the complete independence of Ireland from the British crown.

Gavan Duffy, who knew Lalor personally, described him as "deaf, near-sighted, ungainly and deformed." In the next generation the radical Tory Standish O'Grady was to pay tribute to the socialist Lalor as "the greatest of the Young Irelanders—the deepest, most original and most prophetic. . . . He was small and gibbous," noted O'Grady, "but his speech was far from contemptible." No doubt what O'Grady really admired in Lalor was not his economic theory but his unflinching courage.

In 1848, after Mitchel's arrest, Lalor started a journal of his own in Dublin—a paper that he defiantly named the *Irish Felon.* "Unmuzzle the wolfhound," he exhorted his fellow countrymen. "There is one at this moment in every cabin throughout the land. He will

---

*Happily, this statement was belied by subsequent events, for Mitchel returned to Ireland in 1875 and was even elected M.P. for Tipperary, although he did not live to take his seat in parliament.

be savager by and by." Just before Young Ireland rose, Lalor boldly asked: "Who will draw the first blood for Ireland? Who will win a wreath that shall be green forever?" These were the last words of the *Irish Felon,* for the government promptly suppressed the paper and put Lalor in prison. Next year he died in Dublin of consumption.

In his own lifetime, Lalor's name even among the Young Irelanders was little known; but thirty years after his death Henry George, who had read him in America, came to Ireland to rescue Lalor's ideas from the oblivion that had fallen upon them. It was not, however, until another self-taught workingman, James Connolly, browsing through the yellowing pages of old newspapers, rediscovered Lalor, that the pioneer socialist was given his rightful place in the history of Irish nationalism. Connolly reprinted Lalor's spirited essay, "The Faith of a Felon" and exalted the hunchback recluse as "the keenest intellect in Ireland of his day." John O'Leary, too, despite his own aversion from socialism, expressed admiration for "the active and fertile brain that presided over the frail body of James Fintan Lalor." Still later, in the slums of Dublin, Sean O'Casey rediscovered the originality of Lalor's thought, paying him a tribute in his autobiography that will endure as long as O'Casey's name is remembered.

The Young Ireland Rising of 1848

John Mitchel and Fintan Lalor represented the extreme left wing of Young Ireland, a movement whose leaders were for the most part aristocratic in outlook, having little inclination to cooperate with the contemporary English workingmen's movement known as Chartism. "We desire no fraternization between the Irish people and the Chartists," announced *The Nation* in 1846. "Between us and them there is a wide gulf fixed. We desire not to bridge it over, but to make it wider and deeper." Most of the leaders of Young Ireland—in this respect like their antagonist O'Connell—ignored the agrarian question and were without a program of agrarian reform.

This was especially true of Smith O'Brien (1803-64) who, after the disappearance of the fiery Mitchel, emerged as the undisputed leader of Young Ireland. Educated as an English gentleman at Harrow and Cambridge, O'Brien was a Protestant landowner who had represented the county of Limerick since 1835. Tall and handsome but "grave and frigid in manner," he seemed like a throwback to the days of the Volunteers and reminded some of Grattan. In the House of Commons, where he had always defended Irish interests and opposed the coercion of Ireland, O'Brien was respected as a brave and honorable man. Socially, he was the most distinguished member of Young Ireland. Indeed it was said that, lacking the personal magnetism of men like Mitchel and Meagher, it was his direct descent from Brian Boru that had given him the leadership of the movement.

Though willing to hazard for the sake of Irish freedom all that he possessed—wealth, social status, and personal happiness—Smith O'Brien as a landlord was strongly opposed to the idea that peasants should withhold their rents. During the Famine he had resisted suggestions that starving tenants should seize their landlords' grain. Even in the last days of the 1848 revolt, with inevitable failure in sight, O'Brien still refused to bid for popular support by advocating nonpayment of rent.

The misfortune of Young Ireland was that when in 1848, because of the February revolution in Paris, the most favorable moment for an uprising since 1798 presented itself, the country lay prostrate after the Famine and hence incapable of concerted national action. The year of 1848 saw the most profound upheaval, both political and social, since the original French Revolution of 1789. A powerful wave of nationalist sentiment swept through Germany, Austria, Hungary, and Italy, as well as through France herself. Even in England that year, the long-threatened rising of the Chartists seemed likely to tie down British military forces at a crucial moment. The Chartists, moreover, were known to be sympathetic toward Ireland, Feargus O'Connor, their leader at this time, being himself an Irishman. Plans were even formulated by an ardent Young Irelander, Thomas d'Arcy McGee (1825–68), to send help to an Irish rebellion, should it occur, from ships to be seized on the Clyde and the Mersey.

In March, 1848, Young Ireland sent O'Brien and Meagher to Paris to congratulate the provisional French government on the success of the Revolution. Ledru-Rollin received them warmly, but Lamartine, the Foreign Minister, was cold and unsympathetic. Anxious for British diplomatic support, the second French Republic refused to make any move on behalf of Ireland, lest it should give offense to London. All that O'Brien and Meagher brought back from Paris was the Tricolor and the "Marseillaise," which was sung henceforth in Ireland together with "The Wearing of the Green." In England the collapse of the Chartists in April, 1848, strengthened the position of the government and undermined the hopes of Young Ireland.

Though the situation was clearly hopeless, in defiance the Young Irelanders nevertheless determined to rise. Since Dublin was full of informers and occupied by a strong military garrison, they chose as their center Kilkenny, seat of the Confederation in 1642, and a city, as Meagher wrote proudly, that stood "on the frontier of the three best fighting counties in Ireland—Waterford, Wexford and Tipperary." No doubt Meagher was thinking of the hard-fought Wexford rising of 1798.

This time, however, in a country largely drained of its manhood by death and emigration, history failed signally to repeat itself. Not only, as might have been expected, did the Catholic hierarchy once more condemn rebellion, but even the local priests, ignoring the memory of the hero of ninety-eight, Father Murphy of Boolavogue, prudently decided to remain aloof. Just as in 1795 Pitt had taken out insurance against the United Irishmen by a grant of £9000 to Maynooth, so now Peel followed his example by raising the amount of the subvention to £26,000. Cardinal Cullen later denounced Young Ireland as "a most dangerous party" because of its adherence to the pernicious principles of Kossuth and Mazzini "so often idolized in the pages of the *Nation.*" By a curious chance, on the very day on which Young Ireland collapsed (August 5, 1848), Pius IX formally warned against the movement in an official statement from Rome.

In Kilkenny the Young Irelanders were greeted with wild demonstrations and deafening cheers of welcome. Bonfires were lighted and houses decked with laurel. Ardent young girls embraced the rebel leaders. Thomas Davis had praised what he called "our darling Irish green," and now the Young Irelanders planted on many a rath the green banner of Erin—"the flag of the proud old Irish race," as Meagher was wont to call it. On the slopes of Slievenamon in Tipperary, and at nearby Carrick-on-Suir, Meagher addressed large crowds and received tumultuous acclaim. In exile he would long recall that brief exhilarating moment, for him inseparably entwined with the memory of women's hair—"disordered, drenched and tangled, streaming in the roaring wind of voices."

But for all the excitement, few volunteered for danger and fewer still possessed arms. Passing the ruined windmill on Vinegar Hill, Meagher contrasted the desperate courage of Wexford in ninety-eight with its fatal lassitude now. Too late he realized how the Famine had drained away the spirit of a people—"how cold and nakedness, hunger and disease, to the last extremity had done their work."

Michael Doheny, one of the younger leaders, has left in his autobiography, *The Felon's Track,* a graphic recollection of the enthusiastic dreams that inspired the revolt and of the chilling awareness of reality which gradually dissipated these fantasies. As he rode into Carrick-on-Suir on the morning of the rising, it struck him forcibly how "centuries had gathered into moments" at that fateful hour. "That which was then present to my mind, and occupied all its faculties," he recalled "was the hope of satisfaction, or vengeance if you will, for so many ages of guilty tyranny. The tears, the burning and the blood of nearly one thousand years seemed to litter the eastern sky, as day dawned on my way. Apprehension I had none. From earliest childhood to that hour, I never met one Irishman whose hope of hopes it was not to deliver the country forever from English thrall."

Rude was the awakening from such patriotic fancies. When all was over, Doheny, hunted through the mountains of Munster, a felon with a price on his head, attributed the failure of the rising at Carrick largely to the opposition of the priests. It was with sadness that he recalled the first rapture of the rising, so quickly changed to despair. "As I approached that town in the grey of morning," he wrote, "and the past and future in burning recollection thronged on my brain, I envied the destiny which God had awarded to its inhabitants, in breaking the first link of the slavery of nearly twenty generations. This, also, was a dream. The people of Carrick had already, with shrinking hand, marred their immortal lot."

The end came quickly. After some halfhearted fighting at Ballingarry, County Tipperary, on August 5, 1848, Smith O'Brien and a handful of ill-armed followers surrendered. Preserving his dignity to the last, the chivalrous O'Brien refused to countenance useless killing, whether of friend or foe. "The people," he explained, "preferred to die of starvation at home, or to flee as voluntary exiles to other lands, rather than to fight for their lands and their liberties." Meagher was captured a week later. Less than six hundred people had participated actively in the rebellion.

In October, at the Clonmel Assizes, O'Brien and Meagher were found guilty of high treason and sentenced, like their forerunners the United Irishmen, to be hanged, drawn, and quartered. Victorian England, however, as a result of the mingled if contending influences of Evangelicalism and Utilitarianism, was less barbarous than the England of George III, and the sentences were commuted to transportation for life. So it came about that one day in 1849, out in the Tasmanian bush, O'Brien and Meagher were reunited with their fellow-convict John Mitchel, who from afar had followed their fortunes with avid interest. "Brave men," he called them, "who sought for an honorable chance of throwing their lives away."

Thomas Francis Meagher

As in the eighteenth century the "Wild Geese" had been dispersed over the face of Europe, so now in the diaspora of 1848 the Young Irelanders were scattered to the ends of the earth—from the Antipodes to the American Far West. Four of their leaders were to acquire brilliant reputations in the English-speaking world—Meagher by the sword, Mitchel by the pen, Gavan Duffy and Thomas d'Arcy McGee in the field of colonial politics. In so doing they did much to redeem Young Ireland from the ridicule that, after 1848, had inevitably attached to it.

In the opinion of Arthur Griffith, founder of Sinn Fein and later first executive of the Irish Free State, Thomas Francis Meagher (1823–67) was the most accomplished orator in Ireland in the nineteenth century, not even excepting the Liberator. If Meagher lacked the overwhelming personal impact that O'Connell had had upon his hearers, he also lacked O'Connell's coarseness and scurrility. Yet he, too, had the power to move an audience profoundly—as in the "speech of the sword" in 1846, or in his oration from the dock in 1848, delivered just after he had been convicted of treason. "Even here," he declared, in a phrase that echoed the last words of Emmet, "the hope which has beckoned me to the perilous seas on which I have been wrecked, still consoles, animates and enraptures me." His only wish had been to make Ireland "a benefactor to humanity, instead of being the meanest beggar in the world." For his "treason" he acknowledged no guilt: on the contrary, he felt it "sanctified as a duty; it will be enrolled as a sacrifice."

In Meagher's own account of the role he played during the rising, he sounds the authentic note of Tone's lighthearted insouciance. "I gave myself up," he wrote, "to the gay illusion of a gallant fight. I was full of life and hope, and welcomed the struggle with a laughing heart." Like Tone he had daydreams of entering Dublin in triumph at the head of thousands of followers; like Tone, also, he was prepared to lay down his life for Ireland, "whose freedom has been my fatal dream."

In Tasmanian exile—"those clouded days of solitude, silence and captivity"—Meagher was homesick for "the exquisite wild Liffey as it flowed near Clongowes Wood . . . deepening . . . under ruins and raths," its dark waters teeming with red salmon and speckled trout. Nor could he forget the miserable hovels dotting the plain of Kildare "in the drenching black rain of December." Even at the other end of the world, that recollection chilled him to the heart. Yet though Ireland was inexpressibly dear in memory—and never again was he to behold sunlight and cloud upon her mountains—on no occasion did Meagher ever express regret for what he had done or wish that he had acted otherwise. In Tasmania he was constantly preoccupied with thoughts of Ireland and absorbed by what he termed "the jealous love with which I sit in sorrow by her tomb, awaiting her resurrection."

Sometimes he would foregather with his fellow exiles under the Southern Cross to sing Irish songs and talk about old times, recalling "the red griefs, and the golden memories of our sad, beautiful old country." In the presence of strangers, however, they would all keep silence. "Before the leering eyes of such a community," wrote Meagher, "I would rather die than unveil the bleeding figure of our poor country, and for her wounds and agonies beseech a single tear."

In 1852, Meagher escaped from captivity and made his way across the Pacific to America. He settled in New York and was admitted to the bar of that state; but he refused a public reception in his honor, since Ireland still "remained in sorrow and subjection." When the Civil War broke out, he at once raised an Irish Brigade to fight for the Union. "Never," he declared, "never, I repeat it, was there a cause more sacred, nor one more great, nor one more urgent." Meagher was commissioned with the rank of Brigadier General in the United States Army. His intention was not only to vindicate the Union but to create a combat-tested force that might liberate Ireland once the Civil War was over.

Unfortunately for such hopes the Brigade, which fought with reckless courage, suffered frightful losses at Antietam, where two horses were shot from under Meagher, and again at Fredericksburg, in 1862. After the latter engagement, where the corpses of exiled Irishmen were piled in mounds before the Confederate cannon, the effective strength of the Brigade was reduced from 1,200 to 280. Finally, at Chancellorsville on May 3, 1863, after furious fighting, the Brigade was virtually annihilated. After the war, Meagher was appointed Acting Governor of the Montana Territory, where at Fort Benton on July 1, 1867, he was accidentally drowned in the flood waters of the Missouri, whence his body was never recovered.

Mitchel's Jail Journal

Unlike Meagher, who was a southerner from Waterford and a Catholic, John Mitchel was a dour, saturnine northerner from Newry,

County Down. He had been brought up a Unitarian by his father, formerly a member of the United Irishmen. As a child he had become familiar with the tragic history of Ireland and brooded passionately upon her accumulated wrongs. Mitchel's dark gray eyes were described, by one observer, as "full of dreams and melancholy." In complexion he was "sallow, colourless, bloodless." Self-centered and impetuous, quarrelsome and cantankerous, he was a man of indomitable will and a most formidable opponent.

By profession, Mitchel was a practicing barrister, but on settling in Dublin in 1845, he gave up the law for journalism, succeeding Thomas Davis as editor of *The Nation*. His highly personal style—violent, vituperative, and loaded with invective—was modeled on that of Carlyle. It quickly made him the best-known journalist in Ireland and by drawing down upon him the unwelcome attentions of the British government, made inevitable his arrest and transportation. From O'Connell, who had been the idol of his youth, Mitchel turned away with scorn and almost loathing. He exhorted his fellow countrymen no longer to attend to words but to put their trust in weapons. "I know very well," he wrote satirically, "that this whole idea and scheme of mine wears a wonderfully silly and feeble aspect in the eyes of statesmanlike revolutionists. . . . We must openly glorify arms, until young Irishmen are born to handle them, and try their temper; and this we must do in defiance of 'law.' "

Hatred of England and of the British Empire was a lifelong obsession with John Mitchel. Through all the vicissitudes of his turbulent career—in Ireland, in Tasmania, in America, in France—it comforted and sustained him. It satisfied his deepest emotional needs. In a changing world it was his one fixed point of reference. Such hatred was but the reverse side, however, of a passionate love of Ireland, and it was nourished not only by his recollections of the cruelties he had suffered but also by his memory of the cruelties to which for seven centuries his beloved country had been subjected.

The turning point of his life came when, in his early thirties, during the course of his travels through Ireland, Mitchel witnessed the horrors of the Famine. In every fiber of his being he revolted against a system that was responsible for such suffering as he saw. Even in 1848 when the worst was over, Mitchel's imagination was haunted by the memory of "bands of peasants trooping to the already too full poor houses; straggling columns of hunted wretches, with their old people, wives and little ones, wending their way to Cork or Waterford, to take ship to America; the people not yet ejected, frightened and despondent, with no interest in the land they tilled, no property in the house above their heads, with the slavish habits bred by long ages of oppression ground into their souls and that momentary proud flash of passionate hope kindled by O'Connell's agitation, long since dimmed and darkened by bitter hunger and hardship."

In the pages of his journal written in a Tasmanian convict station, Mitchel's hatred for England burns at white heat. Yeats's friend Lady Gregory used to say that one could learn more about Irish history from Mitchel's *Jail Journal* than from any other source whatever. Sir Desmond MacCarthy, the well-known Bloomsbury critic, advised Englishmen to read it if they wished to understand why the Irish hated England. But it is equally true that one can hardly understand the passion of the *Jail Journal* without an antecedent knowledge of Irish history.

Mitchel considered the British Empire to be "the most base and horrible tyranny that has ever scandalized the face of the earth." "Empire of Hell!" he inveighed. "When will thy cup of abominations be full?" When he thought of Ireland and her wrongs, he echoed the terrible hope of the Psalmist, "that thy foot may be dipped in the blood of thine enemies, and that the tongue of thy dogs may be red with the same." He excoriated the British government as "a ferocious monster—the most authentic agent and vice-gerent of the fiend upon earth." "While I hold a pen," he raged, "it must forever by my most sacred duty to expose the cant of that diabolical Power."

The Famine itself he held to have been the result of a diabolical conspiracy to exterminate the Irish people—a conspiracy "hatched in the bloodthirsty dens of Downing Street" and put into effect by "a gang of ruffians in coronets and ermine." When in 1854 the Crimean War broke out, Mitchel at once saluted Nicholas I, the most ruthless autocrat of the Western World and the destroyer of Poland's freedom, as a true champion of liberty. For Mitchel it was sufficient that Nicholas was England's enemy. "O Czar," he exulted, "I bless thee. I kiss the hem of thy garment. I drink to thy health and longevity. Give us war in our time, O Lord. . . . Who can tell what the chances and changes of this blessed war may bring us?" Even after the Crimean War had ended in a bloody stalemate, Mitchel never ceased to hope that some future conflict would humble the pride of the empire he detested. Grimly he would console himself with the thought that one day "England, the enemy of the human race, will come down and sit in the dust like the daughters of Babylon."

Mitchel's capacity for hatred was unhappily not exhausted by his Anglophobia. When he escaped from Tasmania in 1854 and came to the United States, he shocked his American hosts by the violence of his abuse of democracy, humanitarianism, and progress—"this foul spirit of the age," as he called the latter. Just because he stood for Irish freedom was no reason why he should champion people like the Jews or the Negroes, whom, following his master Carlyle, he considered racially inferior. "The right of the Irish people to independence," he proclaimed defiantly, "never was, never is, and never can be dependent upon the admission of equal right in all other peoples." During the Civil War he not only supported the South but gave to the Confederate Army three sons, two of whom were killed in battle.

Yet so stern a misanthropist and self-styled Stoic was capable—where Ireland was concerned—of the utmost tenderness of feeling. While he was in the hold of a convict ship in the Bermudas, Mitchel's thoughts turned fondly toward the cherished island of his dreams. "Well-known to me by day and night," he wrote, "are the voices of Ireland's winds and waters, the faces of her ancient mountains. I see it, I hear it all—for by the wondrous power of imagination, informed by strong love, I do indeed live more truly in Ireland than on these unblessed rocks."

Alone on deck at midnight in the South Atlantic as the ship "tore through the heavy seas under close-reefed topsail," and watching "the grim, white moonlight on the tossing manes of ten thousand breaking billows," Mitchel would comfort himself by remembering how "the winter moon of these southern oceans is no other than the harvest moon of Ireland, shining calmly into the room where my children are sleeping this blessed night." And in Tasmania he had but to recite some lines from Mangan's "Dark Rosaleen," and "through his dreams there shines in upon him the beautiful mournful face of his dark Roisin Dubh, the torn and crushed dark rose that he has worn in his heart from a boy, thrilling him with an immortal passion."

Young Ireland and the Future

In his *History of Ireland,* Mitchel sardonically summarized the reason for the failure of Young Ireland. "The island bristled with 40,000 bayonets. 'Tranquillity reigned in Warsaw.'" Yet it would not be just to dismiss that movement as a total failure. The fiasco of the Widow McCormack's cabbage patch in Ballingarry was soon forgotten, but the ballads of *The Nation* lived on.

In his *Recollections,* written nearly fifty years later, John O'Leary suggested that Young Ireland had not been a failure, since it had kept alive the tradition of national revolt. Fenianism, he maintained, was the logical result of Young Ireland, as Young Ireland had been of ninety-eight.

Young Ireland was poetry in action. Had it produced only the *Jail Journal,* it would have made a notable contribution to Irish history. The words of Mitchel, wrote O'Leary, "have fallen trumpet-tongued on the ears of two generations of his countrymen." In 1883 there appeared the memoirs of the last surviving leader of the movement—Gavan Duffy's history of *Young Ireland*—and Yeats in his autobiography recalled the excitement with which he and his friends had become aware of the romantic poetry to which Duffy had introduced them. Thus Young Ireland became one of the many springs that fed the Irish Literary Renaissance.

Nor, with Irish freedom gained, has Mitchel's *Jail Journal* exhausted its meaning for the modern world. So fierce a hatred and so savage a denunciation constitute a warning to those who tyrannize over their fellow men. In a work like Frantz Fanon's *The Wretched of the Earth* (1965) one hears again the note of outrage provoked by intolerable wrong and sounded by Mitchel more than a hundred years ago. Now, however, the oppressed who are becoming aware of their far from inevitable wretchedness are not the people of a single small island but the majority of the world's population.

Ireland in the 1850s

In England, the 1850s and 60s saw the greatest prosperity that country had yet known; for Ireland, however, they were a period of lethargy and stagnation, marked by a constant stream of emigration abroad, and at home by the eviction of some 300,000 families. Ireland, as John Bright observed, was a "land of evictions."

During this period the single promising event was the founding in 1850 of the Tenant Right League by Sharman Crawford, Gavan Duffy, the last remaining leader of Young Ireland, and others. In the North, as a result of the circumstances of the original Scotch-Irish settlement, tenants had certain customary safeguards—security against the threat of instant eviction, and compensation for improvements made—such as existed nowhere else in Ireland. The aim of the League was to extend this Ulster "tenant right" to all tenants and get it confirmed by statute. These objectives were stigmatized by the Prime Minister, Lord Palmerston, himself a rich absentee Irish landlord, as "communistic." "Tenants' right is landlords' wrong" was the slogan coined by Palmerston to defend the interests of the small class to which he belonged.

"I have loved to see in the North of Ireland," wrote John Mitchel, "the smoke of the homesteads of innumerable brave working farmers, rising from a thousand hills; and often in my summer wanderings . . . from the farthest wilds of Donegal to the pleasant fields of Down and Armagh, we have dreamed that our country's hope lay in the quiet extension of this tenant-right spirit and practice throughout the island."

The League offered John Stuart Mill, who was wholly in sympathy with its views, a seat in parliament for an Irish county, but Mill's duties at the East India House obliged him to decline the proposal. Soon after this, the League was virtually taken over by two self-serving demagogues, John Sadleir and William Keogh, whose followers, from their ostentatious piety and plethora of clerical hangers-on, became known derisively as "the Pope's brass band." Hence the League became discredited. In disgust, Gavan Duffy emigrated to Australia in 1855, and the Tenant Right League wilted away.

It was during this period that Marx and Engels first became interested in Ireland, Engels visiting that country for the first time in May, 1856. Whole villages, he reported, had been "devastated" by evictions; but what chiefly astonished him was the large number of police everywhere, all equipped with carbines, bayonets, and handcuffs. Not even in Germany had he seen so many police. "Gendarmes, priests, lawyers, bureaucrats, squires in pleasing profusion" were the most prominent figures of the Irish social scene, Engels remarked sarcastically.

Partly because of his personal feeling for two Irish sisters, Lizzie and Mary Burns, the former of whom he was to marry in 1864, Engels took an active interest in the welfare of Ireland. He even learned some Gaelic and contemplated writing a history of Ireland, some notes for which were found after his death. Engels' proposed method for improving the condition of the peasantry was simple but drastic—the liquidation of the landlord class. "Those fellows ought to be shot," he told Marx breezily. "Of mixed blood, mostly tall, strong, handsome chaps, they all wear enormous moustaches under colossal noses and give themselves the sham military airs of retired colonels. . . ."

Partly on the basis of what Engels had reported, in the first volume of *Das Kapital* Marx devoted some space to agrarian conditions in Ireland, a country that he succinctly described as "the fortress of English landlordism." He gave statistics to prove, what was in fact the case, that that island was fast becoming "an English sheep-walk and cattle pasture."

In the radical New York *Tribune* he exposed the injustice of evictions and (like Lalor before him, and Davitt in the years ahead) advocated the nationalization of Irish land.

"The landlords of Ireland," Marx wrote in 1859, "are confederated for a fiendish war of extermination against the cotters [peasants]. . . . The small native tenants are to be disposed of without more ado than vermin is by the housemaid." Ten years later, he persuaded the Council of the first Communist International, branches of which had been formed in Dublin, Cork, Kilkenny, and other Irish towns, to pass a resolution approving Irish freedom. Of the Irish who had emigrated to America, Marx correctly observed: "Their sole thought, their sole passion, is hatred of the English." If only English statesmen had analyzed the Irish agrarian problem as objectively as did Marx, much future violence and bloodshed might well have been averted.

The Founding of the I.R.B. (1858)

The Irish Republican Brotherhood was founded in New York in 1858. A revolutionary organization, bound by a secret oath, it was dedicated to the achievement of Irish independence by force of arms. Its moving spirit was John O'Mahony (1816–77), a tall, handsome Tipperary farmer who had taken part with Young Ireland in 1848. After the failure of the rebellion, he had fled to Paris and lived there in abject poverty for four years before settling in New York in 1852.

O'Mahony, a graduate of Trinity, was a fine Gaelic scholar who had translated Geoffrey Keating's seventeenth-century *History of Ireland* from Gaelic into English. From his familiarity with ancient Irish history came a masterstroke of nomenclature—the bestowal upon the I.R.B. of the romantic appellation "Fenian." No other word touched as deep a chord in the national consciousness. It added to the danger of the present the glamor of the imagined past. In America the I.R.B. was also to become known as the Clan-na-Gael.

John Boyle O'Reilly, a leading figure among Boston Irish-Americans, has left a moving description of the founder of the Fenian Brotherhood as he appeared in his later years.

A tall, gaunt figure—the mere framework of a mighty man; a large, lusterless face, with deep-sunken, introverted eyes; faded, lightish hair, worn long to the shoulders; an overcoat always buttoned, as if to hide the ravages of wear and tear on the inner garments; something of this, and something too of gentleness and knightlihood, not easily described, were in the awkward and slow-moving figure, with melancholy and abstracted gaze, so well known to the Irishmen of New York as John O'Mahony.

By the end of the Civil War, it is claimed that there were some 3 million Irish emigrants settled in North America, of whom 200,000 were veterans who had fought in the Union Army; others put the number of soldiers at only half that figure. It was from this reservoir of trained soldiers, most of whom had been born in Ireland, that the I.R.B. expected to raise a force for the liberation of their native land. But in 1867, when the time for action came, few of these veterans, many of whom were married men with families, were willing to hazard all on so desperate an enterprise. Grandiose plans for a Fenian invasion of Canada in 1866 collapsed as ignominiously as the Jameson Raid was to do nearly thirty years later in South Africa.

Almost simultaneously with the founding of the I.R.B. in New York, a similar organization was established in Dublin by James Stephens (1825-1901). Stephens was a mining engineer from Kilkenny who, like O'Mahony, had fought for Young Ireland in 1848 and who combined considerable organizing ability with knowledge of the world. Small, aggressive, and overbearing, Stephens made enemies readily enough. John O'Leary considered him a man of ability, but stubborn, intolerant, imperious, and ill-tempered.

In 1865, Stephens claimed there were some 200,000 Fenians in Ireland, of whom at least 50,000 he believed to be well armed. He counted on military aid not only from America but also from the Irish who were domiciled in Britain. He estimated further that there were about 15,000 Fenians among Irishmen serving in the British Army, an estimate that was shared by Michael Davitt, a poor emigrant from Mayo who had become a Fenian organizer in England. John Devoy (1842-1928), whom Stephens had selected for similar work in Ireland, calculated that out of a British garrison of 25,000, some 7,000 were "sworn Fenians," including 1,000 men out of a Dublin garrison of 6,000.

Stephens created—at least on paper—an elaborate monolithic organization in "circles" (cells) under leaders called "centers," with himself in charge of the whole structure as "Head Center." Some ammunition had been smuggled into Ireland, and the rebels planned at the outset of the rising to seize English arsenals and equip themselves from English stores.

In 1865, Stephens was arrested and confined in Richmond Prison in Dublin, a jail that was supposed to be escape-proof. Such a supposition overlooked the sympathies of the jailers, who were themselves Irish; and in 1866, with the aid of some friendly warders, Stephens made a spectacular escape and immediately became a national hero. Nevertheless, Stephens' dictatorial ways had made so many personal enemies within the I.R.B. that on the eve of the Rising he was deposed from the leadership. One of his feuds had been with Devoy, who was likewise arrested at this time and sentenced to fifteen years' penal servitude. After four years in English prisons, Devoy was released by amnesty in 1871. Devoy, whom Desmond Ryan calls "the most practical, pertinacious and successful of the Fenians," then emigrated to New York, where for the next fifty years he nursed an implacable hatred of England and plotted the overthrow of English rule in Ireland.

The Fenian Rising of 1867

While Stephens and Devoy were actively planning a military uprising, another group of young idealists, some of whom had risen in 1848, sought to arouse public opinion in anticipation of such an attempt. The *Irish People* was founded on November 28, 1863, with John O'Leary (1830–1907) and Thomas Clarke Luby (1821–1901) as joint editors, O'Donovan Rossa (1830–1915) being business manager. This little group was soon joined by Charles James Kickham (1826–82), later to be famous as the author of *Knocknagow,* perhaps the most popular patriotic novel ever written in Ireland, though devoid of literary merit.

The Fenians, on the whole, came from the lower-middle classes and lacked the aristocratic bias that marked Smith O'Brien and other Young Irelanders. Their strength lay among the shopkeepers of the towns rather than among the peasants of the countryside. Superciliously, the *Annual Register* described them as belonging to "a class somewhat above the lowest—medical students, law clerks, shopmen, tavern keepers, commercial travellers, tailors." To aspersions of this sort a proud man of relatively humble origin, such as John O'Leary, was not entirely indifferent. No doubt the urban background of the Fenians accounted, at least in part, for the lack of interest in the agrarian problem which they had in common with Young Ireland.

During the American Civil War, the *Irish People* enthusiastically championed the cause of the Union. Unfortunately, no one approaching Thomas Davis or John Mitchel in literary ability was connected with the paper, and as O'Leary ruefully admitted, his own writing was

incurably discursive. The editors of the *Irish People,* moreover, while
they looked back to Young Ireland with admiration, could not but
recall how that movement, for all its brave words, had failed. The
remembrance made them—like Sinn Fein later—suspicious of rhetoric.
O'Leary, nevertheless, once confessed himself puzzled that the Fenians seemed unable to produce stirring ballad poetry like that which
The Nation had inspired. The complaint was premature, for a rous-
ing new song, "The Rising of the Moon," was soon to sweep the
country and be forever associated with the Fenians.

On September 15, 1865, the *Irish People* was suddenly suppressed
and its editors thrown into jail. Isaac Butt, the brilliant Protestant
barrister who later founded Home Rule, defended the Fenian leaders
with great courage but in vain. O'Leary, Luby, and Kickham received vindictive sentences of twenty years apiece—even Mitchel
had got only fourteen in 1848—while Rossa was sentenced to life
imprisonment. An eyewitness at the trial of John O'Leary long remembered "the flash of fire in his dark eyes and the scowl on his
features" and how he had looked "hatred and defiance at judges,
lawyers and jurymen."

The suppression of their paper, followed soon afterwards by the
arrest of Stephens and Devoy, plunged the Fenians into confusion.
It was soon discovered that the number of recruits on which they
had counted was vastly inflated and that Stephens' much-vaunted
organization existed chiefly on paper. Almost no help was forthcoming from America. When the day appointed for the rising—
Easter Sunday, 1867—finally arrived, the result was an even greater
fiasco than in 1848. As the crowning misfortune, on the appointed
day in March a blizzard of unusual severity swept over Ireland,
immobilizing everything and burying the land under snow. As in the
days of Wolfe Tone, once more Nature seemed adverse to the cause
of Irish independence.

Katherine Tynan, the novelist and poet, long remembered how the
would-be rebels had crept down to Dublin from the mountains, half-
frozen, exhausted, and disillusioned, to be cared for at Whitehall,
her father's hospitable farmhouse just outside the city. Only in Kerry
and Limerick was there even a pretense of revolt. The chief suspects
were quickly rounded up. If 1848 was tragicomedy, 1867 seemed
pure farce.

Some Fenian prisoners were sent to Manchester in England. In
an attempt to rescue them, a guard was killed. Three young Irishmen
who had taken part in the raid—William Allen, Michael Larkin, the
grandson of a rebel who had been flogged in 1798, and Michael

O'Brien, who had emigrated to America and fought as a lieutenant in the Union Army—were arrested and, though none of them was proved to have fired the fatal shot, on the murky morning of November 23, 1867, all three were hanged in Manchester before an enormous jeering mob, drawn from the dregs of the city's slums. This execution, as it happened, proved to be the last public hanging in England.

From a psychological point of view, the hanging of the "Manchester Martyrs"—the first political executions since that of Emmet in 1803—was a serious blunder. Until then, public opinion in Ireland had been indifferent to the Fenians, but overnight, as Sir James O'Connor observes, "the executions wrought the people into a frenzy of rage." Huge protest meetings were held in Dublin, Cork, and many other cities. All Ireland suddenly found itself mourning the death of three hitherto unknown individuals—"those simple but sublime young men," John O'Leary called them, voicing the sentiments of his fellow countrymen.

It had been reported that, when sentenced to death, each of the three had cried out: "God save Ireland." This saying inspired Timothy Sullivan, an ardent nationalist from Bantry, County Cork, to write some banal verses that gained immediate popularity throughout Ireland.

> High upon the gallows tree
> Swung the noble-hearted three
> By the vengeful tyrant stricken in their bloom;
> But they met him face to face
> With the courage of their race,
> And they went with souls undaunted to their doom.
>
> God save Ireland, said the heroes.
> God save Ireland, say we all.
> Whether on the scaffold high
> Or the battlefield we die,
> What matter when for Erin dear we fall.

In this unexpected fashion, John O'Leary's plaint about the dearth of Fenian ballad poetry was answered. "God Save Ireland" became almost a national anthem, endowed with power to generate a high degree of mass emotion. That year, too, the young English poet, Algernon Charles Swinburne, still a romantic rebel, wrote his "Appeal for the Condemned Fenians," an indiscretion that, according to Sir Charles Petrie, may have cost him the laureateship on the death of Tennyson in 1892.

With the execution of the "Manchester Martyrs," the Fenian Brotherhood was consecrated by the shedding of blood—as Young Ireland had never been. As later in 1916, the British government had done for the rebels what they had been unable to do for themselves: it exalted and glorified them. After years of fruitless conspiracy, the spirit of Fenianism swept the country. Alexander M. Sullivan, brother of Timothy and father of the Sergeant Sullivan who was to defend Roger Casement, published the last words attributed to Allen, Larkin, and O'Brien in a volume called *Speeches from the Dock,* a book that also contained the last statements attributed to the United Irishmen and to Robert Emmet. The book went through many editions and became a sort of Bible of modern Irish nationalism.

One unforeseen result of the execution of three obscure Irishmen was the profound effect it had on a young Irish undergraduate then at Cambridge—Charles Stewart Parnell. Brought up by his mother to dislike England, this influence had been partly counteracted by the wholly English education—from prep school to university—that Parnell had received. The vengeance at Manchester, together with the revulsion that a proud and sensitive young man could not help but feel at hearing his countrymen everywhere traduced as criminals and murderers—these experiences combined to convert Parnell to militant nationalism. The "Manchester Martyrs," therefore, played their part in producing the most formidable antagonist—not excluding O'Connell—that had ever crossed the Irish Sea to do battle with the English in the House of Commons.

The Catholic Church and the Fenians

One reason why the Fenians, until the hanging of "the noble-hearted three," had lacked popular appeal was their condemnation by the Catholic Church. The Irish Republican Brotherhood was a secret society, bound by oaths, and openly espoused violence as a means to the end of national liberation. From the beginning, John O'Mahony, the founder of the I.R.B., had foreseen this difficulty. He wrote in 1859:

We must calculate upon a certain amount of opposition from some of the priests. I do not, however, consider it judicious to come into collision with them openly. Those who denounce us go beyond their duties as clergymen. They are either bad Irishmen, who do not wish to see Ireland a nation, or stupid and ignorant zealots.

... Our association is neither anti-Catholic nor irreligious. We are an Irish army, not a secret society.

This somewhat casuistical reasoning, however, did not satisfy everyone, and the problem of secret oaths continued to perplex devout Catholics down to the day of Pearse and De Valera. The acuteness of the dilemma may be judged from the fact that, unlike the sponsors of Young Ireland, the Fenian leaders were almost wholly Catholic in background, Luby being the only exception.

As the Fenians became more militant, so did the opposition of the Church become more pronounced, until—as happened later with Sinn Fein—it ended in the denial of the sacraments and in some cases, excommunication as well. Even before the founding of the *Irish People,* the Catholic hierarchy at a general meeting held in Dublin on August 4, 1863, condemned Fenianism *in toto.* Shortly after, some bishops even declared it a mortal sin to read the *Irish People.*

Then, in a pastoral letter of October 10, 1865, the leading churchman in Ireland—the future Cardinal Cullen—described Fenianism as "a compound of folly and wickedness wearing the mask of patriotism ... the work of a few fanatics or knaves, wicked enough to jeopardize others in order to promote their own sordid views." The editors of the *Irish People,* he declared, had "made it a vehicle of scandal and circulated in its columns most poisonous and pernicious maxims. Fortunately they had not the wit nor the talents of Voltaire, but ... they did not yield to him in desire to do mischief and in malice." When one recalls that the ideology thus condemned was the enlightened liberalism of Mazzini, who, while in control of the Roman Republic of 1849, had protected from possible violence Cullen himself, then rector of the Irish College in Rome, one gets some idea of the arrogance involved in Cullen's invective against the "spirit of diabolical pride" allegedly shown by the Fenians. More hysterical even than the fulminations of Cardinal Cullen was the blast let loose against the Fenians from the mountain fastnesses of Kerry by Dr. Moriarty. "Oh, God's heaviest curse," cried out this excitable prelate, "his withering, blighting, blasting curse on them. . . . When we look down into the fathomless depth of this infamy of the leaders of the Fenian conspiracy, we must acknowledge that eternity is not long enough, nor hell hot enough, to punish such miscreants." Sixty years later, a derisive immortality was conferred on these vaporings when Sean O'Casey put them into the mouth of the Paycock and flung them half around the world.

The climax of ecclesiastical hostility was reached in 1870, when the Sacred Congregation of the Holy Office, otherwise known as the Inquisition, solemnly banned the Fenian Brotherhood as an organization whose members incurred excommunication by the mere fact of belonging to it. In the judgment of the well-known Maynooth theologian, Dr. Walter McDonald—later to have his own difficulties with the Church—"this caused the Fenian spirit to evaporate."

Faced by this clerical onslaught, John O'Leary and his friends were not entirely passive. "It is a well-known fact," wrote the *Irish People* on May 7, 1864, "that priests and bishops were found very ready to serve the enemies of their country in '98 and '48. And Irish Catholic bishops were the accomplices of Castlereagh in the murder of their country." The conflict between patriots and priests, prophesied O'Leary, was "a war which will have to be fought over and over again before Irishmen can possess their souls in peace or their bodies in safety." His colleague, Charles Kickham, was even more outspoken. The conduct of the clergy, he declared, was "a scandal which would not be tolerated in any other country in the world but Ireland."

Michael Davitt (1846–1907). Fenian leader and founder of the Land League (1879–82).

Michael Davitt and Tom Clarke

The failure of the rising in Ireland did not mean the end of Fenianism. On the contrary, the more desperate spirits resolved to avenge that failure by carrying the war into the enemy's camp. Anticipating the I.R.A.—for whom they were to serve as a model—the Fenians planned to attack prisons in England, along with public utilities like gasworks and reservoirs. These ambitious schemes mostly came to nought; but only three weeks after the executions at Manchester, on December 13, 1867, some Fenians tried to blow up Clerkenwell Jail in London, with the object of liberating some Irish political prisoners held there. They succeeded only in killing four people who lived just across the street and in injuring 120 others. The Clerkenwell outrage sent a thrill of horror through the English public, who now for the first time received direct proof of the criminal tendencies they had always attributed to the Irish.

In 1870, Michael Davitt (1846–1907), then a young man of twenty-four, was sentenced at the Old Bailey to fifteen years' hard labor for his part in a plot to seize Chester Jail with its store of arms in 1867. Davitt's parents, who were from Mayo, the poorest county in Ireland, had been forced by famine to emigrate in 1846 to Lancashire, where at the age of ten young Davitt went to work in a cotton mill. Accidents from crude, unfenced machinery were then not infrequent, and a year later the boy lost his right arm in such a mishap. If memories of Irish wrong made him a Fenian—"the most remarkable man thrown up by the Fenian movement," Sir James O'Connor calls him—Davitt's experience of what workers endured in Lancashire textile factories made him a socialist.

Clothed in the broad arrow of the convict, his head shaven, Davitt was incarcerated in a succession of English prisons—Newgate, Millbank, Dartmoor, Portland—where, notwithstanding the loss of his arm, he was forced to pick oakum and break up blocks of granite. In *Letters to a Blackbird,* Davitt later described the ordeal, both physical and psychological, that he had endured, sometimes in solitary confinement—from inadequate and filthy food, putrid meat, and soup with beetles in it. For a time he had been harnessed like an animal to a heavily loaded cart, whose chains galled the stump of his right arm.

The amusement of captives, wrote Thoreau, is full of a desperate contrivance. In Portland prison—hard by "the proud immaculate promontories" of the Dorset coast, beloved by Englishmen like Thomas Hardy and Llewelyn Powys—Davitt tamed a blackbird, which became his cell companion. One fine autumn morning he decided to release the bird, which, with a single scream of rapture, flew off into the sunlight. On the day of his own release—amnesty having been granted after seven and a half years in prison—Davitt declared that the ecstasy of his first day of freedom was worth the long, heart-breaking years in captivity. The severity of Davitt's punishment did not deter other Irishmen.

Born in the Isle of Wight, the son of an English sergeant who had fought in the Crimean War, Tom Clarke (1858-1916) grew up in Dungannon, County Tyrone. Too young to take part in the initial Fenian rising, he emigrated in 1880 to the United States, where he became a clerk in a Brooklyn hotel. In his spare time, this small, soft-spoken, seemingly gentle man trained himself in the knowledge and use of explosives, experimenting in blasting rocks with nitro-glycerine. In 1883 he returned to England with his head full of plans and his trunk full of dynamite. Warned by informers whom they had planted within the I.R.B., the police arrested Clarke immediately upon arrival in England. He was condemned to life imprisonment. Actually he served fifteen and a half years, chiefly in Portland, where he worked at hewing granite.

"Relentless savagery" was Clarke's description of his prison treatment. After forty days of solitary confinement and semistarvation in an icy cell, he could neither stand upright nor walk without reeling; yet on being let out, he was at once put on hard labor again. In extreme hunger he chewed the rags that were given him to clean his tinware. More than half of his fifteen closest associates—all of them Irish—went insane from the ordeal of solitary confinement. Their cursing and shrieking made sleep impossible at night. Clarke saw one Irish prisoner receive thirty-six strokes of the cat-o'-nine-tails for destroying the scanty furniture of his cell.

As Desmond Ryan observes, when he came out of prison in 1898, Clarke was endowed with an iron will and fortified by an implacable desire for revenge. To future generations, though he had been too young to take part in 1867, Clarke came to be the epitome of Fenian defiance. In the Easter Rising of 1916, his name was placed at the head of the seven signatures to the Proclamation of Independence, taking precedence even over those of Pearse and Connolly. To the very end, Clarke designated himself not a Sinn Feiner but a Fenian. If character be the tragic adherence of a man to his definition, Tom Clarke's character achieved perfect integrity when in 1916 the bullets of a firing squad at Kilmainham pierced that indomitable heart.

While Clarke remained in Portland jail, the Fenians continued their campaign of violence in England. "Dynamite, Greek fire, or Hell fire, if it could be had"—such was the recipe of the Fenian exile, Jeremiah O'Donovan Rossa, for expelling the English from Ireland. One of the most audacious attempts was that of William Lomasney. This quiet little man had emigrated to Detroit from Ireland after the fiasco of "sixty-seven." Like Tom Clarke, while in America he had made himself an expert in the use of explosives. In 1883 he landed in England determined to blow up London Bridge. Lomasney swam under the Thames, but something went wrong with his calculations, and instead of blowing up the bridge, he blew up himself.

On one single day—January 24, 1885—a series of explosions, none of which caused serious damage, erupted simultaneously in Westminster Hall, the House of Commons, and the Tower of London. "Really people are safer in Turkey than they are here," complained one exasperated Englishman. The dread of explosions became widespread, and lasted in England for about two decades. In some towns, citizens were sworn in as special constables to keep watch upon the activities of Irish exiles, and the Home Office kept in close communication with the chief constables of all towns where there were large Irish populations.

Naturally enough, in England the Fenians were considered to be simple murderers. In jail they were treated not as political prisoners but as common criminals—"condemned to associate," Alexander Sullivan wrote angrily, "with the vilest of the scoundrels bred by the immorality and godlessness of England." All Irishmen then in England came automatically under the stigma of Fenianism and were regarded as highly dangerous characters. Lord Haldane's sister, Elizabeth, has left us an account of the terror inspired by the Fenians in the minds of English children at this time. For her as for others, the typical Fenian was a sinister figure, larger than life, looking like a coalheaver, his brutish mind intent on murder.

In 1867, in *Culture and Anarchy* Matthew Arnold amused himself by drawing an ironical sketch of the English conception of the typical Fenian: "He is so evidently desperate and dangerous, a man of a conquered race, a Papist, with centuries of ill-usage to inflame him against us, with an alien religion established by us in his country at his expense, with no admiration of our institutions, no love of our virtues, no talent for our business, no turn for our comfort."

Yet just across the Irish Sea, the Fenians appeared to their own countrymen in a very different light—as heroes risking their lives for freedom. Michael Davitt spoke for most Irishmen when he extolled "the intense earnestness of purpose, the spirit of self-sacrifice and utter selflessness, which have been the qualities conspicuous in the great majority of active Fenians"; and the pacifist Francis Sheehy Skeffington spoke for the next generation when he affirmed that it was "impossible to contemplate the reckless enthusiasm of the young Fenians without a predominant feeling of proud admiration for the spirit of daring and self-sacrifice which possessed them."

"Glory O! Glory O! to the Bold Fenian Men," the ballad by Peadar Kearney, uncle of Brendan Behan, was to become as popular in twentieth-century Ireland as "God Save Ireland" had been in the nineteenth. Geographically the Irish Sea might separate two islands by only sixty miles, but measured by the gauge of national psychology the two nations were sundered by a gulf so wide that to bridge it by mutual understanding seemed quite impossible. Put simply, the crux of the matter was that one of these two nations refused to recognize the existence of the other.

The Fenian Funerals (1861–1915)

However much the Fenians had failed in action, their memory was to dominate Irish sentiment during the next half-century that lay between Ireland and independence. The new Fenian mythology owed much to the report of sufferings endured by Irishmen in English prisons, but it was also nourished by the ceremonious tributes lavished on the dead. During these years the technique of organizing public funerals for national ends was fully developed in Ireland.

The first of these occurred as early as 1861, when the body of a Young Irelander, Terence Bellew McManus, who had escaped from Tasmania, was brought back from San Francisco for burial in Glasnevin. The multitudes attending the funeral were said to be greater even than those that had followed the bier of O'Connell fourteen years earlier. As the coffin passed through the streets of Dublin, it was set down before the places hallowed by association with the deaths of patriots like Wolfe Tone, Edward Fitzgerald, and Robert Emmet.

Similar demonstrations marked the funeral of John O'Mahony, whose body was brought home in 1877. Thirty years later Dublin was again draped in mourning for the death of John O'Leary, while thousands marched in reverent remembrance through the streets. When, finally, in 1915 the body of O'Donovan Rossa was returned from New York, to be buried like the rest in Glasnevin, Britain was already at war with Germany, and ardent Irish nationalists were planning another recourse to arms. At Rossa's burial, Patrick Pearse pronounced the oration before the open grave. In this speech, so often quoted in later days, the national fixation on sacrificial death achieved its most concentrated expression. His mind full of the desperate venture that he himself was planning, the future leader of the Easter Rising spoke low and earnestly to those who stood by

Rossa's grave. For the last time in public, before the moment when weapons would supplant words, Pearse solemnly "uttered the Fenian creed and praised the Fenian deed." A special intensity was added to the effect of his words by the premonition, shared by many present, that within a few months the speaker would offer up his own life on the altar of national freedom.

John O'Leary (1830–1907). Fenian leader, sentenced to twenty years imprisonment; the symbol of Irish resistance for Yeats and his generation.

John O'Leary (1830–1907)

The Fenians exerted their influence over a younger generation not only by impressive commemorations of the dead but also by the living presence in Dublin of the most remarkable of their early leaders, John O'Leary. Sentenced in 1865 to twenty years' imprisonment, five of which he served in Portland Jail, John O'Leary had been released on condition that he spend the unexpired portion of his term outside the British Isles. O'Leary, accordingly, had settled for fifteen years in Paris, where he had lived on the Left Bank in the bohemian world of artists and writers, acquiring something of their cosmopolitanism and something of their tolerance for various forms of eccentricity. In Paris he had known Swinburne, Whistler, and Turgenev, the anarchist Prince Kropotkin and the nihilist Boris Stepniak, as well as many of the French Impressionist painters. O'Leary's perceptiveness is admirably illustrated by his comment on the prose style of

Walter Pater. Writing as exquisite and as decadent as that of *Marius the Epicurean* was, he considered, evidence of a civilization already in decline—a circumstance from which O'Leary drew favorable auguries concerning the inevitable decay of empire and resultant hope for Ireland.

At his trial in 1865, O'Leary had been distinguished by a superb physical presence, with mane of coal-black hair and flowing beard. When twenty years later, he returned to his native land, his hair had turned snow white—indeed, it was said that the change had occurred during his years in prison. Fifty years after, like an incantation from the days of his youth, Yeats would summon up the memory of— "beautiful lofty things, O'Leary's noble head." To the generation that grew up with Yeats, O'Leary appeared the incarnation not alone of Fenianism but of the sorrows of Ireland. With massive head and luminous dark eyes laden with smoldering fire, his strong features deeply etched by suffering, his white beard descending like a cataract, the old man seemed the last survivor of an antique world, the last representative of an age more tragic than the present could ever know. To Katherine Tynan he seemed a veritable Don Quixote come to life; to Stopford Brooke, a stately Spanish galleon becalmed in tranquil seas. If Gladstone was the Grand Old Man of contemporary England, O'Leary was his counterpart in Ireland.

Unlike Davitt and Rossa, O'Leary never permitted himself to speak of his sufferings in prison. Even in his *Recollections of Fenians and Fenianism* (1896), he preserved silence on that subject. If questioned directly about his experiences, the only answer he would vouchsafe was the terse comment: "I was in the hands of mine enemies." What so ardent a spirit had suffered in captivity, no man knew; but whatever the suffering, with age he had transcended bitterness and lived now beyond the twin goads of anger and hatred that had tormented the existence of a man like John Mitchel.

O'Leary led a celibate life with his sister, Ellen, whom he adored. Extremely poor, he cared nothing for money or power or reputation. "I have rescued nought but my honour," he once said, "and this aged, lonely and whitening head." Free from rancor and envy, by his gentleness, dignity, and extreme simplicity of daily life, O'Leary established a unique moral ascendancy over all who knew him.

After the death of his sister in 1889, O'Leary lived quite alone in Dublin. "Her death," he wrote, "has, as it were, cut me quite adrift from my own past. There is no one now with common memories of family, friends and country. The last is, I think, the hardest part of the blow, and the part for which there is absolutely no remedy."

Even though he had become the symbol of militant nationalism, as time went on O'Leary became more and more old-fashioned in many of his attitudes. Preoccupied with the problem of ends and means, he deplored the violence of Davitt's Land League and condemned the use of assassination as a political weapon. "There are some things a man must not do," he once said, "even to save a nation." That there should be any difference between the standards of private and public morality he called "the devil's doctrine." "You will not in the long run," he told his followers, "either serve Ireland or hurt England by sin or crime." Parnell was the only man in public life whom he supported, and when in Dublin the Irish leader always visited O'Leary. When the scandal of the divorce suit arose, the old Fenian, himself a lapsed Catholic, was one of Parnell's most uncompromising defenders. "Good God in Heaven," he would exclaim, "you can't depose a man for gallantry."

In the years that lay ahead—the period of militant Sinn Fein—the moral problem posed by O'Leary was to become acute, and Irish freedom was finally to be gained by means the old Fenian would have deplored. Somewhat impatiently, Stephen MacKenna was to characterize the old man as "a flaming ineffective lover of Ireland and Irish freedom." Yet even the aged O'Leary felt a quickening of his pulse when in October, 1899, the Boers declared war on England. In fact, he told John Butler Yeats that he felt better at that moment than he had in twenty years.

If Tom Clarke was the link between the Fenians and Sinn Fein, John O'Leary was to link the Fenians with the poets of the Irish Literary Renaissance. "It is one among the many misfortunes of Ireland," he observed in 1886, "that she has never yet produced a great poet. Let us hope that God has in store for us that great gift." At that very moment such a poet was about to make his appearance, and O'Leary was one of the earliest to encourage him. In 1889 he exerted himself to procure the subscriptions that made possible the publication of Yeats's first long poem, *The Wanderings of Oisin*. For Yeats's Irish readers, his glorification of the Fenians of old may have blended subtly with recollections of more recent conflict. Oisin's defiance of Patrick—"I will sit down with the Fenians, be they in flame or at feast"—foreshadowed O'Leary's challenge to an empire. Thus poetry nurtured by feeling for the nation's past in turn stimulated such feeling in the present. So completely did Yeats identify the heroic tradition of revolt with John O'Leary that he considered the latter's death to be the end of an epoch:

> Romantic Ireland's dead and gone,
> It's with O'Leary in the grave.

BIBLIOGRAPHY

Abramowitz, Isidore: *The Great Prisoners* (1946)
Bourke, Marcus: *John O'Leary* (1967)
Davis, Thomas: *Essays and Poems* (ed.) (1845)
_____: *Writings*, ed. A. Griffith (1922)
Devoy, John: *Devoy's Postbag 1871-1928*, 2 vols. (1948-53)
_____: *Recollections of an Irish Rebel* (1928)
Dillon, John: *Life of John Mitchel*, 2 vols. (1888)
Doheny, Michael: *The Felon's Track* (ed.) (1920)
Duffy, Sir Charles: *Four Years of Irish History, 1845-49* (1883)
Fogarty, L.: *James Fintan Lalor* (n.d.)
Fox, Ralph Winston: *Marx, Engels, and Lenin on Ireland* (1940)
Griffith, Arthur: *James Fintan Lalor* (1918)
Gwynn, Denis Rolleston: *Young Ireland and 1848* (1949)
Lalor, James Fintan: *Writings*, ed. John O'Leary (1895)
MacSuibhne, Peadar: *Paul Cullen and His Contemporaries*, 3 vols. (1965)
Mansergh, Nicholas: *Ireland in the Age of Reform and Revolution* (1940)
Meagher, Thomas Francis: *Meagher of the Sword*, ed. Arthur Griffith (n.d.)
Mitchel, John: *Jail Journal* (1868), ed. Arthur Griffith (1913)
Norman, E. R.: *The Catholic Church and Ireland, 1859-73* (1963)
O'Hegarty, Patrick Sarsfield: *History of Ireland Under the Union, 1801-1922*
        (1952)
O'Leary, John: *Recollections of Fenians and Fenianism*, 2 vols. (1896)
O'Sullivan, T. F.: *The Young Irelanders* (1944)
Phelan, Josephine: *The Ardent Exile* (1957)
Reynolds, James: *The Catholic Emancipation Crisis in Ireland, 1824-29* (1954)
Rossa, Jeremiah O'Donovan: *Recollections* (1898)
Ryan, Desmond: *The Fenian Chief: Biography of James Stephens* (1967)
_____: *The Phoenix Flame* (1937)
Strauss, Emil: *Irish Nationalism and British Democracy* (1951)
Sullivan, T. D.: *Recollections of Troubled Times in Irish Politics* (1905)

XI

Parnell and Home Rule

John Stuart Mill and Ireland (1868)

Despite its failure, the Fenian movement marked a new phase in the
troubled history of Anglo-Irish relations. For the first time, though as
yet on a small scale, the United States appeared as a factor in the
equation; for the first time also, however ineffectually, the Irish struck
back at the enemy in his own homeland. Victorian England was not
accustomed to political violence. Now, a policeman in Manchester and
four civilians in London had been killed. "Fenianism," wrote John
Stuart Mill, burst "like a clap of thunder in a clear sky, unlooked for
and unintelligible." Startled in a security that was thought to be
inviolable, the Victorian public reacted with feelings of outrage that
verged upon hysteria.

The turmoil caused by the Fenians led Mill in 1868 to publish
England and Ireland, an analysis of the Irish question based on articles
that had originally appeared at the time of the Famine. Unlike most
Englishmen, Mill viewed the Irish problem as something more than
an outbreak of criminality: he saw it as a moral issue. "Rebellions,"
he wrote, "are never really unconquerable, until they have become
rebellions for an idea." The Irish, in other words, rebelling against
English rule, were not being merely wanton but were fighting for the
ideal of freedom. Simply by realizing that the Irish—like the Poles or
the Jews or the Negroes—were ordinary human beings, seeking what
any human being in their position would desire, Mill came closer to
understanding the needs of Ireland than any Englishman had yet
done. "The difficulty of governing Ireland," he wrote, "lies entirely
in our own minds; it is an incapability of understanding." As Freud
was later to observe, no other man succeeded as completely as did

John Stuart Mill in ridding himself of the customary prejudices of his time.

Many Englishmen, wrote Mill, explained Irish "disaffection" as the result of "a special taint or infirmity in the Irish character." His own analysis went deeper:

There is probably no other nation of the civilized world which, if the task of governing Ireland had happened to devolve upon it, would not have shown itself more capable of that work than England has hitherto done. The reasons are these: first, there is no other nation that is so conceited of its own institutions, and of all its modes of public action, as England is; and secondly, there is no other civilized nation which is so far apart from Ireland in the character of its history, or so unlike it in the whole constitution of its social economy.

Mill was also the earliest to perceive that, partly on account of the growing importance of the United States, the Irish problem was becoming an international embarrassment to England. "What are we dreaming of," he asked, "when we give our sympathies to the Poles, the Italians, the Hungarians, the Greeks and I know not how many other oppressed nationalities?" "To hold Ireland by the old bad means," he warned, "is simply impossible. Neither Europe nor America would now bear the sight of a Poland across the Irish Channel. Were we to attempt it, and a rebellion so provoked could hold its ground for but a few weeks, there would be an explosion of indignation all over the civilized world." It was impossible, he believed, to return to "the reckless savagery of the Middle Ages."

What then was to be done? Turning first to the agrarian problem, Mill, anticipating Gladstone's legislation, urged security of tenure for the Irish peasant and an end to rack-renting. Ultimately, he proposed that the Irish landlords be bought out and peasant proprietorship established throughout Ireland. "Such a change may be revolutionary," he conceded, "but revolutionary measures are now required."

As for the political aspects of Anglo-Irish relations, surprisingly enough Mill was opposed to the reestablishment of Ireland's legislative independence. He was led to adopt this view not because of any belief in the native incapacity of the Irish for self-government but because he feared lest an independent Ireland become, like Belgium, an international battleground. Perhaps Mill's exaggerated fear of France was the result of his personal detestation of Napoleon III as the man who had massacred the working men of Paris in 1851. Given the altered situation in Europe produced by the defeat of France in

1870, it seems highly probable that, had he lived, Mill would have supported Gladstone's championship of Irish Home Rule in 1886.

As might have been expected, Mill concluded by appealing to the conscience of his countrymen. "I shall not believe until I see it proved," he soberly affirmed, "that the English and Scotch people are capable of the folly and wickedness of carrying fire and sword over to Ireland in order that their rulers may govern Ireland contrary to the will of the Irish people." If, however, in defiance of reason and justice, England continued to hold Ireland by force, in that event, Mill forecast: "We shall be in a state of open revolt against the conscience of Europe and Christendom, and more against our own."

William Ewart Gladstone (1809–98). Four Times Prime Minister of England and Champion of Home Rule.

Gladstone and Ireland (1869–70)

Mill's brief essay was the clearest analysis of the fundamentals of the Irish problem that had yet appeared in England. In the light of Gladstone's high regard for the man he termed "the saint of Rationalism," it seems likely that the future Prime Minister was influenced in his Irish policy by Mill's thinking on that subject. For Gladstone was the first prominent English statesman to regard the Irish problem as basically a moral one.

Yet Fenianism also played its part in changing Gladstone's mind. Hitherto he had viewed Ireland's troubles much as every other En-

glish statesman had done. Shocked though he was by the Clerkenwell explosion, Gladstone now for the first time came to realize how
deep must be the sense of injustice among Irishmen if it could drive
young idealists to risk their lives in such acts of desperation. When
notified in December, 1868, of his appointment as Prime Minister,
Gladstone paused in the act of felling a tree and, looking up to
heaven, solemnly exclaimed: "My mission is to pacify Ireland." The
following year he told the House of Commons that Fenianism had
finally convinced him of the necessity of doing justice to Ireland.

The accession of Gladstone to power was the turning point in
Anglo-Irish relations during the Victorian Age. After a quarter of a
century's soul searching, the brilliant young Oxonian, whom Macaulay
had once saluted as "the rising hope of the stern, unbending Tories,"
had become Liberal Prime Minister. With his profound interest in
history, Gladstone could not help being absorbed in the problem of
Ireland. Her troubles weighed heavily upon his conscience. "I do long
for the day," he told Archbishop Walsh, "when poor Ireland shall
cease to drink the cup of sorrow." As long ago as 1845 he had
described Ireland as "that cloud in the West, the coming storm, the
minister of God's retribution upon cruel and inveterate and but half-
atoned injustice." When in that year the French premier, Guizot, had
reproached him about England's treatment of Ireland, so sensitive
was Gladstone's conscience that twenty-seven years later he confessed
to Guizot that he had never been able to forget that criticism.

Gladstone's initial act of justice to Ireland was the disestablishment
in 1869 of the Protestant Episcopal Church, which Macaulay had
described as "the most utterly absurd and indefensible of all the institutions now existing in the civilized world"; and which John Mitchel
had stigmatized as "the wealthiest church in the world quartered upon
the poorest people, who abhor its doctrines and regard its pastors as
ravening wolves."

Gladstone's Act of 1869 was the logical supplement to Catholic
emancipation and ended an injustice that was three centuries old. That
it had not been extorted by the threat of civil war but had been granted
freely by one who was himself a devout Christian was a hopeful
augury for the future. For this righting of an ancient wrong Gladstone was overwhelmed with personal abuse—a foretaste of what was
to come. The Attorney General of Ireland denounced the act as communistic. In Belfast it was said that if the Queen gave her consent,
"her crown would be kicked into the Boyne."

In 1870, Gladstone passed the first Irish Land Act, which, in the
phrase of George Moore, the novelist, brought the Middle Ages in

Ireland to an end. It marked the beginning of state intervention in the hitherto sacrosanct realm of landlord-tenant relations where the latter had always been at the mercy of the former. In effect, the act at last extended Ulster "tenant right" to the rest of Ireland. No tenant in the future could be evicted without warning, and if evicted, tenants should be compensated for whatever improvements they might have made in their holdings. For granting this measure of elementary justice, Gladstone was assailed by English and Irish landowners as furiously as the ecclesiastics had attacked him the year before.

Isaac Butt and Home Rule (1871–75)

The failure of Young Ireland and the Fenians to win freedom by force of arms not unnaturally produced a reaction in favor of the peaceful agitation for the restoration of an Irish parliament which O'Connell had led. In 1871, Isaac Butt (1814–79), a successful Dublin barrister and member of parliament, founded the Home Rule League. Two years later, John Barry, an ex-Fenian and a prosperous commercial traveler, launched a counterpart of this organization in Britain, where by this time more than half a million Irishmen were living. It was called the Home Rule Confederation of Great Britain.

The son of a country parson, a Protestant, and a graduate of Trinity, Butt was a staunch conservative. Yet he was also a confirmed nationalist, who had won public acclaim by his spirited defense of Gavan Duffy in 1848 and of O'Leary and other Fenians in 1865. Although, like O'Connell, he had won fame at the bar, Butt was too indolent to be a successful politician and too tolerant to be a good partisan. John Butler Yeats, who loved to sketch Butt's leonine head, his "black eyes luminous with kindness which nothing could tire," used to say of his friend that he "loved humanity too much to hate any man and knew too much of history to hate any politician." In the midst of a *cause célèbre* in which he was a principal, Butt might be found alone in his inn, reading Thucydides or *Paradise Lost.*

An old-fashioned gentleman, Butt appreciated the leisurely, aristocratic atmosphere of the House of Commons as it had been in the days before the ruthless assault of Parnell shook it out of its comfortable ways. It is understandable, therefore, that the English members approved of Butt, with his "stately rhetoric, his venerable figure and the play of his fingers twirling his glasses." Tim Healy later recalled "the dignified consideration" with which the English members treated Butt, and Disraeli's "courtly politeness" to him as they walked, arms linked together.

Butt disliked the idea of democracy as much as did any English peer. "There is no people on earth less disposed to democracy than the Irish," he once remarked. "The real danger of revolutionary violence is far more with the English people." It is not surprising that the original Home Rule party was dominated by wealthy landlords, many of them Catholic, thirty-four owning 150,000 acres between them. Not even such safeguards against the dangerous spirit of innovation, however, could satisfy the Catholic bishops, who were for the most part intensely suspicious of Home Rule. "I do not at all like this new movement for what is called Home Rule," wrote that inveterate conservative Cardinal Cullen, "for of this I am convinced, that the first future attack on the liberty of the Church and on the interest of religion will come from a native Parliament if ever we have one. . . . I am convinced that the moving spirit in this new agitation in Ireland is identical with that in Italy, that is the spirit of the Revolution, so loudly and authoritatively condemned by the Holy See."

The real defect of Butt, of course, was not that he moved with the times instead of moving ahead of them, but that he lagged behind. Under his flaccid leadership, the Home Rule movement was lacking in vigor. Hence it was not difficult for Parnell, a much younger and more forceful man, to oust Butt from the effective leadership of the party in 1877. Three years later, Parnell was formally elected head of the Irish Home Rulers. "Poor Butt," wrote J. B. Yeats, lamenting the supersession of his friend, "superb in his weakness as in his strength."

Charles Stewart Parnell (1846–91)

Charles Stewart Parnell (1846–91) was descended from an English family that had gained its lands in Wicklow during the Cromwellian confiscations. His great-grandfather had been Sir John Parnell, Chancellor of the Exchequer during the last years of the Irish parliament. The young Parnell had been educated entirely in England, leaving Cambridge in 1869 under a cloud, without having taken a degree. In speech, manners, and dress, Parnell was a typical Englishman. Tim Healy once remarked that he could not even imitate an Irish brogue. His favorite sport was the English game of cricket. Aloof even among friends—his own followers referred to him as "the Chief" —reserved in manner, laconic in speech, sallow and bearded, Parnell was as unlike the caricature of the stage Irishman as could well be. He was equally removed from the Irish conception of what constituted the typical Irishman—as illustrated, for example, by Daniel O'Connell. The ebullient, extrovert Liberator and the austere *"grand seigneur"*

Charles Stewart Parnell (1846–91). The most successful leader of Home Rule.

from Wicklow—as Tim Healy once styled him—seemed hardly to belong to the same country.

As Gladstone was astonished to discover when he came to know him personally, Parnell was ignorant even of the basic facts of Irish history. Of that romantic exaltation of the past which characterized Young Ireland and the Fenians, he had not a trace. He hardly ever referred to the heroes of former days and seldom mentioned names such as Owen Roe or Sarsfield, Wolfe Tone or Robert Emmet. Nor had he the least interest in poetry, music, or the arts. One unusual idiosyncracy was his strong dislike of green, the national color of Ireland. The bent of Parnell's mind was practical, and mining engineering his favorite study. He spent much of his inheritance in a vain effort to discover gold in the disused mines of Bronze Age Wicklow.

Friend and foe alike agreed that excessive pride was Parnell's dominant trait. "His coldness and reserve," wrote Lord Esher, "were the outcome of insensate pride." In this judgment the rank and file of Irish M.P.s, whom Parnell kept at arm's length, would have concurred. Lord Morley, on the whole a sympathetic observer, noted that Parnell's pride was too great to allow him to feel jealousy of any other person. Parnell "hated flattery," said Healy, "but did not disdain an implied compliment."

On his entering the House of Commons in 1875 at the age of twenty-nine, Parnell's quality that most impressed itself upon his opponents was his cold, implacable hostility to England. "He hated England, English ways, English modes of thought," wrote Sir Charles

Dilke. "He would have nothing to do with us. He acted like a foreigner." Cunningham-Grahame likewise recalled how Parnell always spoke of England as if it were a foreign country, and in speaking to an Englishman, with what venom he would fling out the words: "*Your* country . . . *your* Queen." His own wife, herself an Englishwoman, agreed that he had a constitutional aversion to the English and added that he was incapable of understanding them. Legend attributed to him the doubtless apocryphal remark that there was only one way to speak to an Englishmen—with your hand on his throat.

That Parnell's intense antagonism to England owed its origin to more than one source seems clear. As Francis Hackett put it, it derived partly from Bunker Hill and partly from Vinegar Hill. His mother, Delia, daughter of Commodore Stewart, the "Old Ironsides" of 1812, came from a line of Scotch-Irish emigrants and passed on to her son an obsessive dislike of the English, a feeling that was fully shared by her daughters. This influence was reinforced by memories of "ninety'eight" that were still fresh among the peasantry of Wicklow—stories like that of old Gaffney, the gamekeeper, about how a certain Colonel Yeo had flogged a rebel, not on his back, but on his stomach, till his intestines burst out and the unhappy man died. Parnell's sister Fanny believed that it was the hanging of the Manchester Martyrs while her brother was still an undergraduate in Cambridge that had really set him brooding over the wrongs of Ireland. And then there was the mystery, connected with a girl who was said to have committed suicide, that surrounded his expulsion in 1869 from the university, in what must have been an overwhelming affront to his pride.

The Irish loved oratory, but to Parnell public speaking was a most unpleasant ordeal. When he had to speak, he spoke as simply as possible, eschewing rhetoric and the oratorical tricks that O'Connell had always at his command. Dr. Walter McDonald once heard Parnell in Kilkenny. "He was very nervous; not however as if he were afraid of the audience or doubtful of his own powers, but as if he were one seething mass of energy, seeking to burst into violent eruption, but kept under firm control. He spoke a good deal with clenched right hand, and one could see the nails digging into the flesh, while up along his back the tightly-fitted frockcoat showed the muscles playing as an instrument." The voice was of no great volume, but it rang so sharp and clear that it was easily heard by all. Parnell's eyes glinted with a peculiar cold blue-green light—like the glint of a bayonet, McDonald recalled. T. P. O'Connor, Parnell's colleague, on the other hand, remembered the "terrible lights" had flecked the brown of Parnell's flinty eye.

Like Swift, Parnell combined an intense personal resentment of England with an ardent championship of a class to which he himself did not belong but which none the less idolized him. "Through Jonathan Swift's dark grove," wrote Yeats, "he passed, and there plucked bitter wisdom that enriched his blood." In southern Ireland Parnell, though a landlord and a Protestant, was the object of well-nigh universal adoration. Not even O'Connell had been more blindly worshiped by the peasantry. Though he never flattered his country audiences, they gave him the passionate love and devotion of which perhaps only a simple and long-suffering people is capable. Ragged throngs would press around to touch his garments or to kiss his hands and knees. Nuns would stuff images into his pockets, praying for his conversion.

Women especially felt the power of his magnetism and sensed the elemental force that lay beneath the cold exterior. Gladstone's daughter, Mary, was one who, on meeting Parnell, immediately fell under the spell. "His personality takes hold of one," she wrote, "the refined, delicate face, the illuminating smile, fire-darting eyes and slight, tall figure." Forty years after his death, Virginia Woolf noted in her diary that to read about Parnell was still enough to make one's heart beat faster.

As for his effectiveness in parliament, Lord Haldane has described how Parnell once disposed of so formidable an antagonist as Joseph Chamberlain by speaking deliberately in slow, measured tones "as if he were dropping vitriol down Chamberlain's neck." "The House," wrote Haldane, "was pained, and yet overcome by the power and incisiveness of Parnell's words." No doubt the Irish leader took a special pleasure in humiliating so arrogant and bitter an opponent as Chamberlain. Long after Parnell's fall, Haldane, a lawyer accustomed to precision in speech, maintained that he had been "the strongest man . . . in the House of Commons for 150 years." Asquith, known equally for caution in utterance, conceded soon after Parnell's death that he had been "one of the three or four men of the century." Chamberlain himself admitted that Parnell had been a great man but also, he maintained, an unscrupulous one; while Gladstone, who for half a century had known almost everyone in the public life of England and of Europe, declared that Parnell was "the most remarkable man I ever met. I do not say the ablest man," added Gladstone, choosing his words carefully. "I say the most remarkable and the most interesting."

Parnell and "Obstruction" (1875–82)

What first made Parnell's name known and detested throughout England was the policy of "obstruction." Actually, the systematic obstruction of business in the House of Commons was invented, not by Parnell, but by an elder colleague in the Home Rule party, Joseph Biggar, a provision merchant from Belfast. Taking advantage of the House's archaic rules of procedure, Biggar and a handful of friends had learned to hold up business indefinitely. Any member might speak to a given motion as long, and as often, as he pleased. In his "harsh Belfast rasp" Biggar would drone on by the hour, quoting endlessly and irrelevantly from encyclopedias and Blue Books. Conor Cruise O'Brien refers to "his confident ungentlemanliness and his harsh, untiring garrulity."

When Disraeli first laid eyes on the ugly little short-legged hunchback, tirelessly addressing an almost empty house, he inquired superciliously if that were what was meant by a leprechaun? Others alluded scornfully to "the pork butcher from Belfast," but derision was wasted on Biggar. "The glare of the Speaker's eye," wrote Sir James O'Connor, "the frown of great statesmen, the fury of the members who wanted to go home, the sarcasm and abuse of the press affected him not." On one occasion in 1875, when he saw the Prince of Wales upstairs in the Distinguished Strangers' Gallery, Biggar even insulted the heir to the throne by availing himself of an ancient rule to demand that the House be cleared of strangers. "I spy strangers," Biggar called out loudly.

In 1877 a phalanx of seven Irishmen, including Biggar and Parnell, kept the Commons at bay for twenty-six consecutive hours. After 1880, when Parnell took effective control of the party, the number of active obstructionists increased to over thirty. By assiduous study and diligent attendance in the House, Parnell so completely mastered its antiquated rules that he was able to correct even the Speaker on points of order. "We must show these gentlemen," he said, "that if they don't do what we want, they shall do nothing else."

The Irish members were ready to oppose everything that was proposed—even the customary motion "that candles be now brought," which was the prelude to turning on the gas—so that the House continued to sit through a dusk that deepened into darkness. Tempers were frayed and manners forgotten. Some of the Irish displayed their disrespect by coming to the House in a state of intoxication. Members came in reeling, and deplorable scenes occurred. One M.P. collapsed on the floor of the House in the midst of his speech. Still the oratory continued with maddening prolixity. The Irish members, Gladstone once complained, "sometimes rose to the level of mediocrity, but more often grovelled amidst mere trash of unbounded profusion."

The future leader of the party, John Redmond, later recalled his first glimpse of parliament when he took his seat in February, 1881. The Commons were debating a coercion bill for Ireland. Tired and travel-stained after an all-night journey from Dublin, Redmond arrived at eight o'clock on a dark, cold winter's morning to find the members haggard, sleepless, and ill-tempered after an all-night sitting. The House was "one unbroken scene of turbulence and disorder," the floor littered with paper. It had then been in session continuously for forty hours. A handful of disheveled Irishmen on one side faced a hundred infuriated Englishmen on the other. Against one "continuous roar of interruption," Parnell, pale and drawn, was still attempting to speak. The English members were howling at the impassive figure confronting them; some were almost foaming with rage. Contrary to precedent, the Speaker finally ended the disgraceful scene by putting the closure, at which the Irish in protest shouted "Privilege," a cry that had not rung through the Commons since Charles I had intruded in person in 1642. Thus, in order to control the Irish, the House of Commons was compelled to curtail drastically one of the freedoms it had cherished for more than two centuries—unfettered liberty of debate.

In 1881–82 the House was forced to make permanent changes in its rules in order to make obstruction impossible, and so the old relaxed atmosphere of the best gentleman's club in England disappeared forever. "Nothing," complained Winston Churchill long after, "availed against men whose only object was to inflict an outrage upon Parliament, and who gauged their success by the indignation and sorrow they created."

By the recklessness and audacity of his attack upon the cherished rules of the House, Parnell not only crippled its capacity for business but made the "venerable mother of parliaments" the laughing stock of the world. By the same token he became a hero to his own people. The Irish were delighted to read of the uproar created by Parnell's filibustering. From the Giant's Causeway to Cape Clear, his feats at Westminster were gleefully passed from mouth to mouth. Parnell did more to injure England's dignity than all the plots of the dynamiters. At last the tables were turned on the conquerors and the shame of the Union avenged. Parliamentary methods were redeemed from the stigma of O'Connell's failure. By speaking in the great cities of America, Parnell won over the Irish-Americans and gained their financial support for Home Rule. "It is time," said Devoy, "that we come out of the rat-holes of conspiracy." The prestige and popularity of the Fenians were transferred to Parnell, "the uncrowned king of Ireland."

Even in Ireland, however, some of the older generation were shocked by the tactics of obstruction, which Isaac Butt repudiated as "lowering the dignity of the Irish nation and the Irish cause." Many years after his death, a tribute to the elder statesman was paid from an unexpected quarter. Wrote Winston Churchill:

> Butt honoured and cherished the House of Commons. Its great traditions warmed his heart. He was proud to be a member of the most ancient and illustrious representative assembly in the world. He was fitted by his gifts to adorn it. Parnell cared nothing for the House of Commons, except to hate it as a British institution . . . Butt trusted in argument; Parnell trusted in force. Butt was a constitutionalist and a man of peace and order; Parnell was the very spirit of revolution, the instrument of hatred, the agent of relentless war.

Davitt and the Land League (1879)

For thirty years after the Famine, the social problem in Ireland remained unsolved, until in 1879 and succeeding years another series of bad harvests, accompanied by a sharp rise in the number of evictions, once more called attention to the urgency of the agrarian question. The failure of the potato crop in 1879 was the worst since that of 1846. The basic injustice of the social system, which the Famine had demonstrated so appallingly, had persisted unchanged throughout this period.

The desire for quick profits by the landlords who had purchased their land under the Encumbered Estates Act of 1849 depressed the peasantry still further and increased the pressure on them to emigrate. Between 1846 and 1879 rural life in Ireland was distinguished by three main characteristics—continuous evictions, resulting in continuous emigration (between 1869 and 1882 some 130,000 people were forcibly evicted from their holdings),* the constant conversion of tillage into pasture land, and the handsome profits realized by the sale of cattle and dairy products in England. Until the great agricultural depression

---

*On his second visit to Ireland, in 1869, Friedrich Engels was struck by the depopulation that had occurred since his previous visit in 1856.

of the late 1870s, Irish land had been regarded as a safe and permanent investment. This happy period for the gentry was about to disappear forever.

In 1876 appeared the so-called "Irish Domesday Book," an official analysis of the rents of Irish landowners. It revealed that the soil of Ireland was owned by 32,610 landlords, some twenty percent of whom owned eighty-eight percent of the land. The size of the average estate was 2,726 acres. On the basis of these figures, Michael Davitt, in founding the Land League, maintained that 110 landlords owned 4 million acres (one-fifth of Ireland), and that 12 owned 1 million acres. On the other hand, 5 million peasants owned not one square foot of the soil they tilled—and as Davitt took care to remind his hearers, under the ancient Brehon laws, all land had been held in common by the people.

The Land League, founded by Davitt at Castlebar, County Mayo, in 1879, sought the nationalization of land, allowing due compensation to landlords. To achieve this end, Davitt devised two simple but revolutionary weapons: a universal boycott of landlords and the withholding of rent. Within a year, the Land League claimed about 200,000 members, scattered through Ireland in a thousand branches. Nothing to equal the fervor of the League had occurred since the days of the Catholic Association fifty-five years earlier. The Land League, however, unlike the Association, was not led by priests.

Thus there began what Professor Dicey of Oxford called "a murderous conflict between landlords and tenants for the possession of Irish land." Not since the war of the thirties had Ireland known such violence as between 1879 and 1881—murder, mutilation, arson, houghing of cattle. "The very foundations of the Irish social fabric were rocking," an official of Dublin Castle reported to John Morley. "The demoralization, the terror, the rage, the fierce hatred, had grown to such a pitch that we were in sight of general resort to knife and pistol." "With fatal and painful precision," avowed Gladstone in 1881, "crime had dogged the steps of the Land League."

Davitt himself deplored the use of violence but could not control his followers, who fiercely resented what they regarded as the parasitism of the landlord class. That they had been educated to such ideas was partly the work of the American agrarian socialist Henry George, whose *Progress and Poverty* Davitt had read four times in prison and whom he induced to visit Ireland in 1881. "I got indignant as soon as I landed," George declared, "and I have not got over it yet. This is the most damnable government that exists today outside of Russia." To this clear-sighted American observer, Ireland's quest for freedom was but part of "a world-wide revolutionary struggle." The consternation produced by such views not only in Dublin Castle but among the landlords of the Home Rule League may easily be imagined. "Nothing," as Albert Jay Nock wrote in his life of Henry George, "throws a politician into such an agony of nervous horror as the 'idea of enforced association' with a man of principle." The American, for his part, was equally disillusioned by the Irish politicians he encountered, save for Davitt and Parnell.

The growth of the Land League placed Parnell in an awkward dilemma. On the one hand, he wished to free his party from the dominance of the conservative landowners whose alliance Butt had courted, and put himself at the head of the new forces of democracy: the Reform Act of 1885 would increase the number of Irish voters from 200,000 to 700,000. On the other, as a landlord himself, Parnell had no sympathy with the boycott, the no-rent campaign, and Davitt's demand for the nationalization of land. In an effort to control these conflicting tendencies, Parnell accepted the presidency of the Land League in 1880, with Davitt as its secretary.

Parnell's moderation in social matters did not avail to win him the sympathy of the conservatives in the Home Rule League, one of whom described it as a collection of "communists, Garibaldians, atheists, and criminal conspirators." Their point of view was well expressed by the Unionist historian in Trinity, W. E. H. Lecky: "The Parnellite movement was essentially a treasonable conspiracy, promoting its ends by calculated fraud, violence and lawlessness, by an amount of cruelty and oppression seldom equalled in modern times, and by constant and systematic appeals to the worst passions of the Irish people"—a judgment that shows that distinguished scholars are no more immune from prejudice than ordinary mortals. "Ireland," Lecky maintained in 1880, "is the one country in Europe in which murder is supported by the full weight of public opinion."

Another problem facing Parnell was that of obtaining American support for Home Rule, since the Irish-Americans, whose spokesman was John Devoy, were still militantly Fenian in outlook. During the winter of 1879–80, Parnell went to the United States, where, among other audiences, he addressed the House of Representatives in Washington. By his outspokenness, Parnell succeeded in winning the confidence of Devoy—a success made possible only by a certain measure of duplicity. For while in England the Home Rule leaders stressed their loyalty to the Empire, on American platforms they emphasized their separatism. Thus at Cincinnati, Parnell was reported to have said that he intended to destroy "the last link which keeps Ireland bound to England"—a statement that, had it been made in England, would have been fatal to any chance that Home Rule would be adopted.

The significance of Irish-American support for Home Rule, especially in financial matters, did not pass unnoticed at Westminster. "In former Irish rebellions," wrote Sir William Harcourt, one of Gladstone's chief colleagues in the Cabinet, "the Irish were in Ireland. Now there is an Irish nation in the United States, equally hostile, with plenty of money, absolutely beyond our reach and yet within ten days of our shores." It was a portent full of significance for the future.

The Phoenix Park Murders (1882)

In the second Land Act of 1881, Gladstone attempted by sweeping agrarian reform to end the disorders fomented by the Land League. The statute enacted the measures that John Stuart Mill and the Tenant Right League had urged thirty years before. The three Fs now became law: fixity of tenure, fair rents, and free sale of the tenant's interest in his holding. It was a striking comment on the existing exploitation that the tribunals set up by the act at once reduced rents by an average of twenty percent throughout the country.

Apart from Catholic emancipation in 1829, the second Land Act was undoubtedly the most important piece of legislation affecting Ireland passed by the British Parliament during the nineteenth century. For the first time it gave status to the peasant, and security in his holding. It altered beyond recognition the immemorial relation between landlord and tenant. As it had needed the violence of the Fenians to bring about the first Irish Land Act, so now what Professor Dicey termed "the base and brutal tyranny of the Land League" produced the second. The landowners of England vied with their Irish brethren in furious abuse of Gladstone as a traitor to his class and country. "The power of the landed gentry," wrote Lord Salisbury, who had succeeded Disraeli in the leadership of the Conservative party, "is absolutely shattered."

The hopes of peace in Ireland, however, which Gladstone anticipated as the probable result of the Land Act, did not materialize. Half a million law suits resulted immediately. The benefits of the act were not extended to the 100,000 tenants in arrears of rent, so that more trouble arose on that score. Bad harvests continued, followed as usual by agrarian violence. Gladstone was particularly disappointed by Parnell's failure to endorse the new act, upon which the Home

Rulers had abstained from voting. Blaming Parnell for the continuance of disorder, on October 7, 1881, Gladstone uttered his famous indictment of the Irish leader as "marching through rapine to the dismemberment of the Empire." A week later, the Chief Secretary for Ireland, W. E. Forster, the Quaker, invoked a new coercion act to imprison Parnell in Kilmainham.

By arresting "the Chief," the government made him a martyr and raised him to the highest pitch of popular esteem in Ireland. In Kilmainham—a place of evil omen for ordinary prisoners—Parnell was comfortably lodged, with writing materials placed at his disposal. Nevertheless, Kilmainham crowned his popularity in Ireland. In the language of the popular broadside:

> Before all this wrong, all other wrongs of Erin do grow pale.
> For they've clapped the pride of Erin's Isle in cold Kilmainham
>   Gaol.

Some six months later, Parnell was released by an informal agreement with Gladstone known as the "Kilmainham Treaty" (May, 1882), by which the Irish leader promised to accept the Land Act of 1881 providing that peasants in arrears of rent were included in its terms.

Within a week of Parnell's release there occurred what Sir James O'Connor calls "the most shocking tragedy in Irish history"—the Phoenix Park murders. To inaugurate the era of good will that it was hoped the "Kilmainham Treaty" would produce, Gladstone sent over as new Chief Secretary, a mild-mannered aristocrat, Lord Frederick Cavendish, his nephew by marriage. On the very evening of his arrival in Dublin—May 6, 1882—Lord Frederick was murdered with Mr. Burke, the Under Secretary, as they were walking together in the Phoenix Park.

Parnell and Davitt, both of whom had just been freed from prison, at once condemned "the cowardly and unprovoked assassination of a friendly stranger." So profoundly shocked was Parnell that he at once wrote the Prime Minister offering to resign his seat in parliament and retire from public life. Convinced of Parnell's sincerity, Gladstone magnanimously refused to accept the offer. So fierce, however, was the hostility displayed by the large anti-Irish crowds that gathered outside his hotel in London, that Parnell was forced to apply for police protection. Chamberlain wrote that in England the feeling against Ireland was so strong that it almost rivaled the intensity of anti-Semitism in Russia. The murderers, members of a gang calling themselves "the Invincibles," were caught and hanged in 1885, one of their number, James Carey, having turned informer. Carey himself was soon afterwards tracked down and shot dead on a Union-Castle liner off the coast of South Africa.

The Phoenix Park murders marked the nadir of Anglo-Irish relations in the nineteenth century. In a single terrible moment the assassins' daggers seemed to have destroyed the chance of reconciliation between England and Ireland for which Gladstone had striven so earnestly. To most of the English people—and to all of Gladstone's enemies, whose number was legion—the murders proved the innate and unalterable criminality of the Irish people and the impossibility of governing them except by the most ruthless use of force—according to the prescription of Strafford in the seventeenth century. Joseph Chamberlain is reported at this time to have compared Ireland to the gout—as being both incurable and detestable. Some feared the total breakdown of law and order in Ireland. "In 1882," wrote a highly placed Irish friend of Lord Morley, "Ireland seemed to be literally a society on the eve of dissolution. The Invincibles still roamed with knives about the streets of Dublin. . . . Over half the country the demoralization of every class, the terror, the fierce hatred, the universal distrust, had grown to an incredible pitch."

The First Home Rule Bill (1886)

In 1885, by a tactical move that dismayed his friends and astonished his enemies, Parnell joined with the Conservatives to vote Gladstone out of office. To the Liberals it seemed the height of ingratitude that the government that had done more than any other to secure justice for Ireland should be turned out of office by Irish votes. Lord Randolph Churchill, then emerging as a leading Tory, promised in return for Parnell's support a settlement for Ireland "as favorable as any that the Liberal Party would give."

The new government (1885–86) was headed by Lord Salisbury, leader of the Conservative party since the death of Disraeli in 1881; Lord Randolph was a prominent member of it, making his brief, meteoric appearance as Chancellor of the Exchequer. Churchill's pledge was redeemed by Lord Ashbourne's Land Act of 1885, which advanced £5 million (to be repaid at four percent over a period of forty-nine years) to the Irish peasant to purchase his land in cases where the landlord was willing to sell. Gladstone's Land Acts of 1870 and 1881 had also made provision for land purchase, but since the tenant had been required to furnish most of the purchase money, they had failed in their object. The Ashbourne Act was the first step in the momentous process by which Ireland was to be transformed into a nation of small peasant proprietors. It also represented a new tactical maneuver by the Tories—that of "killing Home Rule by kindness." It was hoped that by improving the economic status of some 600,000 tenant farmers in Ireland their attention would be diverted from the politically explosive issue of Home Rule. The future Conservative leader, Joseph Chamberlain—at this time still leader of the radical wing of the Liberals—characterized the Ashbourne Act as "the most flagrant instance of political dishonesty this country has ever known."

It is possible that the brief alliance of Parnell and the Tories was the catalytic agent that precipitated the dramatic conversion of Gladstone to Home Rule. When the latter was again returned to power in the elections of 1886, he at once announced his intention of bringing in a bill to give Ireland Home Rule. Parnell, who in the past had called Gladstone "a masquerading knight-errant" and was later to term him an "unrivalled sophist," now hailed the Prime Minister as "the illustrious Englishman who towers head and shoulders over all living men," declaring him without equal in history as a statesman. All over Ireland appeared oleographs of the Grand Old Man whose picture took its place on innumerable cottage walls beside those of Parnell and O'Connell.

It was now that Gladstone unburdened himself of his famous attack upon the Union as "a paper Union obtained by force and fraud, and never sanctioned or accepted by the Irish nation—the offspring of tyranny, of bribery and fraud." The Conservatives had long detested Gladstone as one who had deserted them—they might perhaps not have felt so strongly had he left their party out of undisguised self-interest, but they could not forgive his defection on grounds of principle—and now they assailed him with fury. No epithet was too vile to be applied, no rumor too outrageous to fail of credence. Gladtone was called a hypocrite, a lunatic, a frequenter of prostitutes, a Communist, a Jesuit, Judas himself.

Lord Randolph outdid the rest of his party in the vindictiveness and irresponsibility of his abuse. "Mr. Gladstone," he charged, "has reserved for his closing days a conspiracy against the honour of Britain and the welfare of Ireland more startlingly nefarious and base than any other of those numerous designs and plots which during the past quarter of a century have occupied his imagination." Home Rule he characterized as "this trafficking with treason, this condonation of crime . . . this monstrous mixture of imbecillity and extravagance and political hysterics." The bill itself was "a farrago of superlative nonsense, designed to gratify the ambition of an old man in a hurry." Gladstone was then seventy-six. If the House had listened to him, rather than to the ranting of Churchill, much future suffering and bloodshed in Ireland would have been averted.

Unfortunately, Lord Randolph did not rely on words alone. Perceiving that to defeat Home Rule "the Orange card," as he cynically termed it, was the right one to play, he went to Belfast in 1886 with the deliberate intention of inflaming the religious prejudices that lay dormant. As the slogan of the new militancy, he coined the phrase: "Ulster will fight, and Ulster will be right." Seventy-three thousand volunteers in the north pledged themselves to resist Home Rule—by force if necessary.

> The combat deepens; on, ye brave,
> Who rush to glory or the grave.
> Wave, Ulster, all thy banners wave.
> And charge with all thy chivalry.

"So, with these words," wrote an admirer, "he departed as swiftly as he had come, never to return, but leaving an indelible memory behind him." Churchill also left behind him in Belfast scores of Catholics injured and dozens killed, in the first of that city's modern "pogroms" caused by religious bigotry. "There were bloody battles with paving stones and firearms," wrote Sir James O'Connor. "The city was in a state of siege." Not without prescience had Mr. Speaker Brand observed four years earlier: "Of all the evils which have arisen in the House of Commons, Lord Randolph Churchill is the greatest." The full irony of this outbreak of religious strife cannot be realized unless one remembers that less that a century before—in the time of the United Irishmen—Belfast had generated a spirit of tolerance such as had never previously been known in Irish history.

"To a House packed from floor to ceiling, seething with passion and excitement," Gladstone introduced his bill for Home Rule in 1886. Opposition only served to emphasize further the imperious elements in his nature, and he exerted himself now as he had seldom exerted himself in a lifetime of political combat. Yet he failed to carry his own party with him. Ninety-three Liberals, led by Lord Hartington and Chamberlain, voted against the bill, which was defeated by 343 votes to 313. Gladstone at once dissolved parliament and held another election but was defeated. He resigned immediately. Since his recalcitrant followers now broke away to form their own party— the Liberal Unionists—Ireland once again proved itself the nemesis of English political parties, shattering the Liberals now, as it had broken the Tories in 1829 and 1846.

One remarkable feature of the Home Rule controversy at this time was the almost unanimous rejection of Irish freedom by the English intellectuals who, a generation earlier, had supported the Union in the American Civil War. John Bright, the foremost defender of the Union, now deserted Gladstone. Among those who publicly rejected Home Rule were scientists like Huxley and Tyndall; philosophers like Herbert Spencer, Benjamin Jowett, and Henry Martineau; historians like Lecky, Seeley, Froude, and Goldwin Smith; political scientists like Dicey; poets like Tennyson, Browning, and Swinburne; and artists like Millais and Leighton. Supporting the Prime Minister were only a handful of distinguished men—such as the novelist George Meredith and the historians E. A. Freeman and Lord Acton. Even so staunch a friend and admirer of Gladstone as Lord Acton had the gravest reservations about Home Rule. "It is with a mind prepared for failure and even disaster," confessed the great liberal historian, "that I persist in urging the measure." To Mary Gladstone, daughter of the Prime Minister, Acton, a devout Catholic, made the astonishing admission that Ireland was "a country where religion does not work, ultimately, in favor of morality."

To explain the lack of sympathy with Irish aspirations that so strongly characterized English public opinion—as distinct from that of Scotland and Wales, where the majority favored Home Rule—four main reasons may be assigned: first, the fear that a self-governing Ireland become a threat to English security by entering into agreements with some Continental Power—a fear that was entertained by John Stuart Mill and that so eminent a naval expert as Captain Mahan also considered valid; second, the belief, expressed by Winston Churchill as late as 1922, that Irish freedom would damage England's prestige as a world power and result in a general loosening of the imperial bond; third, the fear that Protestant Ulster be subjected to religious discrimination from the Catholic majority in an Irish parliament; and finally, the widespread belief that the Irish (like women and Negroes) were essentially children incapable by nature of governing themselves. "It is in human nature," pontificated Froude, echoing his master, Carlyle, "and above others in the Irish form of human nature, that men should obey and honor their born superiors, however worthless these superiors might be."

The opposition of Englishmen to Home Rule is readily explained on grounds of self-interest. More surprising was the antagonism shown to Irish self-government by a majority of the Irish Catholic bishops, including prelates as powerful as Cardinal Cullen and Bishop Moriarty, both of whom identified Home Rule with democracy and radicalism. The hierarchy disliked Parnell and Gladstone in equal measure

—Parnell, because he was a Protestant and favored removing higher education in Ireland from ecclesiastical control, and Gladstone, because of the private war he was then waging upon the recently declared doctrine of papal infallibility. The bishops' distrust of Parnell, whose authority over the Irish people rivaled their own, was well known. Lord Randolph Churchill was not slow to see his opportunity. "It is the Bishops entirely," he wrote, "to whom I look in the future to turn, to mitigate or to postpone the Home Rule onslaught." The only possible Conservative policy, he maintained, was to win "the confidence and friendship of the Bishops." Their lordships, he believed, "in their hearts hate Parnell and don't care a scrap for Home Rule." The vehement hostility to Parnell shown by the Catholic hierarchy after the divorce suit was by no means of such sudden growth as might have appeared at the time.

Rome, too, used its influence to discourage self-government for Ireland. Even a liberal Pope like Leo XIII was as hostile to Home Rule as Gregory XVI in his day had been to repeal. To the Vatican, England was a world power to be conciliated, whereas Ireland was only a pawn on the chessboard of international politics. Seventy or eighty Catholic votes at Westminster constituted an influence in imperial politics that Rome was understandably reluctant to lose. In 1883 a papal encyclical forbade the Irish clergy to contribute to a fund whose object was to relieve Parnell of his debts.

In England, Cardinal Manning, a strong imperialist and a staunch papalist, used all his influence to thwart Gladstone and defeat Home Rule, a measure that he termed a "Catholic and a world-wide danger." If Henry Edward Manning was an adroit politician, John Henry Newman was a man of principle, yet where Ireland was concerned, both prelates, being English, were agreed. Much as Newman, when he had lived in Dublin, had admired the fervor of Irish Catholicity, he judged Irish politics purely from the standpoint of an Englishman. It never even occurred to him that a moral question, as well as a political one, might be involved.

Agrarian Unrest; Parnell and the Times *(1887–89)*

The defeat of Home Rule in 1886 was followed inevitably by renewed violence in Ireland: "Captain Moonlight," that mythical leader of the wronged, took over once again. The shooting of landlords—or of their agents—was resumed. "Do they think they can intimidate me by shooting my agent?" asked Lord Clanricarde, perhaps the most avaricious landowner in Ireland (his grandson was later to marry the only daughter of George V). An apocryphal story was current to the effect that shooting an agent, if not actually meritorious, was only a venial sin.

Parnell's two ablest lieutenants, John Dillon and William O'Brien, now devised against the landlords a new weapon known as the "Plan of Campaign." If tenants felt their rents to be excessive, they were urged to withhold payment and to set aside the equivalent of a "fair rent" to help any who might be evicted. The Church opposed the plan, Bishop O'Dwyer of Limerick being especially outspoken, whereupon Dillon and O'Brien, both devout Catholics, went down to Limerick and denounced the bishop outside his own residence. In 1888 the "Plan of Campaign" was condemned by papal rescript.

Lord Salisbury, back in office as Conservative Prime Minister from 1886 to 1892, had one sovereign remedy for Irish discontent—coercion. "Rightly or wrongly," he announced, "I have not the slightest wish to satisfy the national aspirations of Ireland." Almost immediately after the defeat of Home Rule, he made the well-known speech comparing the Irish with Hottentots and Hindus, two people whom he regarded as existing on the same cultural level.

Salisbury appointed his nephew Arthur James Balfour Chief Secretary, in order to deal firmly with the Irish problem. Balfour was considered a languid and elegant dilettante whose consuming interests were golf, tennis, and philosophy. In Ireland he astonished everyone by a ruthlessness that won him the sobriquet of "Bloody Balfour." The future statesman of the empire let it be known that in his opinion Home Rule had really no popular support but was simply the work of a handful of agitators such as Parnell, Davitt, Dillon, and O'Brien. If they were put to hard labor in prison, the whole movement would collapse. A jail sentence, he added hopefully to his friend Wilfrid Scawen Blunt, might even kill a man like Dillon, whose health was known to be delicate. Personally, he would tolerate no "ridiculous" leniency like that shown by his predecessor, W. E. Forster, to Parnell in Kilmainham. By 1889, Balfour had arrested twenty-four Irish M.P.s (though not Parnell), whom he insisted on treating not as political prisoners but as common criminals.

The years 1887–89 saw Parnell at the height of his fame. On April 17, 1887, under the sensational headline "Parnellism and Crime," the London *Times* published letters allegedly written by Parnell, condoning the use of murder in general as a political weapon and particularly with reference to the Phoenix Park tragedy. Never doubting the authenticity of documents appearing in a paper as authoritative as "The Thunderer," and thinking that this was the end of

Parnell, his innumerable enemies in England were beside themselves with joy. Convinced, as Voltaire said of Habbakuk, that Parnell was capable of anything, no proof was necessary to establish his guilt.

The Irish leader brought suit against the *Times*. For two long years the case dragged on, but in 1889 Richard Pigott, the key witness against Parnell, broke down in the witness box. After admitting that he had forged the letters, Pigott fled to Madrid, where he committed suicide. The *Times* was ordered by the court to pay £5,000 damages. The vindication of Parnell made him more than ever "the uncrowned king of Ireland," and even in England he was regarded as a deeply wronged man. When he entered the House of Commons after his victory over the *Times,* the whole House rose and gave him an ovation, Gladstone bowing low in his direction. Today in Ireland, whenever the Casement "diaries" are mentioned, people cannot help but recall the infamous attempt to ruin Parnell by forgery.

In December, 1889, Gladstone for the first time invited Parnell to be his guest in his country home at Hawarden. The Prime Minister was charmed by the man whom he had formerly castigated as "marching through ruin to the dismemberment of an empire." Now, Gladstone found that "it was an intellectual treat to do business with him." Exactly one year later, Parnell was a ruined man, deposed from the leadership of his party; and two years later, he was dead.

The Fall of Parnell (1890–91)

On November 15, 1890, Captain O'Shea, nationalist M.P. for Galway, brought suit in London for divorce against his wife, naming Parnell as corespondent. The divorce was quickly granted, Parnell not appearing in court. Thus came to public attention a liaison that had lasted for ten years, causing the Irish leader infinite embarrassment before finally destroying him.

Limitations of space make it impossible to give an adequate account of the notorious case. Suffice to say that when in 1880 Parnell first met Kitty O'Shea in London, she had been living apart from her husband for some years. For Parnell it was love at first sight—a love that lasted until death. The necessity, in Victorian England, for keeping such a liaison secret was reinforced by Parnell's political prominence. Newspaper publicity would have destroyed him. Hence in self-protection he was obliged to lead for years an extraordinary dual existence, concealing his movements, making secret assignations, adopting fictitious names, using invisible ink, and altering his appearance by shaving off his beard.

Kitty O'Shea (1846–1921). Parnell's mistress and later his wife.

William O'Brien has put on record one instance of the almost incredible subterfuges to which Parnell felt compelled to resort. One day in December, 1886, the two men agreed to meet at Greenwich Observatory. The meeting took place in a dense fog. After searching around helplessly, wrote O'Brien,

> I suddenly came upon Parnell's figure emerging from the gloom in a guise so strange and with a face so ghastly that the effect could scarcely have been more startling if it was his ghost I met wandering in the eternal shades. He wore a gigantic fur cap, a shooting-jacket of rough tweed, a knitted woollen vest of bright scarlet and a pair of shooting or wading boots reaching to the thighs—a costume that could not well have looked more bizarre in a dreary London park if the object had been to attract attention. But the overpowering fascination lay in the unearthly half-extinguished eyes flickering mournfully out of their deep caverns, the complexion of dead clay, the overgrown fair beard and the locks rolling down behind almost to his shoulders. It was the apparition of a poet plunged in some divine anguish or a mad scientist mourning over the fate of some forlorn invention.

Despite the ruses employed by Parnell, he could escape neither the threat of blackmail from O'Shea, a disreputable adventurer who lived on an allowance from the wife he had deserted, nor the exploitation of O'Shea for political purposes by Parnell's enemy Chamberlain. When in 1890 the affair at last became public, the Chief was faced on the one hand by a revolt within his own party led by Tim Healy, and on the other by the rupture of his alliance with the Gladstonian Liberals. For at this point Irish Catholics and English nonconformists vied with one another in shrill and scurrilous denunciations of Parnell.

Parnell's immediate response was to write an angry "Manifesto to the Irish People," in which he alluded to the "English wolves howling for his destruction." On December 3, 1890, the Catholic hierarchy in Ireland demanded his resignation as leader of the party. Three days later, there took place the famous meeting in Committee Room 15 at the House of Commons, at which the Home Rule party split into two irreconcilable factions, Parnell's supporters being outnumbered by forty-four to twenty-eight. Just after Redmond's remark that Parnell was still the master of the party, Tim Healy impudently piped up: "And who is to be the mistress of the party?" "The effect of this," wrote one eyewitness, "was indescribable." Some thought Parnell was about to strike Healy, but with a strong effort he forebore, calling his opponent "a cowardly little scoundrel who in an assembly of Irishmen dares to insult a woman."

During the ten months that Parnell had yet to live, Ireland was rent in twain. As Joyce reminds us in a familiar scene in *A Portrait of the Artist,* and O'Casey in his autobiography, throughout the nation the controversy divided family against family. Parnell's marriage to Mrs. O'Shea after the divorce—in a civil ceremony, since no clergyman had been found willing to officiate—only increased the outcry of the orthodox. "In Christian Ireland," declared Bishop O'Connell of Raphoe, "this news only capped the climax of brazened horrors." "Parnellism," thundered Bishop Nulty of Meath, "springs from the root of sensualism and crime." No man, he said, could be both a Parnellite and a Catholic. Parnellism was heresy. "I have flung him away from me forever," announced Dr. Croke, Archbishop of Cashel, boasting how he had kicked Parnell's bust out of his front hall. The charity that had been accorded O'Connell's flagrant indiscretions was withheld from Parnell's single breach of convention. Even the moderate Redmond, a devout Catholic, felt compelled to criticize the bishops' intervention in politics.

A flood of vilification was loosed against the Chief. He was venomously attacked in the press. Priests inveighed against him from the pulpit and threatened his supporters with hell fire. At his meetings, pious youths shouting "Kitty O'Shea" flaunted petticoats on poles. In Castlecomer, County Kilkenny, lime was thrown in his face, half-blinding him. Every corner boy in the nation felt qualified to pass on Parnell's private life. "Securing Parnell's retirement as a necessary national sacrifice is one thing," wrote William O'Brien, who had sided against the Chief. "Hunting him down like a wild beast and hacking him to pieces with all sorts of foul weapons is quite another thing." Mrs. Parnell later recalled how her husband had been "appalled by the intensity of the passion of hate that he had loosed."

Generally speaking, the country districts—strongly under clerical influence—repudiated Parnell, while the towns, more independent, stood by him. There were, however, numerous exceptions on both sides, and a number of priests—and even nuns—remained ardent Parnellites. Women were more often likely than men to be defenders of Parnell, and young people more often than their elders. Dublin, in particular, was loyal to the Chief. Katherine Tynan heard him speak on December 10, 1890, amid wild enthusiasm at the Rotunda. Many years after, she recalled him as he stood on the platform, pale and silent, looking down upon a sea of passionate, adoring faces.

Finding himself abandoned by the more "respectable" elements of society—for example, by wealthy businessmen like William Michael Martin—Parnell in desperation bid for the support of the lower classes and "the hill-side men." Led in Dublin by John O'Leary and James Stephens, in America by John Devoy and Mark Ryan, the old Fenians rallied round him almost to a man. Yet a puritan like Michael Davitt, shocked by the disclosures in the divorce court, could condemn his former ally as "a cold-blooded sensualist," "an insolent dictator," and "a tyrant the most unscrupulous that ever rode roughshod over the hopes and sentiments of a nation." It was a curious turn of events when the ex-Fenian Davitt, who had spent long years in English jails, now attacked Parnell's "criminal folly" in urging "the young men of Ireland to face overwhelming might of England in the field."

Parnell, in fact, never urged open revolt, but now for the first time he began to stress the need for social reform. Four months before his death, he told the railwaymen at Inchicore: "The future is with the working classes." Under the double pressure of personal grief and party bitterness, the young squire of Avondale was transformed into an advocate for the proletariat. Keir Hardie, founder of the Labor Party in Britain, later called Parnell "the one man in politics for whom I was ever able to feel a genuine respect."

For a man of Parnell's extreme reserve and pride, his last months of campaigning, during which he made a splendid but hopeless attempt to retrieve his political fortunes, must have been a well-nigh intolerable ordeal. In an effort to rally his followers he spoke all over the country—sometimes in crowded, overheated rooms, sometimes bareheaded in the pouring rain. He slept in poor and dirty country inns and often remained for hours in wet clothes. Yet his language had lost none of its vigor—as when at Freshford, County Kilkenny, he alluded to "the miserable gutter-sparrows who were once my comrades. . . . I will not waste my time and breath," he added scornfully, "upon such miserable scum."

Not long before the end, when Standish O'Grady saw him for the last time, he was shocked to find Parnell emaciated, stoop-shouldered, ill-dressed, nearly bald, and with his remaining hair long and ill-cut. "I was no friend to his politics," wrote O'Grady, "yet I admired the man extremely." J. J. Horgan of Cork remembered how when Parnell had come to that city, "he looked like a hunted fugitive, his hair dishevelled, his beard unkempt, his eyes wild and restless." When the names of his enemies were mentioned, "the hatred in Parnell's face was terrible to behold."

Mentally and physically, in those last terrible months Parnell drove himself toward the grave. Thoughts of death were often in his mind and on his lips. "If I were dead and gone tomorrow" was a phrase he used at Listowel, County Kerry. At Cleggs, County Galway, he charged his opponents with wanting him buried before he had died. To his mother, he wrote that he was "weary of these troubles, weary unto death." Yet in public he breathed defiance to the last. In the final speech of his life, nine days before his death, he exhorted his followers to continue to fight. Even Parnell's most irreconcilable antagonist paid tribute to his courage. "His old skill, energy and unscrupulousness," wrote Healy, "reburned in his frame. Genius shone like the upcast flame from an expiring candle."

Parnell's heart had been weakened by an earlier attack of rheumatic fever. His doctor later stated that physical overexertion, combined with his distraught mental state, had killed him. The trauma of rejection by so many of his countrymen no doubt hastened the end, which came at Brighton, in Sussex, on October 6, 1891. His wife was beside him to the last. Only with reluctance did she give permission for his body to be buried in Ireland—a country that she, an Englishwoman, had never even visited. Mrs. Parnell survived her husband by nearly thirty years, dying on February 5, 1921, at Littlehampton, in Sussex, with his name upon her lips. During the crisis of her final illness, she suffered from the delusion that Parnell had come back to comfort and draw her out of the dark waves. Though she had three children by Parnell, none of their descendants are alive today.

Four days after Parnell's death, his body was brought back to Ireland in the cold and windy dawn of an October morning. W. B. Yeats and Maud Gonne were among the crowd present at Dunleary for the homecoming of the Chief. All day the body lay in state in the City Hall in Dublin as silent multitudes filed past the coffin. A great storm wailed over the city, but by evening when the funeral took place in Glasnevin, the sky had cleared. People long remembered how at that hour the west had been suffused by a peculiar clear green and golden light. The air was now still and chilly. Signs and portents, which later entered into the symbolism of Yeats's poetry, were not wanting. During the burial a meteor flashed through the sky. Some thought they saw a falling star. As the coffin was lowered into the grave, the air was rent by a woman's piercing shriek. And so the Chief was laid to rest beneath a granite boulder hewn from the mountains of his native Wicklow.

Never before in Ireland had so many Catholics listened to the words of the Protestant burial service. Maud Gonne was among the dense and silent crowd that churned up the mud of Glasnevin that evening. Lord Wolseley, the Commander-in-Chief in Ireland, sensed something ominous in the self-discipline of such a multitude, its somber demeanor concealing feelings of passionate grief. It had been the only crowd in his life, he wrote later, of which he had ever been afraid.

Effect of Parnell's Fall on Irish Opinion

In the conflict between Parnell and his opponents, young Irish writers were almost wholly on the side of the Chief. In the Parnellite paper, *United Ireland,* Yeats came close to writing the official verse of a laureate.

> Mourn—and then onward, there is no returning,
> He guides ye from the tomb;
> His memory now is a tall pillar, burning
> Before us in the gloom.

Later, Yeats was fond of quoting Goethe: "The Irish always seem to me like a pack of hounds dragging down some noble stag."

A few years later, as a student in Dublin, James Joyce was presently to write a little pamphlet, "Et tu, Healy," in which he fiercely assailed Parnell's chief accuser. It seems probable that when in 1904, at the age of twenty-two, Joyce determined to leave Ireland for good, indignation over what he regarded as the shabby treatment of Parnell was an important element in his decision. Dublin he scornfully termed "the centre of paralysis" and Ireland "a country destined to be the everlasting caricature of the civilized world." Long afterwards, in a lecture in Trieste, Joyce was to recall Parnell's appeal to his countrymen not to throw him to the English wolves. "It reflects honor upon his countrymen," said Joyce with savage irony, "that they did not fail his desperate appeal. They did not throw him to the English wolves: they tore him in pieces themselves."

In *The Deliverer,* a play performed at the Abbey in 1911, Lady Gregory identified Parnell with Moses, who had failed to reach the Promised Land. In yet another play she likened him to Diarmid stricken on Ben Bulben, with Grania mourning over him: "He was a good man to put down his enemies and the enemies of Ireland, and it is living he would be this day if it were not for his great comeliness and the way he had, that sent every woman stammering after him and coveting him; and it was love for a woman that brought him down in the end and sent him astray in the world."

Thousands in Ireland felt Parnell's death as a poignant personal sorrow. Frank O'Connor remembered hearing from his mother how as a servant girl in Cork she had sat up all night in the kitchen with her mistress, both weeping and consoling each other. Another Cork man, Lennox Robinson, recalled how his nurse had run distractedly about the house, beating her breast and lamenting loudly: "Parnell is dead! Parnell is dead!" In his autobiography, Sean O'Casey was to recapture something of the wild grief of the Dublin slums that day. "Oh, me white blossom of Ireland's spring," screamed a drunken trollop in *Drums under the Windows,* "cut down as you were openin' to th' sun. . . . May Kilkenny, that threw lime in his bright eyes, go crawlin' down to Hell!" Like many another boy, Jerry, the autobiographical hero of Francis Hackett's *Green Lion,* on hearing of Parnell's death, burst suddenly into tears, feeling his young life destroyed and the light of heaven gone out of the sky.

For the next generation of Irish writers, Parnell was to serve as a heroic symbol; for Yeats he represented the proud, self-confident aristocratic spirit disdainful of vulgarity and demagoguery; for Joyce, the victory of the philistines over Parnell signified the moral and intellectual bankruptcy of Ireland from which the artist must seek refuge in exile. The downfall of Parnell united in a special and enduring comradeship all who had stood by him to the end, no matter what later difficulties might come to divide them.

A contemporary authority, Dr. Conor Cruise O'Brien, sees Parnell as the victim of *hubris*, as a man "dazzled by his own myth, preferring a tragic end to self-effacement and the continuation of his policy." The latest biographer of Gladstone reaches a similar conclusion. "He sacrificed his people," writes Sir Philip Magnus, "on the altars of his passion and his pride." Yet the disaster of Committee Room 15 can no more cancel the most remarkable achievement in Irish parliamentary history than the disclosures of the divorce court can destroy the integrity of Parnell's love. Gladstone himself was moved to doubt "whether any politician had ever suffered so much for his country." Even Parnell's bitterest enemy, Tim Healy, later first Governor-General of the Irish Free State, paid tribute to the Chief's uniqueness. "I never knew such a man," he declared, "nor ever read of such a man."

The Second Home Rule Bill (1893)

In Ireland it was commonly believed that Gladstone had contrived Parnell's ruin in order to rid himself of the political embarrassment of Home Rule. Even today the idea that Gladstone was nothing but a sanctimonious hypocrite is often encountered in Ireland. Such notions, as John L. Hammond in his careful large-scale study, *Gladstone and the Irish Nation,* makes clear, are totally unfounded. So far from wishing to abandon Home Rule after the death of Parnell, Gladstone was all the more determined to get the bill passed into law. His indomitable fighting instinct roused by defeat, Home Rule had become an obsession with him; and at eighty-three, half deaf and partly blind, yet Prime Minister for the fourth time, Gladstone hoped to complete his long, unrivaled parliamentary career with the grant of self-government to Ireland. The consciousness of approaching death was dominant in his mind: Home Rule was not merely a matter of political justice but the crown of righteousness by which he would justify before his Creator the manifold gifts that had been granted unto him. It was in such a mood that the old man introduced the second Home Rule bill in 1893.

As before, in the north the Orangemen loudly proclaimed their defiance. Ulstermen, wrote Lecky in 1893, "are at fever point . . . and thoroughly armed." Never would they accept the authority of a Dublin parliament. Though still alive, Lord Randolph Churchill was now but the wreck of his former self and had withdrawn from public life. The task of instigating violence was taken over by Lord Hartington, the wealthy Irish landowner who led the Liberal Unionists. Significantly, Hartington reminded his old leader, Gladstone, that Ulstermen were the descendants of those who had fought with William at the Boyne. "Who can say," he demanded, "that they have not a right, if they think fit, to resist . . . the imposition of a Government put upon them by force?" These words, anticipating Carson's seditious utterances in 1912, were justly described by Lord Morley as "the high-water mark of the frenzy to which Unionist fanaticism and superstition can bring men of intelligence."

One young Orange diehard, a red-headed engineer named Fred Crawford, even conceived an audacious plot to kidnap Gladstone as he was walking on the esplanade at Brighton, and ship him off to some Pacific island, together with Homer, the Bible, and an axe for felling palm trees. The plan, which did not lack in daring, failed for lack of funds.

In defending the second Home Rule Bill, Gladstone fought virtually alone, most of his party being lukewarm about a measure that he alone had imposed upon them. Once more, strong passions were roused, and fistfights erupted in the House. A doughty Orangeman, Colonel Saunderson, the light of battle in his eye, cast a smoldering look over the Home Rule benches. "There is plenty of the murdherers here tonight," he was heard to say as, with an ecstatic expression, he laid about him right and left among the swarming nationalists. So outrageous was the melée that when order had been restored, the Prime Minister humbly apologized to the Speaker, much like a prefect to a headmaster for having failed to keep his form in order.

As a result of Gladstone's single-handed herculean effort, this time the bill actually passed the House of Commons. It was at once rejected in the Lords by the overwhelming vote of 419 to 41. From remote parts of the island, the "backwoodsmen" among the peers—some of whom had never been in the chamber since their original installation—had come up to London to deliver England from those terrible twin menaces, Gladstone and Home Rule. So incensed was the Prime Minister by this flagrant and irresponsible rejection of the people's will as expressed in the Lower House that but for the infirmities of age he would have moved at once to attack the Lords directly. When the old man prophetically warned that, should Home Rule be defeated, "ruder and more dangerous agencies" would take control in Ireland, the Tories scoffed at his words. Yet the bloodshed of 1916 and the Black and Tan terror were the bitter fruit of the unthinking rejection of Home Rule by the Lords in 1893. With less prejudice and more foresight, the peers who believed that in defeating Gladstone they had saved the empire might have realized that they were condemning to violent and unnecessary death many young men, both Irish and English, in the succeeding generation.

In 1895 the victory of the Conservatives at the polls brought Lord

Salisbury for the third time to the premiership, ushering in a decade of continuous Tory rule. To many it seemed that Home Rule had finally been disposed of—a supposition that was reinforced by the pitiable state of the once powerful Home Rule party. Their leader dead, their morale destroyed, their unity shattered, the Irish nationalists were now an object of derision to those who once had feared their power.

In the next election after the death of the Chief—that of 1892—only nine Parnellites were returned, as against seventy-two anti-Parnellites. The use of such labels among the Home Rulers illustrates the degree to which private feuds had superseded basic issues. In 1894, John Redmond, future leader of the party, described its plight as due to "disunion, squalid, and humiliating personal altercations and petty vanities." Their organization he said, "was shattered, their funds bankrupt and their credit exhausted." As a result, moreover, of Parnell's overthrow, financial aid from the United States, where the Chief's influence had been paramount, had almost ceased. By 1898, in the opinion of Dr. F. S. L. Lyons, the Home Rule party was actually "within measurable distance of extinction." The outbreak of the Boer War in 1899, however, served as a catalytic agent to crystallize Irish sentiment once more, and led to the reunification in 1900 of the warring factions under the leadership of John Redmond, a Parnellite.

BIBLIOGRAPHY

Abels, Jules: *The Parnell Tragedy* (1966)
Brown. T. N.: *Irish-American Nationalism, 1870-90* (1966)
Curtis, L. P.: *Coercion and Conciliation in Ireland, 1880-1892* (1963)
Davitt, Michael: *The Fall of Feudalism in Ireland* (1904)
Good, James W.: *Irish Unionism* (1920)
Hammond, John L.: *Gladstone and the Irish Nation* (1938)
Harrison, Henry: *Parnell Vindicated: The Lifting of the Veil* (1931)
Healy, Timothy: *Letters and Leaders of My Day*, 2 vols. (1929)
Leamy, Margaret: *Parnell's Faithful Few* (1936)
Lyons, Francis S. L.: *The Irish Parliamentary Party, 1890-1910* (1951)
_____: *The Fall of Parnell* (1960)
_____: *John Dillon* (1968)
McCaffrey, Lawrence J.: *Irish Feudalism in the 1870's: A Study in Conservative Nationalism* (1962)
McCarthy, Justin: *Reminiscences,* 2 vols. (1899)
MacDonagh, Michael: *Life of William O'Brien* (1928)
_____: *The Home Rule Movement* (1920)

McDowell, Robert B.: *Social Life in Ireland, 1800-45* (1957)

Norman, E. R.: *The Catholic Church and Ireland, 1859-73* (1965)

O'Brien, Conor Cruise: *Parnell and His Party, 1880-1890* (1957)

O'Brien, R. Barry: *Life of Charles Steward Parnell,* 2 vols. (1898)

O'Brien, William: *The Parnell of Real Life* (1926)

O'Connor, Sir James: *History of Ireland, 1801-1924,* 2 vols. (1926)

O'Connor, Thomas Power: *Memoirs of an Old Parliamentarian,* 2 vols. (1929)

————: *The Parnell Movement* (1886)

O'Donnell, Frank H.: *History of the Irish Parliamentary Party, 1870-90,* 2 vols. (1910)

O'Flaherty, Liam: *Life of Tim Healy* (1927)

O'Hegarty, Patrick Sarsfield: *History of Ireland Under the Union, 1801-1922* (1952)

O'Shea, Katherine: *Parnell: His Love Story and Political Life* (1914)

Palmer, Norman D.: *The Irish Land League Crisis* (1940)

Pomfret, John Edwin: *The Struggle for Land in Ireland, 1800-1923* (1930)

Sheehy Skeffington, Francis: *Michael Davitt* (1908)

Strauss, Emil: *Irish Nationalism and British Democracy* (1951)

Tansill, Charles C.: *America and the Fight for Irish Freedom, 1866-1922* (1957)

Thornley, D. A.: *Isaac Butt and Home Rule* (1964)

White, Terence De Vere: *The Road to Excess* (1946)

XII

Ireland in the Early Twentieth Century

Settlement of the Land Question

While treating Home Rule as a dead issue, the Conservative governments of Salisbury and Balfour (1886–92 and 1895–1905) nevertheless produced much useful legislation. In 1891, a fourth Land Act advanced a further £83 million to the Irish tenants for land purchase, while another statute that year established the Congested Districts Board, whose main object was to eliminate the tiny "uneconomic holdings" of the west by buying them up. By 1914 the board had purchased 2.5 million acres at a cost of £10 million. The board also developed fisheries, built harbors, planted trees, and reclaimed bog land. More than 300,000 people benefited from these measures, which had been recommended nearly fifty years earlier by the Devon Commission, only to be set aside in the sacred name of private enterprise. Parnell himself lived long enough to welcome both the Congested Districts Board and the Land Act of 1891. The tenant who became an owner, he said, "was thereby a stronger soldier and more fit to serve in the ranks of Irishmen." Timothy Healy, ever the envenomed partisan, promptly accused his former leader of being a "tory and an orange agent" and of "blowing the bellows for Balfour."

Then came the great Land Act of 1903, sponsored by the Chief Secretary, George Wyndham, great-grandson of Lord Edward Fitzgerald. The Act sought to encourage land purchase by offering still more favorable terms to the tenants, while giving the landlords a bonus of £12 million over and above the purchase money. It was becoming increasingly clear that in Ireland there was no future for landlords, and that by this time a majority were willing to sell. Under previous land acts, only 74,000 peasants had bought their holdings, but 300,000 more did so under Wyndham's act, which Dr. F. S. L. Lyons terms "possibly the most momentous piece of social legislation passed for Ireland since the Union." The act, said John Dillon in 1910, "had the effect of changing the whole character of the peasantry. Instead of being careless, idle, and improvident, they have become like the French peasantry, industrious and economical, even penurious. Marriages are now contracted later."

In 1909, Asquith's Liberal government (1908–16), in which Augustine Birrell was Chief Secretary, passed the final Land Act, making land purchase compulsory and forcing landlords to sell. In the whole process since 1885, 11.5 million acres—more than half of Ireland—had changed hands and nearly £120 million had been advanced by the government. In this way there ended, by peaceful compromise, two centuries of agrarian conflict, which had embittered the relations between two countries and caused the death of thousands. With good will and common sense, such a solution could have been achieved many years earlier, thereby saving an incalculable amount of human suffering.

With the passage of Wyndham's act, Balfour and the Conservatives believed that they had solved the Irish problem at last—so limited was their knowledge of the psychology of a conquered people. Together with Marx, their *bête noire,* they made the mistake of supposing economic issues to be ultimately more important than political ones. As a reward for his statesmanlike achievement, George Wyndham was driven out of office by the Conservatives in 1904, his career ended.

While Ireland stagnated politically for two decades after the death of Parnell, in fields other than politics a new vitality was stirring. These were the years of the Gaelic League, of Sir Horace Plunkett's cooperatives, of Sinn Fein and the Abbey Theatre.

The Gaelic League (1893)

On July 31, 1893, the Gaelic League was founded in a small room in Dublin by Douglas Hyde, Eoin MacNeill, Father Eugene O'Growney, and four others. Its aim was the revival of the Gaelic language, which was dying out so rapidly that, unless something were soon done, it was evidently doomed to extinction. The census of 1851 showed 319,602 persons whose sole language was Gaelic, and 1,204,684 who spoke some Gaelic (perhaps only a few words) in addition to English; by 1891 the respective figures were 38,192 and 642,053. In forty

Dr. Douglas Hyde (1860–1945).
Founder of the Gaelic League
(1893) and first President of Eire
(1937–45).

years, therefore, Ireland had lost seven-eighths of its purely native speakers. The Gaeltacht—that is, the area in which Irish was spoken exclusively—had shrunk to a few impoverished districts on the western seaboard—in Donegal, Connemara, and Kerry. In 1891 in the whole province of Leinster only eight persons spoke Irish as their only language. After enduring for fifteen centuries, wrote T. W. Rolleston, Gaelic had disappeared like "a rootless flower in a child's garden."

During its first five years, the League established fifty-eight branches; five years later, it had set up more than four hundred, and by that time had published a quarter of a million pamphlets. Successful branches had also been started among the Irish in Britain. Whereas in 1893 some 50 national schools were teaching Irish to about 900 pupils, by 1910 the language was being taught in 1,631 schools to 55,374 pupils. Fifty thousand Gaelic textbooks were now sold in a single year, Father O'Growney's *Reader* having the largest sale. In 1913 Gaelic became a compulsory subject in the National University.

By the opening of the twentieth century, the Gaelic League had become the central focus of Irish nationalism. A tiny group of dedicated men had developed it into an influential organization with branches in every county of Ireland. Its driving force was the idealism that had disappeared from Irish politics with the death of Parnell. Many a young clerk or shop assistant attending evening classes after a day spent behind desk or counter, felt in his daily life the power of a new inspiration. Irish colleges were established in the Gaeltacht, where during summer vacations fluency could be acquired from Gaelic speakers. In summers passed at a small white-walled cottage that he built at Rosmuc in Connemara—it is now a simple, unpretentious national shrine—Patrick Pearse became a fluent speaker and writer in Gaelic, so that he was later able to teach the language in St. Enda's School.

A knowledge of Gaelic was the key not only to folktales stored in peasant memory but also to the saga literature in which the legendary history of Ireland had been preserved. In libraries as well as in cottages, buried ages could be brought to life. Cuchulain was rediscovered as a symbol of nationhood, and Deirdre as an archetype of grief. Yeats wrote that Lady Gregory's retelling of heroic myth was as significant for Ireland as the Arthurian legends had once been for England, or the *Mabinogion* for Wales; and Synge acknowledged that he got the poetic speech of his characters not only from peasant cottages but also from Lady Gregory's *Cuchulain of Muirthemne.* Thus the impulse that began at Kiltartan reached fulfillment in the Aran Isles. Along with the legends of pre-Christian Ireland, there emerged the forgotten Gaelic world of the eighteenth century—the "hidden Ireland" of Daniel Corkery's phrase—so that, among other things, the lyrics of Blind Raftery and the Rabelaisian couplets of the *Midnight Court* were also saved from oblivion.

The League combined the excitement of discovery with the fervor of a crusade. In 1905-7, Douglas Hyde lectured in the United States and brought home £11,000 to carry on the work of the League, which also gained the support of many distinguished philologists, among them Heinrich Zimmer, Kuno Meyer, Ernst Windisch, Sir John Rhys, and Alfred Nutt.

Patrick Pearse once called the Gaelic League "the most revolutionary influence that has ever come into Irish history." Writing in the first number of the *Irish Volunteer,* he maintained that when in 1893 the original seven had met, "the Irish Revolution really began." With this judgment of Pearse the idealist, Michael Collins the man of action later concurred. "Irish History," he asserted, "will recognize in the birth of the Gaelic League the most important event of the nineteenth century."

The intellectual appeal of the Gaelic League was greater than that of any group since Young Ireland and the men of *The Nation.* "There is a passionate urge of expectancy," wrote Ella Young in Dublin, referring to the language movement. The League was strongest in the towns and among the middle classes, particularly among teachers and university students. Like all revolutionary movements it held a special appeal for the young. It was a protest against the petty jealousies of Home Rule politicians, against the general stagnation of

Irish life, and against the commercialism of the English popular press, which was beginning just then to inundate Ireland. As Douglas Hyde remarked, when the peasant lost touch with folk tradition, it was replaced in his life not by familiarity with the great achievements of English literature, but by the vulgarity of contemporary journalism seeking new markets to exploit.

Whatever the selfless devotion of the young men and women of the Gaelic League, they still formed a small minority of the population. Rural Ireland treated them with complete indifference. To peasants with little formal education, working all day in the fields, the acquisition of a new and difficult language required more energy and application than they were capable of.

Most of the formal opposition to the League came, as might have been expected, from official quarters in education and also from that last stronghold of English influence in Ireland—Trinity College, Dublin. For Sir John Pentland Mahaffy, the oustanding scholar of his generation in Ireland, outside of English there was only one language in the world—ancient Greek, and of this he himself had almost a monopoly in Ireland. But Mahaffy was an inveterate snob and despised Gaelic as a language fit only for helots and corner boys. To compare so barbarous a tongue with Homer savored of blasphemy. In 1900 he remarked superciliously that there was not a single Gaelic text that was not "religious, silly, or indecent." Robert Atkinson, Professor of Sanskrit at Trinity and an Englishman, likewise dismissed the Celtic sagas as "metrical rubbish." Yet even in Trinity, some undergraduates met to found a branch of the Gaelic League. When Mahaffy heard that they had invited to address them "a man called Pearse," he forthwith suppressed the group.

From another quarter, too, despite the presence in the movement of Father O'Growney (1863–99), the League met with resistance. Since the time of O'Connell, the Church had never taken any interest in the ancient language, whose value in America or in missionary work— in Africa, India, China, or South America—was precisely nil. Rome, it was said, regarded the League as a form of "Irish Carbonarism."* At Clongowes the Jesuits did what they could to hinder it, and on one occasion at least, some of the more ardent Gaels in the college were sent to Australia to cool their enthusiasm for the language.

"Politics," wrote T. W. Rolleston to his friend Canon Hannay, in 1905, "have now been, like everything else, absorbed into the Church—everything else but one thing, and that one thing is the Gaelic League. The League represents the last effort of the Irish

*The Carbonari were Italian revolutionaries of the early nineteenth century.

spirit for nationality and a personal independence. The Church began by opposing it; it's now, as usual doing its utmost to absorb it—whether the League can resist the Church any better than the politicians did is very doubtful."

From its inception, Douglas Hyde (1860–1949) had been president of the League. The son of a Protestant parson in County Roscommon and a graduate of Trinity, Hyde was at once its inspiration, its organizing genius, and its indefatigable propagandist. A kindly, modest, and unassuming man, Hyde had been one of the earliest to study folklore from the point of view not of the philologist but of the poet. In the language that was dying in the West he discovered the passion of a long-forgotten past. A lyric that he took down from a toothless, pipe-smoking old crone, sitting in a hovel amid the bogs of Roscommon, astonished the contemporary world by its vehemence and simplicity, and by its freshness of language.

> My grief on the sea,
>   How the waves of it roll!
> For they heave between me
>   And the love of my soul!
>
> Abandoned, forsaken
>   To grief and to care,
> Will the sea ever waken
>   Relief from despair?
>
> My grief and my trouble!
>   Would he and I were
> In the province of Leinster
>   Or the county of Clare.
>
> Were I and my darling—
>   Oh, heart-bitter wound!—
> On board of the ship
>   For America bound.
>
> On a green bed of rushes
>   All last night I lay,
> And I flung it abroad
>   With the heat of the day.
>
> And my love came behind me—
>   He came from the South;
> His breast to my bosom,
>   His mouth to my mouth.

Love Songs of Connacht, a small volume of translations from the Gaelic that Hyde published in 1886, inspired a whole generation of Irish writers. Hyde was also the author of the first play in Gaelic ever to be performed in Ireland—*Twisting of the Rope,* which was produced on October 21, 1901.

Conservative in upbringing, Douglas Hyde was slow to accept the idea of Home Rule. So long as he was president of the League, he strove to keep it out of politics. The times, however, were too much for him. In 1915, ardent Sinn Feiners within the League forced him out of the presidency, which he had held for twenty-two years. "From that day," noted J. J. Horgan, "its decline began." Thenceforward, the League became as much a political as a cultural organization. During the Troubles, by its courageous defiance of the British authorities, it inevitably incurred the displeasure of Dublin Castle, and was suppressed on November 25, 1919.

Sir Horace Plunkett and the Cooperatives (1894)

Descended from an ancient Anglo-Norman family and an uncle of Lord Dunsany (the first Baron Dunsany had been created in 1439), Sir Horace Plunkett (1854–1932) is a unique figure in modern Irish history. Perhaps no man worked harder, or accomplished more, for the public welfare than he; yet few men in public life were more shabbily treated. Not, however, that he was altogether without recognition from his countrymen: the Unionist Lecky considered him to be "the only constructive statesman in Ireland," and John Eglinton the nationalist once suggested that it was Plunkett rather than Arthur Griffith who should be remembered as the "Father of His Country."

Born in England, educated at Eton and Oxford, Sir Horace none the less regarded himself as an Irishman, and it was to Ireland that he gave his life's work and his heart's devotion. Like Davitt at the other end of the social scale, Plunkett illustrates a type that is rare in Irish history—the individual who devotes himself wholly to the well-being of Ireland without feeling the necessity of resenting or repudiating England. The lesson taught by the study of Irish history Sir Horace summed up in a single lapidary epigram: Let England remember, let Ireland forget.

Though reared as a Protestant, Plunkett had reacted against the evangelicalism of his childhood by accepting agnosticism—a philosophy that was distasteful to Protestant and Catholic alike. As an aristocrat, Sir Horace detested the snobbishness of upper-class Dublin society and especially the servility and flunkeyism that pervaded the world

Sir Horace Plunkett (1854–1932). Founder of the Irish Cooperative Movement (1894).

of Dublin Castle and the Viceregal Lodge. His moderation in politics was, of course, felt as an affront by extremists on both sides.

A confirmed bachelor, by temperament reserved and aloof, Plunkett altogether lacked personal magnetism. He had sat in parliament from 1892 to 1900 but had not achieved success in the House of Commons. A poor public speaker, he found it difficult to hold an audience; yet he was widely respected for his sincerity and honesty of purpose. In his general attitude to life, Plunkett was a tolerant and progressive cosmopolitan. In early manhood he had gone to the Far West of the United States for reasons of health and had lived ten years in Wyoming, the first state in the Union to grant women the vote. As a result of this western experience Plunkett became a convinced and lifelong supporter of women's emancipation. In other respects, too, Sir Horace showed an unusual willingness to adapt himself to the modern world. He was the first person in Ireland ever to drive an automobile—at what was considered in 1901 the frightening speed of twelve miles per hour. At the age of seventy he was to take up flying.

In Plunkett's lifetime it was said of him that he was recognized as a great man in every country but his own. The circle of his admirers included figures of international repute—among others Jan Christian Smuts, Theodore Roosevelt, Colonel House, Axel Munthe, H. A. L. Fisher, Bernard Shaw, and Sidney and Beatrice Webb—most of whom at one time or another stayed with Sir Horace at his charming country house at Foxrock, Kilteragh, beneath the Three Rock Mountain a few miles outside Dublin.

On April 18, 1894, Plunkett founded the Irish Agricultural Organization Society. Taking Denmark as his model, he sought to modernize Irish agriculture by means of a cooperative movement. The cooperatives dealt with distribution as well as production, for Sir Horace was anxious not only to increase the national wealth but to diminish the gap between poverty and riches. He hoped also to infuse into the countryside a new spirit of pride and self-reliance and thereby lessen its dependence on the towns.

So successful were his efforts that by 1903, there were in Ireland eight hundred cooperative societies, with 80,000 members representing some 400,000 people and an annual turnover of £2 million. By 1916 there were nearly a thousand branches, doing an annual business of £3 million. Although the I.A.O.S. received no financial help from the state before 1912, its conspicuous success led to an important step in 1900—the establishment of an Irish Department of Agriculture, with Plunkett as Vice President. He promptly nominated as secretary T. P. Gill, a former Home Rule M.P. who had also done useful work for the I.A.O.S. The new department soon established agricultural training stations and schools, as well as advanced education in forestry.

One might have supposed that Plunkett's work would have won immediate recognition in Ireland, but such was not the case. The attempt to modernize agriculture not only affronted deeply rooted rural prejudices but also threatened certain vested interests. Those who had previously profited by exploiting the farmer resented his growing social freedom and relative economic independence. In every village the gombeen man—the local shopkeeper to whom so many were in debt—opposed a movement that diminished the peasants' dependence upon him. Fearful lest the success of the I.A.O.S. deflect the farmer's concern from political matters and thereby jeopardize Home Rule, nationalist politicians also looked askance at what Plunkett, a Unionist, was achieving. Arthur Griffith and Sinn Fein saw in Plunkett a rival for the control of rural opinion, which they themselves hoped to dominate.

Although some priests like Father Tom Finlay, the popular Jesuit preacher from the National University, cordially endorsed the work of the I.A.O.S., clerical opinion was in general hostile. The Church was already distrustful of Sir Horace because of his known lack of religious belief. His views on contemporary life, as set forth in his book *Ireland in the New Century* (1904), gave further offense. For Plunkett deprecated what seemed to him an excessive amount of money spent in Ireland on religious institutions. The clergy likewise resented his criticism of the dullness and monotony of village life and his impatience with the restraints enforced upon the social intercourse of young people of opposite sexes, "eyeing one in dull wonderment" on either side of the road on a Sunday. In cheap newspapers Plunkett was described as "a monster in human shape" and "an exterminator" engaged in "hellish work." One of his most malignant critics was the Dublin journalist D. P. Moran, for thirty-six years editor of the *Leader,* a widely read weekly. To an ultra-Nationalist Gael like Moran, everything that Sir Horace stood for—aristocracy, moderation, cosmopolitanism—was necessarily suspect.

Improved conditions of agriculture meant not only material prosperity but a chance to raise the level of education. In his book Plunkett suggested that a certain degeneration of the national character had taken place. By implication at least, he laid part of the blame for this upon the existing educational system, controlled as that was largely by the Church. In Plunkett's opinion, education should include more than learning by rote and the ability to calculate. What he looked for was the training of character, as reflected in moral attributes such as independence, honesty, and integrity. The current system, he wrote, was "calculated to turn our youth into a generation of second-rate clerks, with a distinct distaste for any industrial or productive occupation in which such qualities as initiative, self-reliance or judgment were called for." He deplored the gap between public and private morality, and like John O'Leary, weighed the actions of politicians by the same strict standards he applied to ordinary men in private life.

Plunkett listed what he regarded as some of the chief weaknesses in the Irish national character: "a striking absence of self-reliance and moral courage; an entire lack of serious thought on public questions; a listlessness and apathy in regard to economic improvement which amounts to a form of fatalism; and in the backward districts, survival of superstition which saps all strength of will and purpose and all this too, amongst a people singularly gifted by nature with good qualities of heart and mind." There was far too much truth in such criticism for it to be accepted with equanimity by the conventional-minded.

Sir Horace looked to his own class to furnish the nation enlightened leadership, but its reactionary views gradually convinced him that little was to be expected from that quarter. In 1908, in his *Noblese Oblige,* Plunkett made a final appeal to the landed gentry to cooperate in the shaping of the new Ireland. Their indifference to his message finally converted him to Home Rule, and he regretted not having realized earlier the paramount importance of politics.

Sir Horace had no particular interest in the Irish literary movement,

William Butler Yeats (1865–1939). The great Irish poet and outstanding figure in the Irish literary renaissance.

or sympathy with its work. No more than James Connolly did he believe in the imagined glories of the Gaelic past. For him cooperatives were more important than Cuchulain, and creameries more valuable than the sagas. It was through W. B. Yeats, nevertheless, that Sir Horace met the poet and dreamer who was to be his most useful ally in the cooperative movement, for in 1897 Yeats introduced him to George Russell, a writer already known by his pseudonym, AE.

The meeting of Plunkett and AE was in its way as significant for Ireland as had been the meeting of Yeats and Synge the previous year in Paris: in each case, as a result of the meeting the younger man discovered his life's true vocation. But while Synge realized himself in solitude upon the rocks of Aran, AE became the peripatetic missionary of the gospel of cooperation, cycling—as George Moore portrays him in *Hail and Farewell*—through the villages of Ireland, eloquent, indefatigable, tweedy, and hirsute—"the Hairy Fairy" of Moran's malicious jibe.

The "call" from Plunkett released Russell from the drudgery of a clerkship in Pim's department store at £60 a year and changed the course of his life. Thirteen years younger than Sir Horace, AE had been, like him, the victim of an early evangelical upbringing against which he had rebelled. Again like Plunkett, AE had lived remote from politics; but where the search for physical health had taken Sir Horace to Wyoming, the quest for spiritual understanding had led Russell to the Hindu scriptures. To AE, wrote John Eglinton, the year 1891 was significant not so much for the death of Parnell as for that of Mme. Blavatsky. The insights of theosophy—its sense of the brotherhood of man—were now to be made available to Ireland. AE also admired the New England transcendentalists: what Emerson had done for Boston, he once told Yeats, together they could accomplish for Dublin.

Not without some misgivings did AE exchange the role of seer for that of salesman. Yeats, however, realized that from his new vocation AE would learn more than the economics of rural life. "Remember always," Yeats told him, "that now you are face to face with Ireland, its tragedy and its poverty, and if we would express Ireland we must know her to the heart and in all her moods. You will be a far more powerful mystic and poet and teacher because of this knowledge."

For a good many years the bearded figure clad in homespun pedaled along the country lanes of Ireland, seeking not only to convert cabin and cottage to the techniques of modern dairy farming but also to disseminate a sense of that mystic beauty that he himself had once beheld upon the mountains. Like Synge, AE enjoyed meeting other wayfarers—the motley throng that wandered the roads of Ireland—peasants, tinkers, and mountainy men. "This wild country," he wrote from Belmullet in the desolate west of Mayo, "has infused a wild melancholy into my blood." Six years after the institution of the Congested Districts Board, however, AE still found living conditions in the west "a disgrace to humanity." It was this discovery that awakened the social conscience that was to play so large a part in AE's future life.

In 1905, when Plunkett appointed him editor of the *Irish Homestead,* which Sir Horace had started in 1896, AE found at length the perfect outlet for his energies. The paper gave him an opportunity to combine a gift for writing with an enthusiasm for social reform. In its weekly columns he gained a pulpit from which to fulminate against selfishness and corruption; and in these years he emerged as a sort of Irish Ruskin, eloquently exhorting his fellow countrymen to moral improvement. "The cry of ancient Israel for righteousness," he proclaimed, "rings out above all other passions."

Sir Horace Plunkett lived to see Easter Week in 1916 and the "Troubles" that followed. Much as he deplored the rising, he exerted himself—unsuccessfully—to gain clemency for those who had led it. During the regime of terror instigated by the Black and Tans in 1920-21, he saw the systematic destruction, in certain parts of the country, of many of the creameries he had worked so hard to establish. In the Civil War of 1922-23, he looked on helplessly and in anguish as the leaders on either side—with many of whom he was personally acquainted—sought to destroy each other.

In August, 1922, the night before Michael Collins left on the mission to County Cork that was to lead to his death in combat, he was a guest of Sir Horace at Foxrock, together with the Shaws and the Laverys. In February, 1923, the Republicans burned down the house that had for so long been Plunkett's home in Ireland. The fire destroyed not only the library that had been Sir Horace's special pride and the blue-green frescoes of romantic seas and magic shores with which AE had decorated many of the walls, but also a wide-ranging correspondence of thirty or forty years that would have proved invaluable to future historians. Heartbroken over the loss of Foxrock, yet still uncomplaining, Plunkett, then approaching seventy, quit Ireland for ever. In one of the last letters of his lifelong correspondence with his close friend, Lady Fingall, Sir Horace permitted himself the confession: "My heart is as young as ever, and it is yours."

The Founding of Sinn Fein (1905)

The separatist aims of the Gaelic League and the regeneration of the countryside wrought by the cooperatives were complemented by the political, social, and economic aims of Sinn Fein, a movement launched in 1905 by a dour Dublin journalist, Arthur Griffith (1872–1922), who was ultimately to become head of the first Free State government. Sinn Fein was a protest against the control of public life in Ireland by Redmond's half-moribund Home Rule party—"useless, degrading, demoralizing," Griffith called it. The Union itself, he wrote, was "a nullity, a usurpation and a fraud." Hence Griffith aimed at complete separation from Britain, save for the link of the crown, though he urged peaceful means for the attainment of this end. If on the one hand Sinn Fein looked back to Grattan's parliament of 1782, on the other it anticipated the Dominion status accorded by the Statute of Westminster in 1922. The founder of Sinn Fein was a pragmatic realist. Theories, as such, did not concern him. "We do not care a fig," he once remarked, "for republicanism as republicanism."

In 1904, in a little book called *The Resurrection of Hungary,* Griffith expounded his political ideas. He had become interested in the long struggle of the Magyars for freedom from the Hapsburgs and had been impressed by the virtual independence achieved by Hungary in the Dual Monarchy of 1867. Louis Kossuth and Francis Déak, the leaders of Hungarian nationalism, were his heroes. Griffith envisaged Ireland as part of a Dual Monarchy under the British Crown.

Repudiating Fenian violence since it had failed, Griffith urged the use of the existing electoral machinery to replace the Home Rulers by a new Sinn Fein party, which would then refuse to go to Westminster. Instead, it would meet in Dublin, where it would constitute itself an independent national legislature—just as was actually to happen in 1919. Griffith, no doubt, had in mind how Déak had at one time boycotted the Imperial Parliament in Vienna. In view of Sinn Fein's renunciation of physical force, it is a singular irony that after 1916 its name came to be attached to the extreme I.R.A. men.*

The fifteen points in the program of Sinn Fein included economic, social, and cultural goals. Political separation was to be accompanied by economic and cultural isolation. Sinn Fein urged the establishment of native Irish industries—presumably with money to be obtained from America—which should be enabled to hold their own against British

*Even such historians as Elie Halévy and Lionel Curtis make the mistake of assuming that Sinn Fein had always advocated violence.

competition by high protective tariffs, such as Berkeley had suggested long ago in *The Querist*. Griffith adopted Swift's maxim: "Burn everything English except their coals," and used it as a slogan at the masthead of his paper. By boycotting English products, Sinn Fein hoped to encourage native manufacture such as the weaving of Donegal tweeds. One interested observer of Sinn Fein activities was Jawaharlal Nehru, who came to Dublin in 1910 while on vacation as an undergraduate at Cambridge. As an ardent Indian nationalist, Nehru was strongly sympathetic with Sinn Fein. In his autobiography written a quarter of a century later, he stated that the policy of "swadeshi" (the encouragement of home products and the boycott of foreign ones) had been partly inspired by the example of Sinn Fein.

If Griffith looked to Hungary for inspiration in politics, it was to Germany that he turned for guidance in economics. The Zollverein, the German custom union of 1842, illustrated what might be done for the industries of a small nation provided they were protected by high tariffs. To Griffith, Frederick List, the creator of the Zollverein, was as significant a figure in European history as Kossuth. For having laid the economic basis of German imperial greatness, Griffith called List "the man England hated and feared more than any man since Napoleon."

The demand for Irish tariffs called attention to the problem of Ulster, whose industrial success was based upon free trade with Britain. Far from wishing to injure the northern province, Sinn Fein regarded it with pride as the most prosperous province of Ireland and as a proof that Irishmen were capable of succeeding in business. Griffith himself viewed Ulster's self-discipline, thrift, and capacity for work as a model to be imitated by the rest of the nation. Ulster was, in fact, to be the showpiece of the new Ireland. At its 1914 convention in Dublin, Sinn Fein offered Ulster special guarantees that under such a parliament its industries should not suffer, and suggested that an Irish parliament, if it came into being, should meet alternately in Dublin and in Belfast. When in 1913 the Ulster Volunteers defied the British government, a number of prominent southern nationalists—including Eoin MacNeill, Patrick Pearse, and Roger Casement—applauded the militance of the north as having demonstrated Ulster's independence of spirit.

Apart from tariffs, Sinn Fein advocated land reclamation, afforestation, the development of fisheries and harbors, and the building of canals in order to offer competition to the high freight charges of the railways. By such projects, Sinn Fein hoped to halt the flow of emigration from Ireland. Impressed by Norway's acquisition of independence from Sweden in 1905, Griffith urged the construction of an Irish merchant fleet that should make the flag of Ireland as well known in the ports of the world as was the flag of Norway. Possibly with Norway's new diplomatic status in mind, Griffith demanded that Britain open Irish consulates in some of the leading cities of the world—a policy that Roger Casement attempted partly to realize at Santos in Brazil, thereby incurring rebuke from his scandalized superiors in the Foreign Office. Another form of protest indulged in by some Sinn Feiners, though certainly not by Griffith, was a sartorial one: a few hardy enthusiasts look to wearing saffron kilts instead of Saxon trousers.

A much more important issue concerned the report of the Childers Commission in 1896. This body, composed almost entirely of Englishmen, revealed that ever since the Union, Ireland had been paying in taxation about £2,750,000 a year more than was being spent on services at home. Outraged by the discovery that all along the poorer nation had been mulcted for the support of its wealthier neighbor, Griffith demanded that an equivalent sum be recovered from the Imperial Exchequer and devoted to the financing of projects for the advancement of Irish interests.

As one might expect, the relations between Sinn Fein and the Gaelic League were excellent. Both appealed primarily to idealists and intellectuals, coming often from a middle-class background, usually young, and with a high proportion of teachers and students in their ranks. Many individuals belonged simultaneously to both organizations. The choice of the name—"Sinn Fein," meaning "we ourselves" or "ourselves alone"—was itself a tribute to the ancient tongue. In a contemporary ballad, John O'Hagan used the term as a symbol of the self-reliance and defiance of Sinn Fein:

> Too long our Irish hearts we schooled
> In patient hope to bide.
> By dreams of English justice fooled
> And English tongues that lied.
> That hour of weak delusion's past—
> The empty dream has flown:
> Our hope and strength we find at last
> Is in OURSELVES ALONE.

Though Edward Martyn, playwright and friend of George Moore, had been the first president of Sinn Fein, Arthur Griffith, who succeeded him in that office in 1910, was its chief inspiration. Sinn Fein without him was as unthinkable as the Gaelic League without Douglas

Hyde. It was the indefatigable Griffith who popularized the aims of the movement in his halfpenny weekly, the *United Irishman,* which lasted from 1899 to 1906. During those seven years, the paper was confiscated by the police on twenty-three occasions, being suppressed three times in one year—1900—for its outspoken opposition to the Boer War. Driven out of business in 1906 by the cost of libel actions, the paper was promptly reconstituted as *Sinn Fein,* and managed—notwithstanding its relentless campaign against the recruiting of Irishmen into the British Army—to survive until 1914. Griffith took special pleasure in publishing statistics concerning the high incidence of venereal disease in the armed forces of the Crown, thereby representing enlistment not only as unpatriotic but as a danger to health.

As Griffith had borrowed Mitchel's title for his original paper, so did he reiterate Mitchel's basic thought: England's danger was Ireland's opportunity. As early as 1912, *Sinn Fein* announced that while it opposed all foreign domination, had it to choose, it would prefer German to British rule in Ireland. When in 1914, war finally came, Griffith expressed in *Sinn Fein* his admiration of the German people, "standing alone and undaunted and defiant against a world in arms. We Celts," he wrote, "honored a race which knew how to live and die like men." It is not surprising that *Sinn Fein,* voicing sentiments like these in time of war, was soon suppressed.

One of the limitations of the Sinn Fein movement—a reflection of Griffith's personal limitations—was the narrowness of its patriotism. Sinn Fein looked askance, for example, at most of the writers in the Irish Literary Renaissance on the ground that they failed to put patriotism before everything else. Griffith attacked Synge's *Playboy of the Western World* as damaging to the good name of Ireland, and Sinn Feiners were active in disgraceful scenes that occurred when that play was presented at the Abbey in 1904. Pearse, however, refused to condone such philistinism and publicly defended the *Playboy.* Few of the patriots, Sean O'Casey complained in his autobiography, had intellectual interests or cared a thraneen about such things as literature or science.

Griffith himself was much offended when the young James Joyce severely criticized the patriotic verse of Griffith's young friend, William Rooney. Patriots considered Rooney to be the "Thomas Davis of Sinn Fein" and were outraged when Joyce observed sensibly enough that love of country was no excuse for bad poetry. Rooney, wrote Joyce, might have done better had he not "suffered from one of those big words that make us so unhappy." To Sinn Fein, the "big word"—in this case, "patriotism"—was everything.

The selfless idealism of Sinn Fein was admitted even by those who were opposed to its objectives. "The strength of these people," wrote the poet T. W. Rolleston to Lady Aberdeen, wife of the new Liberal Viceroy, in 1906, "lies in the fact that they have more sincerity, more high-mindedness, more principle, and very much more education and intellect, than any other section of the Nationalist party at present possesses. Hence their great and growing influence over all the active young minds now coming to maturity in Ireland. Young people are usually impassioned for ideas and for reason, when they have the education to grasp them."

Despite the undoubted truth of these observations, when put to the test at the polling booths, Sinn Fein did not fare well. It had little appeal for businessmen in Dublin, or for the petty traders and gombeen men in the small towns. Though it contested several parliamentary elections against the Home Rule party, before 1917 it failed to win a single one. By 1910, a hundred and thirty branches of Sinn Fein had sprung up all over Ireland, some of them in the north; a year later, there were only six, and by 1912, only one. Well might Professor R. M. Henry write that "from 1910 to 1913, the Sinn Fein movement was practically moribund." But for the unexpected stimulus afforded by the European war in 1914, followed by the injudicious executions of 1916, Sinn Fein might well have expired completely.

One reason—apart from the ingrained conservatism of rural Ireland—for the early failure of Sinn Fein to make headway in the nation at large was no doubt a strain of anticlericalism in the movement, deriving partly from the Fenians and partly from resentment at the Church's treatment of Parnell. Though Griffith himself was a Catholic, the Jesuits accused the *United Irishman* of being lukewarm in its Catholicism; and when in 1899 the Church condemned Yeats's play *The Countess Cathleen,* Griffith volunteered to bring in "a lot of men from the quays" to applaud those passages that clerical critics had resented. The young men in Sinn Fein, observed Rolleston later, embodied "the rising force of resistance to clerical dictation in Ireland. The Bishops," he continued, "have reduced the Parliamentarians to mere puppets, but they have no influence at all over the Sinn Fein people, to whom a Bishop, when he is dealing with secular affairs, is no more sacrosanct than a Resident Magistrate." Canon James Hannay, the Protestant clerical novelist known as George A. Birmingham, a conservative in politics, was one of those who, according to Rolleston, saw in Sinn Fein "the one force that can . . . make head against the domination of the clerics."

The Third Home Rule Bill (1912–14)

After the death of Gladstone in 1898, the Liberals privately hoped that the embarrassing issue of Home Rule had been buried along with him. Even while the old man had still been alive, Henry Herbert Asquith (1852–1928), future Liberal Prime Minister, had described Home Rule as a policy of "ploughing the sands." In 1901, Lord Rosebery, who had succeeded Gladstone as leader of the party, expressed his pleasure that the Liberals were free at last from the alliance with the Home Rulers to which Gladstone had committed them in 1886; and when, twenty years later, the Liberals won by a landslide, they had not even mentioned Home Rule during the campaign.

In 1907, Augustine Birrell, a successful barrister and a genial man of letters, was appointed Chief Secretary for Ireland. Probably no English official in Anglo-Irish history had even approached his task more conscientiously or with greater concern for the benefit of the subject people. The average tenure of a Chief Secretary was two years, but Birrell lasted for nine, until he was suddenly ruined by the 1916 rebellion. Already before his appointment he had read widely in Irish history. He was familiar with the works of Edmund Spenser and Sir Jonah Barrington, with Wolfe Tone's *Autobiography* and Mitchel's *Jail Journal,* and had read Thackeray, Lecky, and Froude on Ireland; he knew the novels of Maria Edgeworth and William Carleton; he had even read Davitt's *Leaves from a Prison Diary.* When Birrell went to Dublin, he was already acquainted with the work of Yeats and Synge, and went to the Abbey Theatre nearly every week. The new Chief Secretary was free from political prejudice, had a lively curiosity, and a real desire to learn. After his fall from office, great play was made with a remark he had made in 1907—that Ireland had never been so peaceful for four hundred years; but though this came to sound fatuous in 1916, no one questioned its correctness at the time the remark was made. If Birrell failed to realize the potential strength of the underground currents—Sinn Fein and the Gaelic League, for example—that were agitating Irish life, neither did the Home Rule leaders, who were far more closely in touch with Irish opinion that Birrell could ever hope to be.

The crisis at Westminster produced by Lloyd George's budget of 1909 had profound results for Ireland. In the stalemate produced by the two elections of 1910, the Irish members under Redmond found themselves, for the first time since 1886, holding the balance of power in the House of Commons. To complete their program of social reform—the first installment of what is now known as the "Welfare

State"—the Liberals led by Asquith needed Irish votes, in return for which they were compelled, however reluctantly, to take up the issue of Home Rule once more.

In order to overcome Conservative resistance to the financing of the new social reforms, the Liberals found it necessary to pass the Parliament Act of 1911, which reduced the absolute veto of the Lords upon legislation to a limited veto of two years only. The Tories were furious at what they termed "a betrayal of the Constitution." The future Lord Birkenhead declared that Asquith's campaign against the Upper House had been "almost obscene in its class hatred." A prominent Ulster politician, Ronald MacNeill, later Lord Cushendun, compared the curbing of the peers to the forethought of "the careful burglar, who poisons the dog before breaking into the house." Since the peers alone had saved Ulster in 1893, the frantic concern of the Orangemen over the Parliament Act is understandable: the last great barrier against Irish self-determination had been removed.

In pursuance of his pledge to the Irish members, Asquith introduced the third Home Rule Bill in 1912. Between 1912 and 1914, it passed the Commons three times in three successive sessions, was three times rejected by the Lords, and finally, as prescribed by the terms of the Parliament Act, went to George V for his signature. On September 15, 1914, the bill—which Sir Edward Carson, the Ulster leader, called "the most nefarious measure that ever has been hatched against a free people"—became law. It is interesting to note that the Home Rule Act was approved by nearly every prominent politician in the Dominions and that every one of the Dominions passed an official resolution endorsing it.

The mild and gentlemanly Redmond appeared to have succeeded where much more forceful leaders like O'Connell and Parnell had failed. In August, 1912, accompanied by Redmond, Asquith paid a triumphal visit to Dublin: it was the first time that any Prime Minister, while still in office, had officially visited Ireland. The rejoicings were premature, for a grim struggle lay ahead—one that threatened to involve Britain in civil war for the first time in nearly two and a half centuries. The events of the next two years may perhaps be regarded as a study in political pathology, a somber prelude to the violence of twentieth-century dictatorships.

Ulster's Opposition to Home Rule (1912–14)

During the crisis of the first Home Rule Bill in 1886, Professor Dicey of Oxford, one of the most learned constitutional lawyers in England, had pronounced Home Rule unconstitutional. To desert the Southern

Unionists, wrote Dicey, would be "vile treachery," "an indelible disgrace" like the abandonment of the American Loyalists in 1783. While Dicey was writing, the House of Lords still served as an insuperable barrier between Ireland and Home Rule. By 1912, however, when the third Home Rule Bill passed the Commons, this obstacle had been removed. Dicey's tone, which in 1886 had been lofty and magisterial, now became hysterical. In a frenetic little pamphlet entitled "A Fool's Paradise," Dicey termed Home Rule "a political Majuba,"* which "threatened ruin to every part of the United Kingdom." He foresaw the day when Dublin would become a second Monte Carlo. He hinted cautiously that even armed revolt might be justified by the attempt of the Liberals "to carry through revolution by fraud." All his life the eminent Oxonian jurist had preached obedience to law. His treatises on constitutional practice were quoted as the highest authority on the subject. Now, because of political partisanship, the professor repudiated the teaching of a lifetime without recognizing what he was doing.

The defiance of the politician soon succeeded the pusillanimity of the don, as the stern reality of the Covenant swept aside the pious platitudes of All Souls. Belfast was prepared to act where Oxford only talked. Carson openly advocated treason—Dicey had only glanced timidly in its direction. On September 28, 1912, Ulster took the first step. In Belfast Cathedral, Carson and other Ulster leaders signed a document called the "Solemn League and Covenant," in which they swore to use all means necessary "to defeat the present conspiracy to set up a Home Rule Parliament." Above their heads hung the faded yellow flag that had accompanied King Billy at the Boyne. In all, nearly half a million Orange men and women signed the Covenant—some, like Fred Crawford, with their own blood. Ulster, commented the London *Times,* seemed to have made "an offensive and defensive alliance with Deity." Throughout the North, the Orange drum was beaten, while massed bands played: "O God, Our Help in Ages Past."

The signing of the Covenant was followed by the recruitment of a private army, complete with General Staff. The Ulster Volunteers began to drill and train, preparing themselves for war. Lord Roberts, the most distinguished soldier in England, personally selected as their commander-in-chief General Sir George Richardson, a retired veteran of Poona and the Northwest frontier of India. By 1914, they claimed 110,000 men. Dr. D' Arcy, future Protestant Primate of Ireland,

*The Transvaal Boers had destroyed a small British force at Majuba in 1881.

Sir Edward Carson (1854–1935). Leader of the Ulster Unionists (1912–14).

solemnly blessed the machine guns that had been acquired. Finally, on September 25, 1913, a Provisional Government of Ulster was formed, with Carson as its head. For nearly a million Orangemen, Carson was Ulster and Ulster was Carson.

Sir Edward Carson (1854–1935) was not an Ulsterman by birth or ancestry. Born in southern Ireland, a graduate of Trinity, he had gained fame and fortune as a ruthless and successful barrister in Britain. Oscar Wilde had been one of the earliest victims of his cold forensic skill. Lord Birkenhead, first Carson's friend and later his enemy, called him "the greatest advocate the English Bar has produced since Erskine."* Lloyd George spoke of "the lash of Carson's terrible tongue." As M.P. for Trinity, Carson had fought not only Home Rule but every other piece of liberal legislation as well—old-age pensions, social insurance, protection for trade union funds, and the Parliament Act of 1911.

Fundamentalist in religion, hypochondriac in temperament, Carson had no use for democracy or for most aspects of the modern world. He was given to extolling the virtues of "blood" and "race." In

*Thomas Erskine was the famous Whig barrister who had successfully defended the London working men charged by Pitt with treason in 1794.

debate, he preferred to overcome an opponent by force rather than attempt to convince him by argument. Like Mussolini he was by temperament a bully; and perhaps there is truth in Mary Colum's observation that he was "the first fascist leader in Europe." From his portraits one may still see what George Dangerfield describes as "the dark eyes brooding above the heavy mouth and brutal chin." Carson was a man of limited ideas but indomitable will. His complete lack of interest in the humanities—in literature, art, music, or philosophy*— made him a fit leader for the dour, hard-working, graceless northern city that took him to her flinty heart. Neurotic like Bismarck, Carson was also prone to tears in public when he dramatized himself to Ulster audiences as a new undaunted Gideon leading a little faithful band against the Midianite hosts of evil.

Once established as leader, Carson proceeded by a series of calculated insults to defy the British government. He frequently proclaimed his contempt for Asquith and for parliamentary leaders in general. "They are such a lot of scoundrels," he wrote in 1914, in what was no doubt an unintended revelation of himself. "I believe they are capable of anything." Carson boasted of the treason he was uttering and taunted the government for failing to prosecute him. In June, 1912, just before leaving for Belfast, he told a London audience "that he intended when he went over there to break every law that was possible." He was not afraid of the cabinet, "for a more wretched, miserable, time-serving opportunistic lot never before sat in Parliament." Warned in Ulster that the Volunteer movement was treasonable, Carson brazenly replied: "I do not care twopence whether it is treason or not." At Glasgow he quoted the Attorney General as having said that the course he was taking would lead to anarchy. "Does he think I do not know that?" sneered Carson. To an English audience at Plymouth, in what sounded like a deliberate threat of civil war, Carson avowed: "I do not even shrink from the horrors of civil commotion." In 1914, Tim Healy reported Carson as announcing that, if necessary, he would march the Volunteers through Ireland "from Belfast to Cork." While Carson was making these seditious statements, Ulster was flooded with pictures depicting him as a knight in shining armor, holding aloft the dripping head of Redmond severed from the scaly dragon of Home Rule.

Under the Treason-Felony Act of 1848, which had sent Mitchel to Tasmania as a convict, Carson's language was clearly treasonable. Neither Young Ireland nor the Fenians had uttered more overt

---

*In old age he turned for solace to P. G. Wodehouse and Edgar Wallace.

incitements to violence. Even so moderate a man as Sir Horace Plunkett criticized Asquith for not arresting Carson. No doubt the premier hesitated to make a martyr out of the Ulster leader. Augustine Birrell, Asquith's chief adviser on Irish affairs, took the comforting view that Carson was only bluffing—a delusion shared by the Nationalist leader, John Redmond, who saw in the Orange defiance nothing but "a gigantic game of bluff and blackmail."

It is important to note that Carson was fighting not to exclude Ulster from Home Rule but to make Home Rule impossible for the rest of Ireland, even if the majority of Irishmen desired it. "I entirely agree with you," wrote Carson's friend, Lord Arran, "that we must use all our physical and armed forces to prevent Home Rule, not only for Ulster, but for the whole of Ireland, as sworn by the Covenant."

The mentality of the Ulster leaders at this time reveals certain almost pathological traits. Their attitude to history showed an extreme alienation from reality; their attitude to the present was a combination of persecution mania with delusions of grandeur. William of Orange was the incarnation of virtue, the Pope—of evil. Hatred of Rome was the first article in the creed of every good Orangeman. Home Rule would mean Rome rule. Some zealots seriously believed that if Home Rule should become law, the Pope would take up his residence in Dublin—to spite the Orange Order. No less a figure than Rudyard Kipling lent his name to such absurd fantasies, as when he wrote in 1913:

> We know the war prepared
> On every peaceful home,
> We know the hells prepared
> For such as serve not Rome.

According to Bonar Law, Ulster regarded the rule of a Dublin parliament with greater loathing than the Poles had ever felt for the rule of the Tsar.

After praising the energy and determination that characterized Belfast at this time, Lord Morley commented that it "harbored a spirit of bigotry and violence for which a parallel can hardly be found in any town of western Europe." To spiritual pride was added the arrogance of Mammon. Ulster looked down upon the rest of Ireland not only because it was Catholic but because it was poor. In the prosperity of Belfast shipyards—where the *Titanic* had been built—Orangemen were wont to see the visible proof that they constituted the Lord's Elect. The northern capital, with "its monstrous array of factory chimneys, flaunting plumes of smoke above diminished spires of churches," laid no claim to elegance or social grace. Rather, it deemed such qualities proper only to an enervating, easygoing city like Dublin, the especial object of Belfast's scorn. The battery of whistles, hooters, and sirens that regulated the hours of the working day was sweeter than music in the ears of a northern captain of industry. Belfast was thrifty, hard-working, and justifiably proud of the wealth it produced: it was also aggressive, boastful, and complacent.

Carson and his friends deliberately set themselves to foment religious discord in Belfast. The inevitable result was a renewed outbreak of anti-Catholic rioting—the first since that instigated in 1886 by Lord Randolph Churchill. On July 12, 1912, and for several days following, an Orange terror raged in the northern capital. "Belfast confetti" was the playful name for the iron bolts and rivets hurled by Orangemen at their Catholic fellow workers. A number of the latter were killed and more than a hundred injured.

Ulster's defiance was rooted in a grotesque version of Irish history, which deified the North at the expense of the south. Speeches were filled with denunciations of the Catholic infamies of 1641 and with praise of the heroic warriors of Derry and the Boyne. No dinner was complete without a toast to "the glorious, pious and immortal memory of the great and good King William." Much use was made of the patriotic symbol of the flag. Everywhere in Ulster one saw the Union Jack—flying on public building and factories, on tenements and farmhouses, even on trees. The largest Union Jack ever woven was proudly displayed at some Orange meetings.

The fierce crusading spirit that animated the North was manifest in a little book called *The Soul of Ulster,* written by Lord Ernest Hamilton, younger son of the Duke of Abercorn, one of Ulster's chief territorial magnates. Lord Ernest was an old Harrovian and a former member of parliament, but his book—invaluable as a study of the Covenanting mind—is almost paranoiac in the intensity of its obsessions, delusions, and hatreds.

Lord Ernest begins by justifying the original Plantation on the ground that before 1608, Ulster had been nothing but "a sink of murder, misery and vice. . . . It was clear," he adds, "that a remedy of some sort was called for." Then, "without any provocation" came the horrid rebellion of 1641. Ten lurid pages devoted to atrocities committed by Catholics are followed by a single casual reference to reprisals made against them. The author accepts Cromwell's inflated estimate of 200,000 Protestants slain, following which Lord Ernest blandly observes that extermination is still "the first item in the official Nationalist programme." If Home Rule should become law, the Catholics would immediately confiscate all land held by Protestants; indeed, Lord

Ernest darkly hinted, the spoils had already been divided in anticipation of victory.

Cromwell, we read, was "scrupulously just in his dealings with the natives, and never brutal." His government was "the most popular Ireland had ever known"—a judgment that perfectly illustrates Lord Acton's well-known saying: first comes the soldier with his sword, and then the historian with his sponge. Passing on to 1798, the reader is again plunged into peasant atrocities that reveal "the secret soul of the Irish people," while the terrible revenge taken by the yeomanry on the peasants is almost completely ignored.

The cause of the Famine was that the Irish had "no genius for agriculture," hence "many thousands died," but fortunately the charity of the Protestants and the British government saved the rest. "The policy of the Protestants towards the natives," writes Lord Ernest with unaffected candor, "is, and has always been, honestly pacific. . . . They only want to live and let live." The motto of the "natives," however, he interprets as being: "To hell or to the sea with every bloody Protestant."

Having established, by well-chosen examples, that the Irish have always been a murderous race, Lord Ernest concludes: "The soul of the native Irish has not at the present day changed by the width of a hair from what it was in 1641, and again in 1798. . . . The basic nature of the native Irish remains the same today as it was in the days of Elizabeth, the same as it was in the days of Strongbow, and probably very much as it had been in the days of Noah."

The unmistakable import of this inflammatory little tract was to convince loyal Orangemen that beneath the benign aspect of John Redmond lurked the instincts of a criminal. For Protestants, however, the idea of revenge was out of the question, since—the pogroms in the shipyards notwithstanding—"Protestants are not built that way." *The Soul of Ulster* throws a harsh light upon the primitive mentality of many Orangemen and compels one to realize the intractable nature of the problem faced by the British government in 1914. In the annals of any nation, it would be hard to find a more blatant example of the debasement of history for purposes of propaganda.

The English Conservatives and Home Rule

That Ulster should have talked treason is not surprising; what is astonishing is that the English Conservative party—the loyal Opposition supposedly devoted to responsible government—should have condoned such treason, urging Ulster to the brink of civil war—and beyond. For the sake of party advantage, the Tories were prepared to wreck the constitution.

Andrew Bonar Law, leader of the Conservative party since 1911, had been born in New Brunswick, the son of an Ulster Presbyterian minister. While his parentage gave him a natural bias in favor of the north, few could have prophesied the lengths to which he would go in encouraging sedition. At Easter, 1912, in Belfast, he took the salute from 100,000 Ulster Volunteers marching past him in military formation. On July 29, 1912, he told a huge Conservative rally at Blenheim, the Duke of Marlborough's palace near Oxford: "I can imagine no lengths of resistance to which Ulster will go which I shall not be ready to support, and in which they will not be supported by the overwhelming majority of the British people." This incitement to revolt Asquith justly characterized as "the reckless rhodomontade of Blenheim, which furnished forth the complete grammar of anarchy." Next year, Bonar Law ridiculed Asquith's lawfully elected government as "a Revolutionary Committee which seized by fraud upon despotic power." Not until more than forty years later did it become known that Bonar Law was at this time trying to intimidate a frightened king (George V) into using the royal veto—a constitutional device that had been obsolete for two centuries.

Walter Long, a prominent Conservative, candidly told Bonar Law that he wanted civil war. "I hope there will be no quarter," he said, "but war to the knife against a Parliament not of statesmen but of cold-blooded murderers." Long's close friend, Lord Esher, gave it as his considered opinion that the House of Commons was "a Constituent Assembly of a revolutionary character and not a parliament at all." Lord Curzon, who as ex-Viceroy of India was better qualified than most to appreciate the need for law and order, was one of the loudest in urging violence. "The contest," he told Lord Esher, "must finally be allowed to solve itself in battle on the soil of Ireland." At the mere mention of Home Rule, Lord Hugh Cecil, son of the former premier, Lord Salisbury, himself a product of Eton and Oxford and a pillar of the Church of England, became like a man possessed. Home Rule, he declared, was Jacobitism. An autonomous Ireland within the British Empire would be like sewage in milk.

If such was the language of grave elder statesmen, it may be imagined how little there was to restrain so unscrupulous a recruit to the Tory party as F. E. Smith, later Lord Birkenhead. Eighteen years younger than Carson, "F.E." became his chief lieutenant in England. Where Carson was brutal, "F.E." was urbane. The fanaticism of the former was matched by the opportunism of the latter. Both were insolent, and both were bullies. Ulster must be defended, "F.E." proclaimed, "though the whole fabric of the Commonwealth be convulsed." Echoing Bonar Law at Blenheim, he asserted that there would be "no length to which Ulster would not be entitled to go— if the quarrel were wickedly fixed upon her." If he were an Ulster Protestant, said "F.E.," he would prefer to be ruled by the Sultan of Turkey than by an Irish nationalist. Home Rule itself he termed a piece of "reckless wickedness," "a crazy and criminal gamble."

Only within the last few years has the full extent of the sinister activity of Lord Milner, the *eminence grise* of the Conservative party, been revealed by Professor A. M. Gollin in his book *Pro-Consul of Empire*. Still more extreme than Carson or Bonar Law, Milner was opposed on principle to a peaceful settlement and actually wanted an Ulster rebellion. He urged Sir Edward to strike. Milner detested democracy, his ideal of government being an autocracy like that of Bismarck in Germany. A defeat for Home Rule would be a blow to democracy and hence an additional reason for supporting Ulster. According to his latest biographer, Milner did not care whether he wrecked the British constitution, so long as Home Rule was defeated.

Milner was the leading spirit in the formation in 1914 of an organization known as the British Covenanters, whose object was to support Ulster regardless of the consequences. In less than six months, two million Englishmen signed the Covenant, which Milner himself had drafted. Among those who openly pledged themselves to break the law if necessary were Lord Roberts, the former Commander-in-Chief of the British Army, the Duke of Portland, Viscount Halifax, Rudyard Kipling, Sir Edward Elgar, the composer, Professor Dicey, and Sir Herbert Warren, President of Magdalen College, Oxford. Milner also obtained for the Covenant "very secret" pledges of financial support, including £30,000 from Mr. Astor and £10,000 from Lord Rothschild.

One member of the British Covenanters, Sir William Watson, a more ingenious versifier even than Kipling, rose to the occasion by finding a word to rhyme with "Ulster." The Liberals, he declaimed, had

> Jeered at her loyalty, trod on her pride,
> Spurned her, repulsed her,
> Great-hearted Ulster,
> Flung her aside.

The full irony of the Conservative dalliance with treason can hardly be appreciated unless one remembers that in the past it had prided itself upon being the only party fit to be trusted with the constitution or with the welfare of the nation. Hitherto, whenever there had been a threat to public order, it had always been the Tories who had urged the utmost rigor of the law against the offender. Now, to defeat the Liberals, they put party before country and urged a course of action that they had termed seditious when it had been adopted by socialists or suffragettes.

Founding of the National Volunteers (1913)

While Ulster was girding for war, the southern Nationalists were in a mood of relaxed optimism, content that Asquith's government should bear the heat and burden of the day. John Redmond (1857–1918), the old-fashioned country gentleman who had led the Home Rule party since 1900, was no fighter, though he had once suffered the indignity of prison on account of politics. Indolent by nature, he was without personal ambition. He liked the amenities of rural life and was never happier than at Aughavanagh, his hunting lodge in the Wicklow mountains. "Ireland to him was Aughavanagh," wrote his friend and biographer, Stephen Gwynn. No match for so ruthless an opponent as Carson, Redmond found the easygoing ways of Isaac Butt more congenial than the strenuous guerrilla tactics of Parnell. He also lacked the personal magnetism of the Chief. With the English members he was popular, since, like Butt, he respected the traditions of parliament.

Though a staunch Nationalist, Redmond was also an ardent Imperialist and an admirer of Cecil Rhodes. Granted self-government, he wrote in 1913, Ireland would be Britain's "brightest jewel in her crown of Empire." A year later, on the outbreak of war, he declared that Home Rule would enable Ireland to "become the strongest arm in the defence of the Empire."

In domestic politics Redmond was a conservative, the spokesman for the landlord and business interests in Ireland. He dismissed Sinn Fein as "a temporary cohesion of isolated cranks." He chose to be ignorant of the appalling condition of the Dublin slums and condemned those who, like Larkin and Connolly, sought to abolish the social conditions that made slums possible. In other words, had Home Rule been granted, Redmond and his nationalist followers would quickly have discovered that the English Conservatives, not the English Liberals, were their natural allies. Hence the scornful dismissal of Redmond many years later by Frank O'Connor as the "jelly-fish of Westminster . . . a perfect Irish gentleman."

If Redmond was loath to challenge Carson personally, and willing to leave the Ulster problem to be settled by Asquith, whom he complimented as "the strongest and sanest man who has appeared in British politics in our time," others in Ireland were not so acquiescent. At a huge meeting held on November 25, 1913, in the historic Dublin Rotunda, where Sinn Fein had been founded eight years before, the National Volunteers were launched as a counterpoise to the Volunteers in Ulster. Professor Eoin MacNeill (1867-1937) was chosen head of the new organization, which included among its leading figures men such as Sir Roger Casement, Patrick Pearse, Bulmer Hobson, and Colonel Maurice Moore, brother of George Moore the novelist.

The formation of the National Volunteers owed much to the efforts of the Gaelic League and the I.R.B. The Home Rulers were conspicuous by their absence. The Volunteer movement was strong in Dublin and in the larger cities like Cork and Limerick but showed little strength in the countryside. In the towns its appeal was chiefly to teachers and students, to the lower-middle classes, and to some working men. By July, 1914, about 180,000 Volunteers had enrolled, nearly a third of whom were Ulster Catholics. "The existence on Irish soil of an Irish army," wrote Pearse in jubilation, "is the most portentous fact that has appeared in Ireland for over a hundred years." What the public did not realize was the degree of control which from the start the I.R.B. exercised in the new organization.

The creation of the National Volunteers caught Redmond unprepared. At first he tried to ignore the new movement, but finding it too strong to be disregarded, he sought successfully to gain control over it by getting his own nominees elected to its Executive Committee. This happened on June 9, 1914, despite the efforts of Pearse, Casement and others to defeat the maneuver. Redmond's pretext for his sudden, if belated, interest in the Volunteers was the dramatic change produced early in 1914 in Anglo-Irish relations by the Curragh "mutiny" and the gunrunning at Larne.

The Curragh Incident (1914)

For Britain in 1912, the Irish problem was the unfinished business of the nineteenth century—the business that the folly of the peers had prevented Gladstone from settling. Now the day of reckoning was at hand, and the attention of Europe was fixed upon England. The Prime Minister was by nature cautious, hesitant, and temporizing. Understandably enough, Asquith had no desire to seize the Ulster bull by the horns and be gored by Carson for his pains. As the Archbishop of York told the Lords in 1912: "The figure of Ulster, grim, determined, menacing, dominated the scene." Asquith himself justly commented on Ulster's defiance of parliament, saying that "a more deadly blow has never been dealt . . . at the very foundations on which democratic society rests." The premier's brave words were not followed by acts. Meanwhile the situation steadily deteriorated in Ireland, where by the spring of 1914, two private armies were preparing for combat.

Asquith's outstanding colleague in the cabinet was David Lloyd George, the hero of the victory over the Lords in 1911. Yet for all his avowed sympathy with Home Rule and his pride in his Celtic origin, throughout the Ulster crisis the little Welshman was strangely silent. Into the breach stepped his younger and more impulsive colleague Winston Churchill, now First Lord of the Admiralty. In the Commons, Churchill had already taunted his former Conservative friends about their claim to watch over the constitution. "How much they care for law," he said, "how much they value order when it stands in the way of anything they like." "We must not attach too much importance to these frothings of Sir Edward Carson," he scoffed. "I daresay when the worst comes to the worst we shall find that civil war evaporates in uncivil words."

Never one to flinch from danger, in February, 1912, Churchill decided to go to Belfast to defend Home Rule in person. Because of its association with Lord Randolph in 1886, no name was more highly regarded in the northern capital than the name Churchill. But where Lord Randolph had appeared as an avenging angel, recklessly lashing his audience into partisan fury, now his degenerate son, a renegade from the Conservative party, appeared as the devil's advocate for common sense. Carson asserted that for Churchill to visit Belfast would be "a more criminal act than has yet been prosecuted in any criminal court." Denied the use of the Ulster Hall, where his father had spoken, the First Lord was compelled to speak at the Celtic football ground in the Catholic quarter of the city. Threats were made against his life. According to Ian Colvin, a Unionist journalist, Orange mobs filled the streets uttering "fearful menaces and imprecations." Fortunately for a generation of Englishmen yet unborn, Churchill, protected by a heavy guard of military and police, got away unscathed, although an angry crowd nearly overturned his motor car. But for the presence of Mrs. Churchill, wrote an Orange writer wistfully, "he would have had his entrails kicked out on the stones of Royal Avenue." The frustrated mob vented its fury by burning the First Lord in effigy on the Shankhill Road.

As Hitler was later to discover, Winston Churchill was not a man to be trifled with. On his return to England he advocated drastic measures against Ulster. At Bradford on March 14, 1914, in what Redmond called "a superb speech," the First Lord flung down the gauntlet. Speaking gravely and deliberately (in words that anticipated his mood in 1940) he warned: "If every concession that is made is spurned and exploited, if the loose, wanton and reckless chatter that we have been forced to listen to these many months is in the end to disclose a sinister and revolutionary purpose, then I can only say to you: 'Let us go forward together and put these grave matters to the proof.' "

Unlike Asquith, Churchill was not just a man of words. He followed his denunciations of what he called a "treasonable conspiracy" by ordering two cruisers to Belfast Lough and a battle squadron from the Channel to Lamlash in the Firth of Clyde. In Ulster it was widely believed that these moves signified an intention to blockade Belfast and arrest the Ulster leaders. Later, Sir John French, Commander-in-Chief of the Home Forces in Britain, reported that the choleric Churchill had told him privately that if Belfast were to resist, "his fleet would have the town in ruin in twenty-four hours." To forestall possible action against Ulster, the Curragh "mutiny" occurred six days after Churchill's Bradford speech.

On March 20, 1914, Sir Hubert Gough, commander of the Third Cavalry Brigade stationed at the Curragh, County Kildare, and fifty-seven officers serving under him, resigned their commissions *en masse*. Sir Arthur Paget, Commander-in-Chief in Ireland, had notified Gough that the brigade might be ordered north, by what he called "those dirty swine of politicians," to move against the Ulster Volunteers, who were reported to be on the point of raiding military depots in order to get arms. Known as a hot-tempered and foolish man, Paget had intimated to Gough—incredible as it may seem—that if he should find this order from a Liberal government distasteful, he and his officers might prefer to resign. Gough took the hint and acted accordingly.

The Curragh "mutiny" blunted the spearhead of possible military action against Ulster. It even appeared as though the government had lost control of its armed forces. As might have been expected, military men in Britain wholeheartedly supported Gough.

Lord Roberts told the Upper House that it was "unthinkable that the British Army should have been called upon to fight the Ulster Volunteers"—a statement he followed by inveighing against "idle but dangerous and mischievous assertions" that the army was becoming involved in politics. (Colonel Seely, the Secretary of War, complained that, according to Lord French, Roberts had called him and Asquith "swine and robbers," but perhaps this was merely the bluff talk of an old soldier.)

With only one exception, the senior officers of an army corps at Aldershot headed by Sir Douglas Haig, the future Commander-in-Chief on the Western Front, let it be known that, sooner than proceed against Ulster, they too would resign their commissions. Many added that they themselves would forthwith join the Ulster Volunteers. The upshot of the Curragh incident was that Seely resigned—a scapegoat sacrificed by the government. No move was made against Ulster, and Gough and his officers were presently reinstated in their commands. The government, and with it the principle of democracy, had suffered a serious reverse.

The Director of Military Operations in 1914 was Sir Henry Wilson, an Irishman by birth, an Orangeman by conviction, and like his friend Milner, an implacable foe of democracy. Five years after Wilson's assassination by the I.R.A. in 1922, the publication of his diaries revealed that throughout the Curragh crisis, the D.M.O. had betrayed the very politicians he was supposed to be serving—the "frocks" as he contemptuously called them—by passing on official secrets to Bonar Law and Carson, while encouraging Gough in his defiance. Arrogant, unscrupulous, disloyal, Sir Henry Wilson, the evil genius of the army, was Carson's secret agent in Whitehall. His conduct, wrote Sir Robert Ensor, the historian, was "quite impossible by any ordinary standards of honour to reconcile with the holding of his post."

"The man who saved the Empire is Henry Wilson," said Lord Milner after the Curragh crisis had ended—a claim that was strongly disputed by Gough, who throughout life regarded himself as the hero of the occasion. Sir Henry Wilson's house in Eaton Place, outside which he was later to be assassinated, was the headquarters of intrigue. There, almost nightly, Geoffrey Dawson of the *Times*, Leo Amery, F. S. Oliver, and old Dr. Jameson (with his South African experience of illegal resort to arms) would meet with Milner and Wilson to plot measures against the cabinet whose members Milner abused as "criminals" whom nothing "was going to save." "These people," he wrote scornfully, in the very act of betraying the government, "are capable of every treachery. They are crawling today, but unless we are wary, and give them no chance, they may jump up again tomorrow." Mild-mannered Liberals like Lord Morley he described as "still screaming for Blood, everybody's blood, though how they hope to be able to draw it is not apparent."

Today what makes the Curragh incident instructive is the light that it throws on the almost pathological mentality of political reactionaries in time of crisis. In the minds of seemingly responsible Conservatives, fact and fiction were confounded, the truth inverted, an arrogant militarism aureoled with a halo of innocence, and a weak vacillating government (in which Churchill was the only strong man) transformed into a malignant despotism. It is curious to reflect that it was in peaceful, parliamentary England that the unmistakable menace of Fascism first appeared. A generation later, on the other side of the globe, the Ulster crisis was to be reenacted on a larger scale. In usurping the authority of the Diet in the 1930s, the Japanese militarists professed their unshaken allegiance to the Crown—as did the Ulster leaders in 1914. But where Carson and his friends had no occasion to do more than vilify the civilian leaders of the government, the Japanese warlords removed theirs by assassination.

The lesson was not lost on observers abroad. In Switzerland, Lenin, who closely followed events in Ireland, was gratified to see the upper classes furnishing the workers with a lesson in resistance to the law. In India, Nehru was impressed that Imperialists who preached law and order to the subject peoples of Africa and Asia should take the law into their own hands the moment it suited them. In the United States, Woodrow Wilson, a Presbyterian of Scotch-Irish origin, was shocked by Carson's defiance of the government. "He ought to be hanged for treason," the President tersely commented. He only wished that Asquith had had the firmness of Andrew Jackson.

The Gunrunnings at Larne and Howth (1914)

Five weeks after the Curragh incident another event occurred that moved Ireland closer to the brink of war. This was the sensational gunrunning at Larne, County Antrim, on the night of April 24-25, 1914, when thirty thousand rifles and three million rounds of ammunition for the Ulster Volunteers were smuggled in from Germany. This audacious operation was masterminded by the engineer Fred Crawford, now a Volunteer colonel, who had plotted to kidnap Gladstone in 1893. He was one of twenty zealots who had signed the Ulster Covenant with their own blood. While in Hamburg negotiating for the weapons, Crawford had heard a supernatural voice urging him on. Crawford had, in fact, consulted the Deity—throughout the enterprise. "In simple language," he wrote, "I told God all about it . . . I point out all this to God." When the arms were landed, there was jubilation throughout Ulster and thanks were rendered to the Almighty. Thirty years later, Sir Nevile Henderson, the last British

Ambassador to Nazi Germany, complacently related in his memoirs how he too had violated the law by smuggling arms into the North, and how his brother-in-law, Lord Leitrim, "one of the most fanatical Ulstermen," had played a leading role in the gunrunning at Larne.

The violation of the law at Larne—the importation of arms into Ireland had been banned in December, 1913 (two weeks after the formation of the National Volunteers!)—led the southern Irish to take countermeasures. On Sunday, July 26, 1914, some 2,500 rifles and 125,000 rounds of ammunition—a much smaller haul than at Larne—were landed at Howth, nine miles from Dublin. The leaders in this enterprise were Darrell Figgis, Bulmer Hobson, and Mrs. Erskine Childers, the former Milly Osgood of Boston. Having got wind of the *coup*, the King's Own Scottish Borderers tried to intercept the National Volunteers as they were marching into Dublin with the newly acquired arms. Despite this unforseen difficulty, many of the weapons did reach Dublin, where two years later they made the Easter Rising possible.

That same evening, stones were thrown at the Borderers as they paraded along one of the quays north of the Liffey known as Bachelors' Walk. The troops fired on the crowd, killing three persons and wounding thirty-two. Thus only a week before the European war, bloodshed occurred in Ireland, where feeling was rising dangerously. The southern Nationalists could not help contrasting the "massacre of Bachelors' Walk" with the impunity accorded to the Orange gunrunning at Larne.

Two private armies—now at least partially armed—faced each other in the small embittered island. Civil war in Ireland seemed inevitable. Among those who took this view was the Imperial German government, which counted on strife in Ireland to immobilize Britain in case Germany should violate Belgian neutrality. Baron von Kuhlmann, secretary to the German Embassy in London, paid a secret visit to Belfast. On his return he quoted Orange leaders to the effect that, should the worst come to the worst, Ulster would prefer the rule of the Kaiser to that of John Redmond. In August, 1913, Sir Edward Carson lunched with the Kaiser at Homburg and came away agreeably impressed. The Emperor told him that he had long wanted to visit Ireland, but his grandmother, Queen Victoria, had not allowed him to do so. Since Wilhelm II was the most powerful Protestant ruler in Europe, some Orangemen regarded him hopefully as another William of Orange.

Meanwhile, in the feverish negotiations over Home Rule that took place in London during the months preceding the war, a distinct change had come about in the attitude of the British government. It was becoming increasingly clear that Ireland was going to be partitioned and that at least part of Ulster would be excluded from the operation of the Home Rule Bill—a solution that Gladstone had never contemplated and Carson had always repudiated, but that Churchill and Lloyd George had urged all along. To coerce Ulster into accepting Home Rule, Asquith said on September 15, 1914—the day on which George V signed the bill into law—was "an absolutely unthinkable thing—a thing we would neither countenance or consent to." Such language was very different from the unqualified pledge of Home Rule given to Redmond by the Prime Minister in 1912.

The Dublin General Strike of 1913

While civil war threatened between Ulster and the South, Dublin itself had been convulsed by an unexpected social crisis—the General Strike led by Jim Larkin in 1913. Ever since Emmet's rising, Dublin had remained passive—sullen, brooding, discontented, yet never erupting in violence. The capital had responded neither to the appeal of Young Ireland nor to that of the Fenians. Yet throughout the century Dublin remained a city of appalling slums—filthy, stinking, and verminous. Parnell and the Home Rulers had ignored them completely; some nationalist leaders even profited financially from the exploitation of slum dwellers.

In 1912, Sir Charles Cameron, the Dublin Medical Officer of Health, submitted a report on health conditions in the capital. It revealed that Dublin's death rate was not only the highest in the United Kingdom but the highest in any city in Europe. It was twice that of London and worse even than that of cholera-ridden Calcutta. Dublin had also one of the highest rates of child mortality in Europe, the death rate among slum children being twenty-eight times higher than that among children of professional people. The death rate in workhouses was nearly ten times the average for the city. The chief killer was tuberculosis, a disease that flourished in the airless and fetid tenements of the poor. For many, as for young Mollser in *The Plough and the Stars,* a hacking cough was the prelude to Glasnevin.

In 1913, a government report on Dublin housing was published. It showed that 25,822 families (87,305 individuals) occupied 5,322 tenement buildings, of which nearly a third were totally unfit for human habitation. Between a third and a quarter of all Dublin families lived in single rooms, without running water, and with one lavatory shared by many households.

Jim Larkin (1876–1947). Founder of the Irish Transport and General Workers' Union, and leader of the Dublin General Strike in 1913.

Many eighteenth-century mansions on the north side of the Liffey had been deserted by the aristocracy that had built them. Now, room by sordid room, they were rented to the poor with handsome profits for their latest owners. Sometimes four families would share a single room, each occupying one corner. Elegant cornices, delicate moldings, painted ceilings, marble mantelpieces, looked down upon the squalid litter of the undifferentiated poor. Privacy was impossible. Opportunities for decency did not exist. Drunken men and sluttish women brawled and cursed and quarreled. In the background could be heard the wailing of redundant offspring or the racking cough of the consumptive. In once-fashionable residential areas like Dominick Street, there was scarcely an unbroken pane of glass or a staircase that was not rotted. Broken windows were stuffed with rags or boards. Filthy wallpaper hung peeling from the walls. From open doorways came the stench of unwashed bodies. The cellars were verminous and rat-infested. The stunted race that occupied such dwellings was clad in torn, ragged, or patched garments, filthy with age. Their children ran about half naked. Such people never knew clean linen till the day they were laid out in their coffins.

In his autobiography Sean O'Casey has left an unforgettable picture of the Dublin slums of his youth. His testimony was corroborated by that of Pearse, who reported that "the tenement houses of Dublin are so rotten that they collapse on their inhabitants." To this scandalous state of affairs the public authorities were almost totally indifferent. City government in Dublin was notorious for its venality and corruption.

The respectable citizens who owned slum property were often the employers of labor, the cheapest commodity on the market. A work week of between seventy-two and seventy-eight hours was not uncommon. Nearly a quarter of those who lived in tenements earned less than fifteen shillings (then about $3.50) a week. Manual laborers sometimes got this amount for a ninety-hour week. Upon this shocking state of affairs, Larkin struck like a thunderbolt in 1909. To wealthy men like William Martin Murphy, Larkin was nothing but a brazen-tongued demagogue, but to the denizens of the slums his stentorian voice sounded like that of an archangel. Within four years Larkin had goaded thousands of working men into a consciousness of their servitude and had organized them into the largest union Dublin had ever had. The inevitable result was the long-delayed collision with the employers.

Jim Larkin (1876–1947) was born in Newry, County Down, but grew up in the slums of Liverpool, where his parents had emigrated when he was a child. The boy never had even a primary education. At the age of seven he was already working forty hours a week for half a crown (then worth about fifty cents). At seventeen he stowed away on a ship bound for the River Plate. Finding the conditions of work intolerable, Larkin attempted to organize his fellow victims in the hold of the ship. As punishment he was put in irons and chained to a stanchion, where he claimed that at night rats had gnawed at the nails on his fingers and toes. Such was Larkin's introduction, about the year 1894, to the world of capital and labor.

During the following decade Larkin became familiar with the lower depths in Britain. With typical hyperbole he used to boast that he had slept in every workhouse from Land's End to John o' Groats', or that between Manchester and London there was not a road he had not tramped nor a hedge under which he had not slept. He read eagerly whatever he could get hold of and learned some poetry by heart, which he was fond of quoting. He developed a consuming hatred of injustice, together with a profound contempt for those who allowed themselves to be exploited. A confirmed teetotaler, he was alleged to have wished for the day when grass would grow over the ruins of Guinness' Brewery in Dublin.

Larkin was over six feet tall, strongly built, and possessed of immense vitality. High cheekbones and hollowed cheeks gave him a gaunt, ascetic aspect. Long black hair fell across a wide forehead. As he shouted and gesticulated, sweat poured from his brow. He was a powerful natural orator with an endless flow of words. Sean O'Casey long recalled the "deep, dark, husky voice" of the man he named "the Irish Prometheus," as well as the outstretched arms and sweeping gestures with which Larkin dominated any crowd that he addressed.

From him the workingmen gained their first insight into the shamefulness of their condition. Larkin became the conscience of the Dublin slums, into which he infused his own sense of outrage. He savored his power and was intoxicated by it. Larkin was a born demagogue, his language inflammatory to the highest degree. Invective and abuse were his natural mode of expression. The torrent of words that poured from him inundated every tenement in Dublin. His egotism was unbounded. He was elemental and explosive like some volcanic force. At his bidding the huge inert mass of humanity at last began to move.

"I have got a divine mission," Larkin would announce, "to make men and women discontented." Not having read Adam Smith, his economics were of an extreme simplicity: "To hell with contracts." He vowed that he would not stand to see Christ daily crucified in Dublin by the employers. Any man who starved, and let his family starve, while the shops were full of food was a fool. To him a policeman was "a Cossack—a dirty brute in blue clothes." He often opened his meetings with the old Fenian song, "The Rising of the Moon." "I am a rebel, and the son of a rebel," he would shout. "I recognize no law but the people's law."

Pearse once observed that he didn't know whether Larkin's methods were justified or not, "but this I do know, that here is a hideous wrong to be righted, and that the man who attempts honestly to right it is a good man and a brave man." Pearse welcomed Larkin's son as a pupil at St. Enda's.

Larkin returned to Ireland in 1907 and attempted to organize casual labor in Belfast. Expelled from that city, he came to Dublin and there in 1909 created the Irish Transport and General Workers' Union, which included stevedores (longshoremen), carters (teamsters), and a variety of unskilled and semiskilled labor. Its headquarters were in

Liberty Hall by the north bank of the Liffey. Branches of the I.T.G.W.U. were soon founded in Cork, Wexford, Waterford, Sligo, and other Irish ports.

The propaganda organ of the union was the *Irish Worker,* a weekly founded by Larkin in 1911. Because of its sensational attacks upon capitalists, the paper quickly gained a large circulation—26,000 in the first month, 95,000 in three months—so that it may easily have reached a quarter of a million readers. In its columns Larkin belabored William Martin Murphy, the leading Dublin capitalist, as "a blood-sucking vampire—the most foul and vicious blackguard that ever polluted any country." Larkin also maintained that if the army were justified in shooting deserters, workers were justified in killing blacklegs.

From 1910 onward, Larkin's second-in-command in the I.T.G.W.U.

James Connolly (1870–1916). A self-taught Irish socialist, who commanded the Citizens Army in the Easter Rising and was shot by the British.

was James Connolly (1870–1916). Born in Ballybay, County Monaghan, son of a street cleaner, Connolly grew up in Edinburgh, where his family had emigrated when he was ten. Like Larkin, Connolly had scant education, earning his living as navvy, trampler, peddler—and finally as a garbage collector. Though self-taught, Connolly unlike Larkin was studious in temperament. He read omnivorously and systematically. He learned his socialism not only from the slums but in the libraries of Edinburgh—and later in the New York Public Library and in the National Library of Ireland.

In 1896, having been on the point of emigrating to Chile, Connolly was persuaded by his wife to settle in Dublin, where he helped to found the Irish Socialist party (which Larkin never joined). He also edited *The Workers' Republic*, a Socialist paper that contained what Louis Le Roux calls "the most passionate and precise incitements to revolution since the days of Lalor and Mitchel." Already in 1903, Arthur Griffith, no friend to labor, was writing in the *United Irishman* that Connolly was "opposed by the shoneens, the tenement-house rack-renters of the poor, the publicans and, we regret to say, the priests." Though not a practicing Catholic, Connolly never formally left the Church (in which he was to die), arguing that socialism and Catholicism were not incompatible.

Along with Francis Sheehy Skeffington, Connolly was also one of the earliest champions in Ireland of equal rights for women. "The worker is the slave of capitalist society," he wrote, "and the female worker is the slave of that slave."

In 1903, Connolly was offered the post of organizer for the American Socialist party, as a result of which he lived the next seven years in New York. He lectured on socialism from coast to coast, meeting "Big Bill" Haywood and other leaders of the I.W.W. Homesick for Ireland, Connolly once assured his wife that he would rather be a poor man in Dublin than a millionaire in America. To Dublin, then, he returned with his family in 1910.

Connolly was modest, unassuming, simple, and direct. He was devoted to his wife and adored by his children. The utmost sacrifice that Connolly could make when he joined the Rising in 1916 was to give up this happy family life. His friends respected his absolute integrity. He had no trace of Larkin's vulgarity or egotism. As a public speaker, he delivered himself quietly and without hyperbole, revealing a mastery of his subject. He dealt in facts or theories, not in personalities. By reasoned argument and by his own sincerity, he too could rivet the attention of a working-class audience. He neither needed nor desired to draw attention to himself. The quiet courage with which he eventually faced the firing squad did not surprise his friends. "He was the bravest man I ever knew," wrote Maud Gonne.

Connolly's vision of Ireland was different from that of romantic writers and poets. Where they saw the heroic personalities of the past, he saw only the class struggle constant in all periods of history. Sarsfield meant no more to him than Cuchulain. He censured the Irish Brigade for deserting their country to fight under a foreign king and did not fail to note how in the end they had fought the French Revolution. The vaunted patriotism of Molyneux, Swift, and Lucas he dismissed as only words. Grattan's parliament was little better than a sham. The real heroes in Irish history were the obscure, unsung peasant leaders of the Whiteboys, the Oakboys, and the Hearts of Steel—agrarian societies that Connolly viewed as the real, if rude, precursors of socialism. Connolly's single concession to romanticism was his idealization of the "primitive communism" of Gaelic Ireland.

Connolly's gaze was fixed steadily upon the actual world around him, and on the injustices in which that world abounded. "Ireland without her people," he wrote, "is nothing to me, and the man who is bubbling over with love and enthusiasm for 'Ireland,' and yet can pass unmoved through our streets and witness all the wrong and suffering, the shame and degradation wrought upon the people of Ireland, aye, wrought by Irishmen upon Irish men and women, without burning to end it, is, in my opinion, a fraud and a liar in his heart." He respected among previous writers on Irish history only Fintan Lalor and John Mitchel, and among contemporaries only Alice Stopford Green.

Connolly's own contribution to the study of the Irish past was a little book called *Labor in Irish History,* published in 1910, in which he made his first systematic application of Marxist ideas. As the work of a self-taught man without much formal education, it is a remarkable study—clear, trenchant, and well organized. Inevitably, the author viewed economics as more significant than anything else. Even the long struggle for national freedom concerned him less than the age-old conflict of the peasant with his landlord. In more recent history, for him the class struggle took precedence over both religion and politics. Compared with the crushing weight of agrarian misery, even the wrongs wrought by the Penal Laws seemed secondary. As for the Papacy, it had usually sacrificed Ireland's interests to those of England, regarding Ireland as important only in so far as it might serve as an instrument for the spiritual reconquest of England.

The General Strike of August, 1913, arose out of a direct clash between the I.T.G.W.U. and the Dublin Employers' Federation, organized by William Martin Murphy to lock out employees in any business who belonged to Larkin's union. Murphy had come to Dublin as an almost penniless boy from Bantry; by 1913, when he was seventy, he had become one of the richest men in Ireland—worth £500,000 at his death in 1921. He owned the Dublin Electric Tramways, the *Irish Independent,* the most widely read newspaper in Dublin, and the largest department store in the city. In politics, Murphy was a Home Ruler, but he was also a firm believer "in the commercial value to Ireland of a place in the British Empire." He had, of course, been an outspoken antagonist of Parnell, who, in his opinion, had "proved himself to be filled with some of the worst passions of human nature."

At this time Murphy was a tall, white-haired, kindly looking old gentleman—dignified in manner, and hard as nails. "A strong Irishman and a strong Catholic," wrote Sir James O'Connor, "he was essentially English and Protestant in temperament: cold, reserved, self-controlled." An Irish combination of Samuel Smiles and Horatio Alger, Murphy believed that every ragged gossoon, if only he were willing to work, could one day become rich.

In 1913, Murphy infuriated W. B. Yeats by his opposition to Sir Edwin Lutyens' project to build over the Liffey an imposing picture gallery for the collection of French Impressionists that Sir Hugh Lane wished to present to Dublin. Murphy rejected the plan on three grounds: as a practical man, because money spent on art was wasted; as a religious man, because the collection contained nudes; and as an Irishman, because the architect was English.

Larkin forestalled Murphy's threat of a lockout by calling a tram strike on the busiest day of the year in Dublin, the opening day of Horse Show Week. Larkin's move failed, service on the tramways being restored within the hour. Murphy and his fellow employers retaliated by instituting a city-wide lockout not only against the I.T.G.W.U. but against all unions in Dublin. Between fifteen and twenty thousand men were thrown out of work. The Port of Dublin was closed for several weeks. By the end of September, when the meager funds of the unions were almost exhausted, nearly 100,000 people faced starvation.

The arrest of Larkin on Sunday, August 26, in O'Connell Street was followed by a savage police assault upon an unarmed and helpless crowd. In his autobiography, Sean O'Casey vividly described the mass panic that ensued, with the sickening sound of batons crunching upon skulls. Two men were killed and about five hundred injured, many of them seriously. It was long before the events of "Bloody Sunday" were forgotten in the slums of Dublin.

A commission of inquiry set up by the British government, presided over by Sir George Askwith, recommended arbitration by an impartial committee. Larkin accepted the suggestion, but Murphy, determined to crush the workers, refused. Askwith at this point observed that the Dublin employers were living mentally in a world that was already half a century out of date. By the spring of 1914 the strikers' funds were totally exhausted. Beaten and dispirited, their families on the verge of starvation, the men returned sullenly to work. Even the London *Times,* which had no sympathy for Larkin, condemned the intransigence of the employers.

What the working people resented most was the almost unanimous condemnation of them—by the press, by the Catholic Church, by the Home Rule leaders, and even by Sinn Fein. To the chorus of vindictive abuse there was but one honorable exception—the writers and poets of Dublin: Yeats and A.E., Patrick Pearse and Thomas Mac-Donagh, Tom Kettle and Sheehy Skeffington, James Stephens and Daniel Corkery. The sole discordant note among the intellectuals was struck by Arthur Griffith, who reminded the impoverished workers that they "must make a sacrifice in money for the moral and social gain of living among their own kindred in their own land."

Outside of the small intellectual community, few voices were raised on behalf of charity or sanity. In his "Open Letter to the Masters of Dublin," A.E. delivered a scathing rebuke to Murphy and his capitalist allies.

> You deliberately determined in cold anger, to starve out one third of the population of this city, to break the manhood of the men by the sight of the suffering of their wives and the hunger of their children. We read in the Dark Ages of the rack and the thumbscrew. . . . It remained for the twentieth century and the capital city of Ireland to see an oligarchy of four hundred masters deciding openly on starving 100,000 people, and refusing any solution except that fixed by their pride. . . . Your insolence and ignorance of the rights conceded everywhere to the worker in the modern world were incredible, and as great as your inhumanity.

To many who had long suspected AE of being a Communist, this letter seemed convincing proof.

Not long after the collapse of the strike, Larkin left Ireland for America, leaving Connolly in charge of the I.T.G.W.U. It was due to Connolly that the failure of the General Strike had an unexpected sequel—the founding of the Citizen Army. In Switzerland, Lenin had watched events in Dublin in 1913 with considerable interest. He believed that the General Strike constituted a turning point in Irish social history—the point at which labor in Ireland was beginning to evolve from nationalism into socialism. The opposite, in fact, appears to have been the case, since Connolly, while remaining a socialist, now began to take a keener interest in nationalism than ever before. Sean O'Casey noted the increasingly nationalist tone of Connolly's pronouncements, regretfully (and incorrectly) concluding that Irish socialism had lost a leader. According to R. M. Fox, Connolly, not long before his execution in 1916, remarked: "The Socialists will not understand why I am here. They all forget that I am an Irishman."

The helplessness of the workers on "Bloody Sunday" had made a deep impression on Connolly. He determined, therefore, to arm the men of the I.T.G.W.U. to defend themselves against possible future violence. In the spring of 1914, Captain Jack White, son of the Boer War hero of Ladysmith, was invited to Ireland to take charge of training for the Citizen Army. The latter wore slouch hats imitated from the Boers, looped up on one side and fastened by the Red Hand, the badge of the Union. A flag was also devised—the Plough and the Stars on a dark blue background, the plough symbolizing the dignity of manual labor, the stars, the aspirations of mankind. The main problem faced by the Citizen Army was that of acquiring sufficient weapons. By 1916 the force consisted of some 220 men; this was the number that marched out of Liberty Hall to take part in the Rising. If, as P. S. O'Hegarty and others maintain, the Citizen Army was a fantastic and hopeless project, so too was the Easter Rising itself.

BIBLIOGRAPHY

Blake, Robert: *The Unknown Prime Minister* (1957)

Callwell, Gen. C. E.: *Life of Field Marshal Sir Henry Wilson,* 2 vols. (1927)

Childers, Erskine: *The Framework of Home Rule* (1914)

Churchill, Winston: *The World Crisis, 1911-14,* 2 vols. (1929)

Ervine, St. John: *Craigavon* (1949)

Gollin, A. M.: *Pro-Consul in Politics* (1963)

Good, James Winder: *Ulster and Ireland* (1919)

Griffith, Arthur: *The Resurrection of Hungary* (1904)

Gwynn, Denis Rolleston: *History of Partition, 1912-1925* (1950)

_____: *Life of John Redmond* (1932)

Hamilton, Lord Ernest: *The Soul of Ulster* (1917)

Henry, Robert M.: *The Evolution of Sinn Fein* (1920)

Hyde, H. Montgomery: *Carson* (1953)

Jenkins, Roy: *Asquith* (1964)

Kettle, Thomas M.: *An Irishman's Calendar* (n. d.)

_____: *The Ways of War* (1917)

Larkin, Emmet: *James Larkin, Irish Labour Leader, 1876-1947* (1965)

Majoribanks, Edward, and Colvin, Ian: *Life of Lord Carson,* 3 vols. (1932-37)

Martin, F. X.: *The Irish Volunteers, 1913-15* (1963)

_____: *The Howth Gun-running* (1964)

O'Connor, Sir James: *History of Ireland, 1800-1924,* 2 vols. (1926)

O'Hegarty, Patrick Sarsfield: *History of Ireland under the Union, 1801-1922* (1952)

Paul-Dubois, Louis F. A.: *Contemporary Ireland* (1911)
Phillips, W. Allison: *The Revolution in Ireland, 1906–23* (1923)
Plunkett, Sir Horace: *Ireland in the New Century* (1904)
Ryan, A. P.: *Mutiny at the Curragh* (1956)
Shearman, Hugh: *Not an Inch* (1942)
Stewart, A. T. Q.: *The Ulster Crisis* (1967)

XIII

The Easter Rising and After

Ireland and the First World War (1914–16)

When on August 4, 1914, Britain declared war on Germany, Redmond, without even consulting opinion at home, pledged Ireland's support to the British war effort. England, he said, was defending "the highest principles of religion and morality and right." Like Grattan in 1782, he offered the services of the Volunteers to repel any attempted invasion of Ireland. No wonder that Sir Edward Grey, the Foreign Secretary, glowingly referred to Ireland as "the one bright spot on the horizon of the Empire and the world." Some seven weeks later, in a speech made on September 20, Redmond went even further and pledged the service of the Volunteers in whatever theater of war England might need them.

Two reasons may be adduced to explain why, with few exceptions, Irish public opinion for several months supported Redmond's impulsive offer of aid to Britain. First there was the sense that with the passing of the Home Rule Act Britain had at last honored her obligations toward Ireland; to be sure, the statute granting Home Rule had been accompanied by a second one, postponing the enforcement of the act until the end of the war, but everyone believed the war would be of brief duration. Secondly, there was the effective propaganda made in the name of Belgium and its heroic Primate, Cardinal Mercier, who had defied the Germans. Belgium won the sympathy of southern Irishmen partly as a small nation that, like Ireland, was seeking to vindicate its freedom against a powerful neighbor, and partly as a Catholic people attacked by the strongest Protestant power in Europe. It might also be noted that, through the high prices fetched by Irish dairy products in the English market, the war brought immediate prosperity to rural Ireland and hence was not unwelcome.

In responding to Redmond's offer of help, the British government showed an almost incredible obtuseness. While the Ulster Volunteers were given every encouragement to join the British Army, every obstacle in the way of so doing was placed before the National Volunteers. A special division, the Thirty-sixth, with its own badge, the Red Hand of Ulster, was created for Ulster, whereas the southern Irish were drafted piecemeal into British regiments. The use of the shamrock as a national emblem was prohibited. In the granting of commissions, Catholics were discriminated against. Redmond's close friend and colleague Stephen Gwynn found so many difficulties put in the way of his becoming an officer that in the end he enlisted as a private. "From the very first," Redmond complained, "our efforts were thwarted, ignored and snubbed. Everything almost that we asked for was refused and everything almost that we protested against was done."

Later on, the Prime Minister admitted that in the handling of Irish recruits, "regrettable blunders" and "dreadful mistakes" had been made. Lloyd George commented that these stupidities looked more like "malignancies." The person chiefly responsible for such folly was the Secretary of War, Lord Kitchener—like so many other high-ranking soldiers in the British Army, an Irishman by birth, but one who detested his native land, for which, as he avowed, he had not "a tincture of sympathy." Kitchener was the embodiment of the military mentality that had supported Ulster and the Curragh officers while only too willing to show its contempt for democracy.

Despite the needless insults offered to Irish sensibilities, Birrell told the Hardinge Commission in 1916 that 150,000 Irishmen, from both north and south, had enlisted to fight for Britain. Proportionately to population, Birrell pointed out, this was a higher number than had enlisted from rural England. Actually, the numbers who joined the British Army direct from the Ulster or from the National Volunteers was almost identical—just over 27,000 in either case. On the War Memorial in Dublin, near the Phoenix Park, are recorded the names of 49,000 Irish soldiers who died fighting with the British forces during the first World War—in France and Flanders, in Greece and Italy, in Palestine and at the Dardanelles.

Among those Irishmen who fell in battle were Tom Kettle, M.P. (1880–1916), a gay and good-humored companion, a brilliant scholar and lecturer at the National University, and Francis Ledwidge (1891–1917) "big-boned, ruddy-faced, handsome," a young Meath poet who had been "discovered" by Lord Dunsany. Kettle was killed at the Somme on the shell-pocked uplands of Ginchy, Ledwidge on the opening day of the Third Battle of Ypres. "No words," wrote Major

Willie Redmond, brother of the Irish leader, "could do justice to the splendid action of the new Irish soldiers. They have never flinched." Having enlisted at the age of fifty-three, Redmond himself was killed in 1917 in the gas-poisoned salient of Ypres. Simple justice demands the recognition that Irishmen such as these, who gave their lives believing that an Allied victory would save democracy and bring freedom to Ireland, were just as good patriots, and cared for Ireland as deeply, as those who died in Easter Week. Such recognition, however, has not always been forthcoming.

Ulster shared fully in the burden and the sacrifice. On July 1, 1916, the opening day of the battle of the Somme—Haig's "Big Push" that was to end the war—thousands of young Ulstermen, from the linen mills of Antrim and the shipyards of Belfast, were mown down in batches by machine guns before the almost impregnable enemy dugouts and redoubts. The Ulster Division went into battle shouting the atavistic cries of "No Surrender" and "The Boyne." Later that summer at Thiepval, a notorious sunken lane was more than once filled with Ulster corpses—victims of the deadly machine gun. When the casualty lists of Thiepval were posted in Belfast, it was said that in the poorer quarters of the city nothing but the sound of weeping could be heard. Today, on the low chalk downs above Thiepval rises a red brick replica of Helen's Tower in Antrim—a memorial to Ulster's dead. At Messines below Ypres, where Major Redmond died, Irish Catholics and Orangemen fought side by side to gain a brilliant but barren victory (June 7, 1917). No sooner was the battle over, in which men of both religions had suffered heavily, than the old feuds broke out again between Irishmen from north and south.

By late 1915 the initial enthusiasm in Ireland for the war had evaporated. Recruiting offices were empty. The expected victory had not arrived, and the earliest blood baths had occurred at Neuve Chapelle and Loos. The Western Front was locked in an agonizing stalemate. At the Dardanelles, where the losses in Sir Bryon Mahon's Tenth Division had been very heavy, the Irish had met with disaster. Famous regiments—the Dublin Fusiliers, the Munster Fusiliers, the Connaught Rangers—had suffered crippling losses. By the beaches of Cape Hellas, where they landed, beneath the tawny slopes of Chocolate Hill, which they had stormed, below the bare crest of Achi Baba, where they were never fated to set foot, young men from Dublin, Cork, or Galway now lie forever with their ill-starred English comrades from Lancashire and Wiltshire.

In Ireland it was now muttered on all sides: "The Germans will bate the Alleys." The universal grumbling caused by higher war

Sir Roger Casement (1864–1916). Became world famous for his humanitarian work in Africa and South America, but was hanged by the British for his part in the Easter Rising.

taxation had erased the earlier consciousness of war prosperity. Perhaps, however, what did more than anything else to sour Irish opinion toward the British war effort was the admission into the government in May, 1915, of Bonar Law, Carson, F. E. Smith, and others who not long before had talked treason so irresponsibly.

Sir Roger Casement (1864–1916)

One result of the war was a cleavage in the National Volunteers. On September 30, 1914, under the leadership of Professor Eoin MacNeill, some ten thousand men resigned from the parent body to form a new organization—the Irish Volunteers. The I.R.B. at once assumed the direction of the new movement. Devoy's Clan-na-Gael supplied them with funds from America. If their numbers were small, their morale was high. They were filled with idealism and the spirit of sacrifice. Skillfully they made use of occasions such as the annual pilgrimage to Bodenstown, or the return of Rossa's body to Glasnevin, to proclaim their beliefs and display their numbers—which by 1916, on account of growing resentment against the war, had increased to about fifteen thousand. Above all, however, tired of words, they were determined to act—as soon as the right moment should present itself.

In November, 1915, the Irish Volunteers joined forces with the Citizen Army, which had been drilling and training for two years. Since Connolly's men were manual laborers, while the Volunteers came from the middle classes, there had been some antagonism between them—a friction that is reflected in Sean O'Casey's *History of the Citizen Army,* with its mordant satire on Bulmer Hobson, MacNeill's second-in-command. The Volunteers for their part were apprehensive lest the impetuous Connolly should take the field before they themselves were ready. In January, 1916, the I.R.B. had gone so far as to kidnap Connolly and hold him captive for four days, releasing him only when he promised not to rise until the Volunteers should give the signal.

It may be asked why the British authorities tolerated for so long the activities of the Volunteers, allowing them to parade in uniform through the streets of Dublin—as when on St. Patrick's Day, 1916, five weeks before the Rising, Eoin MacNeill took the salute in front of the old Parliament House on College Green. On this occasion the Volunteers had marched with rifles and fixed bayonets. The fact was that Birrell, the Chief Secretary, and Sir Matthew Nathan, the Under Secretary, found themselves in a dilemma. If they arrested the Volunteer leaders, they ran the risk of making them martyrs, thereby inflaming public opinion. Knowing how poorly armed were the two militant groups—even in 1916 only four thousand out of fifteen thousand had "firearms of sorts"—Birrell and Nathan decided not to interfere with their activities. Just before the Rising, Redmond told a friend that he "could crush all the Sinn Feiners in Ireland, in the hollow of his hand." Who had more knowledge of what was happening in Ireland, Birrell may have reasoned, then his good friend John Redmond? The police reports were far less reassuring, but the Chief Secretary dismissed them as exaggerated. For this mistake Birrell was later to be severely censured and abruptly dismissed from his post.

One factor that was vital to whatever chance of success a rebellion might have had was, of course, the acquisition of arms from abroad. In this connection there came to be associated with the Rising one of the most remarkable men of the twentieth century. Sir Roger Casement (1864–1916) was an Ulsterman by birth and a Protestant in religion (though he was to become a Catholic on the eve of his execution). He had spent twenty-one years of his life in the British consular service, during the course of which he had twice gained immense recognition—first in the Belgian Congo in 1904, and then on the Upper Amazon in 1911. While consul at Boma, Casement had almost single-handedly exposed the systematic terror—involving wholesale murder, mutilation, flogging, and the virtual depopulation of once-prosperous areas—practiced by Belgian officials in the interest of the rubber companies. Published by the Foreign Office in a Blue

Book, Casement's revelations forced King Leopold to abolish the worst abuses perpetrated in his name and with his consent. As a result, almost overnight Casement found himself idolized by the British public and famous throughout the world. Mark Twain was on this occasion his ally in America.

Six years later Casement was given another opportunity to repeat his success by again exposing atrocities involved in the collection of rubber. This time the victims were the Huitotos—a gentle, trusting tribe of Peruvian Indians whom Casement came to know and love—living in the jungles of the Putumayo, a tributary of the Amazon. The Huitotos had almost been exterminated by agents of the Peruvian-Amazon Company. At the cost of his health, and not without risk to his life, Casement again penetrated almost inaccessible reaches of fever-ridden forests, established the truth of the atrocities alleged against the company, and forced it out of business. In 1912 he was knighted for these services. Next year, his health broken by malaria and other tropical diseases, Casement retired from the consular service.

Up to this point Sir Roger, though lionized in London, was little known in his native country. Yet in 1904 he had undergone what amounted to a conversion to the cause of Irish nationality. His experience on the Congo proved the turning point of his life, for his romantic and chivalrous nature was profoundly stirred by the terrible sights he had witnessed. In some obscure fashion, the intense emotional ordeal he underwent in Africa served to release deeply submerged elements of his own personality. "Up in those lonely Congo forests," he wrote to Mrs. Green, "where I went to find Leopold, I found myself—the incorrigible Irishman." From being a moderate Imperialist, like Erskine Childers, he was gradually transformed into an ardent defender of small, oppressed peoples.

Partly through his close friendship with the Irish historian, Mrs. Alice Stopford Green, since 1905 Casement had been interested in Sinn Fein. On his retirement in 1913 he settled in Ireland and devoted himself to Irish affairs, playing a leading part in the formation of the National Volunteers. In that year also he visited Connemara for the first time and was shocked to see the poverty and wretchedness that prevailed along the western seaboard of Ireland. Sometimes he reproached himself for having devoted his life to the needs of other peoples when so much injustice existed at home. Underlying the varied activities of his public life was the same passionate humanitarianism that linked in a single theme the experience of suffering gained in places as unlike and as far apart as the Congo, the Amazon, and Connemara.

Such was the man who, on the outbreak of the European war, determined to hazard everything for the freedom of Ireland. Apart from his handsome appearance and distinguished bearing, what differentiated Casement from most nationalists in 1914 was the conviction, shared with men like Pearse and Connolly, that the time for words was over and the time for deeds at hand. Even before the outbreak of war, on July 2, 1914, Casement had sailed for America to enlist the aid of the Irish-Americans in obtaining arms. On October 31, 1914, having eluded the British naval blockade, Sir Roger arrived in Berlin seeking German military help for Ireland. He also conceived the unrealistic plan of inducing Irish prisoners of war in Germany to enlist in an Irish Brigade for the liberation of their homeland.

In December, 1914, Sir Roger was received by the Imperial Chancellor, von Bethmann-Hollweg, and a "treaty" was signed by which Germany promised to furnish arms to an Irish rebellion. Casement soon discovered what little trust was to be placed in such promises. His hopes for an Irish Brigade were similarly falsified by events. He secured only fifty-three volunteers, whom the Germans placed for training under Captain Monteith in a camp at Zossen, near Berlin.

Disdained by the powerful allies in whom he had trusted, and humiliated by a deep sense of failure, Sir Roger—as we know from his journals—endured agonies of self-reproach. Unlike Pearse, who was determined on "blood sacrifice," Casement desired an Irish rebellion only if it had a reasonable chance of success. By April, 1916, his one thought was how to call off the Rising and prevent useless loss of life. Failing to convert Devoy to his point of view, Sir Roger resolved to retrieve his personal honor by sharing the fate of his comrades who were about to immolate themselves in Dublin.

In the hope of getting word to MacNeill that adequate aid would not be forthcoming from Germany, Casement returned to Ireland in a German submarine. He must have known that his enterprise was as hopeless as that of Wolfe Tone when he had sailed with the French into Lough Swilly in 1798. At dawn on Good Friday, April 21, Sir Roger was put ashore at Banna on the coast of Kerry. Captured within a few hours and dispatched under heavy guard to London, Casement nevertheless managed to communicate with his friends in Dublin, urging them to call off the revolt.

On Saturday, April 22, therefore, Eoin MacNeill issued an order canceling the preparations that had been made to rise on Easter Sunday. The Supreme Council of the I.R.B. promptly arrested both MacNeill and Hobson, postponing the Rising by only a single day.

It was too late, however, to recall MacNeill's order, which had been transmitted throughout the country; and when the Rising did begin on Monday, April 24, instead of the nationwide revolt led by the Volunteers that had been planned, the rebellion was virtually confined to the capital.

Easter Monday being a bank holiday, most Dubliners had gone to the seaside or to the races at Fairymount, and the city wore a deserted holiday look. The Commissioner of Education was reading Pliny in his garden at Ballsbridge. The Commissioner of Police, more surprisingly, was reading Plutarch at Stillorgan. James Stephens was deep in Mme. Blavatsky. Ordinary people were poring over racing sheets to place their bets. Far removed from the bloodshed in France, the citizens of Dublin were enjoying an idyllic April day.

Just before noon, the Irish Volunteers and the Citizen Army marched through the empty streets and occupied without opposition key points in the capital. In a Proclamation, of which 2,500 copies were distributed, the rebels announced the formation of a Provisional Government with Pearse as President and Commander-in-Chief. Pearse established his headquarters in the General Post Office, with Connolly, head of the Citizen Army, as second-in-command. For the next six days the flag of the Republic flew above the rooftops of Dublin.

The Proclamation, chiefly the work of Patrick Pearse, is to modern Ireland what the Declaration of Independence is to the United States. By its clear and emphatic statement of purpose, by its moral elevation of tone, and by the dignity of its language, the Proclamation bears comparison with any statement of nationality formulated in the twentieth century. Seven names were appended to it: Thomas J. Clarke, Sean MacDiarmada, Patrick Pearse, James Connolly, Thomas Mac-Donagh, Eamonn Ceannt, and Joseph Plunkett. With the exception of Connolly, all were members of the I.R.B. Each of the seven must have known that he was signing his death warrant. All, in fact, were dead within three weeks.

Though traitors in the sight of the law, and at first condemned by their own countrymen, the seven who thus hearkened to "ancestral voices prophesying war" were men of unusual courage and of exceptionally high moral character. Three were poets, two were teachers, one a musician, and one a workingman who was also a self-taught scholar and historian. The place of honor was given to the eldest signatory, Tom Clarke, then fifty-eight and the last surviving link with the Fenians. But by far the most indispensable man in the Rising was Pearse.

POBLACHT NA H EIREANN.

THE PROVISIONAL GOVERNMENT
OF THE
IRISH REPUBLIC
TO THE PEOPLE OF IRELAND.

IRISHMEN AND IRISHWOMEN : In the name of God and of the dead generations from which she receives her old tradition of nationhood, Ireland, through us, summons her children to her flag and strikes for her freedom.

Having organised and trained her manhood through her secret revolutionary organisation, the Irish Republican Brotherhood, and through her open military organisations, the Irish Volunteers and the Irish Citizen Army, having patiently perfected her discipline, having resolutely waited for the right moment to reveal itself, she now seizes that moment, and, supported by her exiled children in America and by gallant allies in Europe, but relying in the first on her own strength, she strikes in full confidence of victory.

We declare the right of the people of Ireland to the ownership of Ireland, and to the unfettered control of Irish destinies, to be sovereign and indefeasible. The long usurpation of that right by a foreign people and government has not extinguished the right, nor can it ever be extinguished except by the destruction of the Irish people. In every generation the Irish people have asserted their right to national freedom and sovereignty ; six times during the past three hundred years they have asserted it in arms. Standing on that fundamental right and again asserting it in arms in the face of the world, we hereby proclaim the Irish Republic as a Sovereign Independent State, and we pledge our lives and the lives of our comrades-in-arms to the cause of its freedom, of its welfare, and of its exaltation among the nations.

The Irish Republic is entitled to, and hereby claims, the allegiance of every Irishman and Irishwoman. The Republic guarantees religious and civil liberty, equal rights and equal opportunities to all its citizens, and declares its resolve to pursue the happiness and prosperity of the whole nation and of all its parts, cherishing all the children of the nation equally, and oblivious of the differences carefully fostered by an alien government, which have divided a minority from the majority in the past.

Until our arms have brought the opportune moment for the establishment of a permanent National Government, representative of the whole people of Ireland and elected by the suffrages of all her men and women, the Provisional Government, hereby constituted, will administer the civil and military affairs of the Republic in trust for the people.

We place the cause of the Irish Republic under the protection of the Most High God, Whose blessing we invoke upon our arms, and we pray that no one who serves that cause will dishonour it by cowardice, inhumanity, or rapine. In this supreme hour the Irish nation must, by its valour and discipline and by the readiness of its children to sacrifice themselves for the common good, prove itself worthy of the august destiny to which it is called.

Signed on Behalf of the Provisional Government,

THOMAS J. CLARKE.

SEAN Mac DIARMADA.   THOMAS MacDONAGH.
P. H. PEARSE.   EAMONN CEANNT.
JAMES CONNOLLY.   JOSEPH PLUNKETT.

The Proclamation of the Provisional Government of the Irish Republic (April 24, 1916), written by Patrick Pearse. All seven signatories were shot within three weeks.

Patrick Pearse (1879–1916). An idealistic schoolmaster, first president of the Irish republic and commander of the Volunteer Army in 1916; shot by the British for his leadership of the Easter Rising.

Patrick Pearse (1879–1916)

Patrick Pearse was born in Dublin on November 10, 1879. His father was a native of Devonshire, by profession a monument sculptor and in politics a Home Ruler. The boy, affectionate by nature, grew up with a strong attachment to his mother and devoted to his sisters and younger brother. Yet he was also solitary, reserved, and withdrawn. Many years after his death, his elder sister Emily remembered the chief characteristics of Patrick's childhood as being "his natural reserve, his gentle shyness and his silent thoughtfulness." His earliest reveries, like those of Robert Emmet, were about Ireland. "When I was a child," he recalled, "I believed that there actually was a woman called Erin." During a long illness and convalescence at the age of seven, which he later came to regard as the most important period of his life, his nurse used to croon ballads in Irish and English, "mostly of men dead, or in exile for love of Ireland." When ten years old, Patrick knelt down and promised God that he would devote his life to the cause of the nation's freedom. With him Irish history was not merely an enthusiasm but a passion.

"Two things," wrote Pearse in an unfinished autobiography, "have constantly pulled at cross-purposes in me: one, a deep homing instinct, a desire beyond words to be at home always, with the same beloved faces, the same familiar shapes and sounds about me; the other, an impulse to seek hard things to do, to go on far quests and fight for lost causes."

His earliest hero was Cuchulain, transformed by the force of his ardent imagination into a "small, dark, sad boy, comeliest of the boys of Eire." Pearse's ideal Irishman, wrote Stephen MacKenna, was "a Cuchulain baptized." John Eglinton said that he once heard Pearse assert his belief in the divine inspiration of Cuchulain. Mary Colum recalled Pearse's reciting at Dr. George Sigerson's table—"with intense emotion, his strange eyes aflame"—his host's translation of Cuchulain's lament over Ferdiad, the friend whom he had killed.

Apart from Gaelic Ireland, another influence on Pearse's childhood was the romantic verse of Thomas Davis. "The sorrows of the people," Yeats once wrote, "affected Davis like a personal sorrow"—a statement that was equally true of Pearse.

Reverie apart, Pearse never forgot that the end of life was action. His chief hero, apart from those of Irish history, was Napoleon, statues and pictures of whom were in his study. The two documents of modern Ireland that moved him most were Tone's *Autobiography* and Mitchel's *Jail Journal.* It was said that he knew the former almost by heart and that he carried it with him as others carried the Bible. Tone, he declared, in a phrase that revealed his own feeling for Ireland, was "the Irish nation in action, gay and heroic and terrible." In 1913, Pearse delivered the oration over Tone's grave at Bodenstown. "We have come to the holiest place in Ireland," he told his hearers that Sunday morning in June, "holier than the place where Patrick sleeps in Down. Patrick brought us life, but this man died for us." Mitchel he ranked next to Tone as a revolutionary leader. "These two shall teach and lead you unto the path of national salvation. For this I will answer on the Judgment Day."

Pearse was also a good classical scholar, being especially devoted to Cicero and Horace. He had traveled on the Continent—in France, Belgium, and Germany—and knew French and German, as well as some Spanish. In English literature, he particularly admired Shakespeare; and in contemporary Ireland he was interested in the work of Yeats and Synge. He was educated at University College, Dublin—where he was three years senior to Joyce—and after finishing his B.A., got a degree in law, though he found actual practice repellent.

Abandoning a legal career, Pearse discovered his true vocation as a teacher. The enthusiastic idealism of the Gaelic League was a revelation to him, and he became an early member. As a boy, he had visited the Aran Islands. Later, he returned often to the west and wandered through the desolate Irish-speaking parts of Connemara. One typical memory of the west of Ireland stayed with him throughout life—the springing of a myriad larks from the flaming furze-covered mountains, and their triumphant song.

At Rosmuc, by the Galway coast, Pearse built a small, white-walled cottage, where during successive summers, he perfected his knowledge of Irish. A Gaelic scholar wrote that Pearse's knowledge of the native idiom was "very rich and expressive" and recalled that he had so delighted Connemara people with his command of the vernacular that they would go home repeating phrases he had used. Such was Pearse's proficiency in the language that at twenty-three he was appointed Lecturer in Irish at University College, Dublin. Among his pupils were a future Chief Justice and a future Minister of Education of the Irish Free State. About this time Pearse visited Belgium, and with the problem of Gaelic in mind studied the Belgian system of bilingual education.

In 1908, at the age of twenty-eight, Pearse founded St. Enda's school and in so doing, discovered himself as truly as Casement had done on the Congo. In 1910 the school moved out to Rathfarnham among the foothills of the Dublin mountains—a place associated with the last fugitive days of Emmet. Pearse used to say that it was the spirit of Emmet that had led him to Rathfarnham. There were seventy boys at St. Enda's, most of whom, according to Pearse, came from families with "traditions of work and sacrifice for Ireland." Although mathematics and science were taught in English, Irish was the official language of the school and served as the medium of instruction for most subjects. Much emphasis was placed upon Irish history, the study of which became a training in militant nationalism.

Pearse's avowed ideal was to revive the Gaelic system of education as he conceived it to have existed in Ireland two thousand years before. The boy Cuchulain was exalted as the hero-model of the school. At St. Enda's the savage warrior who gloried in death and battle was transformed into a prefiguration of Christ. In the heroic age, Pearse persuaded himself, Ireland had honored the hero possessed of the most childlike heart. In the main hall of the school was a large oil painting of Cuchulain, depicted as a slender youth with spear and sword; beneath it was a challenging sentence in Gaelic: "Though I live but a year and a day, I will live so that my name goes sounding down the ages."

Notwithstanding this idealization of an imaginary past, education at St. Enda's was strenuous as well as sentimental. Pearse rejected the idea that modern society had outgrown the need for force. If the individual's first duty was to be virtuous, his second was to be strong.

"We want again the starkness of the antique world," wrote Pearse. A motto attributed to the Fenians was also impressed upon the boys: "Strength in our hands, truth on our lips and cleanness in our hearts." The curriculum at St. Enda's included swimming, boxing, wrestling, fencing, hurling, and shooting. The school became known for its athletic victories as well as for its academic prowess. English games like cricket were forbidden. Pearse strove also to impress upon his pupils an image of Finn—careless and laughing, with his characteristic light-hearted gallantry.

At St. Enda's, education did not consist merely in the imparting of knowledge. It recognized the unique value of every single pupil and attempted to develop each one's potentialities. For Pearse conceived of man as being primarily not a unit in a group but a solitary, irreplaceable being—"a shivering human soul with its own august destiny, lonelier in its house of clay than any prisoner in any Bastille in the world." A grave responsibility, therefore, lay on the teacher to discover the true individuality of each pupil committed to his care. Pearse claimed to know the character of every boy at St. Enda's as well as he knew the people of the Gaelic-speaking west.

Prevailing modes of education he spurned, protesting "against the system which tolerates as teachers the rejected of other professions, rather than demanding for so priest-like an office the highest souls and the noblest intellects of the race." As a teacher of history and literature, he himself knew how to re-create the past. "In the fire of his personality," wrote Desmond Ryan, "he could make platitudes live again." Gaiety and laughter were not discouraged at St. Enda's, for Pearse did not aim to produce sanctimonious prigs. One of his favorite quotations characterized the Gael as in his fighting always merry, in his feasting always sad.

If those who listened to Pearse had not been convinced of his total integrity, and of the perfect congruence for him of word and deed, he never could have gained over them the influence he had. The headmaster of St. Enda's might easily have seemed a forbidding figure. Dressed invariably in black, even on the playing field Pearse wore the scholar's attire. He never attempted to ingratiate himself with his pupils. Instead he strove to raise them to his own intellectual plane. Their judgment on "the grave tenacious idealist in the black gown" may be taken as proof of his quality. "To know him," wrote one of them, "was to love him, to be inspired and to see a glamour in the most humdrum details of ordinary life." Later on, General Blackader, who presided at Pearse's court-martial, was so impressed by his dignity and composure that he observed: "I don't wonder that his pupils adored him."

The secret of Pearse's success lay partly in the unwavering trust he placed in his students. The honor system prevailed at St. Enda's. No teacher ever doubted a boy's word. It was no fun trying to deceive Pearse, said one of the boys, since no matter what the falsehood, he always believed it. Yet the presence of the headmaster was everywhere felt, and when he appeared, the noisiest room fell silent. Pearse used to say that in all his years at St. Enda's, he had never lost his temper—no small claim for one who was reputed to be impulsive and hot-tempered, but also childlike in contrition.

The only problems at St. Enda's were financial ones, but they were ever present. The masters included Pearse's younger brother, Willie, who taught art, and Thomas MacDonagh, who taught literature—both of them to be executed after Easter Week. The staff was not always paid, yet such was their dedication that most of the masters remained none the less. In the spring of 1914, Pearse went on a lecture tour to the United States to raise funds for the school.

Politics apart, Pearse was repelled by the vulgarity and materialism he conceived as characterizing modern civilization. Like Wordsworth, he longed for solitude. Like Synge, he sought the company of simple people. He desired the peace that dwells on mountains and in lonely places. For him the appeal of the west was not only that it had kept the ancient language, but that it preserved an earlier and nobler way of life.

In speaking of a man like Mitchel, Pearse would pass from the cherished hatred of the convict to the exile's nostalgia for the sound of falling water in his homeland, which in turn would lead him to descant upon Columba's love of Irish waterfalls: "He would croon to us," wrote Stephen MacKenna, "in that peculiar voice of his about birds and mountains and misty lakes, and of the ancient Irish love of colour in costume and of bodily beauty in hero and hero's lady love."

Yet Pearse, for all his romantic preoccupation with the past, was well aware of the injustices of the contemporary world. In the General Strike of 1913, he defended the working men of Dublin against their employers. "It is not amusing to be hungry," he wrote. "Twenty thousand Dublin families live in one-room tenements. . . . The tenement houses of Dublin are so rotten that they periodically collapse on their inhabitants." In the face of criticism, he insisted upon keeping Larkin's son at St. Enda's.

All that William Martin Murphy stood for was repugnant to Pearse and to his vision of what Ireland ought to be. As much as William Blake, he distrusted respectability. "Prudence is the only vice," he wrote. "The great enemy of practical Christianity has always been respectable society." As between the pharisee and the publican, one could never doubt which Pearse preferred.

His concern with the General Strike brought him into contact with James Connolly—the last considerable influence upon his thought. Through his friend Connolly, Pearse discovered Fintan Lalor, whose appeal for self-sacrifice was congenial to his own temperament. As may be judged from his pamphlet, "The Sovereign People," and from the Proclamation of Easter Week, Pearse now began to develop a sense of social responsibility. Connolly also persuaded Pearse to espouse women's suffrage, a cause to which he had hitherto been indifferent. As may be supposed, Pearse admired the spirit of the English suffragettes—their courage and constancy, their devotion to a cause and willingness to suffer for it.

In person, Pearse was heavily built and of more than average height. According to Stephen MacKenna, while not handsome and with "no particular charm of manner," he had "a strikingly thoughtful face" and had great personal magnetism. "People," wrote MacKenna, "hung on his slow, melodious words, dreamed his dream and very largely did his will." Seumas O'Sullivan, the poet, wrote of "the strange prophetic glance of Pearse, the half-averted eyes"—a phrase that suggests the reserve of an introverted nature. Darrell Figgis speaks of him as "a grave, priestlike man," with a "curious, heavy gait." Like most men absorbed by their inner vision, Pearse had no capacity for small talk. All who knew him were agreed about his gentleness of manner and his consideration for others. Unlike Yeats, he was never arrogant.

Apart from his dedication to a lofty, self-imposed duty, the outstanding quality of Pearse's moral nature was the identification with suffering that he had in common with St. Francis. He could not bring himself to take the life of any living thing—beast, bird, fish, or even insect. He was careful not to trample upon wild flowers. The paradox remains that for the sake of an ideal he was willing to shed not only his own blood but also the blood of others—including that of some he loved. "I saw a dreamer, I saw a poet," wrote Dora Sigerson on hearing of his death.

> On the red battlefield fell my slow tear.
> "Lover of birds and flowers, singer of gentle songs,

Dying with men of war, what do you here?"
He replied: "I fell to earth, grasping at stars."

Unlike Parnell, he had a natural gift of language. As an orator, Pearse spoke slowly and deliberately. His speeches, carefully prepared, were effective despite the impediment of a slight lisp. Darrell Figgis praised his "slow and simple eloquence." The poet Ella Young recalled that even his silence was powerful and that by his mere presence he could dominate a roomful of people. Desmond Ryan characterized his utterance as "precise, cold, kindling, culminating in some terrific revelation of the gospel of sacrifice for an ideal." His effect was due chiefly to the sincerity with which he spoke, for no one doubted that Pearse would give his life for his beliefs.

His best-remembered speech was that which he delivered in Glasnevin on August 1, 1915, over the remains of O'Donovan Rossa. There, looking steadily into the open grave, Pearse for the last time "uttered the Fenian creed and praised the Fenian deed."

> I propose to you [he told his hearers], that here by the grave of this unrepentant Fenian we renew our baptismal vows; that here by the grave of this unconquered and unconquerable man, we ask of God, each one for himself, such unshakable purpose, such high and gallant courage, such unbreakable strength of soul as belonged to O'Donovan Rossa.
>
> . . . . .
>
> They think they have pacified Ireland. They think that they have purchased half of us, and intimidated the other half. They think that they have foreseen everything. They think that they have provided against everything; but the fools, the fools, the fools! they have left us our Fenian dead, and while Ireland holds these graves, Ireland unfree shall never be at peace.

A large crowd had assembled that day, special trains having brought people from all parts of Ireland. Pearse spoke "very quietly, almost gently," wrote Batt O'Connor. "I was moved, uplifted, listening to that soft voice breathing a holy fervor." He too wished that he might suffer, and if necessary die for Ireland. O'Donovan Rossa's daughter was present and spoke of Pearse's "vital, thrilling, electrical word that winged to the heart." After he finished speaking, there was "an intense all-pervading silence," and then, although they were in a cemetery, there came a sudden outburst of cheering.

The central theme of Pearse's life—of all his speeches, poems, and plays—was that of redemption through blood. It was a theme that accommodated itself to the Christian sentiment of his hearers. "Except a corn of wheat fall into the ground and die, it abideth alone; but if it die, it bringeth forth much fruit." In his play *The Singer,* written six months before his death, the central figure of MacDara is evidently an idealized self-portrait of Pearse. MacDara leaves his sweetheart, saying: "I have to do a hard, sweet thing and I must do it alone." A friend objects that it is a foolish thing for fourscore men to fight forty thousand. "And so it is a foolish thing," replies MacDara. "Do you want us to be wise?" "This is strange talk," mutters a bystander. "I will talk to you more strangely yet," is the reply. "One man can free a people as one man redeemed the world. I will take no pike, I will go into battle with bare hands. I will stand up before the Gall [the foreigner] as Christ hung naked before men on the tree."

Inseparably connected for Pearse with sacrifice was readiness for war, of which he wrote in almost Nietzschean terms: "War is a terrible thing, but war is not an evil thing. It is the things that make war necessary that are evil. Many people in Ireland dread war because they do not know it. Ireland has not known the exhilaration of war for over a hundred years. When war comes to Ireland, she must welcome it as she would the angel of God." "Shall this generation," Pearse asked his countrymen, "alone of all the generations of Ireland, be incapable of the ultimate sacrifice?"

In his speech over Rossa's grave, Pearse touched upon the mutuality of life and death. He meditated on the riddle of the interdependence of cruelty and beauty, and on the harshness of nature which imposes form, and thereby beauty, upon living things to assure their survival. "Red murder in the greenwood," Pearse termed the struggle for existence. "It is murder and death that make possible the terrible beautiful thing that we call physical life. Like springs from death, life lives on death." So, from the ashes of Dublin a terrible beauty would be born.

All through life Pearse felt driven to seek out death, to exalt her as an ideal and woo her as a mistress. A quest so relentless was far removed from the pose of being "half in love with easeful death" and wishing "to cease upon the midnight with no pain." Two short poems written in the last months of his life clearly reveal this absorption.

> A rann I made within my heart
> To the rider, to the high king,
> A rann I made to my love,
> To the king of kings, ancient death.

Brighter to me than light of day
The dark of thy house, though black clay.
Sweeter to me than the music of trumpets
The quiet of thy house, and its eternal silence.

> Long to me thy coming
> Old henchman of God,
> O friend of all friends,
> To free me from my pain.

> O syllable on the wind,
> O football not heavy,
> O hand in the dark,
> Your coming is long to me.

No rebellion was ever more openly proclaimed ahead of time than that of 1916—not only by armed Volunteers marching through Dublin but also by the defiance that rang through Pearse's premonitory verse, as in the last Christmas greeting that he sent his friends:

> O King that was born
> To set bondsmen free,
> In the coming battle
> Help the Gael.

Yet there was also what one might call the Franciscan side of Pearse's nature—his praise of laughter and the joy of life—as evident in a poem like "The Wayfarer," written on the eve of his execution. It was this aspect of Pearse which endeared him to O'Casey, always suspicious of sham and intolerant of humbug. Few reputations emerge from O'Casey's scrutiny as intact as that of Pearse, "sensitive, knowledgeable and graceful . . . a doer of things noble, and a lover of things beautiful." Thirty years later, O'Casey wove some lines from Shakespeare into a final tribute. "Ah! Patrick Pearse, you were a man, a poet, with a mind as simple as a daisy, brilliant as a daffodil; and like these, you came before the swallow dared, and took the *Irish* winds of March with beauty."

Without Pearse the Easter Rising is unthinkable. As the sun's rays are sometimes caught in a burning glass, so in the personality of Pearse centuries were fused in a moment of intensity, from which independence was born. No other figure was the focus of so many traditions inherited from Irish history. In Pearse, pagan and Christian Ireland were reconciled, past and present fused. Slumbering traditions woke to life, and were endowed with new vitality.

> When Pearse summoned Cuchulain to his side,
> What stalked through the Post Office?

Almost alone among those who cherished the sagas, Pearse remained a fervent Catholic. But what Christianity meant to him was not what it meant to such a one as William Martin Murphy. Pearse admired in Christ the lonely idealist, the rebel against authority, the champion of the poor and the oppressed. "I came not to bring peace but a sword" was one of his favorite quotations. As Sean O'Casey remarks, Pearse's Catholicism was that of Columba, Brigid, and Kevin, not that of Loyola, Gonzaga, or De Sales. Pearse's ardent Catholicism and his identification with the Gaelic past make him a more representative figure than any other in the Rising or in the Literary Renaissance.

To the pagan and Christian elements of Pearse's thought was linked the Fenian revolutionary tradition. Although a Catholic, Pearse was a member of the Irish Republican Brotherhood—the secret society anathematized by the Church. Through the Fenians, Pearse identified with the long tradition of patriotic revolt—with Young Ireland and "ninety-eight," with Mitchel and with Tone.

In the twentieth century, too, Pearse represented the convergence of influences thought incompatible, if not antagonistic. While he was moved by the wretchedness of Connemara, he was stirred also by the misery of the Dublin slums. Between Sinn Fein and the Abbey Theatre, he was almost the sole link. He defended the *Playboy* against the philistinism of Sinn Fein. Yeats in turn admired St. Enda's and staged some of Pearse's plays at the Abbey. Finally, through Connolly, Pearse developed a sympathy for socialism and defined the aims of Irish nationalism less narrowly than Smith O'Brien or John O'Leary had done. It was Connolly, too, who enlisted Pearse's interest in another cause inseparable from liberal democracy—the emancipation of women.

In one respect alone, Pearse was untypical of the nationalist tradition: he never invoked cherished symbols such as those of the Dark Rosaleen or Cathleen ni-Houlihan. He wrote no love poetry.* His friendships were always with men. When he does symbolize Ireland it is not as a young girl but as an old woman.

---

*Though he never married and is never known to have been in love, when young he is said to have been attracted to a girl student from University College, Dublin, Eileen Nichols, who was drowned off the Blaskets trying to rescue another girl.

I am Ireland:
I am older than the Woman of Beare.
Great my glory:
I that bore Cuchulain the valiant.
Great my shame:
My own children that sold their mother.

Almost to the end, Pearse remained quietly at St. Enda's supervising the work of the school. On March 21, 1916, he made his farewell speech to the boys, reminding them that it had taken the blood of the Son of God to redeem the world and that it would take the blood of the sons of Ireland to redeem their country. He made no reference to the fact that he was soon to exchange the scholar's gown for the soldier's uniform. Yet when the school closed for the Easter holidays, he must have known that he would never see his pupils again.

On Easter Monday, Stephen MacKenna heard Pearse read the Proclamation under the portico of the post office. It was the culminating moment of his life—the moment Pearse had dreamed of for twenty years. "Very pale he was, cold of face as he scanned the crowd," wrote MacKenna. "The response was chilling; a few perfunctory cheers, but no enthusiasm whatever. . . . A chill must have gone into his heart."

The Easter Rising (1916)

The usual estimate accepted in Ireland for the number of those who took part in the Rising is 1500—and this includes not only the Volunteers but some two hundred men from the Citizen Army. On that Easter Monday there were sixteen thousand British troops in Ireland, of whom three thousand were stationed in Dublin. There were also ten thousand armed men scattered throughout the country in the R.I.C. By midnight of the first day of the Rising, two thousand troops had been rushed into Dublin from the Curragh. Each day the mailboats brought further reinforcements from England, so that by the end of the week there were fifty thousand soldiers in Ireland, well supplied with machine guns and artillery. Against such numbers, prolonged resistance was hopeless, and after six days' courageous resistance, the rebels surrendered late in the afternoon of Saturday, April 29. De Valera, commandant at Boland's Mill, was the last to lay down his arms.

As the result of the fighting, the center of Dublin was partially destroyed. Four hundred and fifty people (including 130 British soldiers) had been killed and 2,614 wounded. The Volunteer losses were relatively light—fifty-six dead, according to one estimate. Civilians caught in the fighting suffered most—216 being buried at Glasnevin that week. Some $10 million damage was done to property.

Few of the Volunteers had had any experience of actual warfare, and whatever his other qualities, Pearse was no military genius. Dublin Castle could have been taken easily had the attack not been bungled at the start. If the Castle had fallen, no doubt the English would have retaken it within a few hours. Yet the moral and psychological effect of having captured, however briefly, what Pearse called "the Bastille of Ireland," would have been immense. No previous rebellion had ever accomplished it. By another blunder, though most telephone lines leading into Dublin were cut, the rebels never attempted to seize the central exchange, so that the military authorities were able to communicate freely with England all week. The insurgents also neglected to seize printing presses, by means of which they could have flooded the city with propaganda. A single small printed sheet, the *Irish War News,* was issued by the rebels from the post office.

It has been suggested that instead of occupying public buildings, the Volunteers should have conducted guerrilla warfare in the streets. This was the course urged by Sean O'Casey in the Citizen Army, but for arguing with his superiors he was forced out of the I.R.B. Captain Monteith, the commander of Casement's Brigade, who had had military experience during the Boer War, later criticized the military dispositions of the Volunteers. He too favored guerrilla war with "no company drill or close order nonsense." Connolly is said to have defended the seizure of public buildings on the ground that capitalists would never willfully destroy their own property. If so, he attributed to the British military authorities a concern for the feelings of Irish businessmen that they did not possess.

A dramatic gesture, regardless of consequences, was what Pearse wanted. He was thinking primarily not of military considerations but of the moral effect of so bold a defiance of British rule. "We are about to attempt impossible things," he told his men, "but only impossible things are worth doing." Despite the failure of the Rising, the fact that the flag of a free Ireland had waved above Dublin for nearly a week was bound to capture the imagination of generations to come, and 1916 would always be honored together with 1798 and 1848 in the annals of the nation. Shortly before the final surrender, Pearse paid tribute to the Volunteers. "They have redeemed Dublin of many shames, and made her name splendid among the names of cities."

The rebels had fought with courage and resolution. They had proved themselves adept at roof warfare and in house-to-house fighting. Nine

Sean O'Casey (1880–1964). One of the great playwrights of the twentieth century, he found his material in the Dublin slums as Synge had found his in the peasants of the West of Ireland.

men from De Valera's command at Boland's Mill had held up the advance guard of the Sherwood Foresters for nine hours. The insurgents had also heeded Pearse's injunction to fight honorably. Not a single act of looting or of indiscipline was reported. Pearse had made them thoroughly aware that Ireland's honor rested with them and that modern Ireland would be judged by their behavior. Asquith himself, while condemning their action, complimented the rebels on their "clean fighting." The majority of them were practicing Catholics, many of whom, like Pearse himself, neither smoked nor drank. On the Saturday before the Rising, Dublin confessionals were crowded, and on Easter Sunday many went to communion in full kit, with rifles slung over their shoulders. Amid the fire and smoke and flying bullets of the post office, brown-robed Capuchin friars moved about ministering to the wounded and the dying.

Grim-faced, unshaven, and exhausted by the strain of six days' constant fighting, with little sleep or rest, the Volunteers at length laid down their arms. Their once smart uniforms now hung in grey and grimy tatters, coated thickly with dust. Sean O'Casey described their "haggard faces chipped into bleeding jaggedness by splinters flying from shattered stones and brick." Some were limping from their wounds; others could scarcely stand. For the leaders, surrender meant almost certain death.

Twenty-four hours after their capitulation, the Volunteers were herded into the Rotunda Gardens beneath the open sky. All week the weather had been warm and sunny, but on Low Sunday and the two following days it turned cold, and torrents of rain fell from gloomy skies. "There will be no blossom on the hawthorn today," Ella Young noted in her diary. That Sunday, dejected and sodden, without cover or sanitary provision of any kind, cursed and taunted by their guards, the unwashed prisoners huddled in the pouring rain. Some, like old Tom Clarke, were stripped naked and subjected to personal indignities. At length the prisoners were removed to the dank chill of the cells in Kilmainham.

Then the military courts went into action. Pearse was court-martialed in Richmond barracks. Even the judges admired the courage he showed throughout the trial. Lady Fingall reported that General Blackader, president of the court, was "terribly affected by the work he had to do." "We seem to have lost," Pearse told his judges, "but we have not lost." His mother was refused permission to see him, but on a scrap of paper that may still be seen in the National Museum, he scribbled for her a last brief prayer, in which occurs an implicit identification between the Savior and himself.

> Dear Mary that didst see thy first-born son
> Go forth to die amid the scorn of men
> For whom he died,
> Receive my first-born son into thy arms
> And keep him by thee till I come to thee.
> Dear Mary, I have shared thy sorrow
> And soon shall share thy joy.

Pearse was the first to be executed. Early on Wednesday, May 3, he was stood up against one of the great wooden gates of the prison and seventeen bullet holes were drilled through his body. The spring morning was bright with sunshine and alive with the song of birds. It was exactly thirteen days since Pearse had left his desk at St. Enda's. That same morning, old Tom Clarke, the unrepentant Fenian, and the young poet Thomas MacDonagh joined Pearse in death under the high wall of Kilmainham. Never again would men come from all over Dublin just to buy tobacco at the "weeshy" shop in Parnell Street from "the wiry little figure" with "the sunken cheeks and the very quick and powerful eye." That link with the revolutionary past was gone forever. Nor would students at the National ever again hang on MacDonagh's words as he spoke of his hopes and ideals, or mark the "bony thumb" that lingered in Yeats's memory. From the trenches in Flanders where he himself was soon to die, Francis Ledwidge wrote a poignant lament for his friend.

> He shall not hear the bittern cry
> In the wild sky, where he is lain
> Nor voices of the sweeter birds
> Above the wailing of the rain.

> Nor shall he know when loud March blows
> Through slanting snows her fanfare shrill
> Blowing in flame the golden cup
> Of many an upset daffodil.

> But when the Dark Cow* leaves the moor.
> And pastures poor with greedy weeds,
> Perhaps he'll hear her low at morn,
> Lifting her horn in pleasant meads.

The next day, four more executions took place. Among the second batch of victims were Pearse's adoring younger brother and inseparable comrade, Willie, and another poet, Joseph Plunkett, son of Count Plunkett, later the first Sinn Feiner to be elected to parliament. At midnight before his execution, handcuffed, Plunkett, "a tall, delicate, fair youth," his face already marked by the pallor of the consumptive, was married to Grace Gifford, whom Orpen had once painted as "Young Ireland." Brooding much on death, Plunkett, like Pearse, had composed his own epitaph.

*One of the many symbols for Ireland.

Because I know the spark
Of God has no eclipse,
Now death and I embark
And sail into the dark
With laughter on our lips.

On the third day John MacBride was shot. The estranged husband
of Maud Gonne, MacBride did not even know that a Rising had been
planned, but happening into Dublin that Easter Morning, he saw the
boys out on Stephen's Green and joined them at once. In the Boer
War he had commanded an Irish Brigade against the British, but the
death that had eluded him under the Southern Cross at Spion Kop
was waiting for him all the time at home in Dublin. "Unlike the
usual Sinn Feiner," wrote the brilliant journalist H. W. Nevinson,
"he was something of the old-fashioned stage Irishman, a swash-
buckler, dissipated, devoid of character." By putting him to death,
the British transformed Yeats's "drunken, vainglorious lout" into a
hero and a martyr. MacBride's last request (not granted) was that he
not be blindfolded. "I have been looking down the barrels of rifles
all my life," he said.

On May 8, another of the seven signatories, Eamonn Ceannt
(Kent), was shot. By profession a clerk of the Dublin Corporation,
Ceannt had a passion for the music of the bagpipes. Darrell Figgis
recalled him as "a dark, proud, aloof man of so extreme a sensitive-
ness that he had schooled himself to wear for mask a cold and rigid
manner." Stephen MacKenna described him as "tall, handsome, always grave, coolly self-possessed," with a "gentle, brooding face,"
always with "some depth in his quiet smile, some singing music in
the soft voice." Not long before the Rising, MacKenna heard Ceannt
play the pipes at the Antient Concert Rooms and left an unforgettable
vignette of the occasion. "Piping as it were without enthusiasm, as a
duty, as a solemn declaration of faith, almost ritually," wrote Mac-
Kenna, "he appeared before my mind as the grave ghost of the old
Ireland rising to haunt the new, and to awe it into homage and
obedience."

Finally on Friday, May 12, the protracted tale of executions came
to an end when the two surviving signatories of the Proclamation
slumped before the bullets of the firing squad—Sean MacDiarmada
and James Connolly. Although crippled by polio MacDiarmada
(MacDermott), a tireless organizer for Sinn Fein, had traveled all
over Ireland. His infectious high spirits later reminded many of Michael
Collins, and in fact Collins cherished a special devotion to his memory.

An intense love of Ireland, wrote Figgis, burned in MacDiarmada "like a flame shining in a slight, crystal-like lanthorn of a body."

James Connolly was the last to die. The court-martial that sentenced him had met at his bedside in the hospital of Dublin Castle. Wounded in the leg, still in pain and unable to walk, he was shot sitting in a wheel chair. The surgeon who attended him was full of admiration for his fortitude. When his wife visited him in prison, Connolly asked her at parting: "Hasn't this been a full life, Lillie, and isn't this a good end?" Shortly before death he received Communion and prayed for those about to shoot him. Pearse had long hoped that Connolly, who had ceased to practice religion, would finally be reconciled to the Church. After a life spent in unremitting hard work, Connolly left behind him as his sole worldly wealth the sum of thirty shillings.

> I write it out in a verse,
> MacDonagh and MacBride,
> And Connolly and Pearse,
> Now and in time to be.
> Wherever green is worn,
> Are changed, changed utterly:
> A terrible beauty is born.

When the Rising began, AE was in Clare. He hurried back to Dublin and from his rooftop office in Merrion Square beheld his beloved city in flames. Like Yeats he admired the bravery of those who gave their lives, while deploring what he took to be their folly. "High words," he wrote, "were equalled by high fate." In December, 1917, he published a tribute "To the memory of some I knew who are dead and who loved Ireland."

> Their dream hath left me numb and cold
> And yet my spirit rose in pride,
> Refurbishing in burnished gold
> The images of those who died.

Lady Gregory remembered those who had given their lives in previous rebellions, and brought past and present together in a spontaneous verse:

> The ballad-singers long have cried
> The shining names of far away;
> Now let them rhyme out those who died
> With the three colours, yesterday.

The dead were buried in quicklime in Arbour Hill barracks, where Matthew Tone and some of the rebels of ninety-eight had long ago been laid to rest. Their sepulture put Joseph Campbell, the poet, in mind of an ancient Irish saying: "If we are dead, it is for the great love we bore the Gael." The month of May was chill and wet. "The rain of springtime," wrote Ella Young, "is cold and wind-tormented. Not so the rain with which Ireland took farewell of her lovers. That rain was warm and passionate, the trees have burgeoned because of it."

Public Opinion and the Rising

General Sir John Maxwell, sent over from England to put down the rebellion, knew from long experience in India and Egypt how to deal with "natives." Naturally enough, he saw in the Rising nothing but an act of disloyalty to England. Ignorant of Irish affairs, he viewed himself as the strong man who was going to teach "these infernal fellows a lesson they would not soon forget." "I am going to ensure," he told the Viceroy, "that there will be no treason whispered for a hundred years." Within six years the treason he was going to stamp out had so far succeeded as to compel the surrender of Dublin Castle and the end of 750 years of British rule in Ireland.

More than 3,500 people were arrested on charges of complicity in the Rising, of whom about 1,500 were released without trial. A hundred and twenty men and one woman were court-martialed. Ninety death sentences were handed down, but of these only fifteen were carried out. Among those whose sentences were commuted were the Countess Markievicz, who had commanded the insurgents in Stephen's Green, and Eamon De Valera, later President of Eire, allegedly because he had been born in New York—a circumstance that made it inadvisable for the British to affront American opinion in time of war. About 1,800 men including De Valera and Michael Collins were deported to England—a blunder of the first magnitude since in the internment camps prisoners from all over Ireland, hitherto unacquainted, forged bonds of comradeship that were to prove their worth when hostilities against Britain were resumed in 1919. Branches of the Gaelic League blossomed amid the grimness of the camps, from which also there emerged the cadres of the future Irish Republican Army.

Since the Rising erupted at a time when the war was going badly for the Allies, and when the Empire itself seemed in peril, it cannot fairly be claimed that the execution of fifteen men was punishment unduly harsh. The mistake lay in the protracted nature of the executions. General Maxwell had forgotten the precept of Machiavelli—that if blood must be shed, it should be shed quickly and all at once. Day after day those who lived near Kilmainham were roused in the early morning by death volleys rattling against the prison walls. Day after day the names of fresh victims were passed by word of mouth throughout the city. Old memories of former wrongs and victims, fertilized by blood, sprang into life once more.

The Rising was condemned throughout the country. "If Ireland as a whole could have got hold of Tom Clarke and his comrades during that week," wrote P. S. O'Hegarty, "it would have torn them in pieces." As the weary and dispirited Volunteers were marched through the streets as prisoners, they were spat upon by the citizens of Dublin. Scornful epithets—"gun-shy ganders," "fine Sunday afternoon soldiers"—were flung at them by those who had never in their lives faced danger. Women in particular, James Stephens noticed, were "viciously hostile" to the captives. One frequently heard the remark: "I hope every man of them will be shot." In Stephen's Green, Maurice Headlam heard an old woman scream over a dead rebel's body: "Let the carrion rot, bringing disgrace on the fair name of Ireland." The husbands of many of these women, it must be remembered were fighting the Germans on the Western Front. Their wives—"separation women," they were called, from the government allowances on which they lived—were understandably resentful of the Volunteers.

The Rising was also condemned by the Church. Not even the fact that most of the Volunteers were devout Catholics saved them from clerical vituperation. The *Irish Catholic* called Pearse "a crazy and insolent schoolmaster," and ridiculed his followers as "rogues and fools." Many bishops deplored what they termed the "mad and sinful adventure" of the rebels. Others, ignoring the I.R.B., blamed everything on Connolly and socialism.

Respectable people were not slow to express their abhorrence of what had occurred. William Martin Murphy, having lost in the Rising a hotel and a department store, led the clamor for vengeance. "Weakness to such men at this stage," he raged, "may be fatal. Let the ringleaders be singled out." Public bodies shared Murphy's demand for blood. Ballyclare Urban District Council called Pearse and Connolly "traitors of the meanest and most cowardly type . . . who richly deserved the severest punishment." Naas animadverted upon "the wickedness and insanity of the rebels." Tralee "deplored with horror the outbreak which brings the blush of shame to every honest Irishman." The Unionists were naturally the most vindictive of all, many urging the execution of every single rebel taken in arms. All this

Pearse had foreseen. The hero of his play, *The Singer,* had prophesied that many would "curse him in their hearts for having brought death into their houses."

The Home Rule members of parliament likewise deplored the Rising. Redmond expressed his "horror and detestation" and approved of the executions; John Dillon, however, who had been in Dublin during Easter Week, was deeply moved by the tragedy he had witnessed. On May 11, speaking under great emotion in the House of Commons, he granted that the rebels had been misguided but paid tribute to their courage and integrity. As for the shootings, he accused General Maxwell of having waded "through a sea of blood."

Following the executions, a swift and unexpected change came over public opinion in Ireland. People recalled how after the 1914 rebellion in the Transvaal, no one had been put to death, not even the intransigent De Wet. By the time the first batch of prisoners were shipped to England from the quays of Dublin, they were already popular heroes. People broke through the police cordon to grasp the hands of the very men they had spat upon two weeks before. One of the prisoners, Batt O'Connor, attributed the change more to Pearse's execution than to any other single factor. By June 10, wrote Tim Healy, the revolution in opinion was complete, Pearse being universally regarded as a martyr. "His executioners would give a good deal," wrote Healy, "to have him and his brother back in jail alive." William Martin Murphy did not fail to register the change in sentiment. While he had not yet recovered from the loss of his store, he nevertheless confessed that when he heard Protestants gloating over the executions, "every drop of Catholic blood in his veins surged up," and he felt his blood begin to boil. People now recollected, especially when they saw British soldiers drunk and using foul language to women, how sober and well disciplined the Volunteers had been.

The first account of the rebellion was written within ten days of its collapse by the poet-novelist James Stephens. He viewed the Rising as "the first day of Irish freedom, and the knowledge," he added, "forbids me to mourn too deeply for my friends who are dead." He took special pride that though many had known the plans of the Volunteers, not a single informer had betrayed them. In this respect the Rising was unique in Irish history. Moreover, Stephens believed that even in defeat the rebels had succeeded in making the Irish question an international one. From the fact of failure, Stephens plucked new hope for Ireland's future. "Her heart which was withering will be warmed by the knowledge that men have thought her worth dying for."

After the Rising, nothing in Ireland was ever the same. Easter Week became the central point of modern Irish history, and events were dated according to whether they had happened before or after that event. "Right down to the heart of Irish nationality it cut," wrote Lennox Robinson, "and two generations to come will feel the piercing terror of that sword thrust." The playwright likened the effect of the Rising on Irish life to the sudden surge into a brackish pool of a great salt wave, tearing and rending the fragile forms that sheltered there, but at the same time cleansing and invigorating the life of the pool.

Though the fifteen leaders lay in a mass grave, the roll of victims was not yet complete. Sir Roger Casement was still a prisoner in the Tower of London, charged with high treason. Outside of Ireland, Pearse and Connolly were virtually unknown, but Sir Roger was a familiar figure throughout the Western World. In England, Casement was now, of course, universally execrated. In the prevailing mood of war hysteria—one that afflicted all Europe—he had become the most hated man in Britain. Admiration had turned into revulsion, love into loathing. "It is a cruel thing to die," wrote Casement not long before his execution, "with all men misunderstanding—misapprehending—and to be silent forever."

From a purely legal point of view, Sir Roger's treason was manifest. From a moral standpoint, however, the reverse is true. Although he had served many years as a British consul, at least since 1904 he felt that he owed ultimate allegiance not to England but to Ireland. It was this belief that brought him to the scaffold. Sentence of death having been passed, in a final statement to the court Casement vindicated his actions and made a final passionate plea for Irish freedom. His last speech from the dock ranks with that of Emmet as a classic of Irish history.

> If English authority be omnipotent, Irish hope exceeds the dimensions of that power, excels its authority and renews with each generation the claims of the last. The cause that begets this indomitable persistency, the faculty of preserving through centuries of misery the remembrance of lost liberty, this surely is the noblest cause that men ever strove for, ever lived for, ever died for. If this be the cause I stand here today indicted for . . . then I stand in a goodly company and a right noble succession.

The sacrifice of Roger Casement, wrote Jawaharlal Nehru many years later, in his *Glimpses of World History*, "laid bare the passionate enthusiasm of the Irish soul."

Early on the morning of August 3, 1916, Casement was hanged at Pentonville Jail in London. Like so many before him, he died with perfect dignity and composure. In New York the poet Padraic Colum wrote a moving lament for his dead friend, in which he recalled

> That noble stature, the grave and brightening face,
> In which courtesy and kindness had eminence of place
>
> . . . . .
>
> They have hanged Roger Casement to the tolling of the bell,
> Ochone, och, ochone, ochone!

In Ireland the news of Casement's execution was received with sorrow and indignation. The trauma caused by the shootings at Kilmainham was renewed and deepened by the hanging at Pentonville. So mild a man as Lennox Robinson was moved to write a protest called "In Silence and Tears," in which he asserted that the death of Casement made Ireland realize clearly that the nature of the enmity between her and England was undying.

On account of his earlier humanitarian accomplishments, Casement was still greatly respected in America and in other parts of the world. Hence the British government felt it necessary not only to take his life but to destroy his reputation. While he lay in prison under sentence of death, "diaries" (which neither Casement nor his solicitor were allowed to see) purporting to reveal his moral depravity were circulated by the authorities. As soon as these documents had served their ignoble purpose of discrediting a doomed man, they were withdrawn from circulation and were not allowed to be seen, even by Casement's biographers, for more than forty years. During the half-century that followed Casement's death, Anglo-Irish relations were bedeviled by a controversy over the "diaries" that lasted throughout the period. Not even the belated production of the documents in 1959 has ended this sorry affair, nor is it likely that the controversy will ever finally be resolved. For the Irish people, the attempt to ruin Parnell by forgery is still too well remembered for anyone to credit the authenticity of charges made surreptitiously against a defenseless political enemy. Casement's last fervent wish had been for burial in his native Antrim. "Do not let me lie in this dreadful place," he entreated in one of his last letters from prison. In February, 1965, after nearly fifty years of constant agitation for the return of his remains, they were at length transferred from the prison yard at Pentonville to the national burying place of Glasnevin.

Aftermath of the Rising (1916-18)

In December, 1916, Lloyd George displaced Asquith as Liberal Prime Minister. Next year, seeking to placate all shades of opinion, he summoned an Irish Convention to Dublin to discuss the future of Ireland. The ninety-five delegates to the Convention were nominated by bodies as various as the Home Rule party, the Ulster Unionists, the Southern Unionists, the Irish peers, the Catholic Church, the Church of Ireland, the Presbyterian Church, labor organizations, and Chambers of Commerce. Even Sinn Fein received an invitation, which it ignored. In order to create an atmosphere of good will in which the meeting might have some chance of success, most of the prisoners who had been interned after the Rising—many of them at Frongoch in Wales—were released under amnesty.

Sir Horace Plunkett, an Anglo-Irishman who had deservedly won universal respect, was chairman of the conference, which opened in Trinity College on July 25, 1917. After meeting at intervals for about eight months, in April, 1918, the Convention came to an end without any agreement among the contending parties. Sinn Fein, naturally, was jubilant, having prophesied all along that it must fail.

A month before the end of the Convention, John Redmond died, convinced finally that the British government had outwitted him over Home Rule. An utterly disillusioned man, not long before his death he told his good friend Lady Fingall: "Do not give your heart to Ireland, for if you do you will die of a broken heart." How complete was the repudiation of the old Nationalist leader by the younger generation—largely because Redmond had refused to intercede for the leaders of the Rising—may be judged from the harsh comment of James Stephens, that Ireland must have been "guilty of abominable crimes in the past to be afflicted with Redmond now." Redmond was succeeded in the leadership of the Home Rule party by John Dillon.

Meanwhile a pressing issue had arisen to unite Ireland finally against the war—the issue of conscription. When in 1916 the draft had been introduced in Britain, Ireland had been exempt from its operation. But after the terrible losses sustained in the third battle of Ypres in the autumn of 1917, and especially after the disaster that befell Gough's Fifth Army in March, 1918, Sir Douglas Haig was insistent in urging the drafting of Irishmen to replenish his depleted ranks. "It was not only to get more men," the Field Marshal explained ingenuously to the king, "but for the good of Ireland." In

June of that year, the French premier, Clemenceau, asked Lloyd George why the Irish had not yet been conscripted. To the astonishment of the bystanders, the latter dryly murmured: "Mr. Prime Minister, you evidently do not know the Irish."

In July, 1918, the government announced that, apart from privileged categories such as priests and members of religious orders, all able-bodied men in Ireland between the ages of eighteen and fifty, and in certain occupations up to fifty-five, would be drafted forthwith. In Ireland the news was greeted with a storm of indignation. Nothing had so united the country since the time of O'Connell—and then the North had opposed Catholic emancipation, whereas now even the North joined with the rest of the nation to oppose conscription. The Home Rulers joined with Sinn Fein, Dillon and Healy with De Valera and Griffith, in opposing the measure. In protest Dillon withdrew the Nationalists from parliament, while De Valera called the act "a declaration of war upon the Irish nation." Public bodies proclaimed their intention to defy the law. The bishops took the lead in resistance to the government: not since Catholic emancipation had the hierarchy put itself at the head of a truly popular cause. Wrote Dr. O'Dwyer, Bishop of Limerick:

> It is very probable that these poor Connacht lads know nothing of the meaning of the war. Their blood is not stirred by memories of Kossovo, and they have no burning desire to die for Servia. They would much prefer to be allowed to till their own potato gardens in peace in Connemara. . . . Their crime is that they are not ready to die for England? Why should they? What have they or their fathers ever got from England that they should ever have died for her? . . . It is England's war, not Ireland's.

Faced by almost unanimous opposition both in the North and in the South, conscription could not possibly be enforced. The act therefore was a dead letter. Once again, in its ignorance of Irish psychology the British government had misread the situation and committed an egregious blunder. The impatience now shown toward Ireland by Lloyd George, who was heard to wish that "damned country were put at the bottom of the sea," is understandable.

The beneficiary of the government's mistake was Sinn Fein, which received a further impetus when in the summer of 1918 the Prime Minister declared that he had discovered a "German plot" in Ireland and promptly arrested seventy-three Sinn Fein leaders, including De Valera. No proof of such a plot was ever forthcoming.

Already by the autumn of 1917, there were twelve hundred Sinn

Fein clubs in Ireland, having an estimated enrollment of 250,000 members. At the annual convention that year, Arthur Griffith, the founder of Sinn Fein, who had opposed the Rising and taken no part in it, gracefully relinquished the presidency to De Valera. The change in leadership dramatized that Sinn Fein had abandoned its old policy of passive resistance in favor of a new militancy, especially since De Valera was chosen as commander of the Volunteers in 1917.

After the Rising, the Volunteers had been declared illegal, but in 1917, in defiance of the government, they were reconstituted. As the Irish Republican Army of the future, a year later they were rumored to number 100,000 men. Inspired by the sacrifice of Pearse and his comrades, and moved by a sense of dedication, their morale was high and their discipline admirable. The majority were devoutly religious, drunkenness among them being almost unknown. Lennox Robinson confessed himself impressed by their "young, dark, eager, vivid" faces as he saw them marching through the streets. If these young men were unwilling to fight in France against a foe with whom they had no quarrel, they were only too willing to fight in their own country against the power they regarded as their hereditary enemy.

The first unmistakable sign of Sinn Fein's new strength was a string of victories gained against the Home Rulers in a series of by-elections. Before 1917, Sinn Fein had not won a single parliamentary contest. In 1917–18 it was successful in every election it fought, returning five M.P.s, of whom—in accord with Griffith's original prescription—none took their seats at Westminster. Its initial success was in North Roscommon, where Count Plunkett, father of the young poet executed in 1916, defeated the Nationalist candidate. Sinn Fein's most significant triumph, however, in 1917, was that of De Valera in East Clare. Not since O'Connell's victory in 1828 had Ennis, that little gray county "town of streams and graceful bridges" gone so wild with joy; not since Catholic emancipation had so many bonfires blazed over "cold Clare rock and Galway rock and thorn." De Valera now found himself Ireland's most popular leader since Parnell.

After the First World War, in the "Victory Election" of December 1918, Lloyd George gained the greatest parliamentary triumph ever won by a British Prime Minister. For Ireland that election was equally momentous, since at one stroke the Home Rule party was shattered. Sinn Fein swept the nation, returning seventy-three M.P.s as against six Nationalists and twenty-six Unionists in the North. Among those who now lost their seats was John Dillon. Since East Mayo had returned him at every election since 1885, the stunning nature of the defeat suffered by the party once led by Parnell is evident.

Out of the total number of votes cast, Sinn Fein won 971,945, as against 235,306 cast for Home Rule and 308,713 for the Unionists. Among the victorious Sinn Feiners was the first woman ever elected to the House of Commons—Constance Markievicz, who had been sentenced to death in 1916 for her part in the Rising. She, too, refused to take her seat—leaving the way open for Lady Astor to become the first woman in parliament.

On January 21, 1919, those Sinn Fein M.P.s who were neither in prison nor 'on the run' met at the Mansion House in Dublin and there proclaimed themselves Dail Eireann, parliament of an independent Ireland. There the twentieth century was at the birth, and its travail would be bloody.

Beginning of the Anglo-Irish War (1919-20)

When the Dail met in Dublin, of seventy-three members eligible to attend, thirty-six (including De Valera) were in jail, six were "on the run," and three had been deported from Ireland. The twenty-seven deputies who were present drafted a Declaration of Independence naming Ireland a Republic and calling on Britain to evacuate the country.

At a second session held on April 1, De Valera was elected president of the Dail, which was accepted as equivalent to being President of the Republic. He immediately chose a cabinet of eight including Arthur Griffith (Home Affairs), Cathal Brugha (Defense), Michael Collins (Finance), and Count Plunkett (Foreign Affairs).

No doubt owing to the influence of Connolly, the original Declaration revealed a strong social awareness. "We re-affirm that all rights to private property must be subordinated to public right and welfare." National sovereignty was defined as extending to the soil and to "wealth-producing processes." No child should suffer, through lack of food and shelter, from hunger or from cold. There should be free universal public education. The hope was also expressed that legislation would be passed to bring about "general and lasting improvements in the conditions under which the working classes live and labour."

Local courts were set up throughout the country to take the place of British judicial tribunals. They proceeded to arbitrate disputes, assess damages, and impose fines. By 1920, partly as the result of intimidation and partly through genuine public support, their decisions were accepted throughout the greater part of southern Ireland; a year later, however, many had been suppressed by the British.

On the very day the Dail met in Dublin, Dan Breen and some

Eamon De Valera (1882–   ). President of the Irish Republic, 1959 to the present.

Volunteers ambushed a small detachment of police at Soloheadbeg, County Tipperary, killing two of them. This was the beginning of a series of hostilities against the British which was to prove the final episode in the 750 years' struggle for national freedom. Attacks on police and police barracks took place in many parts of the country. "Here is our chance," said Dan Breen, "let us start the war soon, or the army will lose heart." These attacks were not authorized by the Dail, but were instigated by local commanders. Not without hesitation, the Dail finally assumed responsibility for them, tacitly recognizing the Volunteers as the Irish Republican Army.

Even so, the Dail shrank from a formal declaration of war upon

Britain, nor did it ever take such action. The caution of the Assembly was in marked contrast to the impetuosity of the Volunteers. Ten days after the opening of the Dail, the Volunteer paper, *An t-Oglach,* edited by Piaras Beaslai, declared that a state of war between Britain and Ireland existed, adding that it would last "until the British military invader evacuated Ireland." "The state of war," *An t-Oglach* continued, "justifies the Volunteers in treating the armed forces of the enemy—whether soldiers or policemen—exactly as a National Army would treat the members of an invading army."

Two years were to pass before both President and Dail were willing to admit publicly that Ireland and England were at war. Soon after his return from the United States in December, 1920, however, De Valera, troubled by the anomalous relations between the Assembly and the I.R.A., persuaded the former to accept responsibility for the war. Even this was done indirectly. On March 30, 1921, the President gave a statement to the press about the attacks made on the British forces. "From the Irish Volunteers," he said, "we fashioned the Irish Republican Army to be the military arm of the Government. . . . The Government is, therefore, responsible for the actions of this army. These actions are not the acts of irresponsible individuals or groups." De Valera went on to accuse the English of "waging upon us not only an unjust but a barbarous war." Even so, no formal declaration of war was made; and two years later in the Dail, General Mulcahy could maintain that that body had never accepted responsibility for the I.R.A., which had acted on its own in waging guerrilla warfare against the British. In this divergence between the Dail and the army lay the seeds of the civil strife that was to convulse Ireland after the treaty with England had been signed.

The man who made the decision to resort to systematic violence was Michael Collins, backed by the Irish Republican Brotherhood, which he now dominated. Collins later congratulated Dan Breen on being "the man who began the war." As a young man of twenty-four, Collins had fought in the post office during Easter Week and had then been interned with hundreds of other Volunteers in the camp at Frongoch. It was there that he first evidenced his qualities of leadership, establishing his personal ascendancy among the prisoners. Physically large, and endowed with abundant vitality, Collins was fearless, shrewd, quick-witted, and intelligent. In De Valera's absence, he proved to be the outstanding personality of the first Dail.

From his secret headquarters in Dublin, Collins organized an expert intelligence service that gave central direction to the guerrilla operations. Without this the war could not possibly have been carried on.

Despite a large reward offered by the British government for his arrest, Collins continued to move freely about the streets of Dublin, constantly changing his headquarters, which at one time were reported to be located just across the street from Dublin Castle. His agents were actually within the Castle itself, and on one occasion Collins was taken inside that citadel of British rule to inspect the dossier that the government had collected upon him. Collins, it seemed, bore a charmed life—at least until the day when he would be shot by his own countrymen in his native county of Cork.

As Minister of Finance, Collins also succeeded in raising within Ireland the astonishing sum of £380,000 as a loan to finance the war effort; while at the same time, De Valera was securing a loan of $6 million from Irish-Americans in the United States.

The undeclared Anglo-Irish war lasted for nearly two years—from September, 1919, to July, 1921. Groups of police were ambushed and individual policemen shot without warning. Barracks were raided for supplies of arms and ammunition. On December 19, 1919, an ambush of Lord French near Dublin almost succeeded in killing the Viceroy. The I.R.A. regarded the killings of police as acts of war; the British considered them as acts of murder. "The first shootings," wrote P. S. O'Hegarty, "stirred and shocked the public conscience tremendously." Newspapers were intimidated by the I.R.A. and their premises wrecked if they dared use words like "murder" to describe the shooting of the police. Bishops such as Dr. Cohalan of Cork, and many individual priests, condemned the I.R.A. campaign of violence.

At this stage, the I.R.A. operated chiefly against the Royal Irish Constabulary, who were well armed with carbines, grenades, and revolvers. The unarmed Dublin Metropolitan Police were left alone; so, too, were soldiers off duty. It soon became difficult to keep the R.I.C. up to its regular strength of about ten thousand men. A grim warning, adapted from a British recruiting slogan, began to appear on the walls of Irish buildings: JOIN THE R.A.F. AND SEE THE WORLD. JOIN THE R.I.C. AND SEE THE NEXT. The younger policemen—all of them Irish—began to resign in considerable numbers from the force. Older men, who would soon qualify for a pension, stayed on and braved the consequences. To conserve the strength of the R.I.C., in the spring of 1920 all outlying barracks were evacuated. In the largest concerted operation yet undertaken by the I.R.A., 315 of these buildings were burned down in a single night—April 3, 1920, which happened to be Easter eve. A month later, on May 1, 1920, the conservative *Irish Times* declared: "The King's government has virtually ceased to exist south of the Boyne and west of the Shannon."

The attacks on the British, though widespread, were the work of a small minority. Though rumored to be much larger, the I.R.A. could never claim more than 15,000 men; and Collins later admitted that he had never had more than 3,000 effectives at any one time. Opposed to them were some 40,000 British troops in Ireland, increased by 1921 to 80,000. Playing into the hands of their elusive and resourceful enemy, the authorities absurdly exaggerated the strength of the I.R.A. Lord French in 1921 put it at 100,000 men, and Ian Macpherson, the Chief Secretary, at twice that number.

To make good the depleted ranks of the R.I.C., two new police units were brought into Ireland—the Black and Tans and the Auxiliaries, the latter being known also as the Cadets. Though officially classified as police, the "Tans" and the "Auxies" were so heavily armed as to constitute, in fact, a paramilitary force. The first Black and Tans landed in Ireland in March, 1920. They got their name from the manner in which their uniforms had been hastily assembled out of inadequate supplies, combining in some cases the black of the old R.I.C. tunics with the khaki trousers of the military, or *vice versa*. Estimates of their maximum strength vary between 5,800 and 7,000. The Auxiliaries, who first appeared in Ireland in July, 1920, wore dark blue uniforms and Glengarry caps. They never numbered more than 1,500 men.

Almost all were veterans of the European war who, after being demobilized, could not or would not find civilian occupation. They enlisted in Ireland either for what was then regarded as high pay (ten shillings a day for the "Tans," one pound for the "Auxies") or for the hope of adventure and loot, or else because they had already become so brutalized that no other existence appealed to them. The Auxiliaries were an elite corps of ex-officers, many of whom had attended English public schools. They were given the privilege of choosing their own officers and were concerned lest people mistake them for the Black and Tans. Some of the Tans had been shell-shocked; others had prison records—about three hundred were ex-convicts. Frank Owen, an English journalist and former M.P., describes them as an "early kind of SS guard." While the Tans and the Auxies were equally brutal, the latter were eventually even more loathed by the Irish because of their swaggering and insolent manner. Churchill observed sardonically of the Tans that "they acted with much the same freedom that the Chicago or New York police permit themselves in dealing with armed gangs."

The Black and Tans (1920–21)

The Black and Tans ushered in a reign of terror worse than any known in Ireland since 1798. A systematic policy of reprisals, never officially avowed, was adopted under which, after an ambush or the death of a single policeman, the nearest town, village, or creamery was burned to the ground—according to the whim of the usually drunken avengers, who were nominally subject to military discipline. The earliest large-scale example of this was the partial burning on September 20, 1920, of Balbriggan, County Dublin, and of the hosiery factory on which the livelihood of the little town chiefly depended. Sir Hamar Greenwood, who had become Chief Secretary in April, first denied and then defended in the House of Commons the policy of reprisals practiced by the police—and on four separate occasions by the military as well—against innocent civilians.

During the next eighteen months, terror prevailed in Ireland. Martial law was in force over large areas. Populous cities like Dublin and Cork were placed under curfew—a seemingly minor restriction but one that was grievous for those forced to remain indoors on summer evenings to swelter in the fetid air of slum tenements. Houses were broken into without warning and their contents ransacked. Jails were filled with suspects, often left for weeks without trial. Pogroms against Catholics broke out again in Belfast. Lorries and tenders roared at high speed through city streets and country lanes, their occupants shooting wildly at anything they saw. Thomas MacCurtain, Lord Mayor of Cork, and George Clancy, Mayor of Limerick, were murdered by night in their own homes. The murder on November 1, 1920, of Ellen Quinn, a young mother sitting by the roadside in Kiltartan with her child in her arms—she was shot from a lorry filled with Tans as they raced through the village—inspired the revulsion of Yeats's poem "1919."

> Now days are dragon-ridden, the nightmare
> Rides upon sleep: a drunken soldiery
> Can leave the mother, murdered at her door,
> To crawl in her own blood, and go scot-free.
> We pieced our thoughts into philosophy
> And planned to bring the world under a rule,
> Who are but weasels fighting in a hole.

The morning of the day that Mrs. Quinn was murdered in County Galway, Kevin Barry was hanged in Mountjoy Jail in Dublin. A lad of eighteen, student at the National University, and a member of the I.R.A., he had participated in an ambush in which several soldiers had been killed, though no evidence was produced that he himself had fired a fatal shot. The execution of so young a boy moved the nation more than anything since the executions following Easter Week. Many of Barry's fellow students hastened to enroll in the I.R.A. A ballad extolling the bravery of young Kevin Barry was sung throughout the country and soon came to rival "God Save Ireland" in its appeal.

Perhaps the most shocking day of the war was Sunday, November 21, 1920, still remembered in Dublin as "Bloody Sunday." As the church bells in the city were striking nine that morning, fourteen British officers were murdered simultaneously, some in the presence of their wives. A wave of horror and resentment spread through England, arousing in older people memories of the shock occasioned by the Phoenix Park murders nearly forty years earlier. Michael Collins, who had ordered the executions, had positive information that the officers, wearing mufti, were espionage agents who, only a short time before, had almost discovered his headquarters and had just missed arresting him—a *coup* that might have ended the guerrilla campaign overnight.

That same afternoon, in reprisal, some Black and Tans opened fire on a crowd gathered to watch a hurling match at Croke Park, killing twelve people and wounding sixty. That evening, Richard McKee and Peadar Clancy, two prominent members of the I.R.A. then imprisoned in Dublin Castle, were summarily shot after being tortured. So the vicious cycle of terror and counterterror continued. Churchill, in his narrative of these somber events, mentions the killing of the officers but does not mention the reprisals that followed.

Exactly a week after "Bloody Sunday" came the biggest I.R.A. success in the war, when at Macroom, County Cork, a body of Auxiliaries that had terrorized the countryside was ambushed by Commandant Tom Barry's Third Cork Brigade, eighteen of the hated Auxies being killed. Two weeks later, on the night of December 11–12, no doubt in reprisal for the disaster at Macroom, a number of drunken Tans and Auxies went berserk in Cork, burning down the center of southern Ireland's second city. More damage was done that single night than in the whole week's fighting in Dublin in 1916. In parliament, Sir Hamar Greenwood solemnly affirmed that the people of Cork had burned down their own city, but by this time no one paid attention to the repeated falsehoods of the Chief Secretary.

A major sensation was created the following February when General

Frank Crozier, commander of the Auxiliaries, unable to control his men or to enforce their punishment by the authorities, resigned in protest against what he termed "the reign of chaos, murder, arson, robbery and drunkenness" instigated by the Black and Tans. The burning of Cork he characterized as "one of the most disgraceful affairs in the history of the British Army." "Law and order," wrote no less a person than General Gough, former leader of the Curragh "mutiny," "have given way to a bloody and brutal anarchy, in which the armed agents of the Crown violate every law in aimless and vindictive and insolent savagery. England has departed further from her own standards, and further from the standards of any nation in the world, not excepting the Turk and the Zulu, than has ever been known in history before."

The guerrilla war was confined chiefly to the city of Dublin and to the province of Munster, where by this time the I.R.A. was operating on a considerable scale, sometimes in "flying columns" of twenty or thirty men. These columns, of which Ernie O'Malley has given so vivid an account in his autobiography, *On Another Man's Wound,* constantly harassed the British forces from hideouts in the mountains or the bogs. They attacked barracks, ambushed lorries, and blew up roads and bridges. They struck swiftly and disappeared as swiftly as they had come. They were adept at evasion tactics. They were everywhere and nowhere. They operated with equal success in crowded Dublin slums and in the desolate mountains of the West. They were, of course, sheltered by the people of the countryside through which they moved; without such aid they could not possibly have survived. They had no heavy weapons of any kind. The few arms they did possess—mostly rifles, revolvers, and grenades—either had been captured from the enemy or else had been manufactured in primitive workshops.

The Crown forces, as Major Florence O'Donoghue has written, were "housed in well-fortified and comfortable barracks, many of their officers were veterans of the European war, most of the troops had received adequate military training, they were armed with modern weapons." They were superior in every respect save one—that of morale. For whereas the British forces were usually mercenaries serving for pay, the I.R.A. was composed of youthful idealists facing danger and death for the sake of a cause in which they were willing to lay down their lives. "The Sinn Fein leaders," wrote Lord Haldane, who visited Dublin in 1919, "are not murderers. They are idealists with a fanatical belief in what they believe to be principles, tempered by a shrewd recognition of realities. . . . The Sinn Fein rebels whom I met," he added, "were friendly and intelligent, and I saw only the best of them, but I thought highly of their quality and their sanity." Many of the I.R.A., like Ernie O'Malley, were inspired by the knowledge that in their guerrilla warfare they had far surpassed anything attempted by the Fenians, Young Ireland, or the men of ninety-eight.

Watching the struggle from a distance in India, Nehru expressed the view of millions of outside observers when he wrote that "a mere handful of young men and women, with the sympathy of their people behind them, fought against fantastic odds; a great and organized empire was against them—Ireland became one huge field of conflict where both parties vied with each other in violence and destruction; behind one of the parties was the organized strength of an empire, behind the other was the iron resolve of a handful of men."

Public Opinion in Britain and America (1919-21)

Yet for all their bravery, by 1921 it was beginning to be doubtful how long the I.R.A. could continue the unequal contest. An exploit like the burning of the Dublin Customs House on May 25, 1921— which destroyed the records of British Local Government in Ireland— cost the lives of sixty men, a loss so serious that the exploit amounted almost to a pyrrhic victory. The shortage of arms was acute and growing worse: by 1921 it was no longer easy, as it had been at the outset, to capture arms from the enemy. Lloyd George, moreover, was reported on the point of increasing the military forces in Ireland to 100,000 men.

What turned the scale in favor of the Irish was the gradual revulsion in public opinion, both in Britain and elsewhere in the Western World, wrought by the increasing revelations of terror as practiced by the Tans and the Auxiliaries. In February, 1921, the Archbishop of Canterbury, while condemning the violence of the I.R.A., likewise deplored the lawlessness of the Crown forces. Intrepid English journalists like Henry Nevinson and Hugh Martin, and outspoken editors like C. P. Scott of the *Manchester Guardian,* made the English people aware of the horrors being perpetrated in their name. The influential London *Times* criticized the government severely. "The whole world," wrote G. K. Chesterton, "thinks that England has gone mad." At the Oxford Union a passionate speech by W. B. Yeats persuaded the undergraduates to repudiate the misdeeds of the Black and Tans in Ireland.

The Liberal and Labour parties charged Lloyd George with evasive-

Terence MacSwiney (1879–1920). Lord Mayor of Cork, who died in London on hunger-strike, November, 1920.

ness and dishonesty in defending his Irish policy. In 1920, Labour sent a commission to Ireland which produced abundant evidence from eyewitnesses of the atrocities being committed in the name of the Crown. The event that perhaps did more than any other to produce a change in British public opinion toward Ireland was the death of Terence MacSwiney, Lord Mayor of Cork, in Brixton Jail in London on October 25, 1920. Arrested not for any act of violence but on a charge of possessing allegedly compromising documents, MacSwiney at once announced his intention to go on a hunger strike. For the almost incredible period of seventy-four days, sustained only by water and by the daily eucharistic wafer. the courageous Lord Mayor lived on, his body slowly wasting away, as Britain and the world watched with anxious sympathy his long-protracted ordeal. When MacSwiney's body was returned to Cork for burial, it was the occasion in Ireland for a nationwide outpouring of grief.

Opinion in the Dominions was also favorable to Ireland and strongly desirous of peace. Archbishop Mannix of Melbourne, the leading Catholic prelate in Australia, was a pertinacious critic of British rule in Ireland. Jan Christian Smuts, who had once taken up arms against Britain but was now Prime Minister of South Africa and Field Marshal of the British Empire, used his great personal influence with Lloyd George to press for peace negotiations. Most of all, however, Britain was embarrassed by the extreme unpopularity of her Irish policy in the United States. In December, 1920, and January, 1921, an American Commission on Conditions in Ireland, whose members included such influential figures as Senator George Norris, Jane Addams, and Norman Thomas, heard evidence in Washington, D.C., on the state of Ireland and published a report that, while condemning the violence by the I.R.A., condemned even more severely the actions of the British government. In the United States, it was not merely Irish-Americans that were critical of Britain but the nation as a whole. At a time when Britain was heavily in debt to the United States and anxious for the best settlement possible, American good will was of vital importance to the Lloyd George government.

The Irish Free State and the Civil War (1922–23)

In 1920 the Prime Minister had already made one attempt to end the war, when by the Government of Ireland Act he had offered Home Rule both to South and North in Ireland. The Dail in Dublin had ignored the offer, but the Orangemen reversed their prewar policy of total opposition to any form of Home Rule and accepted the act. Under the terms of this statute six counties (Antrim, Down, Londonderry, Armagh, Tyrone, and Fermanagh) were to constitute the government of Northern Ireland, with a Governor General, a parliament of two Houses (at Belfast), a cabinet, and a considerable measure of self-government. Northern Ireland, however, was still to remain part of the United Kingdom and to send twelve members to Westminster. On June 22, 1921, George V opened the new Belfast parliament and made an urgent plea for peace in Ireland.

Meanwhile, secret negotiations—in which Smuts played a leading role—had been going on behind the scenes between De Valera and emissaries from Lloyd George. At noon on July 11, 1921, to the intense joy of all Ireland, hostilities ceased and a truce went into effect. The negotiations were now transferred to London, and after five months of feverish activity, on December 6, 1921, the Irish delegation, headed by Griffith and Collins, reluctantly accepted the peace terms offered by Lloyd George under threat of immediate resumption of large-scale hostilities. The terms were quickly ratified by the British parliament and embodied next year in the Statute of Westminster. In Ireland, however, they were accepted in January, 1922, only after heated and protracted debate in the Dail by a vote of 64–57, when the pro-treaty deputies headed by Arthur Griffith and Michael Collins defeated the opposition led by De Valera and Cathal Brugha. The result was the immediate establishment of the Irish Free State, with Griffith as president of the Dail and Collins as head of the new Provisional Government.

The result of the split in the Dail was a brief but fierce civil war in Ireland, lasting from June, 1922, to April, 1923, in which De Valera's followers were defeated by the newly created army of the Free State. During the course of hostilities in Dublin, the brave but irreconcilable Cathal Brugha was killed in savage fighting in O'Connell Street on July 5; while on the other side, Michael Collins was shot in ambush on August 22 at Beal-na-blath in his native county of Cork. The feuds of brothers are more grievous than the conflicts of strangers, and the grim struggle between men who were so lately allies risking their lives in a common cause is one of the most poignant episodes in the tragic history of Ireland. Seventy-seven followers of De Valera, including Rory O'Connor, who had begun the civil war by seizing the Four Courts on June 28, 1922, were put to death by the government—a larger number than the British had executed in the course of the Black and Tan War. One incidental victim of the hatreds unloosed by the Civil War was Field Marshal Sir Henry Wilson, former Chief of the Imperial General Staff, who was shot and killed outside his London residence in 1922 by two Sinn Feiners.

Blood calls for blood, and in revenge for the shooting of Rory O'Connor, the friends of the latter bided their time for nearly five years before settling accounts with the man whom they regarded as his murderer—Kevin O'Higgins, the strong man of the Free State whom Yeats regarded as the outstanding Irish statesman of the twentieth century. On July 10, 1927, O'Higgins, at whose wedding Rory had been best man, was murdered by Rory's friends while walking to Sunday mass. For this crime no one has ever been brought to

Kevin O'Higgins (1892–1927). Strong man of the Free State, greatly admired by Yeats; murdered July 10, 1927.

justice. Even today in Ireland, recollections of what happened forty years ago still poison the national life. Not until a new generation shall have taken over direction of the nation's fortunes will the last traces of these malign influences cease to embitter politics in Ireland.

Perhaps the saddest episode of all was the vindictive killing of Erskine Childers, a most courageous and honorable man. Sentenced to death by a military court, he was straightaway shot by the Free State government on November 24, 1922, before an appeal could even be lodged. There are some interesting points of resemblance between the careers of Erskine Childers and of Roger Casement: the former, half Irish (on his mother's side) and wholly Irish in sentiment, had been, like Casement, a distinguished and much respected British civil servant. By joining Sinn Fein, Childers incurred the implacable hatred of Englishmen who had formerly admired him. When he was taken prisoner by the Free State, Churchill among others clamored loudly for the execution of "the mischief-making, murderous renegade, Erskine Childers." This, perhaps, was only to be expected, but that comrades in arms like Griffith and O'Higgins should scorn Childers as an Englishman—Childers who had also risked his life fighting the Black and Tans—shows how deep were the rancors of the time and how normally chivalrous men had become estranged from reason. In the long, tormented stretch of Irish history there is no lonelier figure than that of Erskine Childers.

The Irish Free State (1922-37)

By the "treaty" that ended the Anglo-Irish war, Southern Ireland gained much more than the old Home Rule party had ever dreamed of demanding. For in 1922 Dominion status—a position in the Commonwealth exactly equal to that of Canada—was conferred upon the newly created Irish Free State. Save for the nominal link with the Crown, against which De Valera had fought in vain, this constituted virtual independence, with a separate cabinet and parliament sitting in Dublin. The Irish Free State was to have complete control over its own foreign policy and diplomatic relations, over taxation, customs and excise, as well as over its military forces and police—the latter now renamed the Civic Guard. Such a settlement went far beyond anything for which O'Connell, Parnell, or Redmond could have hoped. Tim Healy, one of the last survivors from the days of Parnell, was named first Governor General of the Free State.

The price paid by Ireland for the establishment of the Free State was the partition of the country. For by the "treaty," the northern parliament, set up in 1920 by the Government of Ireland Act, was given the right to vote itself out of the newly established State—an option that Northern Ireland, under the leadership of its first Prime Minister, Sir James Craig (1921-40), exercised within twenty-four hours. The result is the existence today in Ireland of two separate governments—one at Dublin for the twenty-six counties of the South, and one at Belfast for the six counties of the North (which, it may be noted in passing, are not the same as the six counties named in the Plantation of Ulster in 1608).

Included in the "treaty" was a promise that the boundary between Northern Ireland and the Irish Free State would be redrawn. The southern Irish certainly believed that this would be done in accordance with the wishes of the majority of the inhabitants, but they neglected to obtain a formal guarantee of this. Without such a guarantee, it is doubtful whether Griffith and Collins would ever have signed the document, or whether the Dail would later have ratified it. Two of the six counties of Northern Ireland—Tyrone and Fermanagh—have substantial Catholic majorities, and the Free State government had reason to believe that when the boundary between North and South was finally established, it would mean the return of these counties to Southern Ireland. When, in 1925, however, the Boundary Commission reported its decision, it was found to involve only minor changes, so that the two Catholic counties remained—as they remain today—

under the control of Belfast. In protest against this award, Eoin MacNeill, once head of the National Volunteers and now Free State representative on the Boundary Commission, resigned in disgust.

Apart from Partition, which still remains the chief cause of dissention between North and South, the two clauses in the "treaty" that gave most offense to the Republicans were the oath of loyalty to the king, compulsory upon all office holders and on members of the Dail, and the retention by Britain of three naval bases on Irish soil—Lough Swilly, Berehaven, and Cobh.

Unwilling to take the oath of allegiance, De Valera, who had been captured and briefly imprisoned by the Free State in 1923, refused at first to enter the Dail. In 1927, however, he changed his mind, declaring as he signed the oath that it was only a meaningless formula. Such a decision, had it been taken in 1922, would have spared Ireland the agony of civil war and would have obviated an immense amount of bitterness.

For ten arduous years (1922–32)—a period devoted to the successful rebuilding of Ireland's ravaged economy—William Cosgrave ably headed the Free State Government and reestablished public confidence. For the last five years of this critical period, De Valera, having founded a new party called Fianna Fail, was leader of the opposition. At length, in 1932, in the wake of the Depression, De Valera defeated Cosgrave in a general election. On taking office, without consulting Britain he forthwith abolished the oath, terminated for all practical purposes the office of Governor General, and ended the annuities to Britain that were still being paid under the series of Land Purchase Acts (1881–1909). Britain retorted by attempting to cripple Irish trade through the imposition of high customs duties on Irish dairy produce.

Ireland in turn retaliated by increasing her tariffs on imported goods from Britain. The "trade war" that followed lasted six years, from 1932 to 1938, and caused more loss to English merchants than to Irish farmers. It was ended in 1938 by an agreement between De Valera and Prime Minister Neville Chamberlain, by which the Free State agreed to pay ten million pounds in final settlement of the annuities, in return for which Britain—much to the chagrin of Winston Churchill—finally relinquished the three naval bases in Ireland.

In 1937, by popular vote, the Free State was formally brought to an end, the name of the country being changed officially to "Eire," which was described in the new constitution as "a sovereign, independent and democratic state." As a tribute to his pioneer work in the Gaelic League, Douglas Hyde, a Protestant, was named first President of Eire. Although the constitution of 1937 contained no reference whatever to the Crown or the Commonwealth, the use of the word "republic" was still avoided. This anomalous situation lasted until 1949, when the Dail voted to designate Eire a republic and to withdraw Ireland completely from the Commonwealth. Thus were terminated the last traces of the legal connection that had bound Ireland to her stronger neighbor for nearly eight hundred years. While giving due credit to the courage and valor of those who fought between 1916 and 1922 for the independence of Ireland, it seems probable that but for the decline of the British Empire and the rise of the United States as a world power, the freedom of Ireland could not have been won during that generation.

BIBLIOGRAPHY

Beaslai, Piaras: *Michael Collins and the Making of Ireland,* 2 vols. (1926)
Bennett, Richard: *The Black and Tans* (1960)
Bromage, Mary: *Churchill and Ireland* (1964)
_____: *De Valera and the March of a Nation* (1956)
Caulfield, Max: *The Easter Rebellion* (1963)
Clarke, Thomas J.: *Glimpses of an Irish Felon's Prison Life* (1922)
Colum, Padraic: *Ourselves Alone* (1959)
_____: *Poems of the I.R.B.* (1916)
Connolly, James: *Labour in Ireland; Labour in Irish History* (1917)
Desmond, Shaw: *The Drama of Sinn Fein* (1923)
Figgis, Darrell: *Recollections of the Irish War* (1927)
Fitzgerald, Redmond: *Cry Blood, Cry Erin* (1966)
Gallagher, Frank: *Days of Fear* (1928)
Greaves, C. Desmond: *Life and Times of James Connolly* (1961)
Gwynn, Denis Rolleston: *Traitor or Patriot, the Life and Death of Roger Casement* (1931)
Henry, Robert Mitchell: *The Evolution of Sinn Fein* (1920)
Holt, Edgar: *Protest in Arms* (1960)
Le Roux, Louis N.: *Life of Patrick Pearse* (1917)
_____: *Tom Clarke and the Irish Freedom Movement* (1936)
Lynch, Diarmuid: *The I.R.B. and the Insurrection of 1916* (1957)
Macardle, Dorothy: *The Irish Republic* (1937)
Markievicz, Constance: *Prison Letters* (1934)
Marreco, Anne: *The Rebel Countess* (1967)
Martin, F. X.: *The Irish Volunteers, 1913-15* (1963)
O'Brien, Conor Cruise: *The Shaping of Modern Ireland* (1960)
O'Broin, Leon: *Dublin Castle and the Easter Rising* (1966)
O'Callaghan, Sean: *The Easter Lily* (1956)

O'Casey, Sean: *The Plough and the Stars* (1926)
O'Connor, Sir James: *History of Ireland, 1798-1924*, 2 vols. (1926)
O'Faolain, Sean: *De Valera* (1949)
O'Flaherty, Liam: *The Informer* (1926)
_____: *Insurrection* (1950)
O'Hegarty, Patrick Sarsfield: *The Victory of Sinn Fein* (1924)
O'Malley, Ernie: *Army Without Banners* (1937)
Pakenham, Frank: *Peace by Ordeal* (1935)
Parmiter, Geoffrey de Clinton: *Roger Casement* (1936)
Pearse, Mary Brigid: *The Home Life of Patrick Pearse* (1934)
Pearse, Patrick H.: *Collected Works: Political writings and speeches* (1917)
Phillips, W. Alison: *The Revolution in Ireland, 1906-23* (1923)
Ryan, Desmond: *The Man Called Pearse* (1917)
_____: *The Rising* (1957)
Stephens, James: *Insurrection in Dublin* (1916)
Taylor, Rex: *Michael Collins* (1958)
Wells, Warre B.: *A History of the Irish Rebellion of 1916* (1916)
White, Terence De Vere: *Kevin O'Higgins* (1958)
Williams, Desmond; ed.: *The Irish Struggle* (1966)

Epilogue

Since for centuries English officials had maintained that Ireland was inherently unfit for self-government—Field Marshal Sir Henry Wilson once declared that "the Irish could not administer two typewriters"— it is of interest to consider briefly the successes and failures that have attended self-government since its inception in Ireland in 1922.

From a political point of view, the most remarkable feature of recent Irish history has been the stability of the central administration and the relative peacefulness of a country long notorious for violence. The lawlessness that had been endemic under British rule and that had flared so disastrously during the first year of the new State's existence were now succeeded by a respect for law and order comparable to that on which Britain had for generations prided herself.

Since 1922 only five individuals—William T. Cosgrave (1922-32), Eamon De Valera (1932-48, 1951-54, 1957-59), John A. Costello (1948-51, 1954-57), Sean Lemass (1957-66), and John Lynch (1966-) —have served as actual head of government; and since Eire came into being in 1937 only three men—Douglas Hyde (1938-45), Sean T. O'Kelly (1945-49), and De Valera (1959-) have served as President.

This smooth and uninterrupted functioning of politics for nearly half a century would never have been possible had not Ireland inherited from Britain an invaluable dual legacy—the two-party parliamentary system and a civil service that was both efficient and honest. Neither the bitter personal feuds carried over from the civil war of 1922-23 nor voting by proportional representation—a device that strengthens minorities while weakening the party in power—has impaired the stability of successive Irish administrations. For nearly forty years now, two major parties—Fianna Fail (Party of Destiny) and Fine Gael (United Ireland)—have contended for power, with the Labor party and other smaller parties sometimes in a position to hold the balance between them.

Since the health of democratic institutions depends ultimately upon the spirit in which they are operated, it is well to remember how much Ireland owes to the magnanimous precedents set by Cosgrave in 1927 and by De Valera in 1932: on each of these occasions, the government in office laid aside rancor and thoughts of revenge, thereby permitting the opposition to function in a normal parliamentary manner without the risk of being prosecuted or purged.

It is hardly to be expected of any nation whose history for centuries has been one of violence that immediately on winning independence, lawlessness will cease. After the defeat of the Republicans in the civil war, the threat of further violence came chiefly from the I.R.A., many of whose members—like demobilized soldiers in other countries—had no desire to return to civilian life, and some of whom had cached their weapons instead of surrendering them.

In 1925 the I.R.A. at length broke with De Valera, whom until then they had continued to regard as President. Their attempt to found a new political party (Saor Eire) in 1929 was thwarted by a Public Safety Act two years later, and after some years of sporadic violance, including the murder of a retired British admiral, De Valera himself felt obliged in 1936 to suppress the organization and put its leaders in prison. The outbreak of the Second World War saw a revival of I.R.A. outrages in England, in which Brendan Behan (then a boy of sixteen) was among those involved. The most serious of these attacks occurred at Coventry on August 25, 1939, when five people were killed and seventy wounded. For this, two I.R.A. men were executed the following year.

Apart from the braggadocio involved in blowing up the Nelson Pillar in O'Connell Street in 1966 to commemorate the fiftieth anniversary of Easter Week, the only real violence indulged in by the I.R.A. during the past thirty years has been the series of attacks launched against the border of Northern Ireland between 1956 and 1962. These attacks caused damages amounting to about £1,500,000 and cost the lives of seven Northern policemen. The Eire government did its best to discourage such outbreaks, while Belfast was able to prevent its own extremists from mounting retaliatory attacks against the South—the very object at which the I.R.A. had aimed. Fifty years after the Dublin Rising it seems probable that the revolutionary impulse, so long a central theme in Irish history, has almost exhausted itself.

In the sphere of religion, fears that the attainment of Home Rule would lead to the persecution of Protestants in the South have fortunately not been realized. Nevertheless, the small Protestant minority—so long the ruling power in Ireland—now finds itself relegated to a position of political inferiority and living in a social and cultural atmosphere that is in many ways uncongenial. The prohibition of divorce in Ireland—against which Senator W. B. Yeats fought so strenuously—and the establishment in 1929 of a severe and illiberal censorship—against which Senator Owen Sheehy Skeffington, son of the martyred pacifist of 1916, protested in vain—are examples of the problems that are apt to arise in any society under clerical dominance. Writers of any independence of mind, whether Catholic or Protestant, find themselves penalized by a censorship that is at once arbitrary and capricious, and that is one of the least attractive features of the new State. While Protestants still control a considerable part of the nation's wealth and are conspicuous among the professional classes, many of them suffer none the less from a malaise of spirit, which, it is said, has resulted in about two-thirds of their number leaving Eire since 1922.

The chief weakness of the new Ireland has been its failure properly to develop its economic resources. In the period after 1932, De Valera did attempt by protective tariffs to achieve the economic self-sufficiency at which Griffith had aimed in founding Sinn Fein in 1905. By encouraging the development of industry, De Valera also hoped to redress the balance between town and countryside. But the tariff war of 1932–38 gravely hampered these plans and produced much unemployment.

The economic policies followed both by Fianna Fail and Fine Gael were cautious, orthodox, and pre-Keynesian. In a country whose main economic handicap was its chronic lack of capital investment, little attempt was made to attract foreign capital or to stimulate economic growth. For nearly forty years the economic growth rate was only one percent—one of the lowest in Europe, if not in the world. Private capital was timid, while public capital was lacking on any sufficient scale. The result was chronic unemployment—often amounting to seven percent of the labor force—stagnation in manufactures and commerce, as well as an all-pervading inertia.

This accumulation of ills—economic, social, and moral—was reflected by the reappearance in Ireland of a familiar malady—a constant stream of emigration often averaging forty thousand people a year, most of them young and able-bodied persons. The pattern of the new emigration, however, changed from what it had been before the First World War. Very few emigrants now proceeded to the United

States. The majority, attracted by the benefits of the welfare state, were content to settle in Britain. Perhaps some two million people have left Ireland since she attained self-government in 1922; and of these, more than half have gone to Britain since the close of the Second World War. This endless flow of the nation's most valuable resource—its youth—to the homeland of the ancient enemy constitutes at once a betrayal of the ideals of those who died in 1916 and an indictment of the economic, social, and cultural attitudes of the new Ireland—for the causes of emigration were not purely economic: they reflected also the rigid and repressive attitudes of an all-powerful Catholic hierarchy and clergy from whose excessive dominance young people sought to free themselves by flight.

Not until 1958 did the government take measures to deal with these grave socioeconomic evils. In that year T. K. Whitaker, head of the Civil Service and secretary to the Finance department, published a document entitled *Economic Development,* which drew attention to the urgency of increasing capital investment in Ireland and implied that this could be accomplished only through careful economic planning. Professor Oliver MacDonagh has characterized the Whitaker plan as revolutionary—"comprehensive, rational and coherent" to a degree hitherto unknown in Irish economics.

The government of Sean Lemass endorsed Whitaker's proposals and put them into effect in its two Programmes for Economic Expansion—the first from 1958 to 1963, the second, projected from 1964 to 1970. The result of this tardy acceptance of the necessity for economic planning in a free society was an increase in the rate of economic growth from one percent to four percent, a stimulus to employment and a slackening in the flow of emigration—reduced to sixteen thousand a year by the middle sixties. In these years also, the development of the tourist industry by judicious investment was vigorously promoted and proved to be a valuable source of revenue.

During the period of the first economic program, the gross national product rose by almost seventy-five percent and investment doubled. By means of various inducements, considerable amounts of foreign capital were attracted to Ireland—even from countries like Germany and Japan. It is, incidentally, a curious fact—one that is understandably resented in Ireland—that Irish-Americans, for all their sentimental attachment to the Auld Sod, have been reluctant to invest their money in a country where the return upon investments has always been meager.

A hard-headed realist in economics, Sean Lemass showed imagination in his dealings with Great Britain and Northern Ireland. In

January, 1965, braving the displeasure of political extremists, he paid the first visit to Belfast that had ever been made by the head of a Dublin government. He and Captain Terence O'Neill, Prime Minister of Northern Ireland since 1963, discussed in a friendly atmosphere matters of mutual concern to both governments; a few months later, O'Neill returned the visit. This was the first sign of a thaw in the frozen and uncompromising attitudes that had divided North and South for half a century.

In December, 1965, showing even more initiative, Lemass negotiated with Harold Wilson's Labour government in London an agreement that envisaged uniting Eire to Britain in a single free-trade area. By the terms of this understanding, Britain promised to abolish existing tariffs upon Irish imports, while Eire agreed to reciprocate by gradually lowering tariffs on British imports over a period of fifteen years, so that there would be complete free trade between the two countries by 1980. A probable by-product of such economic rapprochement would be a further relaxation of tension between Eire and Northern Ireland. This belated recognition of the essential community of interest between two neighboring islands may be regarded as a victory for common sense over centuries of prejudice. It also pointed the way to a still more fruitful collaboration, for when in 1962 Britain applied for membership in the European Common Market, Ireland made her application the very next day. Such membership would immensely benefit Irish agriculture.

From an international point of view, independent Ireland has occupied a unique position. While never legally a colony, she had nevertheless been subjected to what was in effect colonial rule. Hence, in her struggle for freedom Ireland had the sympathy of subject peoples throughout the British Empire, Both Gandhi and Nehru expressed their admiration of Sinn Fein. A generation later, the leaders of both Israel and Egypt studied the tactics of the I.R.A. and put them into practice. In all probability, no state ever became a full-fledged member of the international community with a greater fund of general good will than did the Irish Free State in 1922.

Next year the new State was admitted to the League of Nations, and in 1930 it was elected to membership of the Council of the League. In 1932, De Valera became President of the Council, in which capacity he constituted himself the spokesman at Geneva for small nations in general as opposed to the greater powers, and gained a considerable international reputation.

To the dismay of many of his supporters at home, and not withstanding his own devout Catholicism, De Valera followed Britain's lead in condemning Mussolini's conquest of Abyssinia and in voting for sanctions against Italy. He likewise resisted strong pressures at home to support Franco's dictatorship in Spain; nor did he succumb to the hysterical anti-Communism that was to be the stock-in-trade of so many demagogic politicians for the next generation. In 1934 he joined with Britain in recommending the admission of the Soviet Union to the League.

Within the Commonwealth, Ireland took the lead in pressing for the equality of all its member States. At the Imperial Conference of 1926, Kevin O'Higgins—the strong man of the Free State and the most impressive personality in Irish politics (as Yeats was quick to realize)—made his mark by securing, with Canadian help, the passage of a resolution affirming that the various dominions were "equal in status, in no way subordinate to one another in any aspect of their domestic or external affairs." This paved the way for the Statute of Westminster, passed by the British parliament in 1931—a constitutional landmark that conceded the right of each dominion to legislate for itself, without being bound by any previous laws enacted at Westminster. Winston Churchill opposed this statute on the grounds that the Irish Free State would use it to abrogate unilaterally the clauses of the 1922 "treaty" involving the oath of loyalty to the Crown and the office of the Governor-General—as indeed happened. In these conferences, Ireland took a major part in reshaping the outlook and the framework of the Commonwealth.

On the outbreak of the Second World War, De Valera reaffirmed the neutrality of Ireland. While this meant the denial of Irish naval bases to Britain (a restriction that galled Churchill so sorely that more than once he contemplated using force against Eire), it also meant that Ireland—as De Valera made clear to London—would not be available to Germany as a base for the invasion of England. So consistent was De Valera in his pursuit of neutrality, that he lodged a formal protest with President Roosevelt when in 1942 the United States established an important naval base at Londonderry in Northern Ireland.

In certain respects the neutrality of Eire brought benefits to Britain. Apart from volunteers from Northern Ireland, where by the desire of the British government conscription was never applied during the Second World War, thirty thousand Southern Irishmen enlisted in the British armed forces, some of them, like Brendan Finucane winning distinction by serving in the Battle of Britain with the R.A.F. In addition, tens of thousands of young Irishmen—no doubt for reasons of self-interest—crossed the Irish Sea to work in English munition factories and in other industries vital to the war effort.

Since Britain was the sole force interposed between Ireland and the ruthless exploitation practiced by the Nazis in Czechoslovakia, Norway, and Denmark, the Low Countries, and other small states, it might be said that for the first time in history, Ireland now profited immeasurably from the English connection. The war years were in fact a period of great prosperity for Eire. On the one hand, she provided the dairy products and agricultural supplies so badly needed in England, threatened as Britain was with starvation from the U-boat blockade, and on the other she benefited greatly from remittances transmitted by the thousands of Irishmen working in Britain.

Because of the hostility of Stalin's Russia, Eire was not admitted to the United Nations until 1955. Since then, Ireland has naturally sympathized with the aspirations of new nations in Africa and Asia struggling to be free from colonial domination. As the victor in the first national "war of liberation" waged in the twentieth century, she was in the unique position of being able to identify with colonial peoples while still remaining an integral part of the European community.

During the sixties Eire gave wholehearted support to the United Nations. In 1960, Frederick Boland was elected president of the General Assembly; while Conor Cruise O'Brien, one of Ireland's ablest diplomats and Dag Hammarskjold's second-in-command at U.N. headquarters in New York, played a leading role in the Congo crisis of 1962. Eire responded to the U.N. appeal for participation in international peace-keeping operations, as a result of which Irish soldiers were sent to Cyprus and to the Congo, where some of them lost their lives.

Ireland never became a member of the North Atlantic Treaty Organization and avoided formal political alliances in the postwar world. Yet by virtue of the special circumstances of her history, Ireland could not help but be bound to the United States by ties of unusual affection and gratitude. There was universal joy in Ireland when John Fitzgerald Kennedy was elected President of the United States in 1960. It signified the final acceptance in America of a people and a religion once despised and rejected, the final vindication of the hardship and suffering endured by generations of exiles seeking in the New World a happiness they had never known at home.

During the last four days of June, 1963, John Fitzgerald Kennedy spent in Eire what were perhaps some of the happiest days of his public life. A hundred and fifteen years before, his great-grandparents,

(COURTESY OF RADIO TELEFIS EIREANN)

John Fitzgerald Kennedy (1917–63). At the grave of the 1916 men, Arbour Hill Barracks, Dublin, while the Irish National Anthem is being played, June, 1963.

fleeing from the Famine, had left the little fishing port of New Ross, County Wexford, to seek a new life in America. Now, the descendant of those poverty-stricken emigrants, and the first Catholic ever to be elected to the White House, was returning to the land of his forebears to receive a rapturous welcome in which pride and affection commingled. President Kennedy visited the ancestral farm in County Wexford and relived among his own people the still fresh memories of "ninety-eight." He addressed the Dail in Dublin and captivated its members by his charm and wit. He went to Arbour Hill and stood to attention by the graves of Pearse and Connolly and their colleagues while the once-forbidden "Soldiers' Song"—now the anthem of the Republic—was played.

From Ireland, on the last day of June, President Kennedy flew immediately to London, there to confer on international problems with Harold Macmillan, Prime Minister of Britain, whose feelings toward the President were said to be almost paternal in character. While ever since childhood in Boston John Fitzgerald Kennedy had been familiar with the long tragedy of Irish history, he had also grown up to admire Britain's contributions to the modern world—her parliamentary institutions, the traditions of the Common Law and the practice of democracy.

President Kennedy felt no less at home in London than in Dublin, and the English people, though not so demonstrative as the Irish, were equally sincere in the welcome they accorded him. After his death the young American President was mourned with equal feeling on both sides of the Irish Sea—in Ireland by a people that felt it had just lost its greatest son, in England by a people who had come to regard him as *their* leader almost as though he were also their own Prime Minister. Perhaps it is not too fanciful, therefore, to see in the life and death of John Fitzgerald Kennedy a symbol of reconciliation between two ancient antagonisms—for the President, while he lived, was witness to the truth that one might love Ireland without hating Britain, and that one might admire Britain without being faithless to the memory of those who, through so many generations, had died for Irish freedom.

GENERAL HISTORIES AND DESCRIPTIONS

Arensburg, Conrad: *The Irish Countryman* (1937)

Beckett, James C.: *The Making of Modern Ireland, 1603–1923* (1966)

Carty, James: *Ireland, a Documentary Record,* 3 vols. (1951)

Curtis, Edmund: *A History of Ireland* (1937)

Danaher, Kevin: *In Ireland Long Ago* (1962)

Evans, Emyr Estyn: *Irish Folkways* (1957)

———: *Irish Heritage* (1942)

Falkiner, Caesar Lytton: *Essays Relating to Ireland* (1909)

Freeman, Thomas W.: *Ireland* (1960)

Gray, Tony: *The Irish Answer* (1966)

Green, Mrs. Alice Stopford: *Irish Nationality* (1911)

Hull, Eleanor: *History of Ireland,* 2 vols. (1928)

Jackson, Thomas: *Ireland Her Own* (1946)

Kettle, Tom: *Irish Orators and Oratory* (1915)

MacDonagh, Oliver: *Ireland* (1968)

McDowell, Robert and Curtis, Edmund: *Irish Historical Documents, 1172–1922* (1943)

Meenan, James and Webb, David: *A View of Ireland* (1957)

Mitchel, John: *History of Ireland* (1868)

Moody, T. W., and Martin, F. X.: *The Course of Irish History* (1967)

O'Clery, Helen: *The Ireland Reader* (1963)

O'Connor, Frank: *A Book of Ireland* (1959)

O'Faolain, Sean: *The Irish* (1949)

O'Grady, Standish: *The Story of Ireland* (1894)

Pokorny, Julius: *History of Ireland* (1933)

Prager, R. Lloyd: *The Way That I Went* (1947)

Sullivan, Alexander M.: *The Story of Ireland* (1867)

Sullivan, Timothy: *Speeches from the Dock* (n. d)

Webb, Alfred J.: *Compendium of Irish Biography* (1878)

INDEX